The lost Ireland of Stephen Gwynn

Manchester University Press

The lost Ireland of Stephen Gwynn

Irish constitutional nationalism and cultural politics, 1864–1950

Colin Reid

Manchester University Press

Copyright © Colin Reid 2011

The right of Colin Reid to be identified as the author of this work has been asserted by him in accordance with the Copyright, Designs and Patents Act 1988.

Published by Manchester University Press
Altrincham Street, Manchester M1 7JA, UK
www.manchesteruniversitypress.co.uk

British Library Cataloguing-in-Publication Data is available

Library of Congress Cataloging-in-Publication Data is available

ISBN 978 0 7190 9752 2 paperback

First published by Manchester University Press in hardback 2011

This paperback edition first published 2015

The publisher has no responsibility for the persistence or accuracy of URLs for any external or third-party internet websites referred to in this book, and does not guarantee that any content on such websites is, or will remain, accurate or appropriate.

Printed by Lightning Source

*To my parents and grandmother,
and the memory of Elizabeth Reid and Ernest Scott*

Contents

List of figures		viii
Acknowledgements		ix
List of abbreviations		xi
	Introduction	1
1	Family politics and early life, 1864–86	9
2	Exile in England, 1886–1904	33
3	Political cultures and cultural politics, 1904–9	63
4	Home Rule triumphant, 1909–14	95
5	Ireland's sacrifices, 1914–17	126
6	Redmondism's last stand? 1917–18	150
7	Holding the centre, 1919–22	170
8	Spiritually hyphenated, 1922–26	198
9	Experiences of a literary man, 1927–50	220
	Conclusion	242
Select bibliography		250
Index		264

Figures

1 Sketch of William Smith O'Brien, parliamentarian and rebel, by an unknown artist. From Michael Doheny, *The felon's track* (Dublin: M. H. Gill and Son, 1920)   12

2 Stephen Gwynn, *c.* 1885, by Walter Frederick Osborne, oil on canvas. Photograph © National Gallery of Ireland   24

3 Three Redmonds, *c.* 1912: John, Willie and William Archer. Photograph courtesy of the National Library of Ireland   109

4 Mr Stephen Gwynn, 1914. From Max Beerbohm, *A survey* (London: William Heinemann, 1921). Reproduced with permission of the Max Beerbohm Estate   128

5 Nobel laureate, W. B. Yeats, *c.* 1931. Photograph courtesy of the National Library of Ireland   210

6 Sketch of Stephen Gwynn, by Hooper Rowe. Reproduced with permission of Lebrecht Authors   224

Acknowledgements

This book has been five years in the making, during which time I have incurred numerous debts. Roy Foster provided invaluable support during all stages of the project, offering scholarly inspiration and camaraderie in abundance. Likewise, the unflappable enthusiasm and friendship of Richard English sustained me throughout. The faith that both Roy and Richard have shown in me is a debt which will take a long time to repay; I hope this book will act as a small down-payment with which to begin.

During the writing of this book, I have been fortunate enough to work within three stimulating academic bases: the School of Politics, International Studies and Philosophy at Queen's University, Belfast; Hertford College, Oxford; and the Department of History at NUI Maynooth. For their support, encouragement and friendship, I would like to thank my doctoral supervisors at Queen's, Paul Bew and Margaret O'Callaghan, whose patience and good humour were always appreciated. Oxford provided a wonderful backdrop in which to develop my work: I am grateful to Hertford College for electing me Irish Government Senior Scholar in 2008. Since then, I have benefited immensely from the knowledge and generosity of Jackie Hill and Vincent Comerford in Maynooth.

Tracing Stephen Gwynn's life brought me to a range of archives and libraries throughout Ireland, England, Scotland and the United States. I would like to acknowledge the help I received in the following institutions: Belfast Central Library; the Berg Collection in New York; the Bodleian Library in Oxford; the British Library; the Burns Library at Boston College; the Harry Ransom Humanities Research Center in Texas; the Houghton Library at Harvard University; the Irish Jesuit Archive in Dublin (especially Father Fergus O'Donoghue and Ellen O'Flaherty); the Linen Hall Library in Belfast; the National Archives in London; the National Archives of Scotland; the National Library of Ireland; the National Library of Scotland; New York Public Library Manuscripts; the Public Record Office of Northern Ireland; Queen's University Library, Belfast (especially Diarmuid Kennedy); St Columba's

College (especially Mark Brett); and Trinity College Manuscript Department, Dublin. Lord Aberdeen kindly permitted me to examine papers in his possession at the Haddo Estate, Aberdeenshire, for which I am also grateful to Mark Andrew. Warwick Gould was wonderfully generous with both his time and knowledge, going beyond the call of duty by permitting me to see his (not yet published) paper on Irish links with the Macmillan publishing house. I am indebted to the team at Manchester University Press for their professionalism and dedication to this project.

My research brought me into contact with a remarkable set of people – descendants of Stephen Gwynn. For answering my numerous questions about their ancestor, and to acknowledge the kindness I received during my enquiries, I would like to thank Rose Gayner (née Gwynn), Bill and Jean Jordan, Roger Gwynn and his late father, Harold, Fergus Kelly and his family, Anthony O'Brien, and Robin Gwynn. Bill Jordan in particular offered a wonderful insight into the mindset of a Gwynn: 'from Irish High King to an academic in one thousand years, social mobility of a downward kind, I think'.

I have enjoyed numerous thought-provoking and convivial discussions with others within the scholarly community over the course of my research: it is a great pleasure to salute Lauren Arrington, Richard Bourke, Aaron Edwards, Frances Flanagan, Ultán Gillen, James Golden, James Greer, Erika Hanna, Alvin Jackson, Jennifer Kelly, Matt Kelly, Michael Keyes, Peter Leppard, Patrick Maume, Ian McBride, James McConnel, Shaun McDaid, Marc Mulholland, Senia Pašeta, Simon Prince, Jennifer Redmond, Jennifer Regan-Lefebvre, Andrew Sanders, Graham Walker, Mike Wheatley, Mark Williams and Tim Wilson. The Irish Politics Research Cluster at Queen's and the Irish History Seminar at Hertford College provided invigorating forums of debate: for nurturing a sense of community during my stints in Belfast and Oxford, credit must go to Richard English, Graham Walker and Roy Foster.

Finally, my love goes to my family and friends who sustained me in numerous ways during the past five years. I could not have asked for a stronger pillar of support than Caoimhe Nic Dháibhéid, whose devoted companionship provided the highest level of inspiration and motivation. This book could not have been completed without having her in my life. To Fiona, Hugh, Jenny and Holly Reid, and my grandmother, Marjorie Scott, I can only offer my gratitude for the confidence they have entrusted in me. Only I, though, am responsible for the shortcomings of this book.

Colin Reid
Belfast

Abbreviations

AFIL	All-For-Ireland League
BCL	Belfast Central Library
Berg	Henry W. and Albert A. Berg collection, New York Public Library
BL	British Library
Bodleian	Bodleian Library, Oxford
DDA	Dublin Diocesan Archives
HRHRC	Harry Ransom Humanities Research Centre, University of Texas
ICWSA	Irish Catholic Women's Suffrage Association
IJA	Irish Jesuit Archive
INTS	Irish National Theatre Society
IPA	Irish Press Agency
IPP	Irish Parliamentary Party (used interchangeably with 'Irish Party')
IRA	Irish Republican Army
IRB	Irish Republican Brotherhood
IRC	Irish Recruiting Council
ITGWU	Irish Transport and General Workers' Union
IWFL	Irish Women's Franchise League
IWML	Imperial War Museum Library, London
MP	Member of Parliament
NAS	National Archives of Scotland
NLI	National Library of Ireland
NLS	National Library of Scotland
NYPL	New York Public Library
PAL	Parliamentary Archives, London
PRONI	Public Record Office of Northern Ireland
QUB	Queen's University, Belfast
RIC	Royal Irish Constabulary
TCD	Trinity College Dublin

TD	Teachta Dála
TNA	The National Archives, London
UCD	University College, Dublin
UIL	United Irish League
UVF	Ulster Volunteer Force
WSRO	Wiltshire and Swindon Record Office

Introduction

STEPHEN Gwynn is one of Ireland's lost leaders, a Protestant nationalist who anticipated a Home Rule settlement which would have delivered Irish self-government while binding the country to the British Empire. This was an Ireland which never came to pass; political and cultural revolutions destroyed this ideal, replacing it with an Ireland imbued with a very different ethos. Like Isaac Butt before him, Gwynn represented an inclusive and pluralistic Irish identity and a commitment to achieving Irish self-government peacefully; again like Butt, Ireland has not remembered him, favouring instead the memory of the martyred dead of violent rebellion. Even death tormented Gwynn's vision for a reconciled Ireland. His funeral at a small Church of Ireland cemetery in Dublin in 1950 was surrounded by poignant symbolism. The many contours of his life were visible in the company which surrounded his grave: politicians, authors, scholars, the clergy and officers from a disbanded British Army regiment. But behind the public spectacle was a family's grief; and this was even more profound given the clear religious divisions within their ranks. Father Aubrey Gwynn, Jesuit scholar and Stephen's second eldest surviving son, recalled standing outside his father's funeral as an 'outsider', unable to attend because he had not obtained papal authority to enter a Protestant church, as required by the religious law of the time.[1] As Gwynn's wife and children had converted to Catholicism many years before, the family gathering in 1950 was divided along religious grounds; not even death could provide a middle way. The unfortunate irony that lies with Gwynn's bones is that he endeavoured to break down the barriers which divided Ireland. He advocated a moderate form of nationalism which was pluralist, cosmopolitan and conciliatory, a worldview that envisaged a Home Rule Ireland as the jewel of the British Empire, with an imperial identity fusing with the distinctive Irish character. This rubric, Gwynn hoped, had the power to weaken the divisions between Irish Protestant and Catholic, between north and south, while reconciling Ireland with Britain. Yet in death as in life: politico-religious conflict in Ireland broke the man, and followed him to the grave.

The poignancy of Gwynn's long life should not be overlooked. Gwynn was born in 1864 to a well-to-do family with a long line of scholars and clergymen on one side while claiming descent from an Irish High King on the other; his life spanned Ireland's transformation from Union to Republic, via political and cultural upheavals and revolutions. At critical times during the nineteenth and twentieth centuries Irish affairs were blighted by competing zero-sum mentalities, with success and defeat representing more salient features of the political landscape than reconciliation and settlement. In this context, Gwynn is one of history's sidelined participants, having lost most of the political and cultural battles which he contested. The list of Gwynn's advocacies reads as an epitaph of a lost Ireland of his lifetime: moderate and conciliatory nationalism; federalist constitutional arrangements within the British Empire; sympathy for the declining landlord class; non-political cultural programmes; and the promotion of a meaningful *rapprochement* between unionism and nationalism. Each cause was violated by revolution, out of which Ireland emerged partitioned, not only territorially but also in mentality. Yet there was nothing inevitable about these processes, a point which should be emphasised to permit a deeper understanding of the issues at stake. Eric Hobsbawm once pithily observed that 'there is nothing which can sharpen the historian's mind like defeat'.[2] The lost Ireland of Stephen Gwynn records a succession of defeats, total and complete, in Irish life before and after the end of the Union: one of this book's contentions is that in explaining the failure of Gwynn's brand of political and cultural nationalism, the very forces which overwhelmed him come into sharper focus.

Why study Gwynn in this way? This book makes a case for a serious consideration of Gwynn as one of the most significant and articulate observers of the unfolding events of his day. Active in a number of public spheres – political, cultural and journalistic – Gwynn is a compelling figure in his own right. He offers a window into Redmondite politics, the Irish cultural revivals and nationalist propaganda; significantly, Gwynn represented a blurring of all three. Though his analysis of the Anglo-Irish dilemma is often invoked by political historians and his writings are intensively used by literary historians, there are no previous full-scale studies of Gwynn. This book, then, aims to rehabilitate Gwynn's career and rescue him from undeserved obscurity, while providing much-needed context to his political and cultural thought. His continuous presence on history's losing side, coupled with a palette of idiosyncratic characteristics, accounts, partly at least, for his hitherto understated historical legacy. Gwynn adopted unpopular and, at times, seemingly contradictory stances on the major political and cultural issues of his time, for which he was ridiculed, slandered and even targeted by the Irish Republican Army (IRA) during the Civil War. For instance, in 1909, Gwynn denounced plans to impose the Irish language as a compulsory subject for matriculation in the new National University of Ireland; yet he was also a prominent member of the Gaelic League's executive, which fiercely supported the move. He was the most vocal nationalist advocate of Irish recruitment to the Great War effort and served himself in the trenches: he forever celebrated the blood sacrifice on the killing fields of Europe while bitterly condemning that in Dublin of Easter 1916. In 1920, he staunchly backed the British government's plan to partition Ireland, which other Irish nationalists viewed with horror, disdain and disbelief. In tracing these individual stances, wider networks of a lost Ireland come into focus.

There was nothing provincial about Gwynn's Irish nationalism. While he articulated the need to foster a distinct national literature and culture in Ireland, such activities were envisaged as the flowering of a society nearing a communal maturity. Anglophobia or mistrust of the English interest in Ireland did not fuel his nationalism; his drive for political change was born from constitutional thinking. In his reading, the failure to fully integrate Ireland into the United Kingdom and the lack of reconciliation between Irish nationalism and British imperialism were the two great flaws of the Union settlement which existed from 1800 to 1922. Writing in 1926 of his experiences as an Irishman in London during the final years of the nineteenth century, Gwynn was pragmatic when expressing his political thought: 'I was aware then, as I am now, that Scotland under a Union was a distinct nationality and a satisfied nationality, and if changes could be made so that the Union would mean to Ireland what it meant to Scotland, I was quite prepared to be a satisfied Nationalist within the Union'.[3] The Scottish reference point remained a salient one for Gwynn. 'We desire a Walter Scott', he argued in 1897, to 'glorify our annals, popularise our legends, describe our scenery, and give an attractive view of the national character'.[4] A distinctive cultural identity was not incompatible with cosmopolitan citizenship within the Union and Empire. Gwynn had every desire to share in the fruits of a wider 'Britishness', which would complement his Irish identity. In essence, he desired a form of 'banal unionism' that Colin Kidd has identified as marking Scottish constitutional thought through the nineteenth century, in which the Union was accepted as part of everyday life.[5] The weight of history was, however, against him. Ireland was the ambivalent component of the British nation-building project, never an equal member of the United Kingdom, and imbued with a confusing hybrid of colonial and metropolitan mentalities. Defeat, though, was not inevitable: the malleable qualities of Irish nationalism, British imperialism and the constitutional design of the United Kingdom have been apparent at critical junctures of the evolution of Ireland, Britain and Empire.

Gwynn offers a window into the late-Victorian and Edwardian debates surrounding the envisaged (and expected) future of Home Rule Ireland. His political thought was framed by an imperially minded nationalism, which was given significant resonance during the Great War, when he volunteered for active service in the name of Ireland and Empire. He was that most rare breed: a Protestant nationalist in twentieth-century Ireland. While there was a rich tradition of Protestant involvement in nationalist politics in the nineteenth century (the most recent example being the early years of the Home Rule movement under Isaac Butt's leadership in the 1870s), sectarian and political animosities had increased significantly by the turn of the century; Protestant nationalists – and openly Catholic unionists – became the exceptions that proved the rule. Gwynn, then, occupied a critical position within John Redmond's Irish Party: as its most senior Protestant member, he played a leading role in articulating the argument that unionists had nothing to fear from the Home Rule ideal. While Gwynn later claimed that it was an advantage to be a Protestant within Home Rule circles as nationalist constituencies basked in showing their broadmindedness, the maverick commentator William O'Brien forwarded a rather different interpretation: in his view, Gwynn was merely one among a 'little group of tame Protestant Home Rulers maintained for obvious reasons at Westminster as nominees of a Hibernian party to whose inner rites their religion forbade their admission'.[6] The Protestant experience of Home Rule, as it was envisaged by all sides, would never be realised; but Gwynn's prominence in the religious debates surrounding Home Rule offers a lucid insight into the *mentalités* surrounding the arguments of the time.

Gwynn's political trajectory was unique. While seeking to carve out a literary career in London at the turn of the century, he became interested in the work of Horace Plunkett and the Irish Co-operative Movement, which stressed reconciliation and economic development over the divisive national question; Gwynn moved towards the Home Rule movement during the Boer War. As an Irish Party Member of Parliament (MP), Gwynn dabbled with federalist ideas while committing himself to the imperially minded nationalism which Redmond personified; after the electoral obliteration of the party in 1918, he became one of the few prominent Home Rulers to play an active role in public life. Federalism became the foundation stone of the Irish Centre Party, an organisation Gwynn founded in 1919 to challenge the hard-line positions of Sinn Féin and the Ulster unionists; the Centre Party merged with Plunkett's moderate nationalist movement, the Irish Dominion League, later that year. Gwynn thus moved full circle, beginning with ideas of reconciliation under Plunkett's guidance and ending with them. But the relationship between Gwynn and Plunkett was emblematic of the fate of moderate nationalism in Ireland: in both 1903 and 1920, the two men fundamentally disagreed on key issues relating to the powers of an Irish parliament and the position of Ulster in a self-governing settlement. In 1903, Gwynn advocated Home Rule encompassing the entire island of Ireland, while Plunkett was more concerned with economic sustainability; in 1920, Gwynn pressed for a limited measure of devolution and partition, while Plunkett insisted on dominion status for Ireland and Ulster's inclusion within it.

Biography is a valuable methodological tool with which to examine these shifts in political thought. David Gorman, in his history of imperial identity and political thought, has argued that biography is the ideal framework for historians to assess 'the ideas which contemporaries recorded, argued, and propagated'.[7] Yet this is not a universally held assumption: as Hermione Lee, author of an enthralling and piercing study of Virginia Woolf, has recently contended, biography 'is not neutral ground: it arouses strong and passionate feelings'.[8] One critic claims that political biographies traditionally suffer from one of two serious flaws: that they present their subjects either as 'extraordinary and omnipotent' or as 'predictable individuals whose characteristics and actions form the basis for generalisations'.[9] This is, however, a rather myopic outlook; it is not fully apparent *why* these supposed characteristics of biography are necessarily defective. Indeed, examining wider contextual issues through the lens of an individual is one of the more fruitful frameworks open to an historian, particularly when an empathetic and analytical approach is adopted. The most interesting history firmly embeds the lives of individuals into their wider political, social and economic contexts. Such an approach permits an interrogation of how the future was anticipated by key figures, and how this was reconciled with what actually happened.[10]

In Ireland, imagined futures have a special resonance. The Irish revolution of 1916–23 replaced one political elite with another: the old guard of Home Rule, including Gwynn, was sidelined and a younger, more idealistic, national leadership took its place. It also violently shook the foundations of the young and educated Catholic middle-class elite, many members of which were coming of age as the leaders of the next generation who expected a Home Rule Ireland.[11] Young constitutional nationalist leaders – the Cruise O'Briens, Kettles and Sheehys – became the 'dispossessed' of Irish life in the Free State created in 1922. In 1998, Conor Cruise O'Brien, a scion of these three families, reflected on the alternative future lost in the embers of that revolution: 'Our whole family would have been part of the establishment of the new Home Rule Ireland. As it was, we were out in the cold, superseded by a new republican elite.'[12] Gwynn, too, was one of this dispossessed group; a major theme of this book is his expectations of the future and why the reality which came to pass was very different.

Gwynn was a versatile writer, publishing over sixty books, which covered biography, travel, fiction, verse, essays, history, fishing and politics. In addition, he penned hundreds of newspaper, journal and magazine articles over the course of his long life. He fostered ambitions of being a creative force within the Irish literary revival at the beginning of the twentieth century, but his fortes were criticism, history and politics. Several of his more penetrative books – *John Redmond's last years* (1919), *The Irish situation* (1921) and *Irish literature and drama in the English language* (1936) – chronicled the changing contours of contemporary Ireland, imbued with insightful first-hand knowledge. These texts alone are reasons to treat Gwynn as an astute commentator which a political or cultural historian of early twentieth-century Ireland can ill-afford to ignore. Yet this book is the first to examine Gwynn's wider literary canon; crucially, it places his works in the context in which they were written. This is supplemented by engagement with another side of Gwynn's literary dealings, namely his advisory work for Macmillan, the London-based publisher. Gwynn's reputation as a critic led to his appointment as a literary advisor to the respected firm in 1898, a link which expired only with his death. Gwynn used this position to promote authors close to him, but found resistance from within Macmillan to many Irish writers: the most prominent example of this was W. B. Yeats.

The Macmillan papers housed at the British Library are the most complete archive holdings connected to Gwynn. Unfortunately there is no single cache of papers which can be truly be classed 'Stephen Gwynn papers'; the collection with this name held by the National Library of Ireland on the whole contains only minor literary-connected material. In his memoir, *Experiences of a literary man*, published in 1926, Gwynn referred to the elegant handwriting of Nesta Higginson with a line suggesting that he destroyed his papers on a regular basis: 'It always went against me to burn what she had written'.[13] A number of Higginson's letters thus can be found in the Stephen Gwynn papers, but little else of lasting value. This poses obvious problems which shape this book. Very little material has survived which gives an insight into Gwynn's private life; but what can be gleaned is that it was fairly unorthodox, with (at least) several affairs and temporary separations from his wife. The precise nature of Gwynn's relationship with his children when they reached adulthood is also unclear. His second son, Aubrey, wrote warmly of his father in an unpublished autobiography; but Denis, Professor of History at Cork and Gwynn's third son, seems to have been much more distant. If a lack of Gwynn papers is a hindrance, some extremely fruitful avenues continually opened during the research for this book. Gwynn left a massive paper trail in many contemporary publications, and a number of his letters have survived, scattered throughout depositories in Ireland, Britain and the United States. These tend to centre on the public rather than the private, but from these sources a worldview clearly emerges which is ripe for interrogation. The source material relating to Gwynn is concentrated on the most active period of his life: his political career, c. 1904–26. Hence this book focuses most of its attention on these years.

A second factor in the design of this book is the nature of Gwynn's memoir. *Experiences of a literary man* contains invaluable information about his early life but tails off with his entry into Parliament in 1906. Plans to pen a second volume unfortunately came to nothing. There are inevitably aspects of his life which are sharper in the historical record than others. As Gwynn enjoyed a prominent public position during his political career (as much due to his activities as a Gaelic League enthusiast as to his support of the Home Rule cause), his thought, action and significance can be traced; likewise, the press covered his post-Irish Party career (usually negatively) with interest, as he argued the case for partition. The source material covering the final two decades of his life, though, is patchy, as he removed himself from the public eye. Nevertheless, he published a steady stream of books in this period, many of which were biographical in form. Among his subjects were the eminent Protestant Ascendancy men of the long Irish eighteenth century – Swift, Goldsmith, Grattan – powerfully symbolic figures for a Protestant nationalist to habilitate within the increasingly Catholicised Free State.

This book reconstructs Gwynn's life, and the political and cultural milieux in which he operated, restoring this most intriguing – and difficult – of nationalists to the historical record. Scholars have frequently used Gwynn's writings in investigating a range of historical issues, political and literary. This is the first work which places his commentaries into the context of his time. But above all, this book is about an Ireland which was lost in revolution. The hopes and expectations of Gwynn were rooted in the cosmopolitan, intellectual and patriotic; his life's tragedy was the defeat of every sacred ideal.

Notes

1 *Interfuse: Irish province communicating*, 30 (December 1983), p. 20; copy in the Aubrey Gwynn papers, Irish Jesuit Archive (IJA).
2 Eric J. Hobsbawm, *On history* (London: Abacus, 1998; first published 1997), p. 317.
3 Stephen Gwynn, *Experiences of a literary man* (London: Thornton Butterworth, 1926), p. 170.
4 Stephen Gwynn, 'Novels of Irish life in the nineteenth century', in *Irish books and Irish people* (Dublin: Talbot Press, 1919), p. 7.
5 Colin Kidd, *Union and unionisms: political thought in Scotland, 1500–2000* (Cambridge: Cambridge University Press, 2008).
6 F. S. L. Lyons, *The Irish Parliamentary Party, 1890–1910* (London: Faber and

Faber, 1951), pp. 166–7, n. 2; William O'Brien, *The Irish revolution and how it came about* (Dublin: Maunsel and Roberts, 1923), p. 118.
7 David Gorman, *Imperial citizenship: empire and the question of belonging* (Manchester: Manchester University Press, 2006), p. 7.
8 Hermione Lee, *Biography: a very short introduction* (Oxford: Oxford University Press, 2009), p. 100.
9 Patrick O'Brien, 'Is political biography a good thing?', *Contemporary British History*, 10:4 (1996), p. 60.
10 Such an approach permeates Roy Foster's masterful two-volume biography of Yeats: *W. B. Yeats: a life* (Oxford: Oxford University Press, 1997 and 2003).
11 This theme is the focus of Senia Pašeta's important study, *Before the revolution: nationalism, social change and Ireland's Catholic elite, 1879–1922* (Cork: Cork University Press, 1999).
12 Conor Cruise O'Brien, *Memoir: my life and themes* (Dublin: Poolbeg Press, 1998), p. 21. The late Diarmuid Whelan examined the 'dispossession' of the O'Brien family within Irish life in his *Conor Cruise O'Brien: violent notions* (Dublin: Irish Academic Press, 2009), pp. 3–16.
13 Gwynn, *Experiences*, p. 117.

1

Family politics and early life
1864–86

Ireland, oh Ireland! Centre of my longings,
Country of my fathers, home of my heart!
(Stephen Gwynn, 'Ireland', first published 1896)[1]

'IRELAND of yesterday was Ireland before the revolution', wrote Stephen Gwynn in 1918. 'We may well envy those who lived more easily and quietly in the Ireland of yesterday, and held with an unquestioning spirit to the state of things in which they were born'.[2] Born in 1864 and dying in 1950, the massive upheavals – war, revolution and partition to name but three – that Gwynn confronted in his own life places a certain appropriateness on his words. Memories of his youth were treasured, and became more important to him late in his life, as he reflected on the course of his – and his country's – biography.[3] Reading his autobiography from 1926, *Experiences of a literary man*, which does not cover his life after 1906, one gains the impression that Gwynn was nothing more than a competent writer with a playful sense of memory. Yet for all its light-hearted anecdotes, *Experiences* bears the scars of the political and cultural battles that raged through Ireland in the twenty years before the book was published. As a constitutional nationalist and cultural pluralist, Gwynn was on the losing side of Ireland's revolution: the partitioned dominion settlement, won after a campaign of political radicalism and violence, was very different to the Ireland Gwynn had envisaged. Given his experience of the Irish revolution, Gwynn can perhaps be forgiven for envying the past.

The Gwynn and O'Brien traditions

IT began on 13 February 1864 in St Columba's College, close to the hills of Dublin: Stephen Lucius Gwynn was born to the Reverend John Gwynn, the Warden of St Columba's, and his wife Lucy. John Gwynn came from a distinguished family of Welsh descent, with strong ties to the Church of Ireland and Trinity College Dublin (TCD). His grandfather, also called John, graduated from TCD in 1784, before becoming rector of Kilroot and Ballynure, County Antrim, a position he held for an astonishing fifty-two years.[4] This earlier John married Catherine Rolleston in 1789. She was described by the author Dorothea Herbert as 'a Lady of large fortune'[5] and came from the same family that would produce T. W. Rolleston, a literary contemporary of Stephen Gwynn. Gwynne and Rolleston had two children: the first, Stephen, was born three years after their marriage, and would follow his father by gaining an education at TCD before entering the Church of Ireland.[6] The Reverend Stephen Gwynne was the rector of Larne, County Antrim, and the treasurer of the diocese of Connor for much of his career.[7] His life was, however, blighted by tragedy. His first wife, Mary Stevens, drowned in 1837 while bathing in the sea; exacerbating the horror of the incident, the body was washed up in Scotland.[8] Mary and Stephen Gwynne had six children: four boys – John, James, William and Stephen – and two girls – Jane and Catherine.[9] John, the eldest boy, would become the noted biblical scholar and clergyman, the Reverend John Gwynn (it was his generation that dropped the 'e' from Gwynne); he was the father of Stephen Gwynn.

John Gwynn was ten years old when his mother died, but the family's trauma did not end there: bar his sister Catherine, none of John's siblings lived past the age of forty.[10] Stephen Gwynn described his father's early life as being 'under a cloud of calamity' and also noted that he 'was never robust, and with the family history before them no insurance company would ever accept him'.[11] Yet John Gwynn defied the mortal jinx on his family and lived a full and celebrated life, which included fathering ten children, before dying at the age of ninety, in 1917. He held a number of senior posts within the Church of Ireland before and after its disestablishment in 1869, most prominently the deanships of Derry and Raphoe. His academic reputation was cemented by his appointment as the Regius Professor of Divinity at TCD and later the release of his most revered work, an exquisite edition of the ninth-century *Book of Armagh*, a breathtaking work of precise scholarship which took Gwynn twenty years to complete. Stephen Gwynn later recalled that when the *Book* was finally published his father was in his eighty-fifth year and could barely even lift the volume; 'yet in whose pages you would look long before you could find one word redundant'.[12]

After a successful undergraduate career at TCD, John Gwynn became an assistant to the College's Regius Professor of Greek in 1853.[13] Three years later, he accepted the post of Warden of St Columba's College near Dublin. Under his watch, St Columba's expanded its student numbers to unprecedented levels;[14] included in the student body were a number of O'Briens, of the illustrious family from Clare. St Columba's thus was the setting for the first meeting between the Reverend John Gwynn and Lucy O'Brien, the eldest daughter of the Young Ireland leader William Smith O'Brien. John Gwynn later recorded that in 1849, when he was a young divinity student at TCD, he watched William Smith O'Brien, as a convicted felon, being led through the streets of Dublin in chains.[15] Thirteen years after this procession, the rebellion leader became Gwynn's father-in-law.

The family background of Stephen Gwynn's mother could not be more different from the respected line of clergymen and scholars that the Gwynns represented. When the Reverend John Gwynn married Lucy O'Brien in 1862, he entered one of the most ancient family dynasties in Ireland. 'If anybody in Ireland should have been considered as Irish, it was my mother's people', Stephen Gwynn proudly boasted in his autobiography.[16] The clan traced its lineage to Brian Boru, the eleventh-century High King of Ireland. Boru granted the O'Briens a dignified symbol of pride in their clan; in keeping with this tradition, Gwynn fondly described his ancestor as 'the greatest of all Gaelic kings of Ireland'.[17] The subsequent genealogy of the O'Briens after Brian Boru read, to Gwynn at least, as 'the history of Clare'.[18] The clan provided troublesome distractions for the English overlords of Ireland after the twelfth century by occasionally resurrecting their claims to the Irish crown, but they submitted to Tudor authority in 1541. The adoption of Tudor policy implied that the O'Brien clan had to follow Henry VIII's break with the Catholic Church and embrace Protestantism. One official O'Brien family historian, Donough O'Brien, has affirmed that 'The change at the time was entirely a political one, and had no relation to conscience in the participators of the events that were passing at the time'.[19] The conversion triggered a 'private civil war' among the O'Briens, which still reverberated within the clan centuries later.[20] Two years before the birth of Stephen Gwynn, William Smith O'Brien biliously condemned Murrough O'Brien, who had submitted to Henry VIII in the 1540s:

> In common with a large proportion not only of the clan of O'Brien, but also the rest of the Gaelic population of Ireland, I conceive that our progenitor who, in the reign of Henry VIII, accepted English titles in lieu of the royal honours which belonged to his family, submitted to a derogation of dignity by accepting such titles. The lapse of more than three hundred years which has taken place since that humiliation was inflicted upon our family, does not reconcile me to it.[21]

The outspoken views of Gwynn's grandfather in the nineteenth century reveal that the wounds suffered by the O'Briens in the sixteenth century were far from healed. For William Smith O'Brien, his clan's past was still a contemporary issue.

FIGURE 1. Sketch of William Smith O'Brien, parliamentarian and rebel, by an unknown artist. From Michael Doheny, *The felon's track* (Dublin: M. H. Gill and Son, 1920).

Family politics and early life, 1864–86

After the granting of the earldom of Inchiquin to the clan, the O'Briens maintained a habitual presence in the Irish parliament. Sir Lucius Henry O'Brien, the third Baronet of Dromoland, and his son, Sir Edward O'Brien, the fourth Baronet, were active members of the Irish parliament, with a combined career span predating the initial drive for Irish legislative independence and ending with Irish representatives sitting in the British House of Commons. Both O'Briens opposed the concept of Ireland's legislative future being decided in London rather than Dublin: as Stephen Gwynn proudly noted, Sir Lucius was 'one of the leading statesmen who negotiated the establishment of "Grattan's Parliament"', while Sir Edward 'voted against the Act of Union, which led slowly, but surely, to the destruction of all that he and his stood for'.[22] During the tense Union debates, Sir Edward O'Brien married Charlotte Smith, the daughter of William Smith, a successful lawyer who owned the Cahirmoyle estate in County Limerick. O'Brien inherited severe financial debts from his father's estate in Dromoland: these were exacerbated by his entry into politics. The marriage between Sir Edward and Charlotte Smith was arranged to allow the wealthy William Smith to clear the O'Brien debts, in exchange for his entry into one of the most eminent families in Munster.[23] Despite the economic foundation of the union, Sir Edward and Charlotte enjoyed a fulfilling marriage, rich with children. Their first son and heir, Lucius (the future thirteenth Baron Inchiquin), was born in 1800; he was followed by twelve siblings, including the second son, William Smith O'Brien, in 1803.

Given his family's history, politics was the natural vocation for William Smith O'Brien. Several years after graduating from Trinity College, Cambridge – where he was a member of the elite Cambridge Apostles – he was elected MP for Ennis at the tender age of twenty-four. During his parliamentary career, O'Brien would travel through the Irish political spectrum: in his early days he was close to the Tory Prime Minister Robert Peel; he moved to become a hard-working and diligent independent Liberal; he later joined Daniel O'Connell's Repeal movement; finally, and reluctantly, after breaking with the Repealers, he led the doomed Young Ireland revolt of 1848. Much mocked – the 'battle of the Widow MacCormack's cabbage patch' as it was later described[24] – the rising led to O'Brien's sentence of exile to Van Diemen's Land (now Tasmania) for high treason. He was granted a pardon by the British government and returned to Ireland in 1856. Despite his eventful life, the political career of William Smith O'Brien contained little glamour. It has even been argued by one of his biographers that without the turbulent drama of 1848 he 'might have been remembered as a fine parliamentarian and public servant, and one of the more respected leaders of a formidable national movement'.[25] In many ways, O'Brien's standing as a senior Protestant nationalist within an Irish party at Westminster was similar to that of his grandson's in the first two decades of the twentieth century. Both William Smith O'Brien and Stephen Gwynn were high-ranking nationalists with close links to their respected leaders: O'Brien's career was defined by the paradigm established by the 'Liberator' Daniel O'Connell, while Gwynn's political work was moulded by John Redmond's drive for Home Rule.

Smith O'Brien died in Wales in June 1864, several months after his grandson, Stephen Gwynn, was born to Lucy Josephine O'Brien. She was Gwynn's living link to Brian Boru and the rich history of the O'Brien clan; despite her ancestry, however, Gwynn admitted that he did not know whether 'my mother ever formed a political opinion'.[26] In Lucy's warm correspondence with her father after 1848, political issues were not discussed, even though she became her father's amanuensis after his return from exile. Lucy partially suffered from the O'Brien hereditary deafness (her sister, Charlotte Grace, was completely deaf), but revelled in the company of her grandchildren. Aubrey Gwynn, in his adult years, recalled a loving grandmother who admirably stood for religious tolerance.[27] According to Stephen Gwynn, his mother was a Gael; but in 1862 she accepted a marriage proposal from a man of Ulster planter stock. It was a 'strange marriage' that fused the bloodlines of two different varieties of Irishness in their offspring, of which Stephen Gwynn would be the first.[28]

Early experiences

SHORTLY after the birth of Stephen, the Reverend John Gwynn accepted the rectory of Tullyauhnish, a spacious residence owned by TCD, which came with one of the richest livings connected with the College.[29] The journey north to Donegal brought with it the promise of their own living space, a marked difference from the restricted existence of life within St Columba's College. This move is of central importance to the development of Stephen Gwynn: he recorded later that 'All the most part of my knowledge of Ireland came from Donegal; I got my education there'.[30] Donegal was much more than a home for the young Gwynn: it was his fulcrum and frequent source of literary inspiration. He spent only his childhood in the county, but Donegal remained firmly embedded in his mind. Despite the rise of a Catholic democracy throughout the nineteenth century, Gwynn, in his own words, grew up in a 'Protestant world'. 'Within easy reach were ten or a dozen houses belonging to Protestant gentry'. Gwynn was, however, sheltered from the mounting wave of land agitation: he enjoyed a tranquil childhood as his family were 'neither landlords nor tenants'. Reflections of his youth in old age were tinged with sorrow at the loss of the 'old' Donegal. The dynamic he pinpointed for its decline was Gladstone's Land Act of 1881: it 'really ended the whole order that we had grown up in'.[31]

The 'order' was a comfortable one, and with no shortage of company. Two years after his birth, Stephen greeted his first sister, Lucy. Eight further siblings followed in quick succession: Edward in 1868; Charles in 1870; Lucius in 1873; Arthur in 1874; Robert (known as Robin) in 1877; Mary in 1879; John Tudor (known as Jack) in 1881; and Brian in 1883. This generation of Gwynns would distinguish themselves in a number of spheres: politics, academia, the military, the Indian civil service and sports. Stephen enjoyed, by all accounts, a fulfilling childhood. The O'Briens visited the Gwynns in Donegal on an almost annual basis, exposing the young Stephen to the lifestyle of the gentry.[32] His mother's brothers taught him the way of the country squire: he learned the arts of shooting and angling from his O'Brien uncles.[33] This instilled in him his lifelong fascination with fishing, a recurrent theme in many of his published works. The young Gwynn embraced Donegal life with relish. The nine-year-old Stephen wrote to his 'Aunt Lizzie' (Smith O'Brien's sister-in-law, Elizabeth Gabbett), requesting a copy of Mayne Reid's *The forest exiles* for his upcoming birthday, and expressed his love for shooting birds with a catapult, despite being bitten by an avian foe during his pursuits.[34] In a postscript to the same letter, Stephen's mother added that 'He is quite wild about shooting and looks forward to having a gun some time or other as the height of bliss'.[35] In Joyce Cary's autobiographical novel, *A house of children*, which depicts the life of a child growing up in Donegal at around that time, hunting was fundamentally tied to the process of a boy becoming a man: it moved the male adolescent 'towards the glorious existence of a grown-up'.[36] Gwynn's formative years can be read in this way. A youthful interest in guns almost proved costly, however, as a story that was passed down to Stephen's son, Aubrey, reveals. Aubrey recorded that his father enjoyed playing William Tell in his youth; on one occasion, he convinced his sister, Lucy, to place an apple on her head, allowing the boyish hero to snipe at the offending piece of fruit with a gun he was carrying. Lucy, however, did not duck: only a 'kindly intervention of Providence' caused Stephen's shot to miss Lucy (and the apple).[37] Not that this dampened the enthusiasms of the teenage Stephen: while staying with the O'Briens in Cahirmoyle at the age of eighteen, he excitedly wrote to his mother about his Uncle Donough's gun collection, which contained a 'magnificent' Winchester repeater.[38]

Gwynn returned to the theme of Donegal in his writings throughout his life, most particularly in his travel books. These were not merely guides for tourists, as they contain arresting political and social historical commentaries; at times they display quite surprising attitudes. The assassination of Lord Leitrim is a curious case in point. Lord Leitrim, one of the most hated landlords of his age, was brutally killed in 1878 in Donegal. Gwynn was fourteen years old when the murder occurred, not far from his home, but the incident is, surprisingly, absent from his autobiography. It warrants only a brief mention in his 1899 book *Highways and byways in Donegal and Antrim*, but it is a telling one.

The tyrannical Leitrim was assassinated by members of his tenantry on the morning of 2 April 1878. Despite the lure of substantial monetary rewards funded by the British exchequer and the Leitrim family, no one was ever convicted of the killing.[39] His killers are eulogised as liberators of the tenantry by a monument which stands in Fanad, north Donegal. In *Highways and byways in Donegal and Antrim*, Gwynn recognised Leitrim's violent temper and his tyrannical idiosyncrasies, which produced a hate figure among the tenantry. Yet this analysis was tempered by Gwynn's depiction of Leitrim as 'a man by no means wholly bad and [who] possessed qualities which might, under happier circumstances, have made him famous – absolute courage and a perfectly indomitable will. Nothing could be less like the careless, absentee landlord who has been the real curse of Ireland'.[40] This was a prototype of A. P. W. Malcomson's recent revision of Leitrim, which also stresses the paternalism and reforming merits of the 'wicked earl'.[41] In choosing to emphasise Leitrim's virtues, Gwynn stood apart from the traditional nationalist interpretation of the infamous landlord. Elsewhere he even praised Leitrim when he barred the Viceroy, Lord Carlisle, from entering his inn in Connemara as a demonstration of his disgust with the 1870 Land Act.[42]

This cautious support for Leitrim was partly born of a wider sympathy with the declining and desolate landlord caste in Ireland which Gwynn maintained throughout his life, despite his nationalist activism. Nowhere is Gwynn as pro-gentry as in the Preface to his 1903 collection of essays, *Today and tomorrow in Ireland*:

> In all other ways, I do not think there has been a class in Europe more honourable, more courteous, more kindly, more lovable, and in this I know that they [the landlord class] have been simply blinded by an inveterate prejudice. I take them as the lamentable example of what comes to pass when local patriotism is replaced by a conception of Imperial interests so vague that it can always be filled up in detail to fit personal advantage. Their patriotism has been on a par with the patriotism of capitalists on the land.[43]

It was the Act of Union, according to Gwynn, which forced Irish landlords into an irreconcilable position, caught between the ties and kinship of Britain and the interests of Ireland.[44]

His affinity with the landed class was shaped both by his youthful experiences and exposures in Donegal, and by the notion that the lost 'patriotism' (with its eighteenth-century connotations) of Irish landlordism could yet be rekindled. When the land question re-emerged during his Westminster years, Gwynn 'asserted that in an Irish assembly even the landlord interest of Ireland would fare better than in the House of Commons'.[45] Despite the ruptures of the Land War and the rise of a Catholic democracy, Gwynn envisaged the reconciliation between landlordism and nationalism within the framework of Home Rule. 'If self-government is established without dissolution of the Union, is it not reasonable to suppose that there will be a change in men's dispositions?', he asked in 1913, a particularly sensitive time in Irish politics.[46] Donegal gave Gwynn more than emotional bonds with the landlords; the county also instilled his sense of national rapport. Identity in Ireland and how 'Irishness' was defined were key themes throughout Gwynn's discourse, from his earliest works, through his political and cultural careers, to his final writings. The county of his youth – and the Protestant culture in which he grew up – triggered his later pre-occupation with Irishness. The young Gwynn's Donegal represented a 'mosaic of political culture'.[47] In 1871, when Gwynn was seven years old, Donegal was inhabited by 165,003 Catholics and 52,989 Protestants of all denominations, a breakdown of 76 to 24 per cent. Protestants were, though, vastly over-represented in the higher echelons of Donegal society, particularly in the realms of land ownership and the judiciary: the *Londonderry Journal* reported in 1873 that there was one Protestant magistrate for every 375 Protestants, a marked contrast to the one Catholic magistrate for every 41,250 Catholics.[48] Gwynn grew up acutely aware of the distinctions in the social and economic positions between Catholics and Protestants. His father was a handsomely paid Protestant clergyman and academic, while his mother came from a gentry family. His father's parishioners were mostly Donegal's well-to-do Anglicans. But a different world existed a very short distance away from his family home, and this is the crucial point for grasping Gwynn's later interests in Irish identity, history, culture and politics, as he recorded in his autobiography:

> My life has been spent largely in an effort to understand and interpret Ireland, and that corner of Donegal has been the key to all my study. Everything was there. Ten miles walking would take you where at that time nothing was spoken but Gaelic; but in my father's parish the ordinary speech was Scots.[49]

Donegal was a microcosm of Catholic *and* Protestant Ireland: a minority Ascendancy class maintaining a dominant and privileged socio-economic position, while the majority Catholic population formed the rural poor and small tenantry. Despite the divisions within the county, Gwynn argued that, collectively, 'no people were ever more Irish, whether they were Catholic or Protestant, gentle or simple'.[50] 'Irishness', however vaguely defined, was the binding concept in Gwynn's mind throughout his life, the common identity with the potential to bridge wholesale political and religious differences.

The young Stephen Gwynn resembled an apprentice country gentleman. But in 1876, at the age of twelve, he began his formal education outside Donegal, becoming the first of the eight Gwynn brothers to attend St Columba's College in Dublin, the institution connected to the family through the Reverend John Gwynn's past wardenship.[51] Before Stephen commenced his formal studies in Dublin, his father became the Dean of Raphoe, a reward for his work connected with the disestablishment of the Church of Ireland.[52] Unsurprisingly, given his father's educational ties, Stephen 'learnt to learn' at home in Donegal before his first trip to St Columba's. His mother, Lucy Gwynn, taught all her ten children to the start of their formal education; his father 'supplemented with a little Latin and Greek'.[53]

Stephen's return to his birthplace marked the beginning of his generation of siblings' love affair with St Columba's. All eight brothers passed through the College with great academic and sporting success; the family's distinguished record was publicly recognised and celebrated in 1952 with the creation of a new senior house christened 'Gwynn'.[54] But this was far in the future when the twelve-year-old Stephen took his first tentative steps into the world of private schooling. St Columba's College first opened its doors in 1843: its original focal point was a college identity based on the Oxford and Cambridge models.[55] The teachers were called 'Fellows' and the headmaster was addressed as the 'Warden' to promote this sense of Oxbridge life. While this idea began to slacken within the College during the following decade, St Columba's held a unique position in the Irish educational field, seeking to attract boys who would otherwise tend to enter the English public schooling system. This was emphasised by the fact that highly educated Englishmen dominated the numbers of the College's staff during the nineteenth century.[56] It was a very English institution near the heart of Dublin life. Before the disestablishment of the Church of Ireland, the College stipulated that students must belong to the Anglican faith. After disestablishment, this policy unofficially remained in place: the Warden admitted in 1879 that there were no Roman Catholic or non-Anglican Protestant pupils attending the College.[57]

St Columba's sense of Englishness was not lost on Gwynn: he recorded in his autobiography that 'The school was run somewhat on English lines'.[58] Life at the College exposed him to a culture that was very different to both the rural Irish Protestant and Catholic civilisations of Donegal. The Warden of St Columba's during Gwynn's time was the Reverend Robert Rice, an Englishman with outspoken English views; he once described the College as 'this copy of the good old English foundations'.[59] Tellingly, the most popular career of St Columba's old boys between 1870 and 1889 was with the British Army:[60] Gwynn himself would very belatedly join this statistic when he entered the soldiering profession at the age of fifty-one, in 1915. The College represented conservative rather than liberal England: the Debating Club consistently sided with the Conservative Party and stoutly opposed Gladstonian Liberalism.[61] Gwynn's depictions of a Columban contemporary, Vesey Knox, who later held the Derry City Westminster seat for the Irish Party, illuminates the prevailing unionist atmosphere of the College. Knox was a nationalist, even at St Columba's; Gwynn recalled that to all the pupils this 'seemed the most outrageous kind of freethinking'.[62] In a later essay, Gwynn wrote that during his six years at the College, Knox was the only boy 'disgraced by such a departure from the usages of Protestant gentry' – suggesting that Gwynn himself did not hold nationalist views at this point of his life.[63] Knox's activities went sorely against the grain of narrow Anglican life in St Columba's College: before the onset of the Land War in 1879, he was 'the only indication that there could be two opinions about political questions in Ireland'.[64]

The teenage Gwynn received a rounded education at St Columba's College, with a strong religious element. The official College history documents a daily timetable from 1873: it reveals that the pupils spent a considerable portion of their day inside a chapel.[65] Despite this, and his family's connections with the Church of Ireland which stretched back generations, Gwynn remained ambivalent about religious issues throughout his life. Educationally, though, there was little doubt about Gwynn's capacities, as he swept the board the board at St Columba's. The school magazine, *The Columban*, records many instances of Stephen's high-flying endeavours.[66] In 1881, Gwynn was awarded a gold medal for Latin and came second in Greek in the senior grade: when combined, he was the 'Senior Classic in all the schools of Ireland'.[67] Gwynn's name is also immortalised on a plaque in the College's dining hall that lists the senior prefects: he won this distinction in 1881. The striking aspect about the plaque is the number of Gwynns peppered throughout its list of names: many of Stephen's younger brothers also held this role of responsibility. The Gwynn family's successes were such that from 1888 *The Columban* listed a 'Gwynn Prize', which was to be awarded to a young and able scholar of Latin, Greek, French or German; unsurprisingly, the first winner was a Gwynn.[68] Stephen's academic successes within the College were also matched by his extra-curricular activities. He was captain of the College cricket team, a fact omitted from his autobiography; even his son, Aubrey, was not aware of this fact until after his father's death.[69] Stephen often wrote in praise of the sporting abilities of his brother Lucius,[70] who represented Ireland on the rugby and cricket fields, but he never hinted at his own modest achievements within this sphere. Cricket was not young Gwynn's only sporting interest: he also participated in at least one College lawn tennis tournament.[71] The June 1882 edition of the College's magazine also reveals that Stephen Gwynn delivered 'a very powerful recitation' of Clytemnestra's speech in Aeschylus's *Agamemnon*.[72]

Gwynn's academic and extra-circular flair was rewarded with a scholarship to Oxford in 1882. After rejection from two colleges, he managed to win a place in Brasenose to read classics. The young scholar was excited by the prospect of studying in Oxford, particularly after his first visit to the 'delightful old place'.[73] The Oxford adventure was not, however, a particularly happy period in Gwynn's life. While he succeeded academically, he struggled to find his feet at Brasenose, and the wider University. His later writings consistently adopted a belligerent attitude to the subject of his time at Oxford, reflecting the sense of loneliness and detachment he felt at the University, which was, for Gwynn, 'the extreme characteristic expression of English life'.[74] This negative disposition was partly moulded from his own late-teenage mindset. As a youth, Gwynn was rather socially awkward, a trait amplified by his Oxford experience. Some months before leaving for England, Gwynn stayed with the O'Briens at their estate in Cahirmoyle. He spent most of his time with his cousin, Dermod O'Brien. He told his mother, 'Dermod is as far as I can judge one of the very few people of my own age whom I know that I am likely to make a friend of'.[75] This suggests that the young Gwynn struggled to make friends within his own peer group. When recalling his cheerless Oxford experience, Gwynn generally blamed the prevailing social structure of the elite university.[76] But he hinted at the other side of his isolation later when he declared that he was not 'what the Americans call "a good mixer"'. 'I did not', he rued, 'become easily adaptable until I was over thirty'.[77]

In his written accounts of life at Oxford, Gwynn describes several of his fellow students and scholars with little trace of affection, with Walter Pater, then a tutor at Brasenose, coming under particular attack ('the oddest waste of a man that I ever knew').[78] Aubrey Gwynn starkly recollected the thoughts of his elderly father on his undergraduate days: 'My father said to me more than once in his old age that "he never made a friend at Oxford who was any use to me". That is not the memory of a man who was happy at Oxford'.[79] This dismissive attitude became more prevalent in Gwynn's old age.[80] He found the 'Englishness' of Oxford life grating; like Charles Stewart Parnell's experiences in Cambridge a generation before, he felt, and was made to feel, an outsider. Parnell, who endured a miserable time in Magdalene College during the 1860s, would undoubtedly second Gwynn's comments about life in England's elite universities: 'My views formed themselves under the stimulus of hearing my country abused; and scores of other young Irishmen at Oxford and

Cambridge have in the same way been made to realize that they were Nationalists'.[81] Gwynn left Ireland for Oxford at a sensitive time in Anglo-Irish relations. In May 1882, the Kilmainham 'treaty' was negotiated between Parnell and Gladstone, which saw the release of the leaders of the suppressed Land League. Four days later, the Irish Chief Secretary, Lord Frederick Cavendish, and his permanent Under-Secretary, Thomas Burke, were gruesomely murdered in Phoenix Park by a Fenian splinter group. The murders negatively altered the tone of Anglo-Irish relations at a political level, while the English journal *Punch* used the Irish agitation of the early 1880s to repackage stereotypical Irish caricatures, amply demonstrated in its infamous 'Irish Frankenstein' cartoon.[82] It is in this context of increased anti-Irish feeling in England that Gwynn's nationalist identity began to take shape.

Part of the antagonism for Gwynn related to wealth. He claimed that 'the real dividing line was money' within Oxford; financial status separated the great from the good within the University. The leading lights of Brasenose were those with wealth and Gwynn bitterly complained that 'in effect a lack of money acted as a social disqualification and limited one's choice of acquaintance'.[83] Despite the respect that the Gwynn family drew, they were not hugely wealthy, particularly compared with the families of several of Gwynn's contemporaries at Brasenose. An illuminating example of the two-tiered structure of undergraduate life within the College is presented by Douglas Haig. Haig, who was to command the British Army in France during the First World War, was a prominent member of Brasenose, having joined the College in 1880.[84] Gwynn claimed he never met Haig at Brasenose; despite the small size of the student body at the College, 'about a third of it was clean cut off from the rest'.[85] Haig swiftly 'became an intimate friend of the most prominent, that is to say the wealthiest and the gayest, of the undergraduates';[86] Gwynn admitted he did not even know that he had been educated alongside Haig until the First World War.[87] Tellingly, there was no shortage of money in the Haig household.[88] Aubrey Gwynn picks up this theme in his unpublished autobiography: 'My father was not an impecunious student, but the mere fact he came from an Irish parsonage, had not been at any recognised public school and had no money to throw about placed him from the first at a disadvantage'.[89] For Aubrey's father, this was the crux of Oxford life. He did not move in elite circles, which was further accentuated by not rowing or playing football, rugby or cricket, despite his sporting achievements at St Columba's. Haig, on the other hand, was a powerful force within the undergraduate population. In June 1919, Brasenose organised a reunion dinner to honour Haig and the Allied victory. Gwynn attended the dinner, but more than likely grimaced when Haig triumphantly claimed in his speech that 'It is here in Oxford that is found the main stronghold of the opinion that the highest and most important object of education is the formation of character'.[90] Undoubtedly, Gwynn would agree, but for very different reasons: he was later to claim that 'I formed my Home Rule opinion when I went to Oxford'.[91]

When Gwynn was in his fresher year in Oxford, his father accepted the deanship of Derry. Gwynn recalled that he returned to the family's new home in Derry during the first vacation break at Oxford for fishing excursions in Donegal and copious amounts of lawn tennis.[92] A year later, the Reverend John Gwynn won a lectureship in divinity at TCD, which brought the family to Thorndale in Dublin. During vacations, Stephen was exposed to the TCD element which many Gwynns before him had experienced; he garnered many Trinity acquaintances over the next few years, as well as lasting links with the emerging youthful bohemian and literary movements. Equally crucial in the maturing of his worldview was the influence of his extraordinary aunt, Charlotte Grace O'Brien. She was Smith O'Brien's second daughter and, unlike the majority of her siblings, inherited his nationalist tendencies. Her novel, *Light and shade* (1878), dealt with the 1867 Fenian rising; one English newspaper described it as a 'praiseworthy attempt to create sympathy with the Irish'.[93] Charlotte broke with O'Brien Protestant tradition and converted to Catholicism, something her father did not do. After the Irish Parliamentary Party split in 1890, Charlotte resolutely defended Parnell and sided passionately with his faction against the majority of nationalist opinion, including the Catholic Church. After Parnell's death, she found refuge in the Gaelic League,[94] a body in which Gwynn found favour and discord during the Edwardian period.

The Land War had ended by the time Gwynn arrived in Oxford, but population displacement was still a notable feature of the hardship of Irish life. Emigration defines the social history of nineteenth-century Ireland, with huge numbers of people leaving the island before, during and after the Famine. The exodus peaked during the Famine; but the poor harvest of 1879 and the commencement of the Land War occasioned substantial emigration once again. Ireland's economic downturn during the 1880s was marked by a sharp increase in female emigration patterns: some three-quarters of a million young and generally unmarried women left Ireland in the late nineteenth and early twentieth centuries, a figure that outnumbered male emigration.[95] This was Charlotte Grace O'Brien's great concern, and she threw herself into improving the conditions for the women leaving Ireland and increasing public awareness of the plight of many women who were duped into prostitution. O'Brien became a regular sight on the wharf of Queenstown (now Cobh) in Cork, where she opened a refuge for emigrants passing through, offering a bed, breakfast and an evening meal.[96] Gwynn stayed with O'Brien in Queenstown for a portion of his Easter vacation in 1883 and observed the emigrants passing through her refuge. He found the experience a profound one, recording later 'my views ceased to be mere views and became nourished on fact' after this stay with his aunt.[97] He saw the practice of 'state-aided emigration' at first-hand: many of the people who passed through O'Brien's refuge were partly sponsored to leave the country to lessen Ireland's economic troubles. This was not a new practice, as the first major scheme of state financial assistance to emigrants occurred twenty years before the Famine.[98] Yet the sight of Irish people being paid to leave Ireland left an enduring mark on Gwynn, with his anger spilling over into several of his writings much later. The stark reality of state-sponsored emigration opened his eyes to a different reality from the tranquillity of Donegal. In the context of a withdrawn first year in Oxford, Gwynn developed a growing and distinct feeling of 'otherness', which would evolve into nationalism.

Dublin in the 1880s

IN his time away from Oxford during his undergraduate career, Gwynn befriended many young bohemians based in or around TCD. Trinity was a hotbed of literary and political activities during the 1880s. One organ that represented the flowering of youthful intellectualism surrounding the College was the *Dublin University Review*, established by T. W. Rolleston and Charles Hubert Oldham in February 1885. The *Review* was a short-lived journal that collapsed due to monetary problems: the poet Katharine Tynan was perhaps close to the truth when she claimed that it was 'too good to be popular'.[99] Rolleston and Oldham were also pivotal figures in bringing together many members of Ireland's future literary elite in smoke-filled rooms around the College; Gwynn's route into this world came through his family's links to Trinity. Rolleston, who was distantly related to Stephen's family, was a frequent visitor to the Gwynn household in Thorndale after 1883 at the request of the Reverend John Gwynn, who keenly befriended a number of Dublin-based intellectuals, many of whom were strongly nationalistic, over the course of his Trinity career.[100] Rolleston was commencing a career in letters when Gwynn first met him and he played an important organising role in establishing the Irish Literary Society of London in the early 1890s. The studios of artists such as the sharp-tongued Sarah Purser and Walter Osborne (who became a close friend of the Gwynns) became regular haunts; Gwynn's cousins, W. F. P. Stockley and his brother John, also gave Stephen a direct input into Dublin's literary life. They were regulars at the house of Edward Dowden, Professor of English Literature at TCD. Dowden's home, which was several minutes away from the Gwynn household, became an invaluable meeting-point for many

FIGURE 2. Stephen Gwynn, c. 1885, by Walter Frederick Osborne, oil on canvas.

individuals interested in literature, including Gwynn. Dowden was of 'old Protestant stock' and was staunchly unionist; but he also was, in Gwynn's words, 'a chief rallying point for the new literary movement', despite the overt nationalism of many of its prime movers.[101] Dowden's home was the scene of keen debate involving many notable guests, including: his old friend the artist John Butler Yeats and his shy but mysterious poet son, William; Rolleston and Oldham; the Irish-language enthusiast Douglas Hyde; and the promising barrister J. F. Taylor.

The meetings at Dowden's house exposed Gwynn to debate involving the cream of Ireland's young talented literary figures. Dowden was most taken by the young Yeats and focused much of his attention on him: he declared that Yeats was 'an interesting boy whether he turned out much of a poet or not'.[102] The Trinity professor, however, remained aloof from the Irish literary renaissance that Yeats would spearhead: an inwardly focused Irish literature went against the cultural grain of the worldly poet-professor. Nevertheless, Dowden privately encouraged and praised the young Yeats after the publication of *The wanderings of Oisin and other poems* in 1889. Yeats also left an indelible mark on Gwynn when they first met, in 1885, as Gwynn recalled in 1921:

> From my first knowledge of him, there was a poet, not merely the making of a poet, recognisable in that long wisp of a lad, always in black, whom I remember best with a broken straw hat on his long black hair. He always looked a poet, far more completely than any one else I have known, yet naturally and without pose.[103]

He later added that 'Somehow or other, before he had published a line, he had convinced us that he was a poet who would count'.[104] Gwynn and Yeats would remain literary allies for decades after their first meeting, without giving the impression that they were ever particularly close. Yeats was ultimately to become Ireland's most pre-eminent literary figure, whereas Gwynn found a role as an astute commentator of, rather than creative participant in, the Irish literary revival. Dowden correctly gauged Gwynn's temperament in a reference he wrote during the young Stephen's attempts to secure an academic post during the 1890s: 'He has not only knowledge but also sound judgement and refined feeling in things literary'.[105]

Running parallel to the meetings in Dowden's house was a similar gathering in the rooms of Charles Hubert Oldham at TCD. The two groups shared a significant overlap of personnel: Douglas Hyde recorded in his diary, for example, that on 12 June 1885 he attended Oldham's quarters along with George Coffey, Stockley and Rolleston; on 24 June, Hyde went to Dowden's and found all three there.[106] The debates in Oldham's rooms were much more volatile, however, than the refined discussions on Sunday afternoons at Dowden's house. Oldham, according to Mary Macken, was removed from his Trinity quarters because of his commitment to Home Rule politics (Oldham would later become the driving force behind the short-lived Irish Protestant Home Rule Association in 1886)[107] and moved into rooms opposite TCD on Grafton Street.[108] These smoky rooms became the headquarters of the Contemporary Club.

The Contemporary Club was established in November 1885 by Oldham and became the most important political and literary society attached to TCD. Its membership was exclusively male, although women were not completely barred, as Maud Gonne was permitted to join the debates. She recalled that there were 'men of all shades of political opinion at the Club, even one or two Unionists, and the debate became very vehement'.[109] Vehemence of debate was the trademark of the Contemporary Club. Yeats's recollections are similar to Gonne's: 'In Ireland harsh argument which had gone out of fashion in England was still the manner of our conversation, and at this club Unionist and Nationalist could interrupt one another and insult one another without the formal and traditional restraint of public speech'.[110] The Contemporary Club debated the major contemporary political and cultural issues of the day and, as the testimonies of Maud Gonne and W. B. Yeats reveal, it conducted itself in a no-holds-barred fashion. The English socialist, poet and artist William Morris found this to his cost when he visited the Club after lecturing at a workingmen's association in Dublin in 1886. Gwynn had previously encountered Morris at Oxford, where the poet attempted to bolster the doctrine of socialism among the student body of the University. Although Morris was unsuccessful in convincing the young Irishman of a socialist alternative, a party which included Gwynn and Walter Osborne escorted Morris to an extremely packed session of the Contemporary Club on 11 April 1886. There, as Gwynn recalled, he fared poorly against the regulars, even though Douglas Hyde believed that 'there was not much sense to the questions'.[111] The Club clearly was not for the faint-hearted.

The only common theme that united the members of the Contemporary Club was, seemingly, that 'they were all alive at the same moment'.[112] But the Club's membership list was ambiguous: just as it is unclear whether Yeats was a full member,[113] there is no conclusive evidence that Gwynn was either. When he was on vacation from Oxford he certainly attended some of the debates. Like the more sober affairs at Edward Dowden's house, the rigorous conversation of the Contemporary Club offered Gwynn a uniquely Irish experience: the tone of debate was firmly nationalist, and it is difficult to believe that exposure to this environment did not affect the impressionable young Irishman, who resented life in England. The Contemporary Club also offered a handful of valuable contacts. It was through the Club, for instance, that Gwynn met the elder statesman of radical nationalism, John O'Leary.

O'Leary was a member of the Irish Republican Brotherhood (IRB) who had spent fifteen years in enforced exile in Paris for his Fenian conspiratorial activities. He had returned to Dublin in January 1885 with the aim of furthering Ireland's cultural liberation through the medium of a national literature. He frequently attended the Contemporary Club: the best-known consequence of this was his friendship with W. B. Yeats and his father.[114] The younger Yeats quickly fell under the spell of the older man, who represented the 'acceptable face of the extremist Fenian tradition'.[115] Yeats famously described his mentor as 'the handsomest old man I had ever seen'; Gwynn depicted the bearded O'Leary as an 'eagle-eyed, eagle-beaked old man' who looked uncannily similar to his father, John Gwynn.[116] The young classics student and the older Fenian became friends through their associations with the Contemporary Club and soon Gwynn was invited to attend weekly literary discussion sessions at O'Leary's sister's house, where the senior rebel lived.[117] O'Leary used these meetings to encourage young writers and poets – his audience included Yeats, Hyde, Rolleston and Tynan – to embrace a new form of prose and poetry with a powerful national content, which would underpin a future political revolution.[118] O'Leary was sceptical of the literary value of the prose and poetry of the Young Irelanders, believing their writing to be nothing more than propaganda. He was concerned to create a distinctly Irish literature that was *literature* first and foremost: this later became Yeats's mission, which he would take beyond even O'Leary's vision. One of Gwynn's literary commentaries chronicled the essential value of O'Leary to the young writers, as well as Gwynn's own fascination with him: he was 'able to introduce the young men to an amazing link with the past – reaching back past Fenian times to the heart of Young Ireland itself'.[119] O'Leary was the living, breathing link to the Irish-centred literature and the secular politics of Thomas Davis and the *Nation*, and was to plot the early course for the literary revival by inspiring Yeats – whom O'Leary believed was a genius – to adopt Irish themes for his art. The literary revival that started in the 1880s became the most successful nationalist enterprise in which the IRB man was involved.

Yeats famously lamented the death of 'Romantic Ireland', which was 'with O'Leary in the grave', in his poem 'September 1913'. In life, though, O'Leary was intrigued by Gwynn's own link to 'Romantic Ireland': William Smith O'Brien. Given that O'Leary took part in the 1848 rising, it was not difficult for O'Brien's grandson to attract his attention.[120] In 1885, the Fenian took Gwynn and the poets Katharine Tynan and Rose Kavanagh to visit Charles Gavan Duffy, the organising spirit behind the Young Irelanders. Gwynn admitted feeling a tinge of disappointment after meeting the man who was so close to the revolutionary actions of his grandfather: Gavan Duffy, for Gwynn, was morally 'far less impressive than O'Leary'.[121] Tynan reminisced in 1924 that she thought Gwynn came to Duffy 'as a young man out of the ruling classes in Ireland who was a likely recruit to the Irish National Cause'.[122] Gwynn played down any such suggestion in his autobiography several years later, simply suggesting that 'I went with immense curiosity about the man who nearly forty years before had been deep in revolutionary counsel with my mother's father'.[123] Tynan's account was probably distorted by the prism of Gwynn's later involvement in nationalist politics: there is no evidence to suggest that he was keen to embrace the 'Irish National Cause' any earlier than he actually did. Whatever Gwynn's motives, he was disappointed by the Young Ireland veteran, who was 'a completely worn-out force'.[124]

Gwynn completed his studies at Brasenose College in 1886, but his social network clearly lay around the grounds of TCD. This, perhaps inevitably, led to retrospective comparisons of university life in Oxford and Dublin in several of his later writings and, unsurprisingly, TCD was the preference. In 1948, Gwynn claimed that John Mahaffy and Robert Tyrrell, two brilliant classics scholars who were at Trinity during his undergraduate days, 'would have been better worth knowing than any don I met at Oxford'.[125] In an essay from 1907, Gwynn argued that wealth was not a barrier to social networking at TCD: 'The general trend of life in Trinity is towards frugality', argued Gwynn, 'just as at Oxford it is towards extravagance'.[126] Gwynn's retrospective analysis of his university career echoed the attitude of his grandfather, William Smith O'Brien, who in 1852 insisted that his son, Edward, should attend TCD rather than Oxford or Cambridge; at Cambridge, Smith O'Brien, in his own words, learnt 'much that was evil and little that was good'.[127] Yet if Gwynn was 'not sure that [Oxford] is the best place for a young Irishman to learn in',[128] it did not hinder his academic prowess: he left Brasenose with a double first, one year into a Senior Hulmean scholarship.[129] Gwynn was an able classics scholar by the age of twenty-two, although only one book from his vast collection of writings – *The odes of Horace* (1902) – required the use of his academic training. His Oxford years gave him a formal education in classics, which he did not embrace afterwards, and an informal education in matters of identity, which was yet to express itself politically or culturally. He had a remarkable circle of acquaintances, which would set the tone for much of his own cultural activities. But with the completion of his studies, Gwynn reached the first crossroads of his life: there were many options open to an intelligent young Irishman with a newly minted degree from Oxford.

Notes

1 *Spectator*, 12 September 1896; reprinted in Stephen Gwynn, *The queen's chronicler and other poems* (London: John Lane, 1901), pp. 24–5.
2 Stephen Gwynn, 'Yesterday in Ireland', in *Irish books and Irish people* (Dublin: Talbot Press, 1919), pp. 105–6.
3 See especially Stephen Gwynn, 'From Donegal I wandered', *The Bell*, 15:3 (1947), pp. 26–36.
4 George Rutherford, *Old families of Carrickfergus and Ballynure: from gravestone inscriptions, wills and biographical notes*, ed. Richard Clarke (Belfast: Ulster Historical Foundation, 1995), p. 16.
5 Dorothea Herbert, *Retrospections of Dorothea Herbert 1770–1806* (Dublin: Town House, 1988; first published as two vols, 1929 and 1930), p. 139.
6 Bernhard Burke, *Burke's Irish family records* (London: Burke's Peerage, fifth edition, 1976), p. 533.
7 J. B. Leslie, *Clergy of Connor: from patrician times to the present day* (Belfast: Ulster Historical Foundation, 1993), p. 365.
8 Aubrey Gwynn, 'Unfinished history of the Gwynn family, 1660–1903', Aubrey Gwynn papers, Irish Jesuit Archive (IJA), J10/89(50).

9 Burke, *Burke's Irish family records*, p. 533.
10 Leslie, *Clergy of Connor*, p. 365.
11 Stephen Gwynn, 'A scholar', in *Garden wisdom: or from one generation to another* (Dublin: Talbot Press, 1921), p. 114.
12 *Ibid.*, p. 120.
13 Burke, *Burke's Irish family records*, p. 533.
14 G. K. White, *A history of St Columba's College 1843–1974* (Dublin: Old Columban Society, 1980), p. 76.
15 *Irish Times*, 18 July 1974.
16 Stephen Gwynn, *Experiences of a literary man* (London: Thornton Butterworth, 1926), p. 13.
17 Stephen Gwynn, *The charm of Ireland: her places of beauty, entertainment, sport and historic association* (London: George G. Harrap and Co., 1934), p. 151.
18 Stephen Gwynn, *The fair hills of Ireland* (Dublin: Maunsel and Co., 1906), p. 322.
19 Donough O'Brien, *History of the O'Briens: from Brian Boroimhe AD 1000 to AD 1945* (London: B. T. Batsford, 1949), p. 55.
20 Ivar O'Brien, *O'Brien of Thomond: the O'Briens in Irish history 1500–1865* (Chichester: Phillimore and Co., 1986), p. 39.
21 *Munster News*, 10 October 1862; Dunboyne press cuttings, pp. 94–5, William Smith O'Brien papers, National Library of Ireland (NLI), MS 3375.
22 Stephen Gwynn, 'Introductory memoir', in *Charlotte Grace O'Brien: selections from her writings and correspondence with a memoir by Stephen Gwynn* (Dublin: Maunsel and Co., 1909), p. 5.
23 Grania R. O'Brien, *These my friends and forebears* (Whitegate: Ballinakella Press, 1991), p. 102.
24 Paul Bew, *Ireland: the politics of enmity 1789–2006* (Oxford: Oxford University Press, 2007), p. 227.
25 Robert Sloan, *William Smith O'Brien and the Young Ireland rebellion of 1848* (Dublin: Four Courts Press, 2000), p. 303.
26 Gwynn, *Experiences*, p. 15.
27 Gwynn, 'History of the Gwynn family', Aubrey Gwynn papers, IJA, J10/89 (11).
28 Gwynn, *Experiences*, p. 16.
29 *Irish Times*, 4 April 1917.
30 Gwynn, *Experiences*, p. 26.
31 Gwynn, 'From Donegal I wandered', p. 27.
32 Gwynn, 'Introductory memoir', pp. 36–7.
33 Gwynn, *Experiences*, p. 21.
34 Stephen Gwynn to 'Aunt Lizzie', 6 February 1873, Aubrey Gwynn papers, IJA, J10/82 (1) and (2).
35 Lucy Gwynn to 'Aunt Lizzie', 6 February 1873, Aubrey Gwynn papers, IJA, J10/82 (2).
36 Joyce Cary, *A house of children* (London: Michael Joseph, 1955; first published 1941), p. 194.
37 Aubrey Gwynn, 'Draft of an autobiography of Father Aubrey Gwynn', n.d. [1979], Aubrey Gwynn papers, IJA, J10/90 (112).
38 Stephen Gwynn to Lucy Gwynn, 3 October 1882, papers in the possession of Fergus Kelly, Dublin.
39 *Freeman's Journal*, 6 April 1878. The government offered a £500 reward, while Leitrim's heir put up £10,000.
40 Stephen Gwynn, *Highways and byways in Donegal and Antrim* (London: Macmillan and Co., 1899), pp. 170–2.

41 A. P. W. Malcomson, *Virtues of a wicked earl: the life and legend of William Sydney Clements, 3rd Earl of Leitrim (1806–78)* (Dublin: Four Courts Press, 2009), *passim*.
42 Stephen Gwynn, *A holiday in Connemara* (London: Methuen and Co., 1909), pp. 161–2.
43 Stephen Gwynn, *Today and tomorrow in Ireland: essays on Irish subjects* (Dublin: Hodges, Figgis, and Co., 1903), p. xvi.
44 Gwynn, 'The Irish gentry', in *Irish books and Irish people*, pp. 93–4.
45 *Freeman's Journal*, 21 September 1909.
46 Gwynn, 'The Irish gentry', p. 94.
47 Desmond Murphy, *Derry, Donegal and modern Ulster 1790–1921* (Londonderry: Aileach Press, 1981), p. 135.
48 *Londonderry Journal*, 5 February 1873.
49 Gwynn, *Experiences*, pp. 18–19. The Gwynns also had several Catholic household staff.
50 Stephen Gwynn, 'Thoughts about Ireland', *The Bell*, 15:6 (March 1948), p. 55.
51 Gwynn, 'From Donegal I wandered', p. 26.
52 Gwynn, 'History of the Gwynn family', Aubrey Gwynn papers, IJA, J10/89 (7–8).
53 Gwynn, *Experiences*, p. 27.
54 White, *History of St Columba's College*, p. 181.
55 *Ibid.*, pp. 18, 21.
56 *Ibid.*, p. 74.
57 *Ibid.*, pp. 22, 108.
58 Gwynn, *Experiences*, p. 28.
59 Quoted in White, *History of St Columba's College*, p. 84.
60 *The Columban*, 70: 2 (1949).
61 White, *History of St Columba's College*, p. 107.
62 Gwynn, *Experiences*, p. 29.
63 Gwynn, 'From Donegal I wandered', p. 31.
64 Gwynn, *Experiences*, p. 30.
65 White, *History of St Columba's College*, p. 98.
66 Unfortunately, the library at St Columba's College holds the magazine only from 1881, when Gwynn was in his penultimate year.
67 *The Columban*, 2:7 (October 1881).
68 *The Columban*, 9:5 (June 1888).
69 Gwynn, 'Draft of an autobiography', Aubrey Gwynn papers, IJA, J10/90 (112).
70 See, for example, Gwynn, 'From Donegal I wandered', p. 30.
71 *The Columban*, 2:7 (October 1881).
72 *The Columban*, 3:4 (June 1882).
73 Stephen Gwynn to Katherine Stevenson, 5 March 1882, William Smith O'Brien papers, NLI, MS 8665 (1).
74 Gwynn, *Experiences*, p. 52.
75 Stephen Gwynn to Lucy Gwynn, 3 October 1882, papers in the possession of Fergus Kelly, Dublin.
76 Gwynn, *Experiences*, p. 36.
77 *Ibid.*, pp. 34, 36.
78 *Ibid.*, p. 47.
79 Gwynn, 'Draft of an autobiography', Aubrey Gwynn papers, IJA, J10/90 (116).
80 Stephen Gwynn, 'About eating', in *Memories of enjoyment* (Tralee: Kerryman, 1946), p. 53.
81 Gwynn, *Experiences*, p. 33.
82 *Punch*, 20 May 1882. Also see L. P. Curtis, Jr, *Apes and angels: the Irishman in Victorian caricature* (Newton Abbot: David and Charles, 1971), p. 38.

83 Gwynn, *Experiences*, p. 36.
84 D. Cooper, *Haig* (London: Faber and Faber, two vols, 1935), vol. I, p. 19.
85 Gwynn, *Experiences*, p. 36.
86 Cooper, *Haig*, vol. I, p. 20.
87 Gwynn, *Experiences*, p. 36.
88 Philip Warner, *Field Marshal Earl Haig* (London: Cassell and Co., 2001; first published 1991), p. 11.
89 Gwynn, 'Draft of an autobiography', Aubrey Gwynn papers, IJA, J10/90 (114).
90 Warner, *Haig*, p. 271.
91 *Spectator*, 8 October 1910.
92 Gwynn, 'From Donegal I wandered', p. 35.
93 *Manchester Guardian*, 11 November 1878; scrapbook of newspaper cuttings relating to Charlotte Grace O'Brien, O'Brien family papers, NLI, MS 36, 803/1.
94 Anne O'Connell, 'Charlotte Grace O'Brien', in Mary Cullen and Maria Luddy (eds), *Women, power and consciousness in nineteenth-century Ireland: eight biographical studies* (Dublin: Attic Press, 1995), pp. 254–5.
95 J. A. Nolan, *Ourselves alone: women's emigration from Ireland 1885–1920* (Lexington: University Press of Kentucky, 1989), pp. 49, 53.
96 O'Connell, 'Charlotte Grace O'Brien', p. 247.
97 Gwynn, *Experiences*, p. 33.
98 David Fitzpatrick, *Irish emigration 1801–1921* (Dundalk: Dundalgan Press, 1990; first published 1984), p. 17.
99 Katharine Tynan, *Twenty-five years: reminiscences* (London: Smith, Elder and Co., 1913), p. 143.
100 Stephen Gwynn, 'Foreword', C. H. Rolleston, *Portrait of an Irishman: a biographical sketch of T. W. Rolleston* (London: Methuen and Co., 1939), p. vii.
101 Stephen Gwynn, *Irish literature and drama in the English language: a short history* (London: Thomas Nelson and Sons, 1936), p. 117.
102 Quoted in R. F. Foster, *W. B. Yeats: a life. Vol. I: The apprentice mage 1865–1914* (Oxford: Oxford University Press, 1997), p. 38.
103 Gwynn, 'The ageing of a poet', in *Garden wisdom*, p. 13.
104 Gwynn, *Experiences*, p. 66.
105 Reference from Edward Dowden, Stephen Gwynn papers, NLI, MS 8600(4).
106 Dominic Daly, *The young Douglas Hyde: the dawn of the Irish revolution and renaissance 1874–1893* (Dublin: Irish University Press, 1974), p. 57.
107 James Loughlin, 'The Irish Protestant Home Rule Association and nationalist politics, 1886–93', *Irish Historical Studies*, 24:95 (May 1985), p. 344.
108 Mary M. Macken, 'W. B. Yeats, John O'Leary and the Contemporary Club', *Studies*, 27 (March 1939), p. 137.
109 Maud Gonne MacBride, *A servant of the queen: reminiscences* (London: Victor Gollancz, 1974; first published 1938), pp. 89–90.
110 W. B. Yeats, *Autobiographies*, eds William H. O'Donnell and Douglas N. Archibald (Basingstoke: Palgrave, 1999), p. 99.
111 Gwynn, *Experiences*, pp. 43–4; Daly, *The young Douglas Hyde*, p. 76.
112 William M. Murphy, *Prodigal father: the life of John Butler Yeats (1839–1922)* (London: Cornell University Press, 1978), p. 140.
113 Foster, *Apprentice mage*, p. 42.
114 Marcus Bourke, *John O'Leary: a study in Irish separation* (Tralee: Anvil Books, 1967), pp. 181–2.
115 Foster, *Apprentice mage*, p. 43.
116 Yeats, *Autobiographies*, p. 100; Gwynn, *Experiences*, p. 58.
117 John O'Leary to Stephen Gwynn, n.d., Stephen Gwynn papers, NLI, MS 8600 (13).

118 Bourke, *John O'Leary*, p. 183.
119 Gwynn, *Irish literature and drama*, p. 118.
120 Gwynn, *Experiences*, p. 58.
121 *Ibid.*, p. 59.
122 Katharine Tynan, *Memories* (London: Eveleigh Nash and Grayson, 1924), p. 174.
123 Gwynn, *Experiences*, p. 59.
124 *Ibid.*, p. 60.
125 Gwynn, 'Thoughts about Ireland', p. 54.
126 Gwynn, 'Irish education and character', *Irish books and Irish people*, p. 68.
127 William Smith O'Brien to Lucy O'Brien, 27 June 1852, in Richard Davis and Marianne Davis (eds), *The rebel in his family: selected papers of William Smith O'Brien* (Cork: Cork University Press, 1998), p. 60.
128 Gwynn, *Experiences*, p. 54.
129 *Brasenose college register 1509–1909* (Oxford: Oxford University Press, 1909), p. 669.

2

Exile in England
1886–1904

London was in a sense everybody's country. (Stephen Gwynn, 1936)[1]

THE period between Stephen Gwynn exiting Oxford and entering Westminster coincided with the Irish Party's split, Charles Stewart Parnell's fall from the political heights of national leadership, and the flowering of the Irish literary and Gaelic language revivals. In later years, W. B. Yeats, who kept more than one eye on retrospective interpretations of the literary revival and his role in it, famously argued that the fall of Parnell in 1890 was the catalyst for the cultural renaissance which ultimately forged Ireland's independence.[2] This was a brilliant piece of Yeatsian myth: the reality was, in fact, much more sober.[3] Stephen Gwynn's role in these matters is in a way unique. He was part of the literary revival as a critic, contributor and advisor to a major publisher during its formative stage. He also became an Irish-language enthusiast, building friendships with Irish-Irelanders such as Douglas Hyde and Patrick Pearse. In addition, Gwynn became a committed constitutional nationalist, the very creed that Yeats claimed was destroyed by these cultural forces. The life of Stephen Gwynn offers an insight into all these spheres of Irish life worlds, revealing the complications and contradictions inherent within and between them.

The school master

IN a classic statement relating to his inability to plan ahead, Gwynn proclaimed in his memoirs that 'I proceeded to my degree without the least idea of what I should do next'.[4] Almost immediately, though, an opportunity presented itself: several months tutoring in La Gruette, near Tours, in France.[5] Gwynn relished the prospect of living in France, and the country made such an impact on him that he returned time and again over the course of his life. His 1927 book *In praise of France* is testament to a lasting affection for Gallic culture and lifestyle, and it stressed that affection's early roots: 'I fell in love with France just when I left Oxford'.[6] He also fell in love with a French girl, but this met disaster fairly quickly. More important, retrospectively at least, was the counsel of Monsieur Messire, an elderly professor at Tours, whom Gwynn visited for French lessons. The two men remained in correspondence after Gwynn left France, with Messire seemingly the first to suggest to Gwynn that the young Irishman should embrace literature as a profession.[7]

Despite his negative experiences in Oxford and the new attractions that France offered, Gwynn returned to England towards the end of 1886 to embark on several months of cramming for Civil Service examinations.[8] He recorded in his memoirs that the few months he spent in London 'were worth a great deal to me', as he gained the friendship of the colourful Shakespearian W. J. Craig, and Barkley Higginson, whose sister, Nesta Higginson – better known as the poet Moira O'Neill – also became a close confidante.[9] Gwynn took the examinations at the same time as Herbert Read, an acquaintance from Oxford who later rose to the War and Colonial Offices. Unlike Read, Gwynn was not to make his mark in the Civil Service. As his mother told her aunt, Katherine Stevens, Stephen finished thirteenth in a field of eighty-nine applicants: he could take a post 'but of course as there are 12 men above him all the best vacancies will be offered to them'.[10] In the end, Gwynn did not join the Civil Service queue. In January 1887, he accepted a temporary tutorship at an Army crammer in Switzerland, inspired by the chance to spend more time immersed in the French language.[11] He was to be posted in the village of Lucens in the Canton de Vaud, earning the modest sum of £100 per year.[12] Stephen was initially very taken with life in Switzerland, as Lucy Gwynn informed Stevens: 'He is much pleased with his surroundings. A lovely country, light work, and the opportunity of practicing French and learning German'. She added a negative appendage to this idyllic picture, one that would set the tone of Gwynn's life for the next decade: 'He does not care for teaching'.[13]

Switzerland did not make the same lasting impression on the youthful Gwynn as France did: memories of the country do not recur in his writings. His stay lasted only six months and Gwynn returned to Dublin in the summer. He held another temporary post as French tutor at Rossall College in Lancashire in the autumn; but the search for permanent work drew to a close at the beginning of 1888, when he was appointed Sixth Form Master to the idyllic St Andrew's College in Bradfield.[14] Bradfield (as the College was generally known) had a student body of only 141 boys in 1888. Its debating society had become devoted to Irish politics[15] but Gwynn had little time to investigate this, as several months into the post he turned his mind to marrying his partner, Mary Louisa Gwynn (who was better known as May). May

Gwynn, who was Stephen's first cousin, was a formidable presence. She was literarily inclined and became politically engaged; in many ways, she was the perfect companion for Stephen. Bradfield, however, was endowed with a strong Anglican ethos which promoted celibacy among its staff. Gwynn, then, announced his intentions of leaving soon after his arrival.[16] According to his autobiography, Gwynn was offered the post of Charles Ritchie's private secretary in the summer of 1888, but he turned it down out of political principle. Ritchie was a Conservative MP and President of the Local Government Board – a position previously held by Gwynn's later biographical subject, Sir Charles Dilke – and was on the progressive side of the party. The position of private secretary was a potentially influential one: Dilke, for instance, recorded that his private secretary managed the Board's significant powers of patronage.[17] Retrospectively, Gwynn stated that he could not accept the post as he favoured Home Rule, which had become anathema to the Tories by 1888;[18] no surviving contemporary material confirms or contradicts this claim, but there is little evidence of a solidly pro-Home Rule position in Gwynn's mindset until the late 1890s. Nevertheless, he was sympathetic, at least, to the nationalist position.

Gwynn does not mention in his memoir his multiple applications for academic jobs between 1888 and 1893, all of which were seemingly unsuccessful. His account of the end of his university career was blunt: 'I was bored stiff with the academic way of life and I think my chief aim was to get out of Oxford, and on to something new'.[19] Yet his surviving papers are brimming with references from distinguished scholars commenting on his suitability for particular academic posts. In 1889, for example, John H. Bernard of TCD refereed for Gwynn's application for the Professorship of Mental Philosophy at Toronto.[20] Emphasising his TCD links, Edward Dowden wrote in 1893 that Gwynn would be well suited for the position of Chair of Classics and Literature in Newcastle upon Tyne.[21] The Bishop of Salisbury, John Wordsworth, whom Gwynn befriended at Brasenose College, seconded Dowden's opinion of the young Irishman's literary abilities. He wrote a generous reference for Gwynn in 1888, attached to which was a glowing appraisal: 'I shall be very glad if you can obtain congenial work of a higher literary character than is probably open to you as an Assistant Master at Bradfield. I have great confidence that, if you can find your proper sphere, you will make your mark in it'.[22] The great mystery is why Gwynn's 'proper sphere' was not the academy. With a double first in classics from Oxford, he was suitably qualified, but lingered on unhappily in the school mastering profession until 1896. Gwynn never remarked on his early academic job-hunting in any of his writings and it is unclear why his applications were rejected. Perhaps a retrospective self-criticism on his character following Oxford that Gwynn recorded in 1926 contained more than a hint of truth: 'Looking back now, I see a spoilt and discontented young man – amazingly immature even for two and twenty'.[23]

In late 1889, Gwynn's temporary contract at Bradfield expired and he moved to Clifton College in Bristol, where he would hold a teaching position for the next five years. In December 1889, he married May in Somerset. Gwynn gave his profession on the marriage certificate as 'gentleman'.[24] The Gwynns made a home in Clifton, where four of their six children were born: Edward Lucius Gwynn (who was known by his second name) in November 1890; Aubrey in February 1892; Denis in March 1893; and Sheila in March 1894.[25] Aubrey's godfather was Walter Osborne; the artist's playful watercolour entitled *Master Aubrey Gwynn* was completed in 1896, just seven years before his premature death. While the young family enjoyed several years of stability in Bristol, the Gwynns' home life changed drastically after Stephen moved to London in 1896. This would mark the beginning of an unorthodox domestic life for the family in a number of ways.

For now, Bristol provided the surroundings for Gwynn's first forays into parenthood. Clifton College provided the Gwynns with bookish surroundings through its many literary societies and personalities. Both Stephen and May joined the Browning Society and attended numerous literary lectures during their five-year stint at the College.[26] In March 1893, Gwynn addressed the Society on Sir Walter Scott's life and writings, an early literary interest to which he would return for the purposes of biography thirty-five years later. One member of the audience was particularly impressed by this early example of Gwynn's critical prowess.[27] Several of Gwynn's colleagues at Clifton were distinguished names. He befriended C. H. Russell, a 'fine classical scholar',[28] through whom he met the likes of Arthur Quiller-Couch and Arthur Conan Doyle. Inevitably, Gwynn referenced Sherlock Holmes in his first encounter with Conan Doyle: 'Thank God I've killed the brute', was the weary reply, 'don't let me hear a word about him'.[29] Other members of staff at Clifton during Gwynn's time included W. W. Asquith, the brother of the future Liberal Prime Minister, and the poet T. E. Brown. Like Gwynn, Brown seems to have fallen into the teaching profession not from choice but from necessity: his poem 'Clifton', which was penned after his retirement, hints at his unfulfilling school-mastering experience.[30] Gwynn's major memory of Clifton, though, was of a non-educational matter: the death of Parnell.

In 1926, Gwynn recalled the moment when he heard the newsboys around Clifton in October 1891 proclaiming the death of the 'Chief': 'In all my life, no other announcement has conveyed such a shock; and in realising what it was to me, remote then from Irish politics, preoccupied with my own concerns, I can see what it meant to the mass of the Irish people – even to those who had dethroned him'.[31] Gwynn recorded in his memoir that while he was deeply affected by the death of Parnell, he was 'less in touch with Ireland than in any other period of life' during his five years in Clifton.[32] While life in England inevitably isolated Gwynn from Irish affairs, he maintained his links with the Irish literary circles which he had encountered during the 1880s. Gwynn was among the first subscribers to W. B. Yeats's first collection of poems, *The wanderings of Oisin*, even before a publisher was found.[33] Gwynn also sampled the Rhymers' Club in London, an avant-garde literary circle which contained a marked Irish presence. The Club had been established by the now London-based Yeats and Ernest Rhys, who was of Welsh extraction, to provide a forum for poets in the capital. It had a distinctly 'Celtic' feel, encouraged by the founders and other members of the group such as T. W. Rolleston and Lionel Johnston. Gwynn accompanied Rolleston to one meeting of the Club, which he recalled some thirty-five years later in negative tones: 'Poems were read aloud, but left no mark on my memory'.[34] In November 1892, Gwynn attended Douglas Hyde's seminal lecture, 'On the necessity for de-Anglicising the Irish people', in Dublin, which pleaded for 'the Irish race to develop in future upon Irish lines'.[35] The following year saw the foundation of the Gaelic League by Hyde, Eoin MacNeill and Father Eugene O'Growney. Its mission was to promote the Irish language: this took the form of organising classes, pushing for its inclusion in formal education, and sponsoring social events which brought enthusiasts together. The Gaelic League's initial programme did not, however, make an impact on Gwynn: he did not join the movement until the turn of the century. His literary interests at Clifton were decisively un-Irish in influence, as demonstrated in his early article on Robert Louis Stevenson in the *Fortnightly Review* and his first few largely unspectacular verses which debuted in the *Spectator*.[36]

The most notable literary acquaintance that Gwynn made at this stage of his life in England was, however, Irish: Nesta Higginson, better known by her penname Moira O'Neill. Gwynn spotted Higginson's potential at an early stage, and he and his wife offered her critical and practical advice through the 1890s.[37] Higginson, who was Sheila Gwynn's godmother, was extremely fond of the Gwynn clan, and warmly regarded Stephen as her mentor.[38] He brought her to the attention of John St Loe Strachey, the editor of the *Spectator*, who published several of Higginson's poems in 1894.[39] Higginson's literary interests, were, however, guided by financial enterprise as much as the mystery of the Glens of Antrim: she feely admitted to Gwynn that her publishing plans were purely mercenary.[40] Higginson – who married Walter Skrine in 1895 – placed the manuscript of what was to become her most famous work, *Songs of the Glens of Antrim*, into Gwynn's hands in 1899, with the instruction to take it to 'whichever publisher you think best'.[41] The book appeared the following year bearing the imprint of Blackwood. Despite her claim to be a 'stern woman of business', Higginson's verses were praised for their graceful craftsmanship, demonstrating an ability to reproduce the distinct rhythm and pace of the Antrim dialect, providing a particular Ulster slant to the Irish literary revival.[42] The book went through a number of editions; but the friendship between Higginson and the Gwynns faded as she moved to Canada after her marriage, and petered out after the turn of the century.

The final stage of Gwynn's school-mastering career came with a move back to Ireland in 1895. At the beginning of the year, Gwynn was appointed sub-Warden in the place of his birth and own schooling: St Columba's College in Dublin. This was yet another footnote in the distinguished Gwynn family record at St Columba's. But Stephen Gwynn's return to Ireland was to last only a year and a half. In the summer of 1896, Gwynn left the safety of school-mastering to pursue an uncertain future in London's literary scene. There were several indirect hints of this new departure during his time in St Columba's: Gwynn contributed a classical poem and a translation of 'From Sappho' to the school magazine.[43] The other notable event that coincided with the Gwynns' return to Ireland was the birth of their second daughter, Madeline (who was known as Peggy), in February 1896. Despite this additional responsibility, the school-mastering days were drawing to a close. Gwynn was weary of the teaching profession and desired a radical lifestyle change: as he told May, 'I have had enough of the smell of boy'.[44]

Early London days

IN 1918 Gwynn's sister, Mary, married Henry Bowen in Limerick. At the wedding, Henry's daughter, Elizabeth, then a nineteen-year-old aspiring writer, approached her step-uncle Stephen for advice on pursuing a literary career. As she recalled later, chatting with Gwynn that day confirmed a notion she had had in her mind: 'generally, authors lived in London'.[45] This was the voice of experience: in 1896, the thirty-two-year-old Stephen moved to London with literary aspirations. The artistic landscape of the city was rapidly changing during the 1890s, with old habits dying and the emergence of a more flamboyant creative vitality. Celebrated by the novelist Richard Le Gallienne as the 'romantic '90s', the decade witnessed the infiltration of French symbolism into English intellectual life.[46] The *fin de siècle* was also a decade of new publishing opportunities. The end of the 'three-decker' – the three-volume novel – and its replacement with a cheaper, single-volume alternative came in 1894, while a number of new publishing houses, such as John Lane, Edward Arnold and Constable, were established before the turn of the century. There were a healthy number of literary periodicals and journals in circulation at the close of the Victorian era. All this was underpinned by a significant increase in the size of the reading public, as the effects of mandatory elementary education began to surface.[47] London stood as the apex of the English-speaking literary world, with would-be authors flocking to drawing rooms throughout the city, assuming littérateur veneers and engrossing themselves in the many artistic networks on offer.

Gwynn left his family behind in Dublin as he moved to lodgings in Baker Street.[48] May and the children joined Stephen over the winter of 1896–97, taking a house in Walpole Street, off the King's Road in Chelsea. The half a year which Gwynn spent alone in London seems to have been a source of lasting contention for May. She was left to care for five young children while her husband lived the highlife of the London littérateur; their son Aubrey later recalled that Dublin's incessant gossip mill ran wild with reports that Stephen had left his family permanently.[49] The rumours were not without substance. Gwynn had an affair with Mabel Dearmer, children's author and wife of the Reverend Percy Dearmer, which lasted until her death in 1915; he and Mabel first encountered each other at Althea Gyles's studio in the autumn of 1896.[50] While the date on which the affair commenced is obscure, they rapidly became very good friends, at least, after their first meeting.[51] Gwynn initially moved in the same literary circles as the Dearmers. His memoirs record friendships with Evelyn Sharp, Richard Le Gallienne, James Welsh, Max Beerbohm and Henry Harland: these were the personnel of what remained of the *Yellow Book* group.[52] Published by John Lane between 1894 and 1897, the *Yellow Book* was guided by the psychologically flawed genius of Aubrey Beardsley and the uncompromising mettle of Henry Harland. Despite its brevity, the Aesthetic journal left an influential legacy, renowned for pushing the boundaries of public taste.

The *Yellow Book* group was, though, in decline by the time of Gwynn's arrival in London. Evelyn Sharp, who would remain a close friend of the Gwynns, wrote later of the self-obsessive streak that permeated the *Yellow Book* personnel, which granted the movement an importance scarcely deserved within the literary world.[53] As John Gross has shown, the 'romantic '90s' were only a small part of what was happening during the 1890s; more lasting literary achievements came from the likes of Thomas Hardy, Rudyard Kipling and H. G. Wells.[54] Gwynn claimed to have never offered any work to the *Yellow Book*; his only association with the group was his connection with John Lane, which he cultivated soon after finding his bearings in London.[55] Lane was a crucial figure behind the evolution of Aestheticism during the 1890s.[56] Richard Le Gallienne remembered him as more of a 'creative artist' than publisher;[57] Gwynn was more precise with his description of Lane as an individual who had 'the desire to be associated with literature, rather than the feeling for literature'. Lane published Gwynn's first novel, book of essays and collection of verses; but as Gwynn lamented, neither he nor Lane 'was the richer' for their efforts.[58]

Gwynn immersed himself in literary life in his newly adopted city. He forged a lasting friendship with the versatile man of letters E. V. Lucas and his wife Florence.[59] Gwynn also enjoyed a brief camaraderie with the novelist Maurice Hewlett, who was on the cusp of significant success with the release of *The forest lovers* in 1898. Hewlett moved to Wiltshire soon after he first encountered Gwynn, effectively ending their friendship, a fact which Gwynn greatly lamented upon the novelist's death in 1923.[60] From the off, then, Gwynn found himself on the fringes of important components of English society in London, developing crucial contacts and integrating successfully into the late-Victorian literary scene. His reputation was enhanced by a number of short pieces he published in respected journals such as *Blackwood's Magazine, Contemporary Review, Cornhill Magazine, Edinburgh Review, Macmillan's Magazine, Saturday Review* and *Fortnightly Review*.[61] These covered a wide range of interests: analyses of the politics of western Africa jostled for attention beside critical essays on Tennyson and the poetry of Stephen Phillips.[62] Between 1899 and 1903, Gwynn also penned introductions to Methuen's new editions of Thackeray's *Vanity fair, The history of Pendennis, Christmas books* and *The history of Henry Esmond, esq*. Alongside these contributions sat occasional freelance poetic contributions to the *Spectator* and the *Manchester Guardian*. Gwynn wrote a self-deprecating account of his early output some thirty years later: 'I wrote an inordinate deal, much of it about nothing in particular'.[63] This is a rather harsh assessment; while a unity of purpose is difficult to locate in the diversity of Gwynn's early writings, he was more than capable of delivering sound judgements with wit and clarity. He understood the value of controversy, demonstrated by his willingness to enter a minor literary brawl after publishing a negative account of Jane Austen.[64] This brought swift condemnation from the humourless critic Andrew Lang, much to the delight of Gwynn, who believed the storm would help the sales of his first collection of essays.[65] Gwynn's first few books tend to confirm the view that he offered much more as an essayist and critic than as a creative force. His first novel, the deservedly forgotten *The repentance of a private secretary*, published in 1899 by John Lane, failed to make any headway with the literary establishment. His study of Tennyson, which appeared the same year, though, was a success: the *Spectator* commended it as a 'sane' appraisal of the former Poet Laureate.[66] The clear divergence between Gwynn's acute critical abilities and his failings as a novelist (and to a lesser extent as a poet) was, thus, apparent from the very beginning of his literary career.

The respect in which Gwynn's critical prowess was held was recognised by the interest shown in him by one of London's leading publishing houses only two years after his arrival in the city. Gwynn came to the attention of Macmillan and Company through his contributions to the firm's monthly magazine, then edited by Mowbray Morris, a unique literary operator whom Gwynn evoked in his memoir as 'an extravagant version of the man about town, resuscitated from some earlier generation'.[67] In April 1898, George Macmillan asked Gwynn to become a literary advisor to his publishing house, offering a salary of £100 per year. His remit was to 'do your best to extend our connections with new authors, especially of the rising generation, and advise us also from time to time upon MSS etc submitted to us'.[68] Gwynn jumped at the opportunity. It was a position with significant clout: Gwynn was able to use his connection with Macmillan to gain book commissions, generous royalties and recommend his friends to one of the most respected London publishing houses. His literary star was certainly on the rise.

As was stated in the terms of the advisory post, Gwynn was called upon to read book proposals and manuscripts submitted to Macmillan. The most senior readers of the firm at the time were Mowbray Morris and the Liberal statesman John Morley, both of whom had ferocious literary reputations. They thoroughly scrutinised every manuscript placed in front of them, rejecting the vast majority. Both readers disapproved of most of the new literary trends of the 1890s; the pair, for instance, rejected Hewlett's *The forest lovers*, a decision overturned by Frederick Macmillan to the great benefit of both firm and author.[69] But not every writer was so fortunate: Havelock Ellis's *The new spirit* was rejected to the later chagrin of the firm's bosses.[70] Morley in particular was intellectually unequipped for the new age of publishing that emerged at the close of the Victorian era. Conservative in his tastes and trite in his reports, Morley repeatedly failed to bring new talent to Macmillan's attention. While Gwynn read only a fraction of the number of manuscripts submitted to his senior colleagues, he could be every bit as ruthless. He rejected A. R. Sennett's proposed book on journeys across the continent on the grounds that it was 'intolerably written' and (much more seriously) because 'a man who is capable of calling Swiss red wine good is incapable of speaking the truth about anything'.[71] David Sinclair, whose work confused Gwynn, was labelled a 'clever lunatic', while Walter Stephen's *Paradise lost* was such a 'grotesque parody' of Milton that the reviewer could not get past its first page.[72]

Gwynn's connection with Macmillan did, however, benefit several authors. Shortly after being placed on the Macmillan payroll, Gwynn recommended Mabel Dearmer (who was then possibly his mistress) to George Macmillan; the result was the publication of two of her children's book in quick succession bearing the house's name.[73] Gwynn also strongly recommended the English poet Stephen Phillips to Macmillan. Gwynn and Phillips came to London at around the same time with literary ambitions and met in the city around 1896. Gwynn remembered Phillips as 'an unknown penniless man' in his early London days; within four years, though, he had 'publishers competing fiercely for the right to publish his work'.[74] Gwynn first flagged up Phillips to Macmillan in November 1898, confidently describing his friend as 'the immediate future of English poetry' and urging the firm to take his recently completed drama, *Paolo and Francesca*.[75] Gwynn's pitch impressed Macmillan and Phillips was offered an excellent package of £100 and 15 per cent royalties. In a moment of bad form, though, Phillips revealed the offer to John Lane, who bettered it, thus securing the rising poet's services. Macmillan and Gwynn were extremely disappointed by the whole affair.[76] Gwynn took the 'vexed' affair (as he called it) to heart, refusing to draw the £100 annual salary for his advisory work and suggesting instead to Macmillan that he work on a freelance basis.[77] Towards the end of 1899, though, Edward Arnold approached him for similar advisory work; he instead negotiated a new contract with Macmillan worth £150 per year, in exchange for penning literary notes in *Macmillan's Magazine* and general consultative guidance when necessary.[78] And despite the foul taste the matter left in his mouth, Gwynn remained a staunch champion of Phillips's literary output, long after the poet's untimely death in 1915.

Within three years in London, Gwynn had carved out a significant role for himself, deeply embedded as he was in the city's literary world. Despite the hiccup with Phillips, it is clear that this 'mick on the make'[79] enjoyed close ties with the upper echelons of Macmillan, while opportunities continued to open up for his own literary output. Then came the Boer War in 1899, the watershed moment which pushed Gwynn towards a closer identification with contemporary political debate in Britain and Ireland. Gwynn had been interested in African politics for some time, with the adventures of his brother Charles, a British Army officer who served in West Africa in the early 1890s, whetting his appetite. Gwynn published an account of Charles's experience in *Blackwood's Magazine* in 1894, an article which condemned the bloody nature of British imperial strategies in Sierra Leone.[80] Charles conducted intelligence work on the state of West Africa between 1896 and 1898, which fed its way into several more critical articles by his brother.[81] These were detailed yet accessible pieces, lucid and sanely written, casting Gwynn as something of an expert on West African politics; he later claimed that there 'was scarcely a working journalist in London who had learnt the first thing about West Africa and I had few competitors'.[82] This comment obviously did not include the explorer Mary Kingsley, then at the height of her fame. Kingsley was a frequent traveller to Africa throughout the 1890s; her *Travels in West Africa*, published in 1897, revelled in the distinctiveness of African culture and became a bestseller.[83] Kingsley lived in

London between 1898 and 1900, and was a regular attender at a number of literary salons throughout the city. She was a formidable presence; the artist William Rothenstein remembered her as 'a dominating figure' at the parties hosted by Mrs J. R. Green in Kensington, while Gwynn's reminiscences painted her as 'one of the most singular creatures that ever walked the earth'.[84] Gwynn was prompted by George Macmillan to visit Kingsley in March 1898, advice he duly took.[85] A deep friendship was struck up on Gwynn's first meeting with Kingsley, severed only by her death in South Africa in 1900. Gwynn continued to eulogise Kingsley long after her death, celebrating her single-minded pursuit of justice and humane imperialism.[86]

Gwynn and Kingsley were both appalled by the Boer War and the enthusiasm the conflict generated around London.[87] As G. K. Chesterton, who became a neighbour of the Gwynns in London, later wrote, 'What I hated about it [the Boer War] was what a good many people liked about it. It was a very cheerful war. I hated its confidence, its congratulatory anticipation…. I hated its vile assurance of victory'.[88] Chesterton's negative reaction to the jingoism that the Boer War stoked up throughout Britain overlapped with Gwynn's feeling on the matter. 'I was fiercely in revolt against the Imperialism of those days', he later recorded; it was a turning point for the young Irishman in London.[89] The strength of pro-Boer feeling within Irish nationalism greatly perturbed the authorities, with the rabid anti-imperialism the conflict generated feeding into rejuvenation of an 'advanced' nationalist strand starved since the fall of Parnell. The 1898 centenary of the 1798 rebellion, Boer War discontent and opposition to the two royal visits to Ireland in 1900 and 1903 created an atmosphere in which prototypes of Sinn Féin ideology and propaganda flourished.[90] The Boer War, lasting over two and a half years, provided a degree of anti-imperial continuity during this process and alienated even moderate Irish nationalist opinion. 'The Boer war', Gwynn wrote in 1926, 'taught me definitely that I was an Irishman first; and being an Irishman in my sense meant having an outlook other than the Englishman's'.[91] In 1900 he parted ways with the fiercely loyal *Spectator*, a symbolic break with the 'establishment'; his next sustained engagement with the journal came eight years later, when he wrote to condemn its portrayal of Irish nationalism.

Ireland in London

GWYNN's politics at the turn of the century are vague, but certain elements can be teased out. While he retrospectively claimed that his undergraduate days in Oxford and time spent with his aunt, Charlotte Grace O'Brien, were turning points on his journey towards nationalism, at the time he was not involved in any overt political activity. After a period of relative detachment from contemporary Irish affairs in the aftermath of Parnell's fall, Gwynn tentatively expressed an interest in the politics of 'constructive unionism' (the British policy of piecemeal Irish reform short of Home Rule) and Horace Plunkett's agricultural co-operative movement towards the end of the century.[92] He greeted the passing of legislation which created structures of local government in Ireland in 1897 with a verse in the *Spectator*, the lines of which celebrated 'Ireland with England and herself at peace'.[93] In October 1900, Gwynn published an essay in *Blackwood's Magazine* saluting the work of Plunkett and the co-operative movement in developing Irish agriculture, which drew the applause of George Russell (also known by his penname AE), poet, mystic and Plunkett's lieutenant.[94] Gwynn's flirtation with Plunkettite politics ended, however, with the Boer War. 'But for the Boer War', he proclaimed in his memoir, 'I should almost certainly have been drawn into the group which ... followed Horace Plunkett'.[95] There is little reason to doubt the sincerity of Gwynn's claim. Gwynn met John Dillon, a power in the Irish Party, at Dillon's father-in-law's house in London in 1903 and declared his interest in serving the nationalist cause.[96] By this stage, Gwynn envisaged an Irish future under Home Rule, a marked advance on his support for Plunkett. Yet Gwynn stressed the importance of an imperial identity within his brand of nationalism: Home Rule should not be viewed as an isolationist position but rather as the means to permit Ireland to play a full and meaningful role within the British Empire. Gwynn expressed his fledgling philosophy in the introduction of *Today and tomorrow in Ireland*, a collection of his Irish essays, in 1903:

> I call myself a nationalist. But my nationalism has nothing irreconcilable about it. If Ireland had the status of Canada, I should be as good an Imperialist as Sir Wilfred Laurier [the Canadian Prime Minister]. So I believe would nine out of any ten Irishmen who today are most bitter against England.[97]

In Gwynn's analysis, the crux of the Anglo-Irish dilemma rested on the lack of self-government in Ireland, which had two negative impacts: a denial of Irish national dignity and the detachment of Ireland from the Empire. British imperialism was not the problem, but part of the solution:

> if the Colonies make a sacrifice for Imperial interests, that is because the Empire has both a material and sentimental value for the Colonies. When Ireland has the same reasons for being Imperialist, patriotism in Ireland will take on the same aspect.[98]

This was essentially an articulation of John Redmond's argument in favour of Home Rule. Redmond, the leader of the reunited Irish Party since 1900, asserted throughout the Edwardian period that Home Rule was as important for Britain as it was for Ireland.[99] When he entered Parliament, Gwynn provided 'Redmondism' with an intellectual edge which permeated Irish Party propaganda, stressing the values of Home Rule for the United Kingdom and the possibilities of a reformed imperialism.

Irish political autonomy was, however, only one dimension of Gwynn's evolving nationalism; memories and images of his homeland retained a powerful hold over his mind. The *Spectator* published a verse by Gwynn, 'Ireland', as he was settling into London life. This is one of Gwynn's better-known poems, an exploration of sentimentalism:

> Ireland, oh Ireland! centre of my longings,
> Country of my fathers, home of my heart!
> Overseas you call me: *Why an exile from me?*
> *Wherefore sea-severed, long leagues apart?*
>
> ...
>
> Pearly are the skies in the country of my fathers,
> Purple are thy mountains, home of my heart.
> Mother of my yearning, love of all my longings,
> Keep me in remembrance, long leagues apart.[100]

The verse, which Gwynn's son Aubrey described as his finest, captured an early home-sickness underlying the thrill of being part of literary life in London. Ultimately, though, Gwynn moved restlessly between London and Ireland in the decades which followed, and never fully reconciled his two 'lasting desires', as Aubrey put it, and this tinged his life with an itinerant sadness.[101]

While Gwynn's political nationalism was in part a reaction to the popular jingoism of the Boer War, he was active in Irish circles in London before the turn of the century. Among these was the Irish Literary Society of London, which was established in 1891 by, among others, W. B. Yeats; Lady Augusta Gregory recorded in her diaries Gwynn's presence at several Society meetings from 1898.[102] In 1897, *Macmillan's Magazine* carried an essay by Gwynn on 'Novels of Irish life', a critical discussion of the fictional works of Maria Edgeworth, Lady Morgan, William Carleton, Charles Lever, Emily Lawless, Jane Barlow and Sheridan Le Fanu. The great difficulty in assessing nineteenth-century Irish literature was, according to Gwynn, its almost inextricable connection with 'considerations foreign to art'. Even leaving aside the obvious reference point of Thomas Davis and Young Ireland, patriotic sentiment was much more vital to Irish literary life than was meaningful criticism; the resonances of nationalism, argued Gwynn, hindered the emergence of an 'Irish Walter Scott'. This analysis was not made in a vacuum, as Gwynn acknowledged contemporary efforts to challenge this orthodoxy:

> All great writers proceed from a school, and there does exist now undeniably a school of Irish literature which differs from Miss Edgeworth in being strongly tinged with the element of Celtic romance, from Carleton in possessing an admirable standard of style, and from Lever in aiming at a sincere and vital portraiture of Irish life.[103]

He was referring, of course, to the Irish literary revival, spearheaded by Yeats, Lady Augusta Gregory and George Moore; Gwynn was attracted to the re-imagining of the concept of a 'national literature' forwarded by this circle and he emerged as one of its key propagandists. While he also aspired to be part of the literary revival's creative force, it was as its chronicler and critic that he eventually found his niche.

There was also the business side to the Irish literary revival. Gwynn exploited his links with Macmillan to push several Irish authors. George Russell was one success story, with Macmillan taking his *The divine vision and other poems* in 1904 after lobbying by Gwynn.[104] Negative responses were, however, much more frequent. Gwynn aimed to secure an American copyright for Higginson's *Songs of the Glens of Antrim* but had to make do with a limited distribution instead.[105] Likewise, his promotion of William Buckley's *Croppies lie down* to the American wing of Macmillan was rejected.[106] The most important episode of Gwynn's early connection with Macmillan, though, concerns the firm's handling of Yeats. By the turn of the century, Yeats was looking for a major publisher to take his scattered back catalogue; Gwynn essentially acted as his agent in an approach to George Macmillan in April 1900. Macmillan sent material to Mowbray Morris for review, with a note proclaiming that the failure to secure Stephen Phillips the previous year had dented the firm's reputation: 'we feel that we should not like to lose a chance of catching another man of the same stamp if in your judgement his work seems likely to be as far as it goes of some permanent value'.[107] If Macmillan believed that his conservative and cynical senior readers were best positioned to offer a meaningful judgement on Yeats's work, he was, however, mistaken. Between 1887 and 1900, Morley and Morris rejected every book proposal by Irish authors placed before them.[108] Morley urged Macmillan to reject Gwynn's *Today and tomorrow in Ireland* in 1902: while 'intelligently pro-Irish in the right sense', the senior Liberal feared 'that in England the seed will find very stony ground to fall upon'.[109] The book appeared through the imprint of Hodges, Figgis, and Co., a Dublin-based house, although Macmillan distributed it throughout Britain. Yeats, however, was not even shown this degree of leniency.

Morris was given Yeats's *The Celtic twilight* (1893), *Poems* (1895), *The secret rose* (1897) and *The wind among the reeds* (1899) for assessment. He was, however, spitefully dismissive, mocking Yeats's mythological work and condemning the poet's flirtation with 'advanced' nationalism, which Morris overtly acknowledged had influenced his literary judgement.

Yeats had recently helped organise a protest meeting against Queen Victoria's visit to Ireland, a factor very much in Morris's mind:

> It is disquieting, for the purpose we have to consider, to note that Mr Yeats's work does not improve as he grows older. Perhaps since he has taken to playing at treason with Miss Maud Gonne and Mr George Moore he has not found time to cultivate literature.... I would be sorry to think that work so unreal, unhuman, and insincere would be found to have any permanent value.... That he has any real paying audience I find it hard to believe.[110]

Gwynn protested at Morris's treatment; while the letter does not survive, he probably appealed to Macmillan to consider Yeats's most recent dramatic verse, *The shadowy waters*.[111] It was to little avail. Although Macmillan did approach Morley for a second opinion, it did not differ greatly from Morris's:

> In substance, I entirely concur with M[owbray] M[orris].... Neither rhyme nor reason do I find in one single page.... I have really taken pains, after studying Mr G[wynn]'s letter of May 3, to place myself as near as I can to the author's point of view – symbolism accidental, etc. etc. Do what I will, I can see no sense in the thing: it is to me sheer nonsense. I do not say it is obscure, or uncouth or barbaric or affected – tho' it is all these evil things; I say it is to me absolutely *nullity*. I would not read a page of it again for worlds, and I care not how many good judges swear that 'Yeats is the only man who counts'.[112]

Morley had his own political motives for opposing Yeats. He was appointed Chief Secretary for Ireland in 1892, but lost his seat in Newcastle upon Tyne three years later after Maud Gonne masterminded a 'don't vote for Morley' campaign; Gonne targeted the Liberal minister for his failure to honour amnesty promises made to Irish treason felony prisoners in England. In savaging Gonne's admirer, revenge of sorts was harshly dished out.[113]

After Macmillan received Morley's report, Gwynn received a polite message with a firm answer from the firm: 'our referee has reported emphatically against Mr Yeats, and we have therefore definitely decided not to make any offer to take over his books'.[114] Macmillan ultimately took Yeats's work in 1916 (when he had a multi-volume *Collected works* behind him) but the firm's retrospective embarrassment over the affair was palpable.[115] The personal antagonisms and stuffy biases of readers like Morley and Morris made it extremely difficult for Irish authors to break into the publishing mainstream; Gwynn's publishing record with Macmillan in the early stages of the twentieth century therefore represented something of a sea change in contemporary literary trends.

Gwynn published three books concerning Irish life with Macmillan from 1899 to 1903. Two novels, *The old knowledge* and *John Maxwell's marriage*, appeared in 1901 and 1903, respectively; these were preceded by his first book for Macmillan, *Highways and byways in Donegal and Antrim*, published in 1899. Gwynn was asked by George Macmillan in 1898 to contribute to the 'Highways and byways' series, to which Arthur Norway's *Devon and Cornwall* had been the most recent addition.[116] The book had a remarkably quick turnaround: commissioned with the task in February, Gwynn handed in his draft in July, netting £75.[117] Charmingly illustrated by Hugh Thomson (who would work with Gwynn again on travel literature), *Highways and byways in Donegal and Antrim* vividly sketched the people and places of the coastal stretch across the north of Antrim, taking the reader 'from the wild corners of the west, where Irish is still the language even of trade, business, and the schools, into the very neighbourhood of prosperous, commercial, up-to-date Belfast'.[118] James Loughlin has cited Gwynn's *Highways and byways* in his study of the development of a distinctive Ulster unionist identity between the 1880s and 1920s. Casting Gwynn as nationalist commentator and charging him with an attempt to 'shape opinion on a central element of the great constitutional issue of the period', Loughlin argues that Gwynn used his book to deny a distinctive Ulster identity, strangling the political, cultural and religious diversity of the region to emphasise the unity of the 'nation'.[119] This is, however, to ascribe to Gwynn a wholly untrue motive, one which is obscured by Loughlin's mislabelling of him as a nationalist MP between 1900 and 1918; crucially, Gwynn entered Westminster only in 1906 and was, at the time of writing *Highways and byways*, dabbling with co-operative politics.[120] In a bizarrely partitionist argument, Loughlin condemns Gwynn for claiming north-east Ulster for the 'nation', citing the claim in *Highways and byways* that 'a common element of Irish character' permeated industrial Belfast, thus ignoring any truth in the statement.[121] The true importance of *Highways and byways* lies in its role in reconnecting Gwynn with the Ireland it colourfully described: 'I loved the return to what was familiar', he fondly wrote later. After the book was completed, he revisited Donegal at least once a year until his return to Ireland in 1904.[122] Gwynn became enthralled in the pursuit of Ireland's secrets: the folk stories of the peasantry, the mythology of the island, the mystery of its landscapes.[123] Gwynn had 'discovered' Ireland, as had the promising playwright J. M. Synge: immersion in peasant culture altered Synge's artistic and national temperament, as, to him, 'Everything Irish became sacred'.[124] Like Synge, also a Protestant Irishman, Gwynn was both an insider and outsider to the worlds which he described in essays and fiction, allowing for distance and clarity as well as empathy.

Gwynn wrote many Irish travel books during his life, all of which share the vitality and imagery of *Highways and byways in Donegal and*

Antrim. His novels, in comparison, suffer from a pedestrian pace. *John Maxwell's marriage* and *The old knowledge* (which was dedicated, in risqué fashion, to Mabel Dearmer) have, however, been recently reclaimed from historical and literary obscurity by John Wilson Foster.[125] Foster correctly highlights the thread that weaves the books together: both novels act as case studies into the reconciliation of the gentry and peasantry, and the forging of a common identity and purpose for the benefit of the nation. These were fictional accounts of idyllic Donegal imbued with a combination of Gwynn's early co-operative support and evolving nationalism – a somewhat stilted fusion of the 'Celtic twilight' and the practicalities of Plunkettism. The two novels, which were generally well received, bolstered Gwynn's reputation and his identification with Ireland.[126] This was furthered by the publication of his first collection of verses, *The queen's chronicler*, in 1901, which brought together many of the poems which had appeared in the *Spectator* throughout the 1890s. Gwynn's early verses lacked the inventiveness and imagination of the work of his more prominent contemporaries, yet contain melancholic reflections that evoke a sense of uncertainty in his surroundings. W. F. P. Stockley, scholar and distant relation of Gwynn through the O'Brien line, championed the various strands of Gwynn's literary output in a review article for the *Irish Monthly* in 1903:

> Let us consider Mr Gwynn's books as a product of the soil; as a touching revelation of piety for Ireland; as a bearer to us of the lessons of true patriotism which – thank God for all! – seems easier to learn day by day... I hope he will give us, and give Ireland, much more. There are few better patriots today than the man who has written these books.[127]

Gwynn was well rewarded by Macmillan for his two novels: *The old knowledge* came with a 10 per cent royalty and £150 down payment; *John Maxwell's marriage* brought a 15 per cent royalty and £100 in advance.[128] A generous 20 per cent royalty was forthcoming with *Fishing holidays*, published in 1904, the first of Gwynn's many written tributes to his favourite pastime.[129] By the early years of the twentieth century, Gwynn had become a considerable authority on fishing in Ireland, inspiring other keen anglers to seek out his advice. One such was F. S. Oliver, the Scottish advocate of federalist unionism and one of the most sophisticated political minds of Edwardian Britain; a friendship was quickly forged through a mutual love for fishing and political debate.[130]

Gwynn's Irish connections in London were further enhanced in March 1902, when he became the secretary of the Irish Literary Society; around the same time, he joined the Gaelic League, the Irish language revival movement led by Douglas Hyde and Eoin MacNeill. Gwynn claimed in his autobiography that he was badgered into accepting increased responsibility within the Literary Society by its chair, R. Barry O'Brien. O'Brien had written Parnell's biography several years before, a book which Gwynn greatly admired. Gwynn urged Macmillan's American division to commission O'Brien with a study of Daniel O'Connell: 'He has the gift of biography – a very rare one & a great knowledge of Irish history'.[131] The approach unfortunately came to nothing. As an established literary and political figure, O'Brien had all the necessary qualities to head a society of expatriates: according to Gwynn, he was 'an admirable speaker, a good writer, a vehement Irish Nationalist, but not an easy man to get on with'.[132] Indeed, like many branches of the Gaelic League, the Irish Literary Society of London suffered occasionally from a cantankerous spirit, as petty jealousies played out against a backdrop of political and religious hyper-sensitivities.[133] Despite this, Gwynn threw himself into the work of the Society, organising lectures, contributing to an edited volume of its papers[134] and closely following the progress of the Irish Literary Theatre, established by Yeats at the end of 1898. Despite his failure to convince Macmillan to take Yeats in 1900, Gwynn pressed on with the Yeatsian agenda. In March 1901, Gwynn saluted Yeats's verse play *The shadowy waters*, in the *Spectator*. While John St Loe Strachey, editor of the *Spectator*, believed that Yeats was 'too "lovely and dim" for a brutal Anglo-Saxon like me',[135] Gwynn stressed his importance in altering the literary equilibrium of the age: 'Mr Yeats alone will do much to make it as natural and necessary for a cultivated man to know the fate of Edain as that of Daphne or Syrinx'.[136] Gwynn saw the emergence of a distinctive Irish literature in the English tongue as moving hand-in-hand with the language revival spearheaded by the Gaelic League: 'The two men of letters who stand today for the Celtic revival in Ireland are Dr Douglas Hyde and Mr W. B. Yeats'.[137] 'Anglo-Ireland' was not battling 'Irish-Ireland' for the soul of the nation, in Gwynn's mind, as they were mutually compatible, even mutually desirable, philosophies. While Irish-Ireland zealots such as D. P. Moran denied that the literature produced by Yeats and his circle was Irish by virtue of the language in which it was expressed,[138] Gwynn was much more pragmatic. Given the low level of Irish-language proficiency in Ireland, the Gaelic tongue could not reasonably be the medium for an inclusive Celtic literature: 'For the present, and for the next generation at least, the national literature must be written in English'.[139] Indeed, Gwynn's attachment to the Gaelic League ideal was based on an intellectual interest in the Irish language rather than a deep-rooted national insecurity or Anglophobia. As Gwynn claimed in an essay in 1901:

> The League is the most interesting and significant outgrowth of Nationalism that Ireland has seen in my time. It is not political, but it is national; that is to say, it aims at fostering by all means the distinct and separate

national life of Ireland.... The Gaelic League aims at an object which is partly sentimental, if you like, but in reality educational in the highest degree – at a revival of the national life in its intellectual side.[140]

The Gaelic League offered Gwynn another outlet for his rediscovery of all things Irish: 'One of the little [Irish language] primers was always in my pocket, and in buses and trains my study progressed'.[141] Gwynn felt himself to be part of a genuinely inclusive, non-political cultural revival; Irish society was maturing as it looked forward to the seemingly inevitable arrival of Home Rule.

Gwynn was incredibly active during 1902 and 1903. The tie with Macmillan consumed much of his time and effort. In March 1902, a major coup came his way in the commission to write *The masters of English literature*, a textbook for the educational market ('I could do it as well as anybody today except [Edward] Dowden', Gwynn rather pompously told George Macmillan).[142] He continued to read and revise manuscripts for the firm; his suggestion that the wonderfully burlesque G. K. Chesterton should be commissioned to write a study of Robert Browning for Macmillan's well established 'English men of letters' series was accepted. This led to one of the more eccentric books in the series, as Chesterton later recalled: 'There were very few biographical facts in the book, and those were nearly all wrong'.[143] He was not exaggerating. A senior figure within Macmillan was furious when he saw the proofs and condemned Gwynn for aiding the creation of 'a piece of work which would disgrace the establishment'.[144] The book was, however, a commercial success, vindicating the author and his supporter. Gwynn became more involved in Macmillan's American division through 1902 and 1903, offering occasional literary advice and interviewing perspective authors.[145] The most celebrated author whom he interviewed in this role was undoubtedly the science-fiction writer H. G. Wells. Gwynn urged Macmillan to take Wells, one of the hottest literary properties in early-Edwardian Britain: 'His style admits humour, admits beauty'.[146] As he left his meeting with Wells, Gwynn mentioned that his next assignment was an interview with Yeats. '"Yeats!", he said, "Yeats doesn't like Science"'. When Gwynn found Yeats, he divulged from whom he had just come. '"Wells!", he said: "That man has a mind like a sewing machine"'.[147]

While the Macmillan link provided literary kudos and a steady stream of money, Gwynn's unpaid position at the Irish Literary Society demanded more and more of his time. He also continued to contribute articles which were in essence Yeatsian propaganda to respectable English literary journals. These came at a time when Yeats and the emerging Irish theatre movement were on the defensive: with shades of the later controversy over Synge's *Playboy of the western world*, at the turn of the century Yeats's dramatic verse, the *Countess Cathleen*, provoked the ire of many Catholic critics for its blasphemous undertones. The play depicted the coming of two demons to an Ireland suffering famine, offering gold for souls of the peasants; to save her people the Countess Cathleen agrees to sell her own soul, before finding redemption from the Faustian pact through her selfless dignity. The flamboyant cultural activist Edward Martyn needed convincing that the play was not blasphemous; but the religious controversy truly erupted when Frank Hugh O'Donnell, former Home Rule MP and controversialist, published a pamphlet denouncing Yeats for depicting the Irish as 'a crowd of black devil worshippers'. Cardinal Logue then waded into the storm after reading O'Donnell's commentary (but not the text of the play), proclaiming that interruptions at performances of *Countess Cathleen* might be justified.[148] For D. P. Moran, who founded the *Leader* newspaper in 1900, an extreme Catholic nationalist journal which plagued the Anglo-Irish literary movement for years to come, the insensitivities demonstrated by Yeats made his work irrelevant to the majority in Ireland.[149] Gwynn felt the criticisms directed towards Yeats largely missed the point. 'The mind of Mr Yeats and his artistic sympathies had been moulded away from Ireland; the public which he conceived or assumed was the public that applauds [Symbolist playwright Maurice] Maeterlinck'.[150] This was Ireland on another plane, but one essential for the artistic development of the nation. Gwynn felt that Yeats's Irish Literary Theatre – soon to become the Irish National Theatre Society (INTS) – was 'the real thing. It is Irish, and it is literature'.[151] Such support for the Yeatsian agenda inevitably incurred the ill-tempered wrath of O'Donnell: Gwynn came in for punishing attack when the maverick commentator stepped up his assault on the 'pseudo-Celtic' dramatic movement in 1904.[152]

Gwynn backed up his support for the INTS with more than words. As secretary of the Irish Literary Society, he played a leading role in bringing the Theatre's productions to London in the summer of 1903. He had observed INTS performances several times in Dublin, including a scintillating adaptation of Yeats and Gregory's play *Cathleen ni Houlihan*, starring the incomparable Maud Gonne as the Shan Van Vocht. Gonne's performance still vibrantly resonated in Gwynn's mind decades later as he planned his memoir and history of Irish literary and drama movements; his assessment remains one of the most quoted lines in Irish theatre criticism: 'the effect of *Cathleen ni Houlihan* on me was that I went home asking myself if such plays should be produced unless one was prepared for people to go out to shoot and be shot'.[153] Less often quoted is Gwynn's quip that Gonne resembled 'a half-mad old wife in Donegal whom I have always known'.[154] *Cathleen ni Houlihan* was a call to arms more to the emerging Irish theatre than to nationalist Ireland, despite Yeats's poetic re-imagining of the past in his poem 'The man and the echo' from 1938: 'Did that play of mine send out / Certain men the English shot?'[155]

Gwynn was enthralled by *Cathleen ni Houlihan* and the potential of a distinct Irish theatre. Yet he was aware of the practical problem the venture faced: a lack of funding. In an article Gwynn penned for the *Fortnightly Review* in December 1902, he praised the INTS's recent embrace of Irish amateurs in place of English professional actors, but was attentive to the problem that the project was 'absolutely and entirely uncommercial'. It was clear to Gwynn that the INTS could not be a self-sufficient entity; the logic of this was that a subsidy was required for long-term stability.[156] Seeking to showcase the artistic integrity of Irish drama to a wider audience, Gwynn pitched the idea of a London trip to Yeats in January 1903; the invitation stunned George Roberts, a founding member and secretary of the INTS, but was accepted, albeit with a certain amount of 'fear and trembling'.[157] The London show introduced the INTS to Annie Horniman, a wealthy theatre enthusiast, who later provided it with financial backing. Maire Nic Shiubhlaigh, one of the INTS's leading actresses, many years later recalled the importance of the London trip of 1903:

> Now, I cannot over-emphasise the importance of this development.... It marked the first major turning-point in our career.... If Mr Gwynn had not been in Dublin then, if he had not seen our work when he did, our movement might have pursued a completely different course in the years which followed.[158]

The Irish Literary Society secured a venue, the small Queen's Gate Hall in Kensington; as the actors were amateurs and had work commitments during weekdays, two demanding triple bills were planned for a single day in May. Five plays were drawn from the INTS's repertoire: Yeats's morality tale *The hour-glass* (which drafted in the Gwynns' young daughter Sheila and the Dearmers' son Geoffrey as extras); Gregory's comedy *Twenty-five*; the Yeats and Gregory collaboration *The pot of broth*; Frederick Ryan's satire *The laying of the foundations*; and two performances of *Cathleen ni Houlihan*. Yeats and Gregory made sure that influential London literary figures were in attendance; using his contacts in London, Gwynn also encouraged the presence of 'all the mighty' from the literary scene.[159] The tiny hall was packed on the day, and in his memoir Gwynn recollected the feeling of dread that overcame him as he looked out at the small audience and spotted two leading critics, William Archer of the *Morning Leader* and A. B. Walkley of the *Times*.[160] The show, however, ran smoothly; not even the distant backstage sounds of Shelia Gwynn and Geoffrey Dearmer playing football with a bowler hat belonging to the leading man, W. G. Fay, distracted from the performances. As well as attracting a chic and enthusiastic audience, which included Annie Horniman, rave reviews followed in the leading London dailies.[161]

A second London venture for the INTS followed in March 1904, with Gwynn again involved at an organisational level, despite suffering from ill-health.[162] This was a suitably more ambitious affair. Gwynn set out to secure a regular theatre, a first for the INTS: in February, he managed to book the Royalty at a bargain price of £45 for a matinee and evening performance.[163] A glossy programme made from Irish paper was put together at great cost: Gwynn comforted George Roberts with the philosophy that 'No matter if we rob people, they expect it, on a programme'.[164] Annie Horniman was fully involved, helping to design the scenery and costumes for the bill;[165] this included Synge's haunting tragedy *Riders to the sea*, 'the piece which made most impression' on the INTS's second London visit, according to Gwynn.[166] Political sensitivities were also in Gwynn's mind as the date drew closer: he refused an invitation to Lady Aberdeen, wife of the Lord Lieutenant of Ireland in Gladstone's administration, for fear of providing ammunition to Arthur Griffith's 'advanced' nationalist journal, the *United Irishman*.[167] In the event, the London show of 1904 was again a massive success and was followed almost immediately by Horniman's financial commitment to the INTS; impressed by the Irish dramatic movement's dedication and vision, she arranged to purchase a permanent site for the INTS in Dublin and provided a subsidy. Gwynn was rewarded for his efforts with an INTS-sponsored conversazione in April 1904, which included performances of Yeats's *The shadowy waters* and *The king's threshold*.[168] The Abbey Theatre opened its doors in December 1904, but holding together the Irish dramatic movement became more difficult after it gained its base; there was a feeling of unease within elements of the amateur movement as to the influence of Horniman, who was resolutely anti-nationalist, which would result in splits and an increase in the powers of the central triumvirate of Yeats, Gregory and Synge.

Despite the success of the Irish Literary Society's hosting of the INTS in 1903 and 1904, the toil of this bout of intense activity on Gwynn's health was immense. Upon recovering from ill-health in April 1904, he began making plans for a drastic lifestyle change, as he told George Brett, the head of Macmillan in America: 'As soon as I can sell my house we shall be off to Ireland. Whether I shall return to London or not, after a year, remains to be seen. But there is no doubt of the necessity of a change'.[169] Gwynn's workload since the turn of the century had been great and his private life had suffered a number of strains. His brother Lucius died from consumption in Switzerland in December 1902, aged only twenty-eight. Lucius was one of nineteenth-century Ireland's greatest sportsmen, representing his country at cricket and rugby. While his older brother attempted to make a name for himself in literature in the 1890s, Lucius was easily the most famous of the Gwynn clan.[170] The tragedy of losing a brother was preceded only a few days earlier by an immense shock within Gwynn's household: his wife, May, announced that she and their children, now numbering six following the birth of Owen earlier in the year, were converting to Catholicism. May enjoyed many of the same interests as her husband – she too was a member of the Irish Literary Society and Gaelic League as well as a published author.[171] The reasons for her conversion did not perhaps lie in the purely theological or national: Gwynn family lore has it that she became a Catholic partly because of Stephen's adultery and her own growing feeling of neglect[172] (Stephen was most likely having an affair with Mabel Dearmer at this time). In taking his children to the Catholic Church, May undermined Stephen's authority within his household. Unfortunately, no contemporary evidence has survived which gives an insight into the personal nature of the conversion, but Gwynn later claimed that he desired his children to 'go with the one of their parents in whose life religion played an important role'.[173] This might have been the case, but it did not tell the entire story. Given the course taken by several of his children – Aubrey became a Jesuit priest and Peggy a nun – May succeeded in permanently separating the family from Gwynn in a spiritual – and arguably national – sense. Even later in life, it was clear that Gwynn never quite reconciled himself to his wife's actions.[174]

Towards the end of 1903, Gwynn suffered a breakdown. The physician George Sigerson later told him that he suffered from neurasthenia, or extreme fatigue and insomnia.[175] Overwork was one possible trigger, but Gwynn was forthcoming to George Brett:

> The cause of my woes was I have no doubt not simply work, which I think wouldn't hurt anyone but a large dose of worries last year – now happily at rest – which rather drove me to use work as an antidote. I had to be knocked down before I cd make a break, & now hope to get fully fit.[176]

Gwynn was ordered to a sunnier climate for a rest break, which led to his first and possibly only trip outside Europe: a month in Morocco over the winter of 1903–4. He returned well rested and delved seamlessly into organising the INTS's second trip to London, but the scars would remain. After eight years of London life, Ireland was calling him home: retrospectively he stressed the importance of securing a Catholic education for his children and his own interest in serving the Home Rule cause.[177] In April 1904 he bade farewell to the 'Saxon shore' for the opportunities that Ireland offered.[178]

Notes

1 Stephen Gwynn, *Irish literature and drama in the English language: a short history* (London: Thomas Nelson and Sons, 1936), p. 146.

2 W. B. Yeats, *Autobiographies*, eds William H. O'Donnell and Douglas N. Archibald (Basingstoke: Palgrave, 1999), p. 410.
3 See R. F. Foster, 'Thinking hand to mouth: Anglo-Irish literature, Gaelic nationalism and Irish politics in the 1890s', in *Paddy and Mr Punch: connections in Irish and British history* (London: Allen Lane, 1993), pp. 262–80.
4 Stephen Gwynn, *Experiences of a literary man* (London: Thornton Butterworth, 1926), p. 76.
5 *Ibid.*, p. 77.
6 Stephen Gwynn, *In praise of France* (London: Nisbet and Co., 1927), p. xii.
7 *Ibid.*, p. xvi; Gwynn, *Experiences*, p. 79.
8 Gwynn, *Experiences*, p. 82.
9 *Ibid.*, p. 86.
10 Lucy Gwynn to Katherine Stevens, n.d. [January 1887], William Smith O'Brien papers, National Library of Ireland (NLI), MS 8665 (1).
11 Gwynn, *Experiences*, p. 88.
12 Lucy Gwynn to Katherine Stevens, n.d. [January 1887], William Smith O'Brien papers, NLI, MS 8665 (1).
13 Lucy Gwynn to Katherine Stevens, n.d. [1887], William Smith O'Brien papers, NLI, MS 8665 (1).
14 *The Columban*, 9:1 (February 1888).
15 John Blackie, *Bradfield 1850–1975* (Bradfield: St Andrew's College, 1976), p. 88.
16 Gwynn, *Experiences*, p. 104.
17 Stephen Gwynn and Gertrude M. Tuckwell, *The life of the Rt. Hon. Sir Charles W. Dilke: begun by Stephen Gwynn; completed and edited by Gertrude M. Tuckwell* (London: John Murray, 2 vols, 1917), vol. I, p. 504.
18 Gwynn, *Experiences*, pp. 104–5.
19 *Ibid.*, p. 77.
20 Stephen Gwynn papers, NLI, MS 8600 (2).
21 Stephen Gwynn papers, NLI, MS 8600 (4).
22 Wordsworth to Gwynn, 20 August 1888, Stephen Gwynn papers, NLI, MS 8600 (18).
23 Gwynn, *Experiences*, p. 77.
24 Stephen Gwynn and Mary Gwynn's marriage certificate, Aubrey Gwynn papers, Irish Jesuit Archive (IJA), J10/5.
25 Aubrey Gwynn, 'Draft of an autobiography of Father Aubrey Gwynn', n.d. [1979], Aubrey Gwynn papers, IJA, J10/90 (65).
26 Gwynn, *Experiences*, pp. 109–12.
27 Hand-written review by C. Thurple, March 1893, Stephen Gwynn papers, NLI, MS 8600 (17).
28 O. F. Christie, *A history of Clifton College 1860–1934* (Bristol: J. W. Arrowsmith, 1935), p. 217.
29 Gwynn, *Experiences*, p. 111.
30 T. E. Brown, *Poems of T. E. Brown*, eds H. F. B. and H. G. D. (London: Macmillan and Co., 1908), pp. 53–4.
31 Gwynn, *Experiences*, pp. 109–10.
32 *Ibid.*, p. 111.
33 W. B. Yeats to Stephen Gwynn [24 January 1888], in John Kelly (ed.), *The collected letters of W. B. Yeats* (Oxford: Oxford University Press, four vols, 1986), vol. I, p. 44. *Wanderings* was published by Kegan Paul in 1889.
34 Gwynn, *Experiences*, p. 116.
35 Dominic Daly, *The young Douglas Hyde: the dawn of the Irish revolution and renaissance 1874–1893* (Dublin: Irish University Press, 1974), p. 157.
36 Stephen Gwynn, 'Mr Robert Louis Stevenson: a critical study', *Fortnightly*

Review, December 1894, pp. 776–92; 'Dolly', *Spectator*, 4 March 1893; 'Out in the dark', *Spectator*, 18 August 1894.
37 Nesta Higginson to May Gwynn, 14 May 1893, Stephen Gwynn papers, NLI, MS 8600 (7).
38 Nesta Higginson to Stephen Gwynn, 15 February 1894, Stephen Gwynn papers, NLI, MS 8600 (7).
39 Gwynn, *Experiences*, p. 116; *Spectator*, 22 September 1894.
40 Nesta Higginson to Stephen Gwynn, 17 April 1894, Stephen Gwynn papers, NLI, MS 8600 (7).
41 Nesta Skrine to Stephen Gwynn, 3 August 1899, Stephen Gwynn papers, NLI, MS 8600 (7).
42 Nesta Skrine to Stephen Gwynn, 30 December 1897, Stephen Gwynn papers, NLI, MS 8600 (7); *Irish Times*, 15 February 1900.
43 *The Columban*, 16:4 (May 1895) and 17:1 (February 1896).
44 Aubrey Gwynn, 'Unfinished history of the Gwynn family', Aubrey Gwynn papers, IJA, J10/89 (13).
45 Elizabeth Bowen, 'Coming to London', in *The mulberry tree: writings of Elizabeth Bowen*, ed. Hermione Lee (London: Vintage, 1999), p. 87.
46 Richard Le Gallienne, *The romantic '90s* (London: G. P. Putnam's Sons, 1926).
47 Stefan Collini, *Common reading: critics, historians, publics* (Oxford: Oxford University Press, 2008), p. 240.
48 Gwynn, *Experiences*, p. 128.
49 Gwynn, 'Draft of an autobiography', Aubrey Gwynn papers, IJA, J10/90 (73).
50 Gwynn, *Experiences*, p. 135. Althea Gyles was the artist who designed the cover of Yeats's *Poems* (London: T. Fisher Unwin, 1904).
51 Gwynn, though he publicly acknowledged only a friendship, hints at least that the intensity of their affair reached a crescendo shortly before the outbreak of war in 1914, in Mabel Dearmer, *Letters from a field hospital: with a memoir of the author by Stephen Gwynn* (London: Macmillan and Co., 1916), p. 3.
52 Gwynn, *Experiences*, pp. 137–42.
53 Evelyn Sharp, *Unfinished adventure: selected reminiscences from an Englishwoman's life* (London: John Lane the Bodley Head, 1933), p. 58.
54 John Gross, *The rise and fall of the man of letters: English literary life since 1800* (London: Penguin, 1991; first published 1969), p. 227.
55 Gwynn, *Experiences*, p. 142.
56 James Lewis May's biography of Lane reflects his importance in its title: *John Lane and the nineties* (London: John Lane the Bodley Head, 1936).
57 Le Gallienne, *The romantic '90s*, p. 123.
58 Gwynn, *Experiences*, p. 142.
59 *Ibid.*, pp. 145–9. Gwynn aided Lucas with translations from Latin for the latter's work on Charles Lamb: E. V. Lucas, *Reading, writing and remembering: a literary record* (London: Methuen and Co., 1933; first published 1932), p. 139.
60 Stephen Gwynn, 'Maurice Hewlett', *Edinburgh Review*, January 1924, pp. 61–72.
61 Many of these were reprinted in Gwynn's numerous collections of essays which appeared throughout his life.
62 Stephen Gwynn, 'French and English in the basin of the Niger', *Blackwood's Magazine*, October 1897, pp. 557–73; Stephen Gwynn, 'Tennyson', *Macmillan's Magazine*, November 1897, pp. 57–66; Stephen Gwynn, 'The poetry of Mr Stephen Phillips', *Edinburgh Review*, January 1900, pp. 51–75.
63 Gwynn, *Experiences*, p. 154.
64 Stephen Gwynn, 'The decay of sensibility', *Cornhill Magazine*, July 1899, p. 18; reprinted in *The decay of sensibility and other essays and sketches* (London: John Lane the Bodley Head, n.d. [1900]), p. 1.

65 Stephen Gwynn, 'The sensibility of the critics', *Cornhill Magazine*, August 1899, pp. 229–33; Stephen Gwynn to John Lane, 18 August [1899], John Lane papers, Harry Ransom Humanities Research Center, University of Texas (HRHRC).
66 *Spectator*, 7 October 1899.
67 Gwynn, *Experiences*, p. 152.
68 George A. Macmillan to Stephen Gwynn, 25 April 1898, Macmillan archive, British Library (BL), 55456(3)/1136.
69 Charles Morgan, *The house of Macmillan (1843–1943)* (London: Macmillan and Co., 1944), pp. 148–9.
70 For a discussion of the manuscripts rejected by Morris and Morley, see Warwick Gould, '"Playing treason with Miss Maud Gonne": Yeats and his publishers in 1900', in Ian Willison, Warwick Gould and Warren Chernaik (eds), *Modernist writers and the marketplace* (Basingstoke: Macmillan, 1996), p. 44. Ellis's *The new spirit* appeared in multiple editions through various London publishing houses.
71 Readers' reports, 14 December 1898, Macmillan archive, BL, 55958/262.
72 Both dated 23 December 1902, readers' reports, Macmillan archive, BL, 55966/48.
73 Stephen Gwynn to George A. Macmillan, 5 July [1898], Macmillan archive, BL, box M44. The books were *The book of penny toys* (1899) and *The Noah's ark of geography* (1900).
74 Stephen Gwynn, 'A poet under a cloud', in *Garden wisdom: or from one generation to another* (Dublin: Talbot Press, 1921), p. 60.
75 Stephen Gwynn to George A. Macmillan, 18 November 1898, Macmillan archive, BL, box M44.
76 George A. Macmillan to Stephen Gwynn, 14 December 1898, Macmillan archive, BL, 55458(1)/125.
77 Stephen Gwynn to George A. Macmillan, 13 December 1898, Macmillan archive, BL, box M44.
78 George A. Macmillan to Stephen Gwynn, 23 November 1899, Macmillan archive, BL, 55461(1)/203; Stephen Gwynn to George A. Macmillan, 24 November 1899, Macmillan archive, BL, box M44.
79 Foster, 'Marginal men and micks on the make: the uses of Irish exile, c. 1840–1922', in *Paddy and Mr Punch*, p. 282.
80 Stephen Gwynn, 'The Sofa expedition and the West Indian soldier', *Blackwood's Magazine*, May 1894, pp. 699–710, especially p. 709: 'An empire like that which Queen Victoria possesses can only be held by an annual expenditure of blood'.
81 See Stephen Gwynn, 'An unwritten chapter of history', *Blackwood's Magazine*, March 1899, pp. 605–20, and 'The loss of Moshi', *Blackwood's Magazine*, August 1899, pp. 275–94.
82 Gwynn, *Experiences*, p. 160.
83 Alison Blunt, *Travel, gender and imperialism: Mary Kingsley and West Africa* (New York: Guilford Press, 1994), p. 61.
84 William Rothenstein, *Men and memories* (London: Faber and Faber, two vols, 1932), vol. I, p. 210; Gwynn, *Experiences*, p. 165.
85 George A. Macmillan to Stephen Gwynn, 5 March 1898, Macmillan archive, BL, 55456(1)/232.
86 See in particular Stephen Gwynn, *The life of Mary Kingsley* (London: Macmillan and Co., 1932), and 'A lover of justice', in *Garden wisdom*, pp. 77–102.
87 See Mary Kingsley to Stephen Gwynn, 2 February 1900, Stephen Gwynn papers, NLI, 8600 (9).
88 G. K. Chesterton, *Autobiography* (London: Hutchinson and Co., 1936), p. 113.
89 Gwynn, 'A lover of justice', p. 99.

90 On this, see Senia Pašeta's two important articles: '1798 in 1898: the politics of commemoration', *Irish Review*, 22 (1998), pp. 46–53, and 'Nationalist responses to two royal visits to Ireland, 1900 and 1903', *Irish Historical Studies*, 31:124 (1999), pp. 488–504.
91 Gwynn, *Experiences*, p. 172.
92 For these elements of Irish politics in the 1890s, see Andrew Gailey, *Ireland and the death of kindness: the experience of constructive unionism 1890–1905* (Cork: Cork University Press, 1987), and P. J. Mathews, *Revival: the Abbey Theatre, the Gaelic League and the co-operative movement* (Cork: Cork University Press, 2003).
93 'Pacta Hibernia', *Spectator*, 5 June 1897.
94 Stephen Gwynn, 'A month in Ireland', *Blackwood's Magazine*, October 1900, pp. 573–84; George Russell to Stephen Gwynn, 14 September 1900, in Alan Denson (ed.), *Letters from AE* (London: Abelard-Schuman, 1961), p. 35. Gwynn also championed Russell's first excursions into publishing: see the positive review of *The earth breath*, in the *Manchester Guardian*, 2 March 1898.
95 Gwynn, *Experiences*, p. 171.
96 *Ibid.*, pp. 250–2.
97 Stephen Gwynn, *Today and tomorrow in Ireland: essays on Irish subjects* (Dublin: Hodges, Figgis, and Co., 1903), p. x.
98 *Ibid.*, p. xi.
99 Paul Bew, *John Redmond* (Dundalk: Dundalgan Press, 1996), pp. 30–1.
100 *Spectator*, 12 September 1896; reprinted in Stephen Gwynn, *The queen's chronicler and other poems* (London: John Lane, 1901), pp. 24–5, and *Collected poems* (Edinburgh: William Blackwood and Sons, 1923), pp. 5–6.
101 Gwynn, 'Draft of an autobiography', Aubrey Gwynn papers, IJA, J10/90 (75–6).
102 James Pethica (ed.), *Lady Gregory's diaries 1892–1902* (Gerrards Cross: Colin Smythe 1996), pp. 172, 286.
103 Stephen Gwynn, 'Novels of Irish life', *Macmillan's Magazine*, January 1897, pp. 182–191; reprinted in *Irish books and Irish people* (Dublin: Talbot Press, 1919), pp. 7–23.
104 Frederick Macmillan to Stephen Gwynn, 30 September 1903, Macmillan archive, BL, 55474(1)/260.
105 Nesta Skrine to Stephen Gwynn, 3 August 1899, Stephen Gwynn papers, NLI, 8600 (7); George A. Macmillan to Stephen Gwynn, 30 October 1899, Macmillan archive, BL, 55460(4)/1507.
106 Stephen Gwynn to George Brett, 24 March [1903], Macmillan Company records, New York Public Library (NYPL), box 52. For the separate business interests of Macmillan in the United States, see Elizabeth James, 'Letters from America: the Bretts and the Macmillan Company of New York', in Elizabeth James (ed.), *Macmillan: a publishing tradition* (London: Palgrave Macmillan, 2002), pp. 170–91.
107 George A. Macmillan to Mowbray Morris, 24 April 1900, Macmillan archive, BL, 55462(2)/971.
108 See the important forthcoming work on Macmillan and Irish literary circles by Warwick Gould. I am extremely grateful to Professor Gould for sharing this work with me.
109 Readers' reports, 8 December 1902, Macmillan archive, BL, 55966/25.
110 Readers' reports, 15 May 1900, Macmillan archive, BL, 55961/178–83.
111 W. B. Yeats to Lady Gregory, 1 May [1900], in Warwick Gould, John Kelly and Deirdre Toomey (eds), *Collected letters of Yeats*, vol. II, p. 520.
112 Readers' reports, 15 May 1900, Macmillan archive, BL, 55961/178–83. Original emphasis.

113 Gould, '"Playing treason"', p. 52.
114 George A. Macmillan to Stephen Gwynn, 16 May 1900, Macmillan archive, BL, 55462(3)/1382.
115 Morgan, *House of Macmillan*, p. 220.
116 George A. Macmillan to Stephen Gwynn, 8 February 1898, Macmillan archive, BL, 55455(5)/2391.
117 Stephen Gwynn to George A. Macmillan, 14 July [1898], Macmillan archive, BL, box M44.
118 Stephen Gwynn, *Highways and byways in Donegal and Antrim* (London: Macmillan and Co., 1899), p. 3.
119 James Loughlin, 'Creating "a social and geographical fact": regional identity and the Ulster question 1880s to 1920s', *Past and Present*, 195 (2007), p. 164.
120 To further the error, Loughlin claims Gwynn was the MP for Carlow, when in fact his constituency was Galway City.
121 Loughlin, 'Regional identity and the Ulster question', p. 165; Gwynn, *Highways and byways*, p. 296.
122 Gwynn, *Experiences*, p. 196.
123 These are among the themes in his *Today and tomorrow in Ireland*.
124 J. M. Synge, *Collected works. Vol. II: Prose*, ed. Alan Price (London: Oxford University Press, 1966), p. 13.
125 John Wilson Foster, *Irish novels 1890–1940: new bearings in culture and fiction* (Oxford: Oxford University Press, 2008), pp. 217–22.
126 *Irish Times*, 11 December 1901.
127 W. F. P. Stockley, 'Mr Stephen Gwynn's writings', *Irish Monthly*, June 1903, pp. 308–9, 315.
128 George A. Macmillan to Stephen Gwynn, 22 March 1901, Macmillan archive, BL, 55465(2)/999; George A. Macmillan to Stephen Gwynn, 28 January 1902, Macmillan archive, BL, 55468(2)/969.
129 George A. Macmillan to Stephen Gwynn, 18 May 1903, Macmillan archive, BL, 55473(1)/31.
130 Gwynn, *Experiences*, pp. 220–4.
131 Stephen Gwynn to George Brett, 26 December [n.y.], Macmillan Company records, NYPL, box 52.
132 Gwynn, *Experiences*, p. 203.
133 As soon as Gwynn became the Literary Society's secretary, the organisation became 'threatened with disaster by reason of war' between O'Brien and Charles Russell. *Ibid.*, pp. 203–4.
134 Stephen Gwynn, 'Sarsfield', in R. Barry O'Brien (ed.), *Studies in Irish history 1649–1775* (London: Macmillan and Co., 1903), pp. 253–87.
135 John St Loe Strachey to Stephen Gwynn, 31 December 1900, Stephen Gwynn papers, NLI, MS 8600 (16).
136 *Spectator*, 2 March 1901.
137 Gwynn, *Today and tomorrow*, p. 31.
138 D. P. Moran, 'The battle of two civilizations', in *The philosophy of Irish Ireland* (Dublin: University College Dublin Press, 2006; first published 1905), pp. 94–114.
139 Gwynn, *Today and tomorrow*, p. 92.
140 Stephen Gwynn, 'The revival of a language', *Macmillan's Magazine*, December 1901, p. 238; reprinted in *Today and tomorrow*, pp. 82–3.
141 Gwynn, *Experiences*, p. 213.
142 Stephen Gwynn to George A. Macmillan, 2 March 1902, Macmillan archive, BL, box M44.
143 Chesterton, *Autobiography*, p. 95.

144 Gwynn, *Experiences*, p. 157.
145 Stephen Gwynn to George Brett, 27 March [1903], Macmillan Company records, NYPL, box 52.
146 Stephen Gwynn to George Brett, 6 May [1903], Macmillan Company records, NYPL, box 52.
147 Gwynn, *Experiences*, pp. 158–9.
148 For a detailed outline of the controversy, see Adrian Frazier, *Behind the scenes: Yeats, Horniman, and the struggle for the Abbey Theatre* (Berkley: University of California Press, 1990), pp. 1–23.
149 Moran, 'The battle of two civilizations', p. 103.
150 Stephen Gwynn, 'The Irish Literary Theatre and its affinities', *Fortnightly Review*, December 1901, p. 1052.
151 *Ibid.*, p. 1062.
152 F. Hugh O'Donnell, *The stage Irishman of the pseudo-Celtic drama* (London: John Long, 1904).
153 Gwynn, *Irish literature and drama*, pp. 158–9.
154 Stephen Gwynn, 'An uncommercial theatre', *Fortnightly Review*, December 1902, p. 1052.
155 Yeats was later cruelly mocked by Paul Muldoon, who answered his question, 'Certainly not': 'If Yeats had saved his pencil-lead/would certain men have stayed in bed?', '7, Middagh Street', *Poems 1968–1998* (London: Faber and Faber, 2001), p. 176.
156 Gwynn, 'Uncommercial theatre', p. 1045.
157 W. B. Yeats to Lady Gregory, 13 January [1903], in John Kelly and Ronald Schuchard (eds), *Collected letters of Yeats*, vol. III, p. 302; George Roberts, 'The National Theatre Society', in E. H. Mikhail (ed.), *The Abbey Theatre: interviews and recollections* (London: Macmillan, 1988), p. 20.
158 Maire Nic Shiubhlaigh, *The splendid years: recollections of Maire Nic Shiubhlaigh as told to Edward Kenny* (Dublin: James Duffy and Co., 1955), pp. 36–7.
159 Gwynn, *Experiences*, p. 207.
160 *Ibid.* Gwynn and Yeats were both unhappy, though, at the lack of support on the day from 'our own people' in the Irish Literary Society. W. B. Yeats to Lady Gregory, [8 May 1903], in Kelly and Schuchard (eds), *Collected letters of Yeats*, vol. III, p. 363.
161 R. F. Foster, *W. B. Yeats: a life. Vol. I: The apprentice mage* (Oxford: Oxford University Press, 1997), p. 292.
162 Stephen Gwynn to W. G. Fay, 13 December 1903, George Roberts papers, Houghton Library, Harvard University, MS Thr 24 (42).
163 Stephen Gwynn to George Roberts, 19 February 1904, George Roberts papers, Houghton Library, Harvard University, MS Thr 24 (45).
164 Stephen Gwynn to George Roberts, 5 March 1904, George Roberts papers, Houghton Library, Harvard University, MS Thr 24 (49).
165 Stephen Gwynn to George Roberts, 22 February [1904], George Roberts papers, Houghton Library, Harvard University, MS Thr 24 (69).
166 Gwynn, *Irish literature and drama*, p. 163.
167 Gwynn to George Roberts, 16 March 1904, George Roberts papers, Houghton Library, Harvard University, MS Thr 24 (51).
168 W. B. Yeats to John Quinn, 25 April 1904, in Kelly and Schuchard, *Collected letters of Yeats*, vol. III, p. 586.
169 Stephen Gwynn to George Brett, 7 April [1904], Macmillan Company archive, NYPL, box 52.
170 J. Chartres Molony, *The riddle of the Irish* (London: Methuen and Co., n.d. [1927]), p. 103.

171 May Gwynn published two books: *A birthday book: being a book of wise and pithy sayings for each day in the year* (London: Methuen and Co., [1899]), and the children's book *Stories from Irish history* (Dublin: Brown and Nolan, 1904).
172 Private information from Mrs Rose Gayner (née Gwynn), Stephen Gwynn's niece.
173 Gwynn, *Experiences*, p. 248.
174 *Ibid.*, p. 250.
175 *Ibid.*, p. 226.
176 Stephen Gwynn to George Brett, 27 November 1903, Macmillan Company records, NYPL, box 52.
177 Gwynn, *Experiences*, pp. 248–50.
178 George A. Macmillan to Stephen Gwynn, 29 April 1904, Macmillan archive, BL, 55676(2)/646.

3

Political cultures and cultural politics

1904–9

Yet I keep leisure enough to reflect on the facts which memory brings up, and I see first of all I was a politician always. (Stephen Gwynn, 1921)[1]

Stephen Gwynn had left Ireland for London in 1896 to make a name for himself in the literary world. He returned to his homeland in 1904 with a number of books to his name, crossing the genres of fiction, poetry, essays and travel writing. While not a serious creative force of the Irish literature revival, Gwynn was a gifted organiser and propagandist for both the emerging dramatic movement, under the guidance of W. B. Yeats and Lady Gregory, and the Gaelic League. He was an Irish variation of the quintessential Victorian man of letters so elegantly portrayed in John Gross's masterful survey of literary life in nineteenth-century Britain.[2] Like other examples of men of letters – most prominently John Morley and Augustine Birrell – Gwynn formed a curiosity about politics; the literary man returned to Ireland with a hunger to become a political man. Gwynn's retrospective accounts do not leave any doubt where his loyalties lay at this time: *Experiences of a literary man* declares his younger self a committed Home Ruler by 1904, with entry into the Irish Parliamentary Party (IPP) his primary objective.[3] This may well have been true; but on his return to Ireland, Gwynn certainly did not slow down his literary and cultural work, which continued into his political career after it formally opened in 1906 with his election to Parliament. The spheres of Irish nationalist politics, the Gaelic language revival and Irish literature were becoming increasingly blurred in Gwynn's mindset, a unity of thought that had been forged during his exile from Ireland. The political cultures and cultural politics that Gwynn embraced on his return to Ireland were framed idealistically; the realities of Irish life, however, were not.

The Macmillan link would weaken, but never completely sever, following Gwynn's retreat from London. He took the precaution in advance of his move of informing George Brett in New York that he would be unable to serve as a literary advisor to the American wing of the Macmillan enterprise when he was settled in Ireland, thereby eschewing the small amount of money that came with the post. Ever one to push his literary friends, though, he recommended that Brett should poach E. V. Lucas, then working as an advisor to Methuen, as a replacement, a suggestion that was followed through.[4] Lucas acted as literary advisor to Brett for many years to come; but this did not stop Gwynn from exploiting his American links in later years in several attempts (not always successful) to secure distribution for his own books across the Atlantic. His advisory workload for the London office of Macmillan also decreased over the coming years, as politics and writing became the major outlets of his energies. Macmillan published several of Gwynn's most ambitious works following his departure from England – *Thomas Moore* (1905), *Robert Emmet* (1909) and *The history of Ireland* (1923) all appeared bearing the house's brand – but this is not to say that he was given *carte blanche* on account of his association. Far from it: on the eve of Gwynn's return to Ireland, Macmillan declined his proposal to write another *Highways and byways* book covering Dublin and Wicklow, and also rejected May Gwynn's children's book *Stories from Irish history*.[5]

Irish opportunities

GWYNN was based in Portnablagh, in Donegal, for the first few months of his Irish homecoming. Within days of his return, he received an invitation from the Belfast antiquarian F. J. Bigger to attend a special Gaelic League feis in Cushendall, in the heart of the Glens of Antrim.[6] The festival brought many of the League's most prominent activists to Ulster, as well as an eclectic sprinkling of guests. In attendance were Eoin MacNeill, Sir Roger Casement, Bulmer Hobson and Alice Milligan; more surprising was the presence of Sir Hugh Smiley, the editor of the unionist daily the *Northern Whig*, and Sir Daniel Dixon, later a staunch anti-Home Rule MP. Casement, somewhat inevitably, was the focus of discussion in Gwynn's post-revolutionary recollection of the feis: 'Nothing in this life has surprised me more than the tragic evolution of his career'. Despite Casement's central role in initiating the downfall of the IPP by aiding the organisation of the 1916 Rising, Gwynn remembered him as a 'knight-errant': he was 'one of the most noble creatures I have known'.[7] But rebellion seemed far-fetched from the vantage point of the summer's day in 1904 when Protestants and Catholics mingled easily under the banner of the Gaelic League. With Sir Horace Plunkett, the former unionist MP and head of the Irish co-operative movement, delivering the keynote address on Irish industry, *An Claidheamh Soluis*, the League's official journal, proudly asked

'What other movement could collect on a public platform men representative of such widely different spheres of thought and action?'[8] The Cushendall feis offers a snapshot of the Gaelic League ideal in Edwardian Ireland, with the revival of the Irish language linked with industry, local pride and political pluralism. Gwynn later recorded that he spent the day 'raking out old native speakers and trying to persuade them to come and be judged for their proficiency'.[9] This was, after all, Gwynn at the peak of his Gaelic League zeal, as the essays in his *Today and tomorrow in Ireland* from the previous year attested. Knowledge of the lore, literature and tongue of yesterday (rather than today or tomorrow, despite his book's title) was essential in framing a unity of being for any self-respecting Irish-Irelander.[10] Gwynn's belief in this idealism slackened during his parliamentary years, a reaction to the increasingly myopic assertiveness of the Gaelic League in Irish life. As he returned to Donegal from Cushendall, however, Gwynn was upbeat about the prospects of the Irish-language programme and its role in wider cultural life.

Gwynn spent the summer of 1904 in Donegal finishing his *Masters of English literature* and *Thomas Moore*, both of which were published through Macmillan. *Masters* was a substantial achievement: despite a few wobbles in its drafting (a perplexed George Macmillan queried Gwynn's bizarre insistence that *A tale of two cities* was left unfinished by Dickens and completed by Wilkie Collins),[11] the book stands as a lasting monument to Gwynn's skills as a literary commentator, effortlessly sweeping the landscape of fiction, poetry and drama in the English tongue from Chaucer to Shelley and Keats. Despite the volume of books that Gwynn produced over his lifetime, Aubrey Gwynn recalled his father lamenting that *Masters* was the only book 'from which he had a small, but steady income'.[12] Gwynn certainly never wrote a 'best-seller', a term which was coming into vogue (with some negative connotations) in the late nineteenth century.[13] *Thomas Moore*, not the most obvious candidate to grace Macmillan's well established 'English men of letters' series, proved neither a commercial nor a critical success. It was a rather workmanlike biography, too respectful in content, with the course of Moore's life ably charted without any gritty engagement with the literary context in which he operated. Moore's great achievement, according to Gwynn, was to reproduce 'in English the rhythms of the Irish folk song'.[14] Despite this conclusion, Gwynn did not trace a direct lineage from Moore to the literary revival of his own time, via the Young Irelanders; the book suffered greatly from a general lack of imagination. This represented a missed opportunity for Gwynn to revitalise Moore's modern standing, as his work was out of fashion when the biography appeared, a point George Macmillan sardonically made on the eve of its publication.[15] Ten years before, Yeats had derided Moore's melodies as 'artificial and mechanical when separated from the music that gave them wings'.[16] Despite his obvious admiration for Moore's verse, Gwynn did little to challenge Yeats's negative assessment.

In the autumn of 1904, May Gwynn's mother died and left her daughter a 'considerable fortune' to share with Stephen.[17] This made a move to Dublin possible but, more pertinently, financial security greatly aided his political ambitions, in an age when parliamentarians were unpaid. Several months before, Gwynn published a thoughtful article, in the short-lived intellectual Irish journal *Dana*, in which he explicitly stated his support for the Irish Party and Home Rule. He called on the IPP to take an active role in the then-raging debate over protectionism versus free trade. To force the agenda of self-government for Ireland back into the political mainstream, it would have been logical for Redmond's party to adopt a free-trade stance, if only to support the Liberal champions of Home Rule, such as John Morley and David Lloyd George.[18] 'Traditional' nationalist politics were not, however, Gwynn's only interest at this point. In December 1904, he travelled north to Belfast in the company of Captain John Shawe-Taylor, the progressive Galway landlord and precipitator of the land conference in 1902 which resulted in the following year's conciliatory Land Act. Shawe-Taylor was an active member of the Irish Reform Association, a moderate centrist movement, spearheaded by Lord Dunraven, which advocated devolution for Ireland as a compromise settlement between nationalism and unionism. Shawe-Taylor's trip to the north came about after Thomas Sloan, the independent MP for South Belfast and a proponent of a staunchly proletarian anti-establishment unionism, invited him to address a meeting of the Independent Orange Order. The Independent Orange Order was founded by Sloan in 1903 and dabbled with progressive politics;[19] Gwynn's role in all this arose from a simple curiosity about the movement. He wrote to Shawe-Taylor after the details of the meeting were announced, asking if he could accompany the young landlord to Belfast; the request was accepted. Shawe-Taylor received the respectful attention of his audience at the meeting, appealing to the Independent brethren to 'throw their weight, influence and power on the side of toleration, and fair play for all'. Gwynn was struck by the good spirit which greeted Shawe-Taylor during his address. In a commissioned article for the *Northern Whig* entitled 'Daniel in the lions' den', Gwynn commended the bravery of Shawe-Taylor, praising his efforts in bringing 'the North perceptibly nearer to the South'.[20] Despite his analysis, though, Gwynn was not tempted to join the Irish Reform Association. He claimed in his memoir that he was asked to become secretary of the movement at its inception in 1904 but refused on the basis that he was a Home Ruler. 'I was temperamentally inclined to the policy of conciliation and co-operation', Gwynn proclaimed; he believed then, as he did later with major revisions, that this could be achieved through the rubric of Home Rule. This would become clearer in 1906, as Gwynn faced Shawe-Taylor in a stormy by-election for the Galway City parliamentary seat.

Gwynn's profile within nationalist Ireland was certainly on the rise following his move to Dublin. As well as continually propagandising on behalf of the Irish Party and the Gaelic League, he also attempted to prove his credentials as a serious creative force within the sphere of the Irish literary revival movement, by turning his hand to dramatic writing. In 1905, he completed a play based on Robert Emmet and the 1803 rebellion and sent the script to the newly established Abbey Theatre for consideration. The response was, however, wholly uncomplimentary. William Fay, a leading actor at the Abbey, damned the first draft as 'unactable'.[21] The second draft was little better. Gwynn received a letter of rejection from Yeats, who, with the best intentions of constructive criticism, merely amplified the weaknesses of the effort:

> I am very sorry but I don[']t like your play.... It is all too scattered.... your imagination is hampered by an unfamiliar medium.... Probably you have allowed yourself too many plans, too many people & have there[fore] not got to any one unifying idea.[22]

Following the brutal dismissal, Gwynn did not attempt dramatic work again. He was to be found, however, in the chair of the inaugural meeting of the Theatre of Ireland in May 1906, an openly nationalistic drama society which broke away from Yeats's Theatre Society after Annie Horniman's financial backing forced the movement to abandon its amateur status and (hence) the players' independence. Gwynn played no part in the Theatre of Ireland beyond the first meeting, however; while his attitude to its ethos is unclear, it is not impossible that his early involvement sprang as much from resentment at Yeats's clumsy rejection of his play as from any commitment to amateur dramatics.[23]

A more lasting literary endeavour came on the heels of this disappointment. Along with Joseph Hone and George Roberts, Gwynn founded the Dublin publishing house Maunsel and Company.[24] Forever remembered as the publishing house which rejected James Joyce's *Dubliners* in 1912, Maunsel was in fact an important offshoot of the buoyant early-Edwardian Irish-Ireland mentality of self-reliance: Irish authors desired to see books *about* Ireland published *in* Ireland.[25] The founders all enjoyed connections with the emerging dramatic movement based at the Abbey, and in time Maunsel would publish works by Yeats, Gregory and Synge. Yeats was a formative influence on the fledgling firm and he forced James Starkey, one of the original proposed founders and confidant to George Russell, to step down in favour of Gwynn, as he wryly feared that Russell would exert pressure to 'get all the bad poems in Dublin printed'.[26] Gwynn was named as a director of Maunsel during the summer of 1905, but did not put up any capital: it was Hone's money which enabled the venture to get off the ground.[27] His directorship did not, however, last long: Gwynn resigned the post on becoming a Member of Parliament the following year, although he continued to work closely with Maunsel throughout his political career.

Even as Gwynn was dabbling in Irish publishing, his eye was still on politics. In April 1905, he announced his ambitions to the IPP leader, John Redmond, to serve the nationalist cause in Westminster. Gwynn stressed his financial position, stating that he would not have to draw on party funds for subsidence.[28] Redmond put Gwynn in touch with John Dillon, who was closer to the local organisation of the Irish Party, the United Irish League (UIL).[29] Dillon was impressed with Gwynn's intellectual calibre and was in favour of including him on the nationalist benches in the House of Commons.[30] During the autumn, with a general election looming, Gwynn received an invitation from Monsignor Glynn, the parish priest of Carrigaholt, to declare his candidature for the West Clare seat. Gwynn eagerly accepted. While he had the backing of the national leadership, his candidature could not be forced on a constituency: the UIL locally, in which the Catholic clergy were amply represented, held the power to choose their prospective MP.[31] Local popularity was thus an essential ingredient to securing a constituency, with many grassroots branches resentful of attempts to parachute in 'outsiders'. Seven candidates contested the West Clare candidature; in the end, a local man, James Halpin, won the nomination. Halpin's victory speech made political capital from his roots in the community: 'For the past fifteen years West Clare was represented by strangers', but now the UIL had sent a 'protest against invasion'.[32] It was a tough political baptism for Gwynn, and a demonstration of the gritty nature of local politics and patronage.

Despite Gwynn's failure to secure a parliamentary nomination in West Clare, he was a prominent canvasser for the IPP during the general election. He also continued to build on other nationalist foundations. Gwynn was co-opted into the Gaelic League's executive committee, the Coiste Gnótha, in the summer of 1905;[33] he continued to lecture and propagandise on behalf of the cause of the Irish language. Gwynn was also involved in establishing Maunsel's new journal, the *Shanachie*. Presented as the new house's flagship periodical, the *Shanachie* styled itself as the official organ of the Irish literary revival and it brought together many of its more recognised figures. The first issue contained contributions from the likes of Yeats, Lady Gregory and George Bernard Shaw, as well as Gwynn himself; the second carried a characteristic pencil sketch of Gwynn by John Butler Yeats. Impressive as the cast was, however, the *Shanachie* was short-lived, folding in the winter of 1907 after only six issues. W. B. Yeats predicted its decline early on, citing the journal's editorial vagueness and its timid wish to appeal to a large audience; what was needed was a more direct literary assault, as he spelt out to Gwynn: 'What Dublin wants is some man who knows his own mind and has an intolerable tongue and a delight in enemies and I wish I could see you setting out upon that man's journal'.[34] Gwynn, Roberts and Hone were not the men to carry out this bellicose request – Synge would become Yeats's totem in his delighting in enemies – but this is not to say that Gwynn lacked such faculties altogether. He revealed a more vindictive side to his personality during a Gaelic League controversy towards the end of the year, a dispute not unconnected with his impending candidature for the vacant parliamentary seat of Galway City.

The seething pot of Irish life

THE final chapter of Gwynn's memoir deals with his by-election victory in November 1906, but it opens with the advice that if the reader 'wants to re-constitute the political conditions in Ireland at the time when I was definitely entering Irish politics', he/she should read George A. Birmingham's *The seething pot*.[35] George A. Birmingham was the penname of Canon James Owen Hannay, the Protestant rector of Westport in Mayo, novelist and Gaelic Leaguer. Hannay's first novel was *The seething pot*, published in 1905; its contents provoked questions regarding the true identity of its author. Gwynn's reference to the book is telling, as it deals with the fictionalised character of Sir Gerald Geoghegan, the son of an 1848 rebellion leader who bears more than a passing resemblance to Gwynn's grandfather, William Smith O'Brien. The similarities were so striking that Gwynn – writing from an ironic third-person perspective – felt duty bound to mention them to Hannay:

> Mr Stephen Gwynn presents his compliments and thanks the author of *The seething pot*, but cannot refrain from expressing a grievance. The line of Mr Gwynn's early life having been actively annexed by an author (G. A. Birmingham) for purposes of fiction, Mr Gwynn, who is himself in that line of business, had hoped that at least his grandfather might be spared to Mr Gwynn's own uses.

Gwynn went on to address a rumour that was floating around some Irish literary circles regarding the mysterious identity of 'George A. Birmingham':

> Mr Gwynn's lack of resentment is heightened when he learns that the authorship of the offending book – if the expression may be pardoned – is attributed, in some circles, to himself. His experience does not furnish him with any parallel so complicated a piece of literary injustice.[36]

Given the novel's content, it is unsurprising that Gwynn was a chief suspect in the question of its authorship. Hannay's wife, for example, received a letter from a friend claiming that 'So many people have wanted to know who wrote the book and many think that Mr Stephen Gwynn is the author'.[37]

The seething pot depicts a fictionalised version of the Parnell split. The story brings Sir Gerald Geoghegan, who has lived his whole life in Australia, the country where his father was exiled after 1848, to Ireland for the first time to run the family's large estate in Mayo. Holding romantic notions of nationalism fostered by his father's progressive landlord tendencies and doomed stand in 1848, Sir Gerald arrives in Ireland with hopes of contributing to national life. But he is quickly confused by the political and cultural labyrinths he encounters. A Protestant joining the IPP is clearly a social *faux pas* in the context of Hannay's novel, with the prejudices of the landed unionist class constantly battering Geoghegan's sensibilities. Political nationalism is portrayed as revolutionary blackguardism, while cultural nationalism is viewed from the 'Big House' as a harmless pastime.[38] Hannay's treatment of cultural nationalist pursuits was not, however, the contentious aspect of the book; rather, the negative portrayal of the Catholic Church in the downfall of the Protestant nationalist leader (based on Parnell) was immensely controversial. It was this piece of literary interpretation which contributed to Hannay's forced resignation from the ruling committee of the Gaelic League.

Gwynn's involvement in the controversy provides a case study of what he described as the Gaelic League's 'cantankerous spirit',[39] set against the background of his election campaign in Galway City as an IPP candidate in November 1906. Hannay was a prominent member of the Gaelic League, securing election to its ruling executive, the Coiste Gnótha, in 1904. He advanced the view that promotion of the Irish language was a purely cultural pastime: in a well received lecture in January 1906, Hannay told his audience that the Gaelic League was foremost in 'producing union, amity and love' within Ireland.[40] But his alter ego attracted much attention throughout 1906, particularly after George A. Birmingham's public unmasking by John Dillon at the start of the year. At the end of that September, Hannay attended a meeting of the Gaelic League in Claremorris, which triggered a debate over free speech within the League. The meeting was called to work out the details of a provincial feis in Connaught for the following year, but the chairman, Canon Macken, the parish priest for Tuam, rejected a call for the creation of an organisational committee, citing the presence of Hannay as the reason. This provoked hostility from the floor of the meeting, with the strongest support for Hannay coming from, interestingly, other Catholic priests in attendance. Most raised the point that freedom of speech was being threatened by Macken's stance.[41] The exclusion of Hannay was, however, carried – with Hannay himself voting for it, seemingly to avoid confrontation.

Several weeks later, Macken gave his reasons for opposing Hannay. His objection was not based on the fact that Hannay was a Protestant clergyman, but rather 'that in his books he has virulently and unjustly attacked Catholic priests and institutions'.[42] The affair was deeply embarrassing for the Gaelic League, with Arthur Griffith's journal *Sinn Féin* professing that the 'attack is not on the Rev. Hannay but on the principle of Free Speech, and the Gaelic League has been used as the instrument of attack'.[43] While Hannay's treatment in Claremorris was as unusual as it was unsavoury, the affairs of a provincial branch of the Gaelic League quickly became the concern of the movement at a national level. The fallout of Macken's actions in excluding Hannay was debated at the Coiste Gnótha on 13 October. Here, perhaps surprisingly, Gwynn strongly supported the case of Canon Macken.

Hannay was not able to attend the Coiste meeting, but Gwynn wrote to him the following day giving an account of what had transpired. Macken voiced his objection to Hannay to the executive. For Gwynn, 'he appeared ... to have justification in his attitude'. Gwynn informed Hannay that he had taken an active role in the debate that followed: 'I said to the Coisde[44] that you had used language about the Irish priesthood which was to me the language of insult'.[45] Gwynn quoted from *The seething pot* to the gathered executive members, but did so in a manner that would provoke venom from Hannay. The passage was drawn from a narrative that followed a conversation between a priest and a bishop: 'The Irish priests have schemed and lied, have blustered and bullied, have levied taxes beyond belief upon the poorest of the poor; but they have taught the people a religion which penetrates their lives and which, in its essential features, is not far from the Spirit of Christ'.[46] In Gwynn's account of the meeting to Hannay, the quotation ends at the semicolon after the word 'poor'; when Hannay read the letter, he was furious. Gwynn received a charged reply: 'I myself see no escape from the belief that you deliberately tried to create a prejudice against me by means which you knew to be unjust ... by your own account, you have been largely instrumental in making my position impossible'.[47] Gwynn's defence against the charge of selective quoting is muddy. In his memoir, he claims that he quoted the entire passage but simply did not transcribe it for Hannay;[48] but in his contemporary response to Hannay's 'angriest kind of letter', Gwynn admitted that he did stop after the word 'poor'. He was at pains, though, to balance this by telling the Coiste that Hannay 'had paid a tribute of evident sincerity and eloquence to the work of the Catholic Church'.[49] Hannay accepted this explanation: his correspondence from this point to Gwynn resumes a warmer tone.

In the interests of Gaelic League harmony, Hannay did not appeal to the Coiste Gnótha when the controversy erupted, and even prepared a statement of resignation to free the executive 'from the necessity of a decision'.[50] This was never acted on; but the issues raised were so fundamental that others took up his case. When the matter came before the Coiste, two outcomes were possible, both potentially explosive. The League's President, Douglas Hyde, informed Hannay of the conundrum before the crunch executive meeting. A ruling against Macken 'would turn all the priests against [the Gaelic League] and kill the language',[51] but a decision in favour of him would repulse the majority of the organisation's officers, which could also, in the words of Arthur Griffith, 'mean the death of the Gaelic League'.[52] When the meeting started, a number of resolutions against Macken's stance were aired before a visibly concerned Hyde; but Gwynn's unexpected defence of the Catholic priest allowed the President to propose a delay in reaching a final decision. Gwynn informed the Coiste that Hannay and Macken were in correspondence, which might yet yield a solution; this was the basis for Hyde's eager procrastination.[53] But a private settlement was not forthcoming and Hannay then took the initiative to end the tiring controversy. He wrote to the Coiste Gnótha to say that he would not urge it to decide on the legalities of Macken's actions 'in the event of its being considered wiser to pass the matter over in silence'. The Coiste gratefully accepted this and the matter was considered closed.[54] Hannay wanted to avoid the fight; but when the issue came to the Coiste, as the careful words of his final letter to the body suggest, he was disappointed at its failure to wholeheartedly support him against an unconstitutional exclusion from the League's affairs. He did not seek election to the Coiste Gnótha the following year: as he told Gwynn at the height of the controversy, if he was going to be censored, 'it would be absurd to expect me to attend such meetings'.[55]

What motivated Gwynn to side with a Catholic priest who was attempting to censor a fellow author? Hannay and Gwynn were both liberal-minded Protestants deeply interested in Irish-Ireland; both were men of letters; and both were sympathetic to political nationalism. In his autobiography, Gwynn maintained that his stance was one of principle: a writer should not combine fact and fiction.[56] While a genuine distaste of Hannay's unfairness to the Catholic clergy may account for Gwynn's actions, Arthur Griffith forwarded an alternative hypothesis, which questioned Gwynn's 'principled' stand. Hannay enjoyed a friendly relationship with Griffith and was mildly sympathetic to early Sinn Féin policy.[57] Once the provincial dispute made national headlines, Griffith's *Sinn Féin* newspaper firmly sided with Hannay. But in a letter to Hannay urging him not to resign from the Coiste Gnótha, Griffith queried Gwynn's display, linking it to his 'impeding candidature for Galway'; Gwynn's backing for Macken was, according to Griffith, 'at least suspicious'.[58]

Griffith was unsubtly suggesting that Gwynn used the opportunity created by Canon Macken to bolster his nationalist credentials in the forthcoming Galway City by-election by appearing to defend the Catholic Church against the malicious writings of a Protestant clergyman. The matter was debated on the Coiste Gnótha in the middle of October; the vacancy for Galway City had been announced at the end of September. When Gwynn took to the floor to defend Macken, he was not yet a declared candidate for Galway, but was the IPP hierarchy's first choice for the constituency. The logic of Griffith's view was that Gwynn adopted a stance against Hannay to appeal to the Catholic clergy of Connaught; and, indeed, Gwynn did receive 'considerable assistance from local Roman Catholic clergy' in his campaign in Galway.[59] If Griffith was correct in hinting that Gwynn had used a Gaelic League dispute to prove his pro-Catholic credentials to the clergy in Galway at the expense of Hannay's standing in the League, this would suggest that Gwynn possessed a ruthless side in his pursuit of a political goal that was almost Machiavellian in nature. The Galway vacancy offered him another chance at a parliamentary seat: he stood at a crossroads in the autumn of 1906. Reviewing *Today and tomorrow in Ireland* in 1903, James Joyce viewed Gwynn as a nationalist conundrum: 'It is hard to say into what political party Mr Gwynn should go, for he is too consistently Gaelic for the Parliamentarians, and too mild for the true patriots'.[60] It was time, then, for Gwynn to grasp the nettle. He did not want a repeat of his earlier failure to secure a parliamentary nomination and knew what was required of him. While Gwynn boldly declared to Hannay that 'I am as anti-clerical a man as lives',[61] he was politically astute enough to know that the support of the Catholic Church was fundamental to a successful career in nationalist politics. What better way to win the eye of the clergy than to back the parish priest of Tuam in a dispute with a Protestant writer accused of anti-Catholicism?

The Galway City parliamentary seat became vacant at the end of September 1906 when its sitting member, Charles Devlin, resigned in order to take up a position in Canadian politics.[62] Soon after Devlin's resignation, John Dillon wrote to John Redmond about the impending by-election, naming his favourite for the IPP candidature: 'I am inclined to think Stephen Gwynn would be the best plan – if our friends locally can get to accept him'.[63] While Gwynn had the support of Dillon, local opinion, as the IPP's deputy leader perceptively feared, was against such a candidate. The *Galway Express* opened the campaign with a stark warning to the IPP that would have made Dillon grimace: 'In the constituency there is a very strong feeling in favour of a local candidate.... The universal demand is for a local man to represent Galway'.[64] Rumours about Gwynn's involvement, however, began to circulate publicly from the middle of October, although he was not confirmed as a candidate until a week later. The unionist *Irish Times*, perhaps ironically, responded favourably to Gwynn's connection to the seat, but reminded readers that the 'clerical influence that controls every Convention for the selection of Nationalist candidates' had prevented Gwynn from representing West Clare in 1905 and warned that it could do the same in 1906.[65] Gwynn refuted this and assured the mostly unionist readers of the *Irish Times* of the tolerance of the Catholic clergy in Galway.[66] He seemed genuinely to believe this. In later years, Gwynn told F. S. L. Lyons that Protestant nationalists enjoyed more leverage in the candidate selection process than Catholics: 'If a man had made himself conspicuous for home rule, it was rather an advantage to him as a candidate to be a Protestant. Constituencies liked to be able to say – "See how broadminded we are"'.[67] Unlike the Clare contest, Gwynn won the local UIL's selection competition, in which he was pitted against three other candidates, two of whom were local.[68] There was considerable disappointment in Galway that a local man had failed to secure the nationalist nomination.[69] But a local Independent candidate emerged to challenge the IPP: Captain John Shawe-Taylor, the political centrist whom Gwynn had accompanied to Belfast in 1904.

The *Galway Express* welcomed the introduction of Shawe-Taylor's candidature, declaring him to be 'the man for Galway'. But the *Express* editorial was somewhat confused, as it gave a critique of devolution, the conciliatory policy that Shawe-Taylor was associated with, before calling for the unionist electors of Galway to vote for him.[70] Now forced into an active campaign, Gwynn started to canvass. In his first address he was keen to point out his link to the history of Irish rebellion:

> I was selected because I was known to be a straight-forward Nationalist, because the Leader and the Party were willing to welcome me into their ranks, and last but not least, because I was the grandson of William Smith O'Brien and stood for the same cause for defending which he was sentenced to be hanged, drawn and quartered.[71]

Gwynn eagerly dealt the Smith O'Brien card throughout the campaign. D. P. Moran, for one, believed it was shamefully overplayed: 'Might we say to Mr Gwynn that we are getting tired of hearing of one of his grandfathers?'[72]

Gwynn mercilessly attacked Shawe-Taylor and the politics of conciliation from the electioneering platforms throughout Galway City, which contributed to an ill-tempered atmosphere that permeated the contest.[73] John Dillon's arrival at the end of October to canvass for Gwynn did little to ease the tensions. His first speech certainly was not conciliatory: 'Why should the electors of Galway not elect Shawe-Taylor?... First of all, because Mr Shawe-Taylor has in his veins some of the worst blood in Galway (hear hear) ... do not believe that a man with the black blood of Clan Cromwell in his veins can ever be otherwise than an enemy of

Ireland'. Without a hint of irony, Dillon described Gwynn as 'the concentrated essence of everything that was Irish, good, and noble'.[74] The day after Dillon's 'black blood' speech, trouble broke out when the two candidates held meetings at the same time. There followed a period of sustained rioting between the two factions, with various makeshift weapons freely used, such as sticks, stones and eggs; Gwynn recalled that the occasion also saw the launching of 'Galway's special missile – a rotten herring'.[75]

The final days of the campaign were calmer, if still tense, as the closing appeals to the electorate were made under the watchful eye of an increased police presence. With the close of the poll, Gwynn easily defeated his rival, gaining 983 votes to Shawe-Taylor's 559. In his victory speech, Gwynn claimed that the constituency had around 400 unionist voters, meaning that at least 150 nationalists had voted for Shawe-Taylor.[76] But this analysis assumes that all 400 unionists turned out for Shawe-Taylor, which is difficult to sustain. The London *Times* and the *Galway Express* claimed that most unionists in Galway had ignored the contest;[77] the *Irish Times* also accepted this line, and gleefully pointed out that, as Shawe-Taylor had picked up over 500 votes, 'the boasted unity of the Nationalist Party is a pure figment in Galway'.[78] In a letter to the pro-IPP *Tuam Herald* after the election, Gwynn subtly conceded part of this stinging criticism of local UIL organisation, accepting that it was 'a little unprepared this time'.[79]

Following the tribulations of the Galway election, the year ended on a pleasant note for Gwynn, as his *The fair hills of Ireland* was published shortly after the by-election. *Fair hills* was greeted with widespread critical acclaim: J. M. Synge, reviewing the book for the *Manchester Guardian*, described it as 'charmingly written ... in an excellent patriotic spirit, kept in check by a scholarly urbanity which has been absent too frequently from patriot writings in Ireland'.[80] *Fair hills* blended travel, landscape and history with genuine finesse, illuminating Gwynn's romantic fascination with the hidden Ireland of lore. The book was written chiefly 'for the traveller rather than for the tourist, for Irishmen rather than for strangers'.[81] This was a deliberate move away from the ethos of his last travel book, *Highways and byways in Donegal and Antrim*, which was part of a wider series of travel writings covering Britain and Ireland (and primarily targeted at British readers). Besides its literary merits, *Fair hills*' lasting effect was to bolster the fledgling publisher, Maunsel and Company. As Maunsel specialised in the 'high culture' of the Irish literary revival, Gwynn's book represented a deviation in its publishing direction. Gwynn chose Maunsel, the publishing house which he had helped to establish, to encourage the self-reliant philosophy of Irish-Ireland.[82] He also negotiated a distribution of *Fair hills* in Britain through Macmillan, recognising that the idealistic notion of Irish publishing of Irish books could not be fully self-sufficient.[83]

Gwynn's early career as a parliamentarian was dominated by his ambitions to reconcile the spheres of political and cultural nationalism: membership of the Irish Party could be compatible with membership of both the Gaelic League and other literary movements. The IPP desired Home Rule as the final solution to the Irish question, but the Gaelic League defined the boundaries of the Irish nation on the grounds of language, not political autonomy. The IPP leadership was suspicious of any nationalist movement it could not control, which accounts for its quietly hostile attitude to the Gaelic League. The party thus remained largely aloof from the Irish-Ireland programme, paying lip service to it only when necessary. There were several known Irish-language enthusiasts within the Edwardian IPP, such as John Boland, but Gwynn became the most prominent Irish-Irelander within its ranks. At an UIL meeting in Dublin at the beginning of 1907, Gwynn assaulted the chief planks of Sinn Féin politics – abstentionism and the 'Hungarian policy' – before drawing the conclusion that the Irish Party 'differed from the Sinn Féin people, not on ends but as to means'.[84] In March, he called for members of the Gaelic League and the UIL to work together in the nation-building process; the implication was that they were not.[85] Mutual suspicions aside, political and cultural fusion was difficult to envisage. The IPP, somewhat predictably, refused to take a public stance on the riots that followed the debut of *Playboy of the western world* at the Abbey Theatre in January 1907, despite the scale of nationalist disgust directed at the play's author, J. M. Synge.[86] Gwynn, however, proved to be the exception, and became the only Irish MP to contribute to the debate.[87] In stark contrast to the Canon Hannay controversy only several months before, Gwynn chose to support the author's integrity against what Yeats saw as the mob mentality of the Dublin middle classes. Gwynn believed that the play should be taken as it was intended – as a comedy – and if people did not like what Synge was doing, they should stay away from the theatre.[88] In later years, Gwynn championed Yeats for refusing to back down to Synge's numerous critics during the *Playboy* controversy and for thereby offering a 'courageous service to art'.[89] But such an interpretation put Gwynn at odds with mainstream nationalist opinion – both political and cultural.

The Council Bill and its aftermath

IN the first week of May 1907, Gwynn attended an IPP dinner at the House of Commons in honour of various colonial premiers who were in London on imperial business.[90] For the Liberal Party, the annual colonial conference, the centrepiece of the diplomatic activity, underlined their distinct lack of imperial enthusiasm, as demonstrated by their polite snubbing of the case for closer colonial co-operation forwarded by the Australian Prime Minister, Alfred Deakin, and, more symbolically, Henry Campbell-Bannerman's infamous failure even to recognise the Canadian Prime Minister, Sir Wilfred Laurier.[91] For the Irish Party, however, such shows of unity with the self-governing colonies of the British Empire – Canada, Australia, New Zealand, Newfoundland and the four provinces that were soon to become the Union of South Africa – were important public relation events, providing useful pro-Home Rule propaganda for British consumption. As Gwynn told his friend Roger Casement, the 'Colonial Conference offers a very remarkable occasion for raising the whole question [of Irish Home Rule]'.[92] That Home Rule would have been much more limited in its operation in Ireland than the systems of colonial governance in place in, say, Australia or Canada seemed to be largely irrelevant in Irish nationalist discourse. Gwynn in particular frequently equated Home Rule with the colonial freedoms enjoyed by the self-governing countries of the Empire.

Irish Home Rule was, of course, not on the Liberal government's agenda at the time of the imperial conference, but the granting of full self-government for the former hostile Boer republics of the Transvaal and the Orange Free State at the end of 1906 whetted the appetite of Irish nationalism. Under Redmond's leadership, the imperial dimension was a prominent component of Home Rule discourse. Redmond was unflagging in his attachment to the Empire: he admitted to Gwynn that 'If I were an Englishman, I should be the greatest Imperialist living'.[93] While sentiments linking Home Rule with the Empire could be targeted at British audiences for tactical reasons, Redmond possessed a genuine imperial strain, which Gwynn also represented. The thorny issue that is more difficult to gauge was the wider Irish public's (and even Irish Party's) commitment to the Empire. Benedict Anderson, in his classic study of nationalism, argues that 'print-capitalism' – particularly newspapers – made it possible for individuals to relate themselves to an 'imagined community'.[94] Nationalist newspapers in the Redmondite era rarely, however, shared the IPP leader's enthusiasm for the Empire: even the party's semi-official organ, the *Freeman's Journal*, was largely indifferent to imperial matters.[95]

Such cracks between the leadership and nationalist grassroots could be plastered over by the winning of significant concessions for nationalist Ireland from the British government; but these were not immediately forthcoming. The Irish Council Bill debacle of 1907 – when a very limited form of devolution was offered by the Liberals but rejected wholeheartedly by nationalist grassroots opinion – exposed the party leadership to taunts of incompetence.[96] The IPP was attacked on the matter by all elements on the nationalist spectrum – constitutional dissidents such as William O'Brien and Tim Healy, Sinn Féin and the Gaelic League – and faced dissension within its own ranks, resulting in the defections of Charles Dolan and, more damagingly, the party's chief whip, Thomas Esmonde, to Sinn Féin. The fallout of the Council Bill's rejection proved a testing time for the Irish Party, but Gwynn, writing retrospectively, cast the period as an important one in refocusing nationalist politics: 'The failure of the Council Bill had one good result, and one only. It cleared the way for a definite propaganda on Home Rule'.[97]

During the summer of 1907, Gwynn took the fight to the increasingly jaunty Sinn Féin movement. Although Sinn Féin was more of an ideological threat to the IPP than an organisational one before the Easter Rising of 1916, it nonetheless presented an outlet for discontent with Redmond's leadership. Gwynn delivered a lecture in Dublin on John Mitchel, the most radical of the Young Irelanders and a hero to Arthur Griffith, which not-so-subtly turned into a propaganda drive against Sinn Féin. Gwynn argued that Mitchel's rejection of parliamentary methods made him a disruptive element within Irish nationalism, a force for 'disunion and cleavage'. Parliamentary action and Irish-Ireland 'ourselves alone' politics, stated Gwynn with a very contemporary resonance, 'should go hand in hand and in alliance'.[98] As he made this plea, Gwynn – or rather 'Stiofán MacFhinn' – was successfully re-elected to the Gaelic League's Coiste Gnótha.[99] Despite this, Gwynn was displaying subtle signs of political fatigue with the Gaelic League. From January to July 1907, he attended only one meeting of the Coiste.[100] In August, Gwynn published an article entitled 'Some aspects of Sinn Féin' in the *Freeman's Journal*. As well as detailing further criticisms of Sinn Féin, Gwynn condemned two cultures which he saw prevailing within the Gaelic League. The first was the politically apathetic Leaguer: 'The Nationalist who thinks that his whole duty is done if he joins the Gaelic League and makes a perfunctory study of Irish, is becoming distressingly common, and the Sinn Féin propaganda tends to multiply his like'. The second was more dangerous. This was the Leaguer who was politically aware but who opposed the IPP; the implication was that such a person would be a supporter of Sinn Féin.[101] This was the first time that Gwynn connected the Gaelic League's politics of culture with Sinn Féin's culture of politics, but certainly not the last.

In an attempt to revitalise the Irish Party, Home Rule demonstrations were organised by the UIL throughout Ireland during the late summer and autumn of 1907. These were headed by a small group of energetic MPs such as Tom Kettle, John Gordon Swift MacNeill and Joe Devlin. Gwynn was also a key figure in this drive, appearing all over the country, proclaiming that Ireland had a 'right to be free amongst the nations of the world'.[102] Despite the party's efforts and bluster, though, Home Rule was a political impossibility, as the House of Lords would have rejected any such bill. Nevertheless, if a political vacuum of sorts opened between the failed Council Bill of 1907 and the Liberals' renewed commitment to Home Rule in 1909, it benefited Gwynn in his rise through the Irish Party's ranks. He emerged in the period immediately before the titanic struggle over the third Home Rule Bill as one of the IPP's most skilled and energetic propagandists, culminating in Redmond's choice of Gwynn to head the resurrected Irish Press Agency (IPA) at the beginning of 1908. The IPA had been a propaganda unit attached to the Parnellite machine in Britain until it folded with the split in 1890.[103] It had existed to propagandise the cause of Home Rule in Britain and Redmond envisaged the newly restructured Agency performing a similar function. Part of Gwynn's remit was to challenge unsavoury coverage of the nationalist cause in the British press and to educate public opinion in Britain of the virtues of Home Rule for Ireland. The massive scale of anti-Home Rule propaganda which flooded Britain on behalf of the unionist cause, dating from the 1880s, also provides a crucial context for the revival of the IPA.[104] Unable to contain nationalism in Ireland, unionists instead targeted British opinion; the Irish Party was keen, therefore, to neutralise unionism's propaganda efforts. But the new IPA could not function as the Parnellite organ had done, as Gwynn was quick to point out:

> He [Gwynn] was greatly occupied with the question of the machinery for distributing the literature which had been prepared. In the old days the Liberal Party had been glad to help. But the present Liberal Party were passionately desirous to have as little as possible said about Home Rule today.[105]

The IPA issued numerous short pamphlets stressing the merits of Home Rule for distribution in Britain,[106] while Gwynn regularly appeared in the letters pages of British newspapers. Such media concentration backfired at times on the nationalist cause; no more so than in the case of agrarian radicalism.

After the maverick MP for Meath, Laurence Ginnell, launched a new wave of agrarian agitation in 1907, Gwynn became embroiled in a heated exchange with the *Spectator*. In October 1907, Ginnell denounced the grazing farming system and called for a novel form of action against ranchers: cattle-driving.[107] This triggered the 'Ranch War', the ideological core of which was to undermine the grazing system by ridding farmlands of cattle and replacing them with people, fostering tillage arrangements and a fairer division of the spoils.[108] Such activities, which involved members of the UIL, however, pushed the IPP under Redmond's leadership into an awkward position. On the one hand, agrarian radicalism distracted from the Irish Party's failure to secure Home Rule, while reminding British audiences of the Parnellite agitation of the 1880s; on the other, as Redmond fully understood, cattle-driving was deeply unpopular with the Liberals in Britain, with whom the hopes and dreams of Home Rule were intimately bound. Given this paradoxical duality, the traditional Irish Party approach to agrarian radicalism was to adopt a policy of silence. The scale of the outbreak after the Council Bill debacle, however, rendered silence impossible, as Ginnell sought to shift the eye of nationalism from Westminster to rural Ireland, while the Irish Party moved to give the appearance, at least, of controlling the agitation.

The uncertainties of the situation were reflected in IPP propaganda. At the end of 1907 – coincidently, on the same day that Ginnell was arrested for his part in the renewed agitation – Gwynn and Tom Kettle praised the cattle-driving movement at a rally in Abbeyleix. But Gwynn followed this by declaring that now was the time to end the agrarian campaign, as the Irish Chief Secretary, Augustine Birrell, 'was a man whom people could trust' to rectify land distribution in Ireland.[109] This was the Irish Party attempting to refocus nationalist attention on the high politics of London, a point not missed by Birrell. The Irish Chief Secretary certainly understood the pressures under which the Irish Party laboured, caught as it was between radicalism and respectability while ostensibly gaining nothing for either notion.[110] While senior Liberals were aware of Redmond's tenuous position, however, British public opinion saw only Irish lawlessness, rural brutality and cruelty to animals. Sustained press coverage made it difficult for the Irish Party to deflect criticisms that it supported such unsavoury practices. The *Spectator* was the British journal most hostile to the Irish cattle-driving movement and Gwynn, no stranger to its pages, challenged its negative portrayal of Irish nationalism's tendencies of lawlessness. In a letter in January 1908, Gwynn addressed two points that the *Spectator* had raised in previous weeks. First, he argued that there was no issue of cruelty against the beasts being driven, as they suffered no more 'than if they were being driven to a fair'. Second, he stressed that the agitation was not directed against dairy farmers, but against 'speculators in dry stock' – in other words, farmers who traded in cattle, not those who produced from them. The *Spectator* sneered at Gwynn's defence, pointing out that there had been recorded cases of cattle mutilations, and suggested that the Irish Party's advocacy of cattle-driving was encouraging such crimes.[111]

This was a serious charge, and one which left Gwynn wrong-footed. In 1910, the *Spectator* published a letter from 'Pat' (the penname of P. D. Kenny, the former editor of the *Peasant*) which condemned the Ranch War, arguing that the Irish Party's tacit compliance in the new wave of agrarian disruption had undermined Ireland's claim for responsible self-government.[112] The letter outraged Gwynn, who responded by confronting the journal's editor, John St Loe Strachey. Gwynn condemned the decision to publish what he saw as a misleading letter, referring to 'Pat' as nothing more than a 'falsifier of facts'. Strachey was shaken by the protest: he referred the episode to S. H. Butcher, a

Conservative MP, seeking a second opinion on both sets of claims. But Butcher's reply did not favour Gwynn: the Galway MP, he believed, had been 'utilised to defend the worst actions of the party'.[113] It was a cutting analysis that demonstrated the precariousness of the Irish Party's position in British political circles on this matter, as well as Gwynn's identification with more insalubrious aspects of Irish nationalist life.

The cattle-driving campaign began to tail off in the summer of 1908 when Birrell announced that the government would introduce a new Land Bill for Ireland. But Gwynn's views on cattle-driving are worth considering. He travelled through the west of Ireland during 1908, which resulted in a lively book published the next year, *A holiday in Connemara*. Gwynn used the book to dwell on the contemporary campaigns of agitation in the west of Ireland and fleshed out some of the arguments that he had submitted to the *Spectator*. He claimed in *A holiday* that the cattle-driving campaign (in Connacht at least) was directed at graziers, who were, for the most part, also shopkeepers: they neither worked nor spent any capital on the land they rented, and they profited twice because they frequently accepted stock instead of money for credit. Such a situation, according to Gwynn, was 'against the public interest' and hence it was just to force these shopkeepers out of the livestock business and to replace them with cottiers and tillage farmers.[114] Unsurprisingly, the shopkeeper–grazier class was deeply unpopular and had been the object of hostility in land agitation since the Land War era. Gwynn articulated the classic nationalist critique of the shopkeeper–grazier in *A holiday*, but failed to address several anomalies in his analysis, such as the seemingly paradoxical strength of shopkeeper–graziers in the UIL and the potential benefits of grazing, which included wealthy graziers acting as 'middlemen' between small farmers and the Irish cattle industry.[115] In the world of nationalist politics, propaganda and appearances came first.

Gwynn's support for the cattle-driving campaign may seem paradoxical when positioned against the backdrop of his sympathy for landlordism, best articulated in the prefatory of his 1903 collection, *Today and tomorrow in Ireland*. But Gwynn wrote *A holiday in Connemara* while an Irish MP and this must colour any reading of the book. Gwynn's analysis of the land situation in his *Spectator* letters and *A holiday* read as classic Parnellite propaganda, justifying the new wave of agitation on a class basis. He was, therefore, following Redmond's lead: 'pretending' to be in control of the cattle-driving campaign. The manipulation of 'Ginnellism' was the obvious card to play, even if it made Gwynn a prisoner of his own propaganda. Undoubtedly, Gwynn's conservative land views and cattle-driving are difficult to reconcile, and can perhaps only be explained by the Irish Party's salient imperative to maintain unity.[116] In October 1909, Gwynn would write that 'of all the curses that can befall a country, agrarian revolution is the worst'.[117]

Yet there was no ideological commitment for or against cattle-driving: Gwynn told a nationalist gathering in Galway in 1910, for example, that, following the previous year's Land Act, there was no need for further cattle-driving, but 'If he thought otherwise he would let them know'.[118]

Amid the disarray and dysfunction within the Irish Party over the Council Bill and cattle-driving, early 1908 saw an astonishing display of unity among the nationalist MPs at Westminster. Redmond put feelers out to the renegade nationalist MPs outside the IPP's ranks – specifically William O'Brien and Tim Healy – after the Council Bill's destruction to encourage them to rejoin the party. On 17 January, O'Brien and Healy, as well as other dissident nationalists, attended an Irish Party meeting and formally rejoined. Gwynn keenly welcomed the prospect of O'Brien's return to the IPP, although he warned that it should not undermine the position of O'Brien's enemy, John Dillon, within the party.[119] The return of O'Brien and Healy provided a much-needed boost for the leadership of Redmond. Healy had been expelled from the IPP in 1901 (by a motion forwarded by O'Brien), while O'Brien had resigned in 1903; and in the intervening years, they had been, in the words of Gwynn, 'formidable antagonists' of Redmond and the Irish Party.[120]

Soon after, the reunion was to strike a sour note for Gwynn. At the end of 1907, he published a series of short stories through Maunsel and Company entitled *The glade in the forest and other stories*. One of the tales, 'St Brigid's flood', which had been serialised in the *Spectator*, drew the ire of 'A Connaught Priest', who wrote of his disgust to the *Tuam Herald*. He complained that Gwynn had painted an unflattering picture of a Catholic priest in one passage:

> The priest was standing there, a big, red-faced, coarse-looking man, as you could see. He took a step over, and he caught McCormick by the throat, and shook him like a rat.... Then he threw the man from him, and he faced around, gathering the whole crowd in front of him with a sweep of his arm. Then he made the sign of the cross in the air, and raised one hand.[121]

'A Connaught Priest' could not believe that Gwynn had written such a description of a clergyman, given that the MP for Galway 'depends upon them [the clergy] for his seat in Parliament'.[122] The affair rumbled on for a month in the *Herald*'s pages, with Gwynn himself writing to defend his work. He pointed out that he had concluded the story with the same 'red-faced' priest 'turning an angry mob from their fury to Christian devotion and neighbourly kindness'. Gwynn then asked the readers of the *Herald* to 'judge between this "Connaught Priest" and the object of his censure'.[123]

The dispute seemed minor, but it took a more sinister turn when the *Connacht Champion*, which was owned by John O'Donnell, the O'Brienite MP for South Mayo, became involved. The *Champion*, though hardly a clerical organ, supported the stance taken by Gwynn's detractor, but went one step further by claiming that the Galway MP's story undermined his nationalist credentials: 'the fact that Mr Gwynn has written such a book demonstrates beyond a shadow of a doubt that he is a dangerous man to have in the Irish Nationalist ranks'.[124] Gwynn was shaken by the attack. He wrote two letters to Redmond on the same day that the *Champion* publicly attacked his book, calling it the 'first breach of unity so far as I am concerned'.[125] O'Donnell had rejoined the Irish Party with William O'Brien only one week before; the viciousness of the attack starkly illustrated the precarious nature of the reunion, not least in Gwynn's own mind. He demanded from his leader 'a clear understanding that this gentleman [O'Donnell] is not to have a free hand to make mischief for me in my constituency'.[126] He was asking Redmond for the impossible: discipline within the Irish Party.

Gwynn's clash with O'Donnell was a precursor to wider difficulties within nationalism: the Irish Party soon haemorrhaged under the strain of re-absorbing O'Brienism. At the end of April, William O'Brien forced a vote within the IPP to back his conciliatory land policy – 'a friendly conference with the landlords' – to the anathema of John Dillon, who 'feared that the national struggle would be demoralised by social reconciliation'.[127] Inevitably, O'Brien was defeated, by forty-two votes to fifteen, with Gwynn voting along Dillonite lines.[128] O'Brien was bitterly disappointed that his 'conference plus business' approach was not embraced and had no qualms about publicly criticising the Irish Party's leadership. This drew Gwynn, again, into the faction-fighting. At a UIL meeting in Wexford, Gwynn shot back at O'Brien, claiming that he had failed to convince the Irish Party on the political virtues of his philosophies and now should fully back Redmond and Dillon.[129] O'Brien, always a loose cannon, dismissed Gwynn as an 'ex-Unionist, ex-Sinn Féiner, and ex-Devolutionist'.[130] The divisions could not be cemented over, as Gwynn found out to his cost in September. At a demonstration in Limerick, he and Tom Kettle came under attack from an O'Brienite mob armed with sticks, who proceeded to wreck their platform. Kettle left with a bloodied face, Gwynn received a blow to the head and another Irish MP, Michael Joyce, was knocked unconscious in the ruckus.[131] Literally and metaphorically, it was a heavy blow to nationalist unity.

The university question

THE fate of the Council Bill revealed that Irish nationalism would not be satisfied with half-measures of self-government. Despite this, the Liberals maintained a 'constructive unionist' approach, attempting to steer Home Rulers towards the unresolved university question in

Ireland in the aftermath of the Council Bill disappointment. At the end of March 1908, the government introduced the Irish Universities Bill, which established two new universities in Ireland: the National University, with colleges in Dublin, Cork and Galway, and the Queen's University of Belfast. Trinity College in Dublin was left untouched. The university question in Ireland since the days of O'Connell was never purely an educational matter: it was a highly political issue, with national identities and religious antagonisms at its heart.[132] Historically, it had presented profound challenges to the coalition of forces that composed Irish nationalism; early-twentieth-century nationalism endured its own schisms over the question of third-level education, with huge implications for Gwynn.

Birrell recalled in his memoirs that prior to his appointment to the Irish Chief Secretariat, he had hoped to play some part in establishing a university 'to which the Catholics of Ireland could flock with pride and pleasure'.[133] His Irish Universities Bill looked like achieving this ambitious goal after the Irish Party and the Catholic Hierarchy cautiously welcomed it, despite the non-denominational basis of the legislation. But there was another influential constituency keen to make its voice heard in 1908: the Gaelic League. Many Leaguers were ambivalent about the new Bill, as it did not grant the Irish language special status in the National University.[134] An editorial in *An Claidheamh Soluis* in May 1908 fleshed out the Gaelic League's argument for an Irish-Ireland ethos in the National University:

> We want in the first place Irish as an essential part of the curriculum of every student who passes through the Dublin [i.e. National] University.... It will not do to call for Irish as compulsory merely at matriculation ... due provision must be made for the encouragement of Irish studies throughout the course by the institution on an adequate scale of scholarships, studentships and fellowships in Irish.[135]

The only member of the League's executive who was also an MP did not, however, accept the line advocated by *An Claidheamh*. Gwynn had long opposed compulsion: as early as 1905, he rejected it as a viable policy on the grounds of its divisiveness.[136] When the 1908 Bill was introduced, Gwynn was initially more concerned with the design of the National University's Senate than with the position of the Irish language. He reported details of a conversation he had with Birrell to Dillon shortly after the Bill's introduction, when he ascertained that the University's Senate would be initially nominated rather than elected. Gwynn informed Dillon that he had seen the list of prospective Senators to represent the Galway College, which included Gwynn's own name. Membership of the Senate, which would offer the opportunity to mould the curriculum and ethos of the new University, generated much discussion over the summer of 1908, with political, cultural and religious observers eagerly following the appointments. The Gaelic League was to be represented by its President, Douglas Hyde, and Vice-President, Eoin MacNeill. Despite the non-denominational framework set out by the legislation, the Catholic Church received important nominations to the Senate, such as the Archbishop of Dublin, William Walsh; Gwynn also told Dillon that a handful of influential clergymen were on the list of twenty-four names that he had seen, including the Archbishop of Tuam, John Healy, Father John D'Alton and Father Peter Dooley, a significant figure in Galway's local political scene.[137] Yet the clergy did little in Gwynn's later estimation to erode the ideal of a 'free' university: he even defended the Catholic Church on behalf of the IPA from attacks made on the universities scheme by British newspapers.[138] It was the language movement that undermined Gwynn's conception of a 'National' University.

Shortly after the introduction of the Bill, the executive of the Gaelic League gathered to discuss its position on the university question. Gwynn was unable to attend, but received a warning from Eoin MacNeill as to its uncompromising tone on the issue. MacNeill stressed that if the Bill prevented the new university from recognising Irish studies, the moderate leadership of the Gaelic League would face a mutiny: 'I am certain that the League will promptly declare open hostility and will not allow Hyde or me to represent them'.[139] The League held a special Ard-Fheis in June to confirm its strategy with regard to the new university, which revealed that Gwynn was in a small minority among the organisation's officers in opposing compulsory Irish. He submitted an amendment to the requirement for Irish for matriculation, calling for the language to be put on the same non-compulsory level as Greek within the new university, but a large majority of the conference defeated his revision.[140] By adopting an anti-compulsion stand, Gwynn was cutting a lonely figure within the Gaelic League, although he was in an influential position. Shortly before the Ard-Fheis, he had been appointed by the government to the commission tasked with drafting the new university's statutes and selecting academic staff.[141] Despite the clear differences of opinion between Gwynn and the bulk of the Gaelic League, he was still dedicated to promoting an Irish-Ireland dimension in the new university, albeit one that did not hinge on compulsion. After the Ard-Fheis, Gwynn wrote to Archbishop Walsh, a long-term sympathiser of the Gaelic League who also had been appointed to the statutory commission, to express the Coiste Gnótha's desire to secure a commission 'favourable to the League's views'; his own appointment, Gwynn noted, coupled with Walsh's, had the full backing of the leadership of the Gaelic League.[142]

Gwynn was successfully re-elected onto the Coiste Gnótha over the summer, and he also demonstrated that his personal commitment to the Irish language remained high by sending one of his sons to Patrick

Pearse's new school, St Enda's, which opened in 1908. St Enda's was a secular all-male school which aimed to promote a strong Irish-Ireland ethos through the Irish language, culture and sports, as well as 'Christian virtues' such as 'purity, temperance, fortitude, truth, and loving-kindness'.[143] Gwynn had 'a long talk' with Pearse in August 1908 about the possibility of sending his third son, fifteen-year-old Denis, to him in time for St Enda's first term. As Gwynn told Dillon: 'The thing [St Enda's] is not so cranky as it sounds and I'm seriously of [the] opinion that a boy will have a better education there than is available at any other Catholic school in the country'. Dillon, who was looking for a school for his two eldest sons, was advised by Gwynn to consider Pearse's new institution.[144] But Dillon was not as taken as Gwynn was with some of Pearse's 'methods':

> John Dillon drove out to St Enda's in a cab to inspect the school and interview the principal. However, according to the family story, as they drove up the avenue Dillon saw boys in a playing field, 'playing hockey in skirts', a sight which so dismayed him that he ordered the cab to turn around there and then.[145]

During his two years at St Enda's, Denis demonstrated the classic Gwynn scholarly ability which came almost naturally to successive generations of the family. Academically, he was St Enda's finest product from its initial batch of students, winning the first classical entrance scholarship for University College Dublin in October 1910.[146] He was close to Pearse in these years: as he wrote in the 1920s, 'I was constantly with him on terms of close companionship'.[147] But Denis never adopted Pearse's politics, unlike many of the other boys at the school, and was in fact extremely critical of the course his mentor took in 1916.[148] This was undoubtedly coloured by his experiences during the Great War (he enlisted in the British Army in 1916); sympathy with his father's Redmondite politics was also palpable in his writings on modern Ireland.[149]

Denis was not the Gwynns' only link to St Enda's. From 1910, Stephen's wife, May, served on the board of governors, a body that administered the school's finances. Pearse's finances were always precarious and St Enda's was largely maintained on hand-outs and loans. The inside knowledge of the school's coffers which May gained in 1910 perhaps influenced the decision not to send Owen, the Gwynns' youngest son, to St Enda's at that time; Mount St Benedict was chosen instead. Both Denis and his younger brother Aubrey had previously attended Mount St Benedict; Aubrey recorded later in life that his father had sent the boys there because he insisted that they learn Irish.[150]

The National University Senate met for the first time on 17 December 1908, with all members, including Gwynn, present. Archbishop Walsh was unanimously elected Chancellor, which, symbolically at least, entrenched the new university's Catholic ethos.[151] The Church did not officially back compulsion with regard to the Irish language for matriculation from the National University, although Walsh in particular was keen to avoid an open feud with the Gaelic League. Nevertheless, as Gwynn briefed Dillon, 'how it [the question of compulsory Irish] will go, I can't say'.[152] He was, nonetheless, gearing up to launch himself into the compulsion debate, a decision which had profound consequences for his standing in Irish-Ireland circles.

One week after voicing his doubts to Dillon, Gwynn issued the most articulate critique of the League's scheme from a lay – and Protestant – position. In a letter to the *Freeman's Journal*, he listed a string of concerns: 'My own view is, first, that to exact a knowledge of Irish from all students would be unfair.... And further, that it would weaken and injure the University, and in this way impair the best instrument for restoring Irish to its pride of place'.[153] Gwynn argued that forcing knowledge of Irish for matriculation would bar students coming from Great Britain for the 'Catholic atmosphere' of the National University. But he wanted it both ways: his argument stressed that compulsion would also increase national divisions within Ireland, as the vast majority of Protestants would be excluded.[154] Instead of compulsion, he advocated placing the language on a par with other languages at matriculation: namely, making Irish optional. Gwynn also highlighted the more profound side to the language debate, beyond the practicalities: 'In truth, the Gaelic League is laying stress on the wrong points. It will not really help Irish to exact a smattering from every student.... If everyone has to learn Irish, no one will be learning it for the honour of Ireland'.[155] This was the voice of a committed Irish-Irelander, who learned the language at the age of forty and ensured that his children were well schooled in Irish. Part of Gwynn's opposition to compulsion was, then, a grimly realistic awareness of the spiritual consequences for Irish under such a scheme.

Gwynn was, however, swimming against the tide. After his public rejection of compulsory Irish, Griffith bitterly attacked him in *Sinn Féin*, describing the Galway MP as a 'miserable intriguer' and a 'humbug'.[156] The compulsory campaign had other powerful allies. Eoin MacNeill published an elegant pamphlet on behalf of the Gaelic League that positioned the language debate within the wider context of nationality. While MacNeill was one of the League's leading moderate intellectuals, his message was uncompromising: 'In Ireland there is no possible foundation for a national culture except the national language'.[157] This was, however, put into the shade by the vitriol of another contemporary publication. The title of Father Michael O'Hickey's pamphlet spoke volumes: *An Irish university, or else —*. In spite of the Hierarchy's suspicion of the Gaelic League's goal, compulsory Irish could claim the support of a number of lower clergy and clerical academics, of whom O'Hickey was one, holding a professorship at Maynooth. His pamphlet was a Gaelic call to arms, insisting on the need to make Irish the medium of education.[158]

MacNeill and O'Hickey provided examples of the pro-compulsion arguments that Gwynn faced; in their appeal to national sentiment, even if it was vague or distorted, they were difficult to challenge without being branded as unpatriotic. The intellectual arguments of Gwynn, as well as a small band of dissident Irish-Irelanders such as Mary Hayden and Francis Sheehy Skeffington, were poorly received. MacNeill neatly summarised the status of the debate between the two factions: Gwynn, he contended, 'appeals mainly to facts, while most of the Gaelic League disputants are content to appeal to ideals'.[159] The idealism of the Gaelic League's push for Irish was the major difficulty that the realistic Gwynn and the loose coalition of clerical and secular anti-compulsionists faced. It was clear to most sympathisers of Irish-Ireland which strain *ought* to be supported. This accounts, in part at least, for the Irish Party's aloof position which it adopted during the debate over compulsory Irish, caught in the middle as it was between the Catholic Hierarchy's pronouncements against making the language 'essential' and Irish-Ireland's zealous support for it. The party's leadership was quietly hostile to the Gaelic League, and Gwynn was openly anti-compulsion, but a number of Irish MPs, such as John Boland, Thomas O'Donnell and Richard Hazleton, publicly identified with the League's campaign. Boland, keen to shake the Irish Party into declaring a position for or against the League's ambitions, forwarded a motion for the national convention of the IPP to debate in February 1909.[160]

Just before the convention, Gwynn was appointed to the governing body of the new University College in Galway.[161] But if he had momentum going into the convention, this was lost on the day. Boland, seconded by O'Donnell, introduced a resolution that would have bound the Irish Party to supporting compulsory Irish at the new University. A powerful figure rose, however, to oppose the motion. In his challenge to Boland's motion, John Dillon repeated many of the arguments that Gwynn had previously articulated, but it did little to alter the outcome: Boland was supported by some three to one of those in attendance.[162] Gwynn's anti-compulsion arguments held little sway in the internal debates of either the Gaelic League or the Irish Party. All the components of Irish nationalism – with the notable exception of the Catholic Hierarchy and the leadership of the Irish Party – were in favour of compulsory Irish in the National University.

The decision of the Irish Party's convention did not, however, alter Gwynn's position in the short term: he maintained that to force Irish onto the students of the National University was wrong, particularly if this were to be done on 'national' grounds.[163] Nevertheless, he actively contributed to the design of the new institution, seeking staff on at least one occasion from an English university with technological and commercial experience.[164] Gwynn wanted to see a genuinely cosmopolitan institution established that could live up to the name 'National University'. The Irish Party's acceptance of compulsion, however, altered the dynamics of the debate. Gwynn had little to say on the matter from February 1909; and in 1910 he conceded that he had lost the argument and would vote for compulsory Irish on the Senate.[165] This came in June 1910: the Senate decided that Irish would be an 'essential subject' for the National University's entrance examination from 1913.[166] It was a disappointing end to a frustrating campaign for Gwynn, who resigned his Senate seat in January 1912, as he believed that 'it is useless to remain a deadhead'.[167]

Gwynn formally severed his links with the Gaelic League in August 1909 by not standing in the Coiste Gnótha elections. The debate over compulsory Irish had taken its toll on him personally and his was a lost cause within the movement. His writings from this point – and particularly after the Easter Rising – reflect a sense of hostility to the Gaelic League. For Gwynn, the Gaelic League had become the uncontrollable Frankenstein's monster of Douglas Hyde's naïve creation; in reality, though, it was more an expression of the rising ambitions and expectations of bourgeois Catholicism. The League proved successful in forcing its agenda on the political culture of early-twentieth-century Ireland, despite its formal 'non-political' stance. That the number of Irish-speakers continued to fall after the National University adopted compulsory Irish for matriculation highlighted the shortcomings of the Gaelic League's campaign; but perhaps more damaging was, as Gwynn feared, the severing of the emotional attachment to the old tongue. 'I learnt the language with enthusiasm and pleasure', Gwynn's friend, John Horgan, recorded in his 1948 memoir; 'my grandchildren's generation learn it because they must'.[168] Vindication is perhaps of little compensation, however, as one's fears become reality. And it would not be the last time that Gwynn experienced the pain of defeat.

Notes

1 Stephen Gwynn, 'A lover of justice', in *Garden wisdom: or from one generation to another* (Dublin: Talbot Press, 1921), p. 77.
2 John Gross, *The rise and fall of the man of letters: English literary life since 1800* (London: Penguin, 1991; first published 1969).
3 Stephen Gwynn, *Experiences of a literary man* (London: Thornton Butterworth, 1926), p. 250.
4 Stephen Gwynn to George Brett, 7 April [1904], Macmillan Company records, New York Public Library (NYPL), box 52.

5 George A. Macmillan to Stephen Gwynn, 6 May 1904, Macmillan archive, British Library (BL), 55676(2)/756; Frederick Macmillan to Stephen Gwynn, 29 April 1904, Macmillan archive, BL, 55476(2)/622. May's *Stories from Irish history* was published later in 1904 by Browne and Nolan of Dublin.
6 Gwynn, *Experiences*, p. 257.
7 *Ibid.*, pp. 260–1.
8 *An Claidheamh Soluis*, 16 July 1904.
9 Gwynn, *Experiences*, p. 258.
10 Stephen Gwynn, 'The revival of a language', in *Today and tomorrow in Ireland* (Dublin: Hodges, Figgis, and Co., 1903), p. 76.
11 George A. Macmillan to Stephen Gwynn, n.d. [1904], Macmillan archive, BL, 55477(1)/424.
12 Aubrey Gwynn, 'Unfinished history of the Gwynn family', Irish Jesuit Archive (IJA), J10/89(180).
13 For the origins of the best-seller, see Philip Waller, *Writers, readers and reputations: literary life in Britain 1870–1918* (Oxford: Oxford University Press, 2008; first published 2006), p. 668.
14 Stephen Gwynn, *Thomas Moore* (London: Macmillan and Co., 1905), p. 177.
15 George A. Macmillan to Stephen Gwynn, 4 February 1905, Macmillan archive, BL, 55478(4)/1830.
16 W. B. Yeats, *A book of Irish verse* (London: Routledge, 2002; first published 1895), p. xx.
17 Gwynn, *Experiences*, p. 262.
18 Stephen Gwynn, 'The policy of the Irish Party', *Dana*, 1:3 (July 1904), p. 68.
19 On Sloan and the Independent Orange Order, see Henry Patterson, 'Independent Orangeism and class conflict in Edwardian Belfast: a reinterpretation', *Proceedings of the Royal Irish Academy*, 80:1 (1980), pp. 1–27.
20 *Northern Whig*, 17 December 1904.
21 Joseph Holloway diaries (microfilm), 30 April 1905, National Library of Ireland (NLI), reel 7.
22 W. B. Yeats to Stephen Gwynn, 30 July [1905], in John Kelly and Ronald Schuchard (eds), *The collected letters of W. B. Yeats* (Oxford: Oxford University Press, four vols, 2005), vol. IV, p. 141. Unfortunately (or perhaps fortunately), the script of Gwynn's play has not survived.
23 Theatre of Ireland minute book, NLI, MS 7388.
24 Frances Jane French, 'A history of the house of Maunsel and a bibliography of certain of its publications' (Dublin: TCD MLitt thesis, 1969), p. 9.
25 Clare Hutton, '"Yogibogeybox in Dawson chambers": the beginnings of Maunsel and Company', in Clare Hutton (ed.), *The Irish book in the twentieth century* (Dublin: Irish Academic Press, 2004), p. 37.
26 R. F. Foster, *W. B. Yeats: a life. Vol. I: The apprentice mage* (Oxford: Oxford University Press, 1997), pp. 335–6. Starkey was also known as Seumas O'Sullivan.
27 Draft articles of agreement, n.d. [June 1905], George Roberts papers, Houghton Library, Harvard University, bMS Thr 24 (181).
28 Stephen Gwynn to John Redmond, 3 April [1905], John Redmond papers, NLI, MS 15, 192/9.
29 Gwynn, *Experiences*, pp. 251–2.
30 John Dillon to Stephen Gwynn, 7 August 1905, Stephen Gwynn papers, NLI, MS 8600 (4).
31 Fergus Campbell, *The Irish establishment 1879–1914* (Oxford: Oxford University Press, 2009), p. 141.
32 *Clare Journal*, 15 January 1906.
33 *An Claidheamh Soluis*, 26 August 1905.

34 W. B. Yeats to Stephen Gwynn, 13 June 1906, in Kelly and Schuchard (eds), *Collected letters of Yeats*, vol. IV, pp. 419–20.
35 Gwynn, *Experiences*, p. 280.
36 Stephen Gwynn to James Owen Hannay, 24 March [1905], J. O. Hannay papers, Trinity College Manuscript Department, Dublin (TCD), MS 3454-6/186.
37 Quoted in Brian Taylor, *The life and writings of James Owen Hannay (George A. Birmingham) 1865–1950* (Lewiston: Edwin Mellen Press, 1995), p. 51.
38 'George A. Birmingham', *The seething pot* (London: Edward Arnold and Co., 1932; first published 1905), p. 173.
39 Gwynn, *Experiences*, p. 283.
40 J. O. Hannay, *Is the Gaelic League political?* (Dublin: Gaelic League, 1906), p. 7.
41 *Sinn Féin*, 6 October 1906.
42 *An Claidheamh Soluis*, 3 November 1906.
43 *Sinn Féin*, 6 October 1906.
44 Gwynn uses the alternative spelling 'Coisde' throughout his letters and published works.
45 Stephen Gwynn to J. O. Hannay, 14 October [1906], J. O. Hannay papers, TCD, MS 3455/337.
46 'Birmingham', *The seething pot*, pp. 186–7.
47 J. O. Hannay to Stephen Gwynn, 17 October 1906, J. O. Hannay papers, TCD, MS 3455/343.
48 Gwynn, *Experiences*, p. 283.
49 Stephen Gwynn to J. O. Hannay, 18 October [1906], J. O. Hannay papers, TCD, MS 3455/345.
50 Undated statement of resignation by Hannay, J. O. Hannay papers, TCD, MS 3455/350.
51 Quoted in R. B. D. French, 'J. O. Hannay and the Gaelic League', *Hermathena: a Dublin university review*, 102 (spring 1966), p. 49.
52 *Sinn Féin*, 6 October 1906.
53 French, 'J. O. Hannay and the Gaelic League', p. 49.
54 *An Claidheamh Soluis*, 24 November 1906.
55 J. O. Hannay to Stephen Gwynn, 17 October 1906, J. O. Hannay papers, TCD, MS 3455/342.
56 Gwynn, *Experiences*, p. 282.
57 'George A. Birmingham', *Pleasant places* (London: William Heinemann, 1934), pp. 187–91.
58 Arthur Griffith to J. O. Hannay, n.d. [October 1906], J. O. Hannay papers, TCD, MS 3455/351.
59 *Galway Express*, 10 November 1906.
60 James Joyce, *Occasional, critical, and political writing* (Oxford: Oxford University Press, 2000), p. 65.
61 Stephen Gwynn to J. O. Hannay, 14 October [1905?], J. O. Hannay papers, TCD, MS 3455/337.
62 *Galway Express*, 29 September 1906.
63 John Dillon to John Redmond, 26 September 1906, John Redmond papers, NLI, MS 15,182/12.
64 *Galway Express*, 6 October 1906.
65 *Irish Times*, 17 October 1906.
66 *Irish Times*, 19 October 1906.
67 F. S. L. Lyons, *The Irish Parliamentary Party, 1890–1910* (London: Faber and Faber, 1951), pp. 166–7, n. 2.
68 *Freeman's Journal*, 27 October 1906.
69 *Galway Express*, 27 October 1906.

70 *Galway Express*, 3 November 1906.
71 *Freeman's Journal*, 31 October 1906.
72 *Leader*, 3 November 1906.
73 *Freeman's Journal*, 31 October 1906.
74 *Freeman's Journal*, 1 November 1906.
75 Gwynn, *Experiences*, p. 299.
76 *Freeman's Journal*, 5 November 1906.
77 *Times*, 5 November 1906; *Galway Express*, 10 November 1906.
78 *Irish Times*, 5 November 1906.
79 *Tuam Herald*, 10 November 1906.
80 *Manchester Guardian*, 16 November 1906. Reprinted in J. M. Synge, *Collected works*, ed. Alan Price (London: Oxford University Press, four vols, 1966), vol. II, p. 387.
81 Stephen Gwynn, *The fair hills of Ireland* (Dublin: Maunsel and Co., 1906), p. 2.
82 Gwynn, *Experiences*, pp. 263–4.
83 Frederick Macmillan to Stephen Gwynn, 7 April 1906, Macmillan archive, BL, 55482(4)/1557.
84 *Freeman's Journal*, 18 January 1907.
85 *Irish Independent*, 18 March 1907.
86 See James Kilroy, *The 'Playboy' riots* (Dublin: Dolmen Press, 1971).
87 For the political context of the *Playboy* riots, see Ben Levitas, *The theatre of nation: Irish drama and cultural nationalism 1890–1916* (Oxford: Oxford University Press, 2002).
88 *Freeman's Journal*, 2 February 1907.
89 Stephen Gwynn, *Irish literature and drama in the English language: a short history* (London: Thomas Nelson and Sons, 1936), pp. 179–80.
90 *Freeman's Journal*, 7 May 1907.
91 John Wilson, *C.B.: a life of Sir Henry Campbell-Bannerman* (London: Constable and Co., 1973), p. 595.
92 Stephen Gwynn to Roger Casement, 2 November [1907], Roger Casement papers, NLI, MS 13,073 (7/ii).
93 Stephen Gwynn, *John Redmond's last years* (London: Edward Arnold, 1919), p. 15.
94 Benedict Anderson, *Imagined communities: reflections on the origin and spread of nationalism* (London: Verso, 1983), p. 40.
95 Felix M. Larkin, 'The dog in the night-time: the *Freeman's Journal*, the Irish Parliamentary Party and the empire, 1875–1919', in Simon J. Potter (ed.), *Newspapers and empire in Ireland and Britain: reporting the British Empire, c. 1857–1921* (Dublin: Four Courts Press, 2004), pp. 109–23.
96 Patrick Maume, *The long gestation: Irish nationalist life 1891–1918* (Dublin: Gill and Macmillan, 1999), p. 89.
97 Gwynn, *John Redmond's last years*, p. 34.
98 *Freeman's Journal*, 16 August 1907.
99 *An Claidheamh Soluis*, 17 August 1907.
100 Gaelic League executive attendance book, NLI, MS 5179.
101 *Freeman's Journal*, 31 August 1907.
102 *Freeman's Journal*, 23 September 1907.
103 For the Parnellite IPA, see Maume, *The long gestation*, p. 9.
104 Patrick Buckland, *Irish unionism. Vol. I: The Anglo-Irish and the new Ireland 1885–1922* (Dublin: Gill and Macmillan, 1972), pp. 23–5.
105 *Freeman's Journal*, 28 March 1908.
106 For instance, Stephen Gwynn, 'Why Home Rule is needed for Ireland and for England', NLI, 4B1192.

107 Paul Bew, *Conflict and conciliation in Ireland 1890–1910: Parnellites and radical agrarians* (Oxford: Oxford University Press, 1987), p. 139.
108 Laurence Ginnell, *Land and liberty* (Dublin: James Duffy and Co., 1908), pp. 50, 73.
109 *Times*, 24 December 1907.
110 Leon Ó Broin, *The Chief Secretary: Augustine Birrell in Ireland* (London: Chatto and Windus, 1969), p. 17.
111 *Spectator*, 4 January 1908.
112 *Spectator*, 26 February 1910.
113 John St Loe Strachey to S. H. Butcher, 8 March 1910, and S. H. Butcher to John St Loe Strachey, 9 March 1910, John St Loe Strachey papers, Parliamentary Archives, London (PAL), STR/21/1/5.
114 Stephen Gwynn, *A holiday in Connemara* (London: Methuen and Co., 1909), pp. 109–11.
115 Fergus Campbell, *Land and revolution: nationalist politics in the West of Ireland 1891–1921* (Oxford: Oxford University Press, 2005), pp. 18, 148.
116 Gwynn told Dillon that it was important that the *Spectator* was challenged, but did not, as such, communicate his thoughts on the tactic of cattle-driving. Stephen Gwynn to John Dillon, 6 January [1908], John Dillon papers, TCD, MS 6754/611.
117 Stephen Gwynn, 'Ireland's need', *The Nineteenth Century and After*, October 1909, p. 630.
118 *Freeman's Journal*, 1 June 1910.
119 *Freeman's Journal*, 2 November 1907 and 13 January 1908.
120 Gwynn, *John Redmond's last years*, p. 34.
121 Stephen Gwynn, *The glade in the forest and other stories* (Dublin: Maunsel and Co., 1907), p. 208.
122 *Tuam Herald*, 11 January 1908.
123 *Tuam Herald*, 1 February 1908.
124 *Connacht Champion*, 25 January 1908.
125 Stephen Gwynn to John Redmond, 25 January [1908], John Dillon papers, TCD, MS 6747-9/256.
126 Stephen Gwynn to John Redmond, 25 January [1908], John Dillon papers, TCD, MS 6747-9/255.
127 Alvin Jackson, *Home Rule: an Irish history 1800–2000* (London: Weidenfeld and Nicolson, 2003), p. 97.
128 *Freeman's Journal*, 29 April 1908.
129 *Freeman's Journal*, 21 August 1908.
130 *Freeman's Journal*, 24 August 1908.
131 *Irish Times*, 7 September 1908.
132 Senia Pašeta, *Before the revolution: nationalism, social change and Ireland's Catholic elite, 1879–1922* (Cork: Cork University Press, 1999), pp. 15–16.
133 Augustine Birrell, *Things past redress* (London: Faber and Faber, 1937), p. 194.
134 *An Claidheamh Soluis*, 11 April 1908.
135 *An Claidheamh Soluis*, 16 May 1908.
136 *An Claidheamh Soluis*, 18 February 1905.
137 Stephen Gwynn to John Dillon, n.d. [April 1908], John Dillon papers, TCD, MS 6754/568.
138 See, for example, Gwynn's letter to the *Morning Post*, 9 July 1908, reprinted in the *Freeman's Journal*, 10 July 1908.
139 Eoin MacNeill to Stephen Gwynn, 19 May [1908], John Dillon papers, TCD, 6754/570.
140 *An Claidheamh Soluis*, 20 June 1908.
141 *Freeman's Journal*, 5 June 1908.

142 Stephen Gwynn to William Walsh, 19 June [1908], William J. Walsh papers, Dublin Diocesan Archives (DDA), 375/6.
143 Ruth Dudley Edwards, *Patrick Pearse: the triumph of failure* (Dublin: Irish Academic Press, 2006; first published 1977), p. 116.
144 Stephen Gwynn to John Dillon, 23 August [1908], John Dillon papers, TCD, MS 6754/575.
145 Maurice Manning, *James Dillon: a biography* (Dublin: Wolfhound Press, 1999), p. 17.
146 Elaine Sisson, *Pearse's patriots: St Enda's and the cult of boyhood* (Cork: Cork University Press, 2004), p. 45.
147 Denis Gwynn, 'Patrick Pearse', *Dublin Review*, 172:344–5 (January–March 1923), p. 93.
148 *Ibid.*, pp. 92–105.
149 See Denis Gwynn, *The life of John Redmond* (London: George G. Harrap and Co., 1932) and *The history of partition 1912–1925* (Dublin: Browne and Nolan, 1950).
150 Gwynn, 'Unfinished history of the Gwynn family', Aubrey Gwynn papers, IJA, J10/89 (186).
151 *Freeman's Journal*, 18 December 1908.
152 Stephen Gwynn to John Dillon, 22 December [1908], John Dillon papers, TCD, MS 6754/582.
153 *Freeman's Journal*, 28 December 1908.
154 *Freeman's Journal*, 30 December 1908.
155 *Freeman's Journal*, 28 December 1908.
156 *Sinn Féin*, 2 January 1909.
157 Eoin MacNeill, *Irish in the National University of Ireland: a plea for Irish education* ([Dublin]: [An Cló-Cumann], [1909]), p. 9.
158 Michael P. O'Hickey, *An Irish university, or else —* (Dublin: M. H. Gill and Son, 1909), p. 3.
159 *Sinn Féin*, 2 January 1909.
160 John Boland, *Irishman's day: a day in the life of an Irish MP* (London: MacDonald and Co., [1944]), pp. 131–2.
161 *Tuam Herald*, 30 January 1909.
162 Boland, *Irishman's day*, p. 133.
163 *Freeman's Journal*, 20 February 1909.
164 J. W. Dulanty to Thomas Kettle, 11 February 1909, Thomas Kettle papers, University College, Dublin (UCD), LA34/214. Dulanty wrote to Kettle to ask his advice on taking a position at the new Dublin College after Gwynn 'took me aside to explain that he had suggested to Dr. Coffey [Denis Coffey, UCD's first President] that one's experience of Higher Education and University work in Manchester might be of value in the organisation of the National University in Dublin'.
165 *Freeman's Journal*, 31 May 1910.
166 *An Claidheamh Soluis*, 2 July 1910.
167 Stephen Gwynn to John Dillon, 4 January [1912], John Dillon papers, TCD, MS 6754/591.
168 John J. Horgan, *Parnell to Pearse: some recollections and reflections* (Dublin: Richview Press, 1948), p. 106.

4

Home Rule triumphant

1909–14

> This entanglement of Irish with British affairs at Westminster was now about to display its disastrous consequences. (Stephen Gwynn, 1923)[1]

GWYNN reported on the Irish Press Agency's first year in an open letter in the *Freeman's Journal* to John Redmond at the start of 1909. The assessment was glowing: Gwynn proudly informed his leader of the contribution that the IPA had made to Irish nationalist propaganda. The IPA was occupied with producing leaflets for distribution in Britain for most of its first year and it was also industrious in writing letters to the British press to 'reply to misrepresentations'. Gwynn told Redmond that some 100,000 to 150,000 leaflets had been printed and distributed through 'Irish and English Agencies' in Britain.[2] These leaflets were collected together and released by the IPA in a pamphlet called *What Home Rule means*, which received a degree of notoriety when, in August 1909, it was seized from the Maunsel and Company stalls at an industrial exhibition in Belfast by the organisers because of its 'objectionable' political content.[3]

Gwynn's own imperial sympathies permeated the IPA's propaganda, including *What Home Rule means*. Priced at a penny and intended for a mass British audience, the message was straightforward. Irish nationalists had no desire to injure Britain's power or imperial prestige: 'We claim simply that "local autonomy" which is conceded to white men within the Empire'.[4] Gwynn equated Ireland with the white self-ruling colonies of the British Empire; the uncomfortable fact that non-white colonies also did not possess self-rule was glossed over. In this regard, Irish nationalism – in particular the imperialism of Gwynn and Redmond – was underpinned by an assumption of white racial superiority. Yet Gwynn's focus on Empire was tactical as well as sentimental. He sent a leaflet entitled *Canada and Home Rule* to John Dillon in September 1908. Its main argument was that Canada was a rebellious colony *before* the granting of Home Rule.[5] Gwynn pointed out to Dillon that the perceived threat to the Union and Empire was Home Rule's major stumbling block: 'The question of danger is the one sticking point with all English opponents of Home Rule that I have ever talked to and I think it should be faced fairly and frankly'.[6] The IPA thus attempted to dispel English and imperial fears of Irish nationalism.

An issue arising from this is the attitude of the Irish majority to the Empire. While Gwynn was keen to promote the advantages of Home Rule for British imperialism, the advantages of British imperialism for Home Rule were not overtly stated. A leaflet which Gwynn wrote entitled *Ireland and the Empire* carried the line that 'intellectually, very many of us are convinced that England and the Empire will be the freer and the stronger for granting Home Rule to Ireland'.[7] The leaflet was intended for British consumption; but, even so, the Irish dimension is strangely missing from the argument. Gwynn's pro-imperial sentiments, when unpackaged in an Irish context, can perhaps be described in terms similar to those of John M. MacKenzie's study of propaganda and the British Empire: 'The Empire was remote from everyday experience, yet apparently crucially influencing it for the better'.[8] Gwynn's use of Empire in nationalist propaganda fell into this ambiguous formula: before the First World War, from an Irish perspective, it was largely an intellectual exercise. The Irish nationalist journal, the *Leader*, for one, argued that 'Though we are not out to smash the Empire, the Empire doesn't interest us, and we think that may stand roughly as the attitude of the majority of Nationalists'.[9] The coming of the war would, however, shatter the tenuous relationship between Ireland and imperialism, terminating Redmondite hegemony over nationalism.

The changing contours of political and private life

FROM an Irish nationalist perspective, Westminster politics became very relevant after the introduction of the 'People's Budget' in April 1909 by the Chancellor of the Exchequer, David Lloyd George. The budget introduced a staggering range of new taxes to fund the Liberals' social reform schemes: it was damned as socialist from many quarters and was initially opposed by the Irish Party. Redmond roundly denounced the increase in taxes and duties; Gwynn deplored the programme as 'plainly unjust'.[10] The unofficial Liberal–Irish Party alliance was seriously jeopardised by Lloyd George's budget: at its second reading, sixty-two nationalists sided with the opposition.[11] But as a constitutional stalemate developed, with the Tory-dominated House of Lords threatening to reject the budget and the Liberal government refusing to back down, new opportunities opened for Irish nationalist politics. In a joint meeting with Joseph Devlin in Galway in the autumn,

Gwynn argued that the actions of the House of Lords were being keenly watched by an increasingly optimistic nationalist Ireland: the parliamentary deadlock might usher in the circumstances to bring Ireland within 'measurable distance of Home Rule'.[12] With the very real possibility that the Lords would reject Lloyd George's Bill, the Irish Party tactically abstained from its third reading in early November, despite severe misgivings about the budget. As Gwynn put it, 'Our people in Ireland realise that small issues must be sacrificed to great ones'; in other words, Home Rule was the goal, not budget reform.[13] A consequence of the abstention, though, was to force another split with Tim Healy, who fiercely opposed the budget on all grounds. Healy recalled in his memoirs that Gwynn was ready to join him at an earlier stage of the budget debate in opposing it, but was prevented by T. P. O'Connor.[14] This is entirely plausible, given Gwynn's hostility to the budget at its introduction. But Gwynn recognised that the budget's financial implications had fundamentally altered the political climate to the advantage of Irish nationalism and felt the opportunity should not be lost.

The nationalist gambit paid off when the Tory Lord Lansdowne moved to reject the budget on 22 November and it was thrown out a week later by a majority of 275. A dissolution of Parliament was now certain. With an election on the horizon, Redmond pressed Lord Morley, the intermediary between the IPP and the Cabinet, for a commitment to Irish self-government in the next Parliament, threatening the Liberals with a revolt by Irish electors in British constituencies if this was not forthcoming.[15] Redmond's pressure was effective: at the opening meeting of the Liberals' campaign at the Albert Hall, London, on 10 December, Herbert Asquith committed his government, if returned, to Home Rule.[16] With 1909 drawing to a close, the foul aftertaste of the Council Bill was forgotten: Redmond declared that now was 'the greatest chance that Ireland has ever had in our lifetime of achieving Home Rule'.[17]

The year of the People's Budget was a literarily productive one for Gwynn. In the summer of 1908, he believed his political work was slowing down, permitting him more time for writing. He proposed a political novel to Macmillan, with the British market very much in his mind; in his pitch, he affirmed that 'Irish politics [would be] vigorously barred out'.[18] The idea came to nothing; but Gwynn did publish a number of books in 1909, just before politics reasserted itself as his major priority, when the glittering prize of Home Rule beaconed on the horizon. In this, Gwynn lived up to, and indeed surpassed, his later claim that he modelled himself on the unwavering politician/author template laid down by Irish Party stalwarts T. P. O'Connor and Justin McCarthy.[19] *A holiday in Connemara* followed the proven formula of travel guide-cum-social history of his 1899 book *Highways and byways in Donegal and Antrim*.[20] In it, he noted two important and sharp declines in Connemara's recent history: the socio-economic strength of landlordism and the use of Irish among the young peasantry.[21] Home Rule Ireland would seemingly be built economically on peasant proprietorships and – despite the advances of the Gaelic League – would be increasingly Anglicised.

Gwynn honoured the memory of his favourite aunt, Charlotte Grace O'Brien, who died in June 1909, by editing a collection of her writings and penning a short memoir of her life. While her literary reputation was not great, Gwynn praised the 'classic dignity' and 'noble simplicity' of her work, which he compared favourably to Aubrey de Vere's.[22] Charlotte Grace O'Brien was very much in the mould of her father, William Smith O'Brien; Stephen Gwynn was now their heir in nationalist sentiment. His decision to donate all the profits from the book to the Parnell Statue Fund, which was being gathered to erect in Dublin a statue of the late nationalist leader,[23] was a gesture that would have met with his aunt's glowing approval.

The book in which Gwynn placed most hope, though, was his semifictional *Robert Emmet: a historical romance*. Published by Macmillan, this was billed as a 'true to history' novel: as Gwynn noted in the book's preface, he wanted to create a 'faithful recital of things which happened in the year 1803', the year of Emmet's rebellion and execution.[24] Gwynn's interest in Emmet was long established. The failed stage play that he submitted to the Abbey in 1905[25] was based on Emmet (and seems to have provided the framework for the book); he had also edited the memoirs of one of Emmet's closest lieutenants, Miles Byrne, in 1907.[26] As Gwynn told George Brett, at Macmillan in America, his new book was 'the first authentic account as I have been through all the State Papers etc.... I have invented dialogue etc. of course, but have put in no incident which did not actually happen – or almost none'.[27] Yet fictionalising Emmet, rather than producing a biography or a history of the 1803 rising, resulted in an uncritical narrative tale which, although at times well written, lacked the insight of Gwynn's later 'factual' biographical studies or any sense of drama comparable to that produced by contemporary Irish novelists such as George Moore or George A. Birmingham. What Gwynn produced with his *Robert Emmet* was a weak slice of Thomas Moore-esque story-telling. It was neither a commercial nor a critical success; prior to publication, Gwynn was unsuccessful in extracting an advance of £100 from Macmillan, who cautiously offered only £50, with royalties. This was a lucid piece of foresight by Macmillan, as the book failed to shift on either side of the Atlantic.[28] The novel format was clearly not Gwynn's forte and *Robert Emmet* was his final attempt at it. Aubrey Gwynn was surely correct when he recorded that 'My father's reputation as a novelist was still-born'.[29]

The coming year saw several of Gwynn's children in the public eye. Denis took the lead role in a successful St Enda's production of Standish

O'Grady's *The coming of Finn* in the Abbey Theatre in April 1910, which Joseph Holloway described as a 'unique and inspiring show'.[30] The eighteen-year-old Aubrey joined his father on the campaign trail and in his later years recalled making a speech in Irish on behalf of the Irish Party.[31] He won a scholarship to enter the National University in June 1910, but shocked his father by asking for his permission to join the Jesuit order.[32] Stephen's reply was testy: 'Your letter has been a great surprise to me and I think you will know, not one I am glad of'. He believed his son was too young to make such a decision and asked him to wait a year before taking any action. Gwynn also accused the Church of exerting 'a disproportionate attraction' over Irish youth, as 'society is in a weak and undisciplined state'. 'The drain of emigration', Gwynn starkly informed his son,

> seems to me much less serious that the drain of all the picked young men into the priesthood and the celibate life.... I am fully convinced that an Irishman of onus and character can do more good in all senses, as a layman than as a cleric – unless he has the vocation so strongly that his life would be thwarted and marred by going counter to it.[33]

Despite his father's admonitions, Aubrey entered the Jesuit order soon after and became one of the most distinguished medieval historians in Ireland. But his father's private pronouncements on the matter are worth pondering, as they belie his public proclamations praising the priesthood in Ireland. Gwynn's anti-clericalism was a fundamental part of his secular–nationalist makeup; like Douglas Hyde, he longed for Home Rule's introduction, as, in his view, a self-governing Irish political society would challenge the hegemony of the priesthood over Catholic Ireland.[34] This analysis could not, of course, be voiced in public, given the predominance of the Church within nationalist politics. If May Gwynn converted to Catholicism to punish her husband for extra-marital activities, Aubrey's choice of vocation unintentionally offered a larger cut of revenge than his mother could have ever anticipated.

Heightened tensions

THE Liberal government called a general election for January 1910, seeking a mandate for its budget and constitutional reform of the House of Lords. The Irish Party took a hit in Ireland as a spate of independent nationalists, mainly affiliated to William O'Brien's All-For-Ireland League (AFIL), were elected; that said, the IPP still returned seventy-three members, fifty-three of them unopposed, including Gwynn. All eyes were fixed on the British political scene, however, with the Liberals returning to power, although dependent on Irish nationalist support. Given the anti-Home Rule makeup of the Conservative Party, though, the IPP had little to gain from toppling a Liberal government.[35] As the *Spectator* proclaimed, Redmond was more than aware of the 'folly' of 'proving too hard a taskmaster' in relation to the Liberals.[36] The balance of power that Redmond held could tip in only one direction.

Writing at the height of the violent years of the Irish revolution, Gwynn recalled that Irish nationalist feeling in 1910 was 'strong and confident'.[37] If the close nature of the general election in Britain undermined the Liberals' resolve for radical constitutional reform, this did not affect the Irish Party. Redmond was not, however, tested in the seriousness of his threat to pull the plug on the Liberal administration if it did not introduce a bill to neutralise the power of the Lords: resolutions to this effect were drawn in March, which also marked the final passage of the budget. Following this groundbreaking success, Redmond achieved a Parnell-esque status within Ireland for the first time since he became leader.[38] Francis Cruise O'Brien, for example, delivered a lecture in April entitled 'Two Irish leaders: Parnell and Redmond', which made the prediction that Redmond would finish what Parnell had started.[39] Gwynn was in an optimistic mood. At a propaganda drive at Brasenose College, Oxford (his despised alma mater) in March, Gwynn managed to carry a Home Rule motion by two to one: he was delighted to manage such a feat at what he described as 'one of the most conservative colleges in Oxford'.[40]

Nationalist confidence was rocked, however, by the death of King Edward VII in May. The wave of emotion that followed convinced the Liberals and the Conservatives that a compromise should be found to maintain the pillars of political society in Britain. A constitutional conference, containing only representatives of the two major parties, met over the summer and autumn, but closed in November 1910 without agreement. The conference provoked renewed discussions about the constitutional boundaries of the United Kingdom: ideas of 'Home Rule all round', which would have created regional assemblies in Ireland, England, Scotland and Wales, gained currency during the proceedings. The attraction of federalism was that it offered a mechanism to preserve the Union and Empire at a time of great constitutional uncertainty.[41] A writer using the penname 'Pacificus' effectively articulated this possibility in the letter pages of the London *Times* throughout 1910, with his main points collected in a single volume published at the end of the year.[42] 'Pacificus' was Gwynn's friend F. S. Oliver, a noted imperialist and a member of the Round Table group (a movement dedicated to the idea of imperial federation and wider constitutional reform). Oliver proposed federalism as a means to strengthen the Union and Empire, with Westminster delegating certain functions to each regional parliament, allowing London to focus on the high politics of imperialism.[43] The impact of this debate on Irish policy was obvious. Some commentators, such as the Round Table group, felt that the constitutional conference provided a fitting backdrop 'to settle the Irish difficulty on lines to which both Liberal and Unionist could agree'.[44]

'Home Rule all round' appealed to a section within the Irish Party, and to Gwynn in particular. He recorded that his lasting friendship with Oliver was founded on their common fascination with politics,[45] and the work of 'Pacifus' perhaps encouraged Gwynn's enthusiasm for federal Home Rule. Gwynn was certainly a late convert to federalism: as recently as 1908 he had condemned it out of hand as an insufficient response to the Irish question.[46] But in 1910 – in the context of English imperialist moves towards federalism – he began to advocate 'Home Rule all round' as a possible constitutional solution. In the Commons he argued that he opposed the House of Lords' veto not only for Ireland's sake, but also for the benefit of Scotland and Wales.[47] The Union had nothing to fear from the enhancement of democracy throughout the United Kingdom; with this reasoning, Gwynn turned the unionist argument against Home Rule on its head. 'Home Rule all round' had the potential to strengthen the Union while fulfilling nationalist aspirations. Gwynn's thought on this matter attracted English pro-federal imperialists who wished to seek information on Irish politics: he alone from the Irish Party maintained these links.[48]

While the debate over 'Home Rule all round' appealed to some within the political classes of Britain and Ireland, it was largely an academic exercise. The weakness of its application in Ireland was revealed after Redmond, accompanied by Joseph Devlin, departed for the United States in August to raise funds for the Irish Party. At a speech in New York, the nationalist leader defined Home Rule in terms that could be easily understood by his audience: it would be 'something like you have here, where Federal affairs are governed by the Federal Government and State affairs by the State Government'. When this leaked out, Home Rule traditionalists and enemies such as Healy savaged Redmond, and his definition received little support from nationalist politicians or newspapers.[49] Federal Home Rule was quietly dropped from the Irish Party's agenda, with more 'traditional' definitions (amounting to 'Gladstonian' Home Rule) coming again to the fore. Francis Cruise O'Brien articulated Irish nationalism's discomfort with notions of 'Home Rule all round' in the *Leader*: 'A federated United Kingdom supposes that English and Irish interests are identical. History has something to say on the point'.[50] Redmond's rebuff by nationalist Ireland was an ominous sign for the chances of resolution in the coming year. Gwynn, following nationalist opinion, dropped allusions to 'Home Rule all round' in his speeches, even while in England: at a meeting of Young Liberals in London in January 1911, for example, he made no reference to a federalised United

Kingdom and argued the more familiar line that 'Ireland should be given at least as much fair play as the Colonies had received'.[51]

A general election – the second of 1910 – was called in the aftermath of the constitutional conference's final meeting, in an attempt to clear the political air. For the Irish Party, the election was about the removal of the Lords' veto over Commons' legislation; this was coupled with a drive for nationalist unity. Gwynn and Willie Redmond were drafted to meet the challenge from William O'Brien: they travelled deep into the heart of O'Brienite territory – Cork City – to bolster the Irish Party's campaign.[52] Gwynn himself faced a challenge in Galway from James L. Wanklyn, a former unionist member for Bradford, who was now standing as an Independent Home Ruler. Gwynn regarded Wanklyn's challenge as an 'insult', but easily defeated him, by 1,062 votes to 203, in a contest mercifully free from the violent scenes that marred the 1906 contest.[53] It was a good election for the IPP: the party celebrated taking Healy's North Louth seat and defeating every O'Brien candidate outside of Cork. In national terms, the December 1910 election produced an almost identical result as the January election. The Liberals had won their third successive election, but still needed the support of the Irish Party. The government pressed ahead for substantial reform of the House of Lords and ultimately Home Rule for Ireland, both of which were now on the table. The problem of Ulster, though, threatened its viability.

One of the key planks of the unionist argument against Home Rule was that such a settlement would bolster the political power of the Catholic Church in Ireland: the perception from unionist quarters was that a self-governing Ireland would necessarily be a confessional state, which Protestants should fear.[54] This was heightened after the Vatican issued the *Ne Temere* decree in 1908, which declared that marriages between Roman Catholics and Protestants not solemnised according to the rites of the Roman Catholic Church were void. This had devastating implications for mixed marriages, particularly after the 1910 McCann case provided a real-life example of the decree's effects in Ireland.[55] The McCann case fuelled unionist pronouncements against Home Rule on sectarian grounds: as Gwynn asserted in 1919, it 'unquestionably gave Tory disputants a formidable instrument for evoking the ancient distrust of Roman Catholicism which is so deeply ingrained in the Protestant mind'.[56] But attempts were made to counter this negative perception, and Gwynn was at the heart of many of these. As a committed Home Ruler and a Protestant in a mixed marriage, he seemed perfectly positioned to dispute unionist notions of Catholic intolerance.

Throughout 1910 Gwynn made speeches to assure Irish Protestants that they had nothing to fear from a Home Rule settlement.[57] On Christmas Eve 1910, he published a letter in the London *Times* which argued that Home Rule had the potential to redraw the boundaries of Irish politics. 'Once an Irish Parliament meets', Gwynn proclaimed, 'parties will instantly begin to shape themselves according to material interests and political ideals'. Irish politics in the Home Rule dispensation would be measured on the left–right spectrum, divorced from the abstract complexities of the national question. That said, Gwynn was keen to praise the Irish priesthood and its contribution to Irish life.[58] Despite his private anti-clericalism, Gwynn was sensitive to the necessities of working within a Catholic–nationalist framework until a form of self-government was achieved. But ultimately, he believed that Home Rule would fundamentally weaken the Church's political power in Ireland; the logic of this analysis was, ironically, that it was in the interests of Irish unionism to aid the campaign for self-government.

Unfortunately for Gwynn, Protestant Ireland did not interpret politics in the same manner. Following the slim Liberal victory in December, unionism in Ireland – particularly in Ulster – became more overtly militant, foreshadowing the years of crisis that were to come.[59] On Christmas Eve, the senior Ulster unionist, James Craig, delivered a militant speech in Lisburn, calling for unionists to train men and acquire arms to resist Home Rule. These ominous threats set the tone of unionist discourse for the next few years, but nationalist Ireland immediately rejected them as mere bluster.[60] Gwynn was, however, perturbed by Craig's call to arms. Although he regarded the unionist stance as a bluff – 'They do not, in my opinion, for an instant contemplate actual rebellion', he argued in the *Morning Post* – Gwynn's analysis was much more nuanced and thoughtful than the standard nationalist response. Craig might be a fool, claimed Gwynn, but he was no joke; and the (re-)introduction of the gun into Irish politics had the potential for dire consequences. He wrote:

> Let it once be believed that the Orangemen are arming, and all the powers of earth and air will not stop Mr Devlin's supporters from arming too. Both parties in Belfast have proved their readiness to stand fire. So, one fine day, rifles will go off; and we shall be told that if this happens under the Union, under Home Rule we should have civil war full-blown.[61]

As a Protestant who grew up in Donegal, Gwynn was all too aware of the uniqueness of Ulster and its marked differences – religious, political, industrial – from the rest of Ireland. The picture that he painted at the end of 1910 – an extremely successful year for the Irish Party – was bleak: Ulster unionists would not fight British forces in Ireland, but under Home Rule they would turn their guns on an armed nationalist force. The Ulster question was on the mind of Stephen Gwynn, in sharp contrast to the majority of his colleagues: the crux of that question was, at what price Home Rule?

The eve of battle

STEPHEN Gwynn's extra-marital activities were not far from the lips of Dublin's chattering classes from the beginning of 1911. The surviving sources are scant in depicting his personal life, but he certainly had affairs with at least two prominent women: the author Mabel Dearmer and the artist Grace Henry. Towards the end of his life, Gwynn also lived with E. V. Lucas's wife, Florence (after E. V. died, it should be noted), but it is unclear whether this relationship was intimate. It was not for nothing that Sean O'Faolain described Gwynn as an 'amorist', in the same breath as 'journalist, novelist, poet'.[62] The Dearmer affair seems to have had a particular longevity: Gwynn first encountered Mabel in late-Victorian literary circles, and it seems that their liaison lasted for some time, possibly on and off from the late 1890s to her death in 1915. By 1911, Gwynn appears to have been living with Dearmer, but the balance between wife and mistress became undone that year. Writing to Lady Gregory in February, W. B. Yeats was wonderfully indiscreet on the matter:

> I find everyone here in Dublin talking of the Stephen Gwynn scandal.... He has left his wife, who became jelous [sic] of Mrs Percy Dearmer [Mabel], and has told his children that he will live at home no more. And Mrs Dearmer is supposed to have said that she would always have sent him home every now and then for a couple of weeks if Mrs Gwynn had been sensible.[63]

This saga affected Stephen Gwynn in a number of ways. He had tentatively agreed to write another novel for Macmillan the previous year, but complained in February that he lacked the 'freedom of mind' to complete the task; the novel was subsequently shelved. Moreover, as he told Frederick Macmillan, the affair strained the wider family network, with all his blood relatives siding with May.[64] Gwynn did, however, return to May, only for them to separate again in the early 1920s after his affair with Grace Henry. The damaged marriage provides an intriguing private context to May's later political and religious activism: she supported Sinn Féin during the revolutionary period and became an advocate of the *über*-reactionary Catholic Truth Society, both declared enemies of her husband. Ultimately, though, there was no formal rupture of the marriage: indeed, Gwynn appears to have been permitted to adopt a 'revolving door' policy with regard to living in the marital home, with recurrent absences until May's death in 1941.

Observers of Irish politics were fixated on Westminster throughout 1911, with the introduction of the Parliament Bill in February and various governmental proposals for the shape of Home Rule coming to light. A Cabinet committee, consisting of Augustine Birrell, David Lloyd

George, Winston Churchill, Sir Edward Grey, Herbert Samuel, Lord Haldane and Lord Loreburn, was appointed in January 1911 to examine the entire Home Rule question: its primary focus came to be not Ulster but financial questions and federalism.[65] Both Churchill and Lloyd George favoured 'Home Rule all round' schemes with differing details, but these were strongly opposed by Birrell, who feared the implications of a move away from Gladstonian Home Rule for Ireland. A radical proposal by Churchill to divide the United Kingdom into ten segments, each with its own assembly, was quickly dropped by the Cabinet. In June 1910, Churchill had approached Redmond expressing a desire to saturate himself in Irish history, and was put in touch with Gwynn. The Galway MP loaned Churchill half a dozen books on Ireland, mostly of a nationalist persuasion, including Alice Stopford Green's *The making of Ireland and its undoing 1200–1600* (1908) and R. Barry O'Brien's edited collection *Two centuries of Irish history 1691–1870* (1907).[66] Quite how Churchill came to his quirky proposal for widespread federalism armed with the texts Gwynn provided is something of a mystery.

The Parliament Bill, which ended the Lords' absolute veto over Commons' legislation, was the first major piece of business that the recently re-elected Liberals introduced in 1911. Gwynn struck an aggressive tone during the second reading of the Bill in the Commons, declaring that the reason for the failure of the Union was that Ireland 'has been governed as a conquered country and is governed as a conquered country held by force'. There was, however, light at the end of the constitutional tunnel. Gwynn argued that once Home Rule was conceded for Ireland, the country's nationalist representatives 'will come as the Scotch and the Welsh come, to be a normal part of this Assembly'.[67] The Gladstonian framework had firmly replaced notions of 'Home Rule all round' in the party's thinking: Ireland's historical – and unique – grievances under the Union were emphasised over the need for wider constitutional tinkering.[68] Redmond still left the door slightly ajar for a future United Kingdom federation into which a Home Rule Ireland could fit; but the Irish Party's contribution to the Parliament Bill debates, including Gwynn's, sounded distinctly weary under the weight of nationalist impatience.

As the Parliament Bill undertook its legislative journey, and the constitutional barrier to Home Rule was consigned to history, a new dispensation opened. The political debate over the merits or otherwise of Home Rule heated up: numerous pamphlets, articles and books were published over the next few years, capturing the mood of a generation on the verge of self-government. Gwynn's parliamentary colleague Jeremiah MacVeagh compiled a pamphlet in 1911 which was published by the Irish Press Agency. *Religious intolerance under Home Rule* provided a printed extension of Gwynn's arguments that Protestants had nothing to fear from self-government in Ireland. It contained a number of tributes to this effect from well known Irish Protestants, including the Reverend J. B. Armour, F. J. Bigger, the Reverend James Hannay, Douglas Hyde and Horace Plunkett.[69] This was extremely useful propaganda for the Irish Party; but the contributors to the pamphlet, impressive in number and public status as they were, were hardly representative of mass Irish Protestant opinion, which was bitterly opposed to Home Rule. Despite the coverage given to Protestant issues in the increasing volume of political literature, the Liberal government refused to acknowledge the problem. In the build-up to the introduction of the Home Rule Bill in April 1912, the question of Ulster's distinctiveness, in particular, was entirely ignored.[70]

One of the more vivid publications from this era was Harold Begbie's *The lady next door*. Begbie was an English journalist who travelled through Ireland in 1912, one of many from that profession to embark on such a journey. Gwynn acted a gatekeeper for Begbie, arranging for him to meet Violet Martin ('Martin Ross', of Somerville and Ross fame) in Skibbereen, County Cork, before he moved on to John J. Horgan's nearby house, armed with letters of introduction from the MP for Galway.[71] Begbie travelled north from Cork, capturing the at times incomprehensible mood of unionist and nationalist Ireland through gaudy interview material with clerical and lay sources. *The lady next door* was targeted primarily at an English-reading audience, and the Irish divisions it highlighted most prominently were social and sentimental: romantic rural (and anti-Union) against modernist industrial (and pro-Union).[72] The Irish schizophrenia, as Begbie saw it, was evaluated in his concluding remarks: he declared that both mentalities were understandable, but urged English people to concede nationalist Ireland's demand for self-government 'to make her own destiny'.[73]

Gwynn made his own contribution to the Home Rule debate in late August 1911 with the publication of *The case for Home Rule*, which was commissioned by Redmond to provide the clearest case for the 'common-sense proposal' of Home Rule for Ireland.[74] *The case for Home Rule* confidently probed the history (and potential future) of Anglo-Irish relations from a traditional nationalist framework and brought together many ideas about Irish self-government that Gwynn had been expounding in recent years. It argued that the Union had failed Ireland and Britain; that Catholics in Ireland had been subject to severe persecution; and that under Home Rule national divisions in Ireland would melt away. Like Thomas Kettle's pro-Home Rule propaganda,[75] Gwynn dedicated a large part of his argument to economics: under the Union, 'Ireland has seen the constant recurrence of famine'; 'England had succeeded in crushing out the manufacturing interests in Ireland'; and much more tax had been collected in Ireland than was spent there.[76] Gwynn was at pains, though, to stress that focusing solely on the economics of Home Rule missed the point: 'Even if a country were prospering under foreign rule, its honour and its dignity should force it to demand the privilege of freedom, which is the right to manage its own affairs. The demand for Home Rule rests primarily on that ground'.[77]

Political pamphleteering on the eve of the introduction of the third Home Rule Bill was not monopolised by nationalists. A number of important anti-Home Rule pamphlets emerged throughout the crisis years from Irish unionist circles, revealing its political vibrancy and intellectual underpinnings. In November 1911, Peter Kerr-Smiley, a thoughtful unionist MP, published *The peril of Home Rule*, which served as a reply to many themes that Gwynn touched on in *The case for Home Rule*. Kerr-Smiley queried the colonial analogy frequently forwarded by Gwynn as a sustainable solution to the Irish question, arguing that it would create friction between the mother parliament and the dominion.[78] Kerr-Smiley also probed the religious aspect, concluding that Home Rule would usher in an ascendancy of Roman Catholicism, which would oppress Irish Protestantism. He quoted the editor of the *British Weekly*, Sir William Robertson Nicoll, who declared that the propaganda drive by Irish nationalism, spearheaded by Gwynn, did not find an apathetic unionist audience:

> Thus it is more clear than ever that Home Rule as the Nationalists conceive it means Rome Rule.... Home Rule will not come without the bloodiest of battles, without the last extremity of resistance, and we have to thank Mr Stephen Gwynn and his like for corroborating Protestant convictions and renewing Protestant determination.[79]

'The year 1912, in which the straight fight on Home Rule was to begin, opened stormily', Gwynn recalled seven years later in his study of Redmond.[80] Gwynn was referring to controversy over Winston Churchill's planned speech in February in support of Home Rule at the Ulster Hall in Belfast, the iconic venue – to unionists – where his father, Lord Randolph, had passionately delivered one of his famous anti-Home Rule addresses.[81] But Gwynn had a quite different concern at the beginning of the year. In January, he wrote to John Dillon expressing his distress at the papal decree emanating from the Vatican the previous October, *Motu Proprio*, and, more precisely, the Irish Party's silence thereon, which Gwynn feared could fuel unionist propaganda against the forthcoming Home Rule Bill. The *Motu Proprio* ruling, which followed on the heels of the more notorious *Ne Temere* decree, ruled that any member of the Catholic laity who brought a clergyman into a civil or criminal process in a court of law, whether as defendant or witness, without the authorisation of a bishop, would face excommunication. Furthermore, the decree stipulated that any Roman Catholic legislator who supported a law deemed to intrude on the rights of the Church of Rome would suffer the same fate. Coming on the heels of the *Ne Temere* ruling, Gwynn worried that the *Motu Proprio* decree would bolster the 'Rome Rule' thesis of unionism, all the more so after it became apparent that the IPP leadership was not going to speak out on the matter. He wrote to Dillon: 'I think it extremely demoralising for the country that it should be accepted in silence. Is there any prospect of any prominent lay man making public reference to it?'[82] The following week, he suggested the man and the place: John Redmond, on his planned visit to Belfast in February – with Winston Churchill. Gwynn wanted Redmond to publicly acknowledge Protestant fears about the papal decree and to make a declaration that *Motu Proprio* would not have automatic application in Ireland. Failing this, Gwynn called for the Catholic majority of the Irish Party to pass a resolution to the same effect. Despite acknowledging the sensitivities of the issue, Gwynn warned Dillon, in a striking turn of phrase, that 'if it is not done, I think a very heavy responsibility will rest on *your* people, for neglect[ing] to express the views which you hold'.[83]

Neither of Gwynn's suggestions was taken onboard. At the end of December 1911, Redmond confided in Dillon that he did not want the party to become embroiled publicly in a debate over the decree for fear of its divisiveness.[84] The nationalist chief thus ducked referring to the *Motu Proprio* ruling in his Belfast speech, commenting instead more generally (and vaguely) on the presence of ample safeguards to protect Protestant interests in a Home Rule parliament.[85] The controversial scenes generated by Churchill's arrival in Belfast, with the unionist leadership aggressively double-booking the Ulster Hall, forcing the Liberal minister instead into Celtic Park, overshadowed Redmond's speech anyhow.[86] The Irish Party did not issue a motion rejecting papal authority over civil courts, leaving only the MP for Westmeath, Sir Walter Nugent, to broach the subject, without explicit party authorisation.[87] The silence was indeed deafening, and it presented unionism with very real evidence for the charge of 'Rome Rule'. The emotional power of the religious argument was immense, and was skilfully exploited. Sir Edward Carson, for one, situated the *Ne Temere* and *Motu Proprio* decrees at the heart of his introduction to Simon Rosenbaum's articulate collection of propagandist essays, *Against Home Rule*, arguing that they 'constituted an invasion of the rights hitherto enjoyed by the minority in Ireland'.[88]

Ulster unionist and British Conservative posturing against Home Rule became more militant through 1912, emerging as a significant obstacle to the new Bill's successful operation. As the Bill travelled through the first round of its parliamentary journey, Home Rule's opponents relentlessly attacked the measure, without drawing a special case for Ulster's exclusion. The first call for partition came from a backbench Liberal MP, Thomas Agar-Robartes, who proposed an amendment to exclude four

FIGURE 3. Three Redmonds, *c.* 1912: John (centre), Willie (left) and William Archer.

'Protestant' counties of Antrim, Derry, Down and Armagh from a Home Rule settlement, on the basis that 'Ireland consists of "two nations"'.[89] In an earlier debate, Gwynn rebuffed similar sentiments expressed by Agar-Robartes, pointedly insisting that Ireland did not possess two nations but 'two parties': he discarded any assertion that nationality was a political matter.[90] The Agar-Robartes amendment was rejected; the Irish Secretary, Augustine Birrell, told the Commons that 'it would require a good deal of evidence *from Ulster* to sever itself from the rest of Ireland'.[91] The Irish unionists voted for the amendment, although they had not, by this point, articulated a desire to partition Ireland: their interest in the scheme was 'purely tactical and destructive'.[92] The exclusion of Ulster counties was, in other words, used by unionism in 1912 as a wrecking ball to destroy the entire Home Rule project: only later – Alvin Jackson makes a persuasive case for September 1913[93] – would it become an end in itself.

The Ulster crisis

IN contrast to his reasonably high profile between winning his parliamentary seat in 1906 and the introduction of the Home Rule Bill, Gwynn was notably less active in public politics during the Ulster crisis years. This was in part due to a new literary venture: following the death in 1911 of Sir Charles Dilke, Gwynn commenced researching and writing what would become a dense two-volume biography of the disgraced former Liberal minister, published in 1917.[94] Gwynn completed the bulk of the work by the end of 1913, and aimed for publication towards the latter stages of 1914. This was conditional on one thing: that Dilke's old friend Joseph Chamberlain should have died in the interim, a proviso imposed by Dilke on any biographical project that followed his passing.[95] As so often with Gwynn's major endeavours, his plan did not quite work out as anticipated; while Chamberlain went to his grave in July 1914, Gwynn underestimated the time needed to complete the task. The onset of the Great War, with Gwynn's soldierly involvement, greatly slowed work on the book: so much so that in the autumn of 1916, Gwynn handed over the unfinished manuscript to Gertrude Tuckwell, Dilke's niece and literary executrix, to complete.[96] The book – and the making of the book – is not without controversy. Despite running to over 1,000 pages, *The life of the Rt. Hon. Sir Charles W. Dilke* ignores the Crawford divorce case of 1885, which ultimately terminated Dilke's high-flying political career. Tuckwell seems to have been heavily involved in even the early stages of the project, and her passionate belief that her uncle was the victim of a 'great miscarriage of justice' is evident in the tone of the work.[97] The biography certainly lacks a critical engagement with the subject matter. Wilfred Blunt read the book in 1919 and disdainfully told Lady Gregory that Tuckwell and Gwynn's attempt to 'whitewash' Dilke was 'absurd'.[98] Later biographers of the Liberal radical have accused Tuckwell and Gwynn of ruthlessly omitting key source material, as well as destroying papers that cast a negative light on Dilke.[99] Dilke himself had begun the process of mutilating his papers before he died and gave sanction to his niece to excise material as she saw fit. The papers remained in the possession of Tuckwell during and after Gwynn's research on the Liberal radical, and Gwynn's agreement with the publisher in 1916 to hand over the project to Tuckwell contained a condition that she was to be given 'a free hand'.[100] Tuckwell was ultimately, then, in control of Dilke's papers, and was given scope to 'edit' the final form of Gwynn's book. This is not to exonerate Gwynn from the wrath of Dilke's later biographers, as he acquiesced in these decisions, but Tuckwell should be seen as the driving force of the hagiographic project.

While Gwynn worked on the book, Home Rule seemed to be an apparent certainty as the Ulster crisis rumbled on. This was the era of great nationalist rallies led by Redmond, Dillon and Devlin, which eclipsed other propaganda activities. Ironically, the IPA lost some of its impetus from 1912 and was disbanded in the autumn of 1914 after Home Rule was placed on the statute book.[101] Gwynn was found on few political platforms through 1912, with possibly his most notable public appearance in Ireland coming in July, at a Dublin meeting of the Association of Booksellers of Great Britain and Ireland. Striking a rueful tone, Gwynn questioned whether Ireland had 'kept up' with its literary revival. He hoped, though, that the changing political landscape would stimulate Irish reading habits by introducing a cheerier environment.[102]

Unionism's militant response to the Home Rule Bill, however, did little to cheer Irish nationalism. The centrepiece of the unionist campaign came in September, with the spectacle of 'Ulster Day', which saw the unveiling of the Ulster Solemn League and Covenant, an affirmation of hazy intent that pledged to use 'all means which may be found necessary to defeat the present conspiracy to set up a Home Rule Parliament in Ireland'.[103] During the autumn and winter of 1912, Gwynn commenced a series of conciliatory gestures aimed at dispelling unionist fears. At a House of Commons debate on the design of the proposed Irish parliament's upper house, Gwynn spoke warmly of the potential for the landed gentry to play an active role in the politics of the new Ireland, through weighted membership of a senate, an idea which he fleshed out in an article in 1914.[104] A rally of Protestant Home Rulers was organised by Gwynn in December – symbolically, perhaps, held in London rather than Dublin or Belfast. The major goal of the gathering was to articulate the groundlessness of Protestant Ulster's fears of nationalist and Catholic domination under a Home Rule parliament.[105] To this end, Gwynn arranged an eclectic range of speakers – including George Bernard Shaw, Arthur Conan Doyle and the small band of Protestant IPP MPs – to express their solidarity with Catholic Ireland. Gwynn informed Shaw in November that the Irish Party would not officially involve itself in the organisation of the event, leaving the speakers free from party affiliations. Despite this, Gwynn was determined to enforce his own censorship on the meeting, as Shaw was abruptly warned: 'If you happen to be among the Home Rulers who advocate a separate administration for "Ulster", I want you to stay away'.[106] Gwynn presumably imposed this rigid stipulation on all the participants. The rights (or otherwise) of Ulster were uniformly avoided at the rally; Shaw and Conan Doyle chose to emphasise the tolerant nature of Irish Catholicism.[107] But there was one prominent Irish Protestant notably absent from the platform. Gwynn asked his old friend W. B. Yeats to address the gathering, but received a guarded reply. Despite expressing sympathy with Gwynn's aims, Yeats explained that he could not in all conscience endorse the rally's central theme. 'There is intolerance in Ireland', claimed Yeats, 'it is the shadow of belief everywhere and no priesthood of any church has lacked it'.[108] Yeats did, however, agree to lend his name to the London rally; bizarrely, though, it was reported that the poet was unable to attend 'owing to a railway accident'.[109]

Yeats's private anti-clerical outburst served as a jagged reminder of the barriers that faced Home Rule's acceptance in Ireland, even within elements of Protestant nationalism. The case for the essential tolerance of Catholicism made by the unrepresentative trio of Shaw, Conan Doyle and Gwynn was never likely to be taken seriously by its target audience in Ulster. Gwynn, as we have seen, was privately a fierce critic of clericalism and longed for the establishment of a Home Rule government to weaken the Church's political influence over Irish nationalism. His anti-clericalism focused on the Hierarchy and not Catholicism more generally: he genuinely believed that the laity in Ireland would not sanction the intolerant 'Rome Rule' which unionism feared so much. Convincing other Protestants of that, though, proved an impossible challenge: the potential for Home Rule to act as a conciliatory measure between unionism and nationalism, where both ideologies would cooperate responsibly to further their interests, as Gwynn sketched out in an article in November 1913, never looked like becoming a reality in an increasingly polarised Ireland.[110]

Irish life became increasingly militarised during the Ulster crisis years, with the emergence of Volunteer movements and the politics of threat and force. The melting pot also bubbled with two other contentious issues that at times spilled into violent activism: the campaign for an extended franchise and the clash between capitalist interests and trade unions. Unfortunately for the Irish Party, which sought to focus exclusively on protecting Home Rule from its enemies, women's suffrage and class questions simultaneously reached a crescendo, providing considerable divisive and explosive distractions.

Home Rule and the destruction of the Lords' veto were not the Liberals' only major constitutional reforms in the Edwardian period: the administration also attempted to extend the franchise to all adult males. An amendment was added to the subsequent Franchise Bill to grant voting rights to women, but this created difficulties for sections of the Liberals and the Irish Party. The Irish Women's Franchise League (IWFL) found Redmond entirely opposed to placing a clause in the Home Rule Bill to grant the vote to Irish women; the suffrage bill that came before the Commons in 1913 was killed by IPP votes. The Irish Party's official line was that its MPs were elected to the House of Commons to achieve Home Rule; all other issues were of secondary importance. In November 1912, Redmond described women's suffrage as 'a domestic issue' that should be settled 'in our own parliament'.[111] The message was clear: Home Rule must come first. The bulk of the Irish

Party, tied closer to the fortunes of Asquith's government than ever, were keen to block any divisive legislation which risked compromising the Prime Minister's position: with the Cabinet split on the suffrage question, there was real potential for ministerial resignations.[112] Practical politics and natural conservatism, then, were key elements in the Irish Party's opposition to extending the vote to women – even if this meant that IPP personalities such as John Dillon and Willie Redmond became targets for radical suffragettes.[113]

A small number of Irish MPs did not, though, abide by their leaders' strategies on the suffrage issue. Seven members of the party broke ranks with wider nationalist sentiment in May 1913: Gwynn, Willie Redmond, Richard Hazleton, John Boland, Patrick White, J. J. O'Shee and Arthur Lynch.[114] Gwynn's pro-suffrage stance is worth closer inspection. He had been an advocate of women's political rights for some time and was perhaps the most liberal member within the Irish Party on the matter. The author Edith Somerville identified him as a 'pledged suffragist' who was constricted by the formalities of party politics.[115] At a parliamentary debate in January 1913, Gwynn expressed concern that voting for universal suffrage involved stepping outside the boundaries of accepted opinion within his party, but emphasised what he saw as the common bonds of Irish nationalism and the suffragettes:

> I am going to vote upon a conviction of justice, and that conviction does not concern itself solely with the abstract question whether women should have a vote or not.... The consequence has been, and is now, that we see violence and mob law taking the place of argument, and I say to myself and to my colleague, is there not an analogy between the case of this movement and of our movement? Is there not, first of all, a tremendous claim for justice?[116]

The bulk of the constitutional nationalist movement did not agree: Gwynn and the other dissidents who voted for the bill in May were criticised by the Ancient Order of Hibernians.[117] While Gwynn linked franchise rights with wider concerns of 'justice' in an effort to entice his parliamentary colleagues to consider changing the direction of their vote on the issue, he was also committed to universal suffrage on its own merits. The IWFL, the largest suffrage body in Ireland, identified Gwynn as one of its most prominent advocates within the Irish Party.[118] Gwynn never shied away from receiving suffragette delegations and publicly declaring his support for their cause, as he did in Galway in June 1914, a sensitive time in the Home Rule debate.[119]

While both the constitutional and violent campaigns of the suffragettes focused attention on the question of political rights for women during the years preceding the Great War, Gwynn needed no introduction to the issues at stake. An old literary friend from late-Victorian

London, Evelyn Sharp, had long been a prominent suffragette. More pertinently, Gwynn's wife, May, was also a conspicuous activist for franchise reform: she was a member of the IWFL and, in 1915, a founder of the Irish Catholic Women's Suffrage Association (ICWSA). The ICWSA, as its name suggests, existed to mobilise Catholic women who were alienated by the more extreme forms of protest advocated by the IWFL, headed by Hanna Sheehy Skeffington: its ethos was explicitly non-militant.[120] Despite this, the Association enjoyed a close relationship with the IWFL, aided by the Gwynns' friendship with Sheehy Skeffington.[121] Universal suffrage was one of the few political programmes that united Gwynn and his wife in what was otherwise a complicated marriage.

The politics of suffrage and its militant excesses provided one distraction from Home Rule; another was brewing in trade union circles in Dublin. The bitter battle between James Larkin and his Irish Transport and General Workers' Union (ITGWU) and William Martin Murphy, the owner of the Tramway Company, *Irish Independent* and other businesses, culminated in the Dublin lockout, which began in August 1913. The lockout presented the Irish Party with a huge problem. The party's primary goal (in theory) transcended class interests: the Home Rule programme united the disparate elements within the nationalist bloc, labour, capitalist and agrarian. Many members of the IPP had a background in the Land War of 1879–81 and the party's identification with the politics of land, for good or bad, was indisputable.[122] Disputes between labour and capitalism were, however, much more difficult for the IPP to handle than the nationalist-tinged economics of land, and certainly proved more divisive; because of this, one thoughtful contemporary believed that the IPP 'never had a genuine economic policy, outside land purchase'.[123] In practice, this meant that Irish nationalist MPs tended to remain silent when labour disputes broke out during the Edwardian period: they feared alienating the capitalist element which provided funds for the IPP, while wishing to avoid ensnaring the Home Rule ideal with divisive domestic disputes.[124] The Irish Party did not, then, welcome the intense scenes of class conflict witnessed on the streets of Dublin from the autumn of 1913.

Writing of the Irish Party's official silence on the lockout in October, Gwynn informed Archbishop Walsh of Dublin that 'nationalist members are afraid to move at this juncture for fear for creating disunion'.[125] This had been noticed by observers of the dispute, with the *Leader* commenting in September that the Irish Party 'appears to be divorced from the whole situation' in Dublin.[126] Individual MPs did speak out, but uniformly *against* the strikers: David Sheehy and William O'Malley, for example, fiercely condemned Larkin's tactics and his increasingly militant rhetoric.[127] For Larkin, the Irish Party's attitude was predetermined by the class divide. The *Irish Worker*, Larkin's pro-Labour newspaper, publicly connected a number of Irish MPs to the capitalist interest, claiming that John Boland, Walter Nugent and Patrick Brady were major shareholders in Murphy's business empire.[128] Also included on Larkin's list of shame was Gwynn: it was alleged that the Galway MP held a stake in Murphy's enterprises 'through his wife'. No evidence of this link has survived, but Gwynn did not refute Larkin's accusation. If his silence is taken as proof of his wife's financial connection with Murphy, it did not, however, stop Gwynn from taking a public stand contrary to most within his party.

Gwynn had previously encountered what he interpreted as the intransigence of Murphy and the idealism of Larkin, and this provides an essential context in explaining his attitude to the lockout. In October 1913, Gwynn lobbied Redmond on Yeats's behalf to back the campaign to secure for Dublin the paintings of the art collector Hugh Lane, which, under Lane's terms, required the construction of a grand gallery spanning the Liffey. Redmond's support for the project, however, was not forthcoming, as Gwynn told Yeats, with the current powder keg state of proletarianism cited as the major factor:

> The important point from his [Redmond's] point of view is that there is no use – in fact, that it would be lunacy at the present moment – to discuss in public the spending of money on a gallery in Dublin, with the falling-down of tenement-houses and the general starvation. He thinks that the public, however unreasonably, would be simply furious at the idea.[129]

Over the summer of 1913 the support of wealthy businessmen – expressly William Martin Murphy and Lord Ardilaun of the Guinness family – had been sought to build the new gallery. But they refused to support the venture with money; when this became clear, Lane withdrew his offer and Dublin lost the paintings. The collapse of the campaign was not the fault of Redmond, as Gwynn told Yeats, but the philistine parsimony of Dublin's leading capitalists: 'I hope to God that Murphy and the Ardilauns may be damned to an eternity of the Dublin Corporation.... Altogether, my mouth is full of blasphemies'.[130] This belligerent view of Murphy contrasted with a declaration of sympathy for Larkin that Gwynn made to Redmond during the 1907 trade union agitation in Belfast: 'Larkin is far more right than wrong'. The Galway MP also bracketed Larkin with a number of other nationalist activists who stood outside the Irish Party – George Russell, George Bernard Shaw and Shane Leslie – as 'force[s] that we have should had on our side'.[131] And it was a *Freeman's Journal* assault on Russell and Shaw that forced Gwynn to break his public silence about the lockout.

Russell and Shaw, along with Yeats, were the most prominent Irish supporters of the striking workers, with Russell's iconic open letter 'To the masters of Dublin' standing as the finest expression of bohemian sentiment against the capitalist classes.[132] Gwynn's defence of Russell and Shaw sprang from a major subplot of the 1913 lockout: the 'save the kiddies' campaign. Seven weeks into the strike, Dora Montefiore, an English suffragette and socialist, initiated a scheme to lessen the pressure on the ITGWU's soup kitchens. She proposed to rescue the children of striking workers for the duration of the lockout, boarding them with sympathetic families in England. This humanitarian gesture was, however, greeted with frenzied scenes in Dublin, with angry priests and gangs of Ancient Order of Hibernians physically stopping anyone attempting to leave the city with a child, amid claims that the supporters of Montefiore were manipulating the hardships of the Catholic working class to proselytise their children.[133] Gwynn condemned the 'save the kiddies' crusade, as it distracted from what he believed was the real issue at stake: the labour–employer dispute. The religious fanaticism stoked by the arrival of English socialists undermined the class solidarity of the strikers and weakened public sympathy for their actions; as Gwynn wearily informed Walsh, who was also hostile to the 'save the kiddies' campaign, 'These idiot women have developed a situation which gives victory to the employers'. But Gwynn warned the Archbishop, with whom he enjoyed a good working relationship stretching back to the formation of the National University, that such a victory 'will inevitably be regarded by the Radical section among the workers as won by clericalism'. The Church would be seen merely as a branch of capitalism: even the anti-clerical Gwynn believed that this would be 'the seed of a dangerous growth'.[134]

On 1 November, Russell and Shaw addressed a meeting at the Royal Albert Hall in support of the strikers. The 'Dublin six' – the six nationalist MPs for Dublin – were the targets in a tirade from Russell which accused them of protecting the interests of the Church above those of their working-class constituents.[135] Reporting the meeting the next day, the *Freeman's Journal* struck back, impugning Russell as a socialist radical intent on proselytising the Catholic young.[136] Gwynn was horrified when he read this and issued an irate rebuttal to the *Freeman's Journal*:

> Your article – the leading article of the leading organ of Nationalist opinion – is calculated to set every young man of brains and education in Ireland against the main National movement. What is it? A violent denunciation of two Irishmen of genius – Mr Bernard Shaw and Mr George Russell – both of them strong Home Rulers; both of them loyal lovers of Ireland.

Gwynn categorically backed Russell, proclaiming that he 'rejoiced' in his 'To the masters of Dublin', while condemning the 'save the kiddies' programme as a 'monstrous blunder'.[137] It was a stunning end to a public silence.

With this outburst, Gwynn became the first – and ultimately the only – IPP MP to align himself publicly with the strikers. Russell was euphoric after reading the letter: on the same day as Gwynn's defence appeared in the paper, he wrote to Yeats, from whom he had recently become estranged, to declare his happiness at seeing such a line-up 'on the same side of life'.[138] More representative components of Irish nationalism, however, brushed away Gwynn's complaints: the *Freeman's Journal* showed no remorse, and again queried Russell and Shaw's 'value as Home Rulers'.[139] Another wave of criticism followed after Gwynn wrote again to the *Journal* comparing the ITGWU to the Land League: this provoked the ire of two Land League veterans, David Sheehy and Andrew Kettle, who abruptly rejected any similarities.[140] Gwynn, then, stood outside the mainstream of the Irish Party during the lockout. While his actions were not greeted favourably by many of his parliamentary colleagues, there was one lasting legacy. Throughout the lockout, Gwynn advocated the extension of the Provision of Meals Act of 1906 to Ireland as an alternative to the 'save the kiddies' scheme.[141] With the backing of Hanna Sheehy Skeffington and Maud Gonne in Ireland (who aided the drafting of the bill), a handful of Irish MPs, including Gwynn, P. J. Brady and Hugh Law, secured the extension in 1914, shortly after the strikes ended in defeat.[142]

Another legacy of the lockout was more menacing in design; in Gwynn's retrospective analysis, the labour struggle and its aftermath in Dublin left 'dark embers of revolutionary hate', which contributed to the events of Easter week 1916.[143] In November 1913, against the backdrop of the lockout, two paramilitary groups were established: the Irish Citizen Army, a defence force for the striking workers (and coincidently founded in the Trinity College rooms of Gwynn's brother, Robin, a fellow of TCD and Larkin sympathiser); and the Irish Volunteers, a more directly nationalist militia group, born outside the sphere of Irish Party control, and dominated by elements from the underground Irish Republican Brotherhood. The emergence of both private armies was heavily indebted to the example of the Ulster Volunteers, founded in January 1913, and further accelerated the militarisation of politics in Ireland during the Home Rule crisis.[144] This was the ominous backdrop to the Home Rule Bill's passage through Westminster, as it neared the end of its legislative journey. Without an agreement with unionism, though, the prospects for Home Rule's successful application in Ireland were unclear. The autumn of 1913 hence saw an intensive round of private negotiations, culminating in behind-the-scenes exchanges between the leaders of the Liberals and Tories, Asquith and Andrew Bonar Law, in which both men expressed grave reservations about pressing their respective positions to the brink.[145] The government tested the nationalist waters in November 1913 by issuing Redmond with a proposal for Ulster exclusion from Home Rule.[146] Redmond, however, rejected the suggestion; but as the Home Rule Bill's parliamentary time ticked away, the Liberals pushed him into conceding a form of 'county option' to Ulster, allowing individual counties in the north temporarily to opt out of the framework of Home Rule. The Irish Party leadership reluctantly acquiesced to a six-year exclusion period. While Redmond seemed to win support from northern nationalism for the move, it was a sickening concession for him to make. Crucially, Ulster unionism did not reciprocate on the dilution of the IPP's stance, with Sir Edward Carson colourfully rejecting the temporary nature of the deal.[147]

On the nationalist side, the negotiations to reach a compromise were conducted in almost complete secrecy. Only the four leading members of the Irish Party were involved: Gwynn, like the majority of rank-and-file members, was not party to the discussions and in fact remained upbeat about the possibilities for a deal.[148] His 1919 book, *John Redmond's last years*, however, contains many illuminating insights into the negotiations of 1913–14. For instance, for all of Gwynn's Redmondite loyalties, the book pondered what he considered to be the Irish Party's tactical mistakes during the Ulster crisis. While Gwynn sympathised with Redmond's oligarchic leadership during the critical negotiations, there was also a tinge of regret in his retrospective analysis:

> In my opinion these modifications of the Bill were never adequately discussed in the meetings of the Irish party. All was done between the Government and Redmond's inner cabinet, consisting of Redmond himself, Mr Dillon, Mr Devlin and Mr T. P. O'Connor. The negotiations were most delicate and difficult, and above all secrecy is hard to maintain when a body of over seventy men, each keenly concerned for the view of his constituents, comes to be consulted. Yet I think it a pity that the party never thrashed this question out.[149]

John Redmond's last years also pinpointed the moment when the Irish Party conceded temporary exclusion as a missed opportunity to resolve the Ulster question on mutually beneficial lines. Reviewing Redmond's position five years on, Gwynn came to the conclusion that the party should have offered Ulster permanent exclusion from the start of the 1913–14 negotiations: had such a strategy been adopted, he argued, 'a real effect could have been produced on much moderate opinion in Ulster'. He hypothesised that the Irish Party's standing in Ireland would not have been any worse than it was after the concession of temporary exclusion was made, but would have been dramatically boosted in Westminster and Britain more generally.[150] This issue is explored again later in the present volume, as the context in which it was written is of crucial importance: the analysis reveals more of Gwynn's attitude to partition in 1919 than in 1914.[151] His point, though, should not be missed. In acquiescing to a temporary county option scheme in 1914, Redmond compromised himself and his party in the eyes of nationalists as diverse as William O'Brien and John Quinn.[152] In rigidly insisting on a time limit for exclusion, Redmond also failed to win over unionism. The Buckingham Palace conference of June 1914 – the final peacetime initiative to hammer out an agreeable compromise – came to nothing, with unionism and nationalism at loggerheads over the area for exclusion, a quite separate issue from time limits. Neither side was willing to concede further ground, nor did the long-running series of negotiations resolve any of the substantial issues. Yet the Irish Party had been forced to swallow the poison of partition at the behest of British Liberalism, which had reneged on one of its most sacred principles: Irish unity.

With political stalemate and opposing militia groups, it took the outbreak of war in August 1914 to halt the logical conclusion: violence. The Irish Party annexed the Irish Volunteer movement in June 1914, after it had mushroomed in response to external crises, such as the Larne gun-running and the Curragh 'incident'. With the weight of the constitutional movement formally behind them, the Irish Volunteers would claim over 180,000 members just as the horrors of the First World War began.[153] The Volunteers contained the seed of the bitter fruit which undid much of Redmond's programme in Easter 1916; despite securing a majority within the militia's ruling committee, the Irish Party found that this did not equate to control.[154] Gwynn confided in Eoin MacNeill, the Volunteers' figurehead, that he believed the IPP made a fatal error in not 'taking hold of the Volunteer movement from the first'.[155] There was much in favour of this argument: the Volunteers, after all, were, as Gwynn pointed out retrospectively, an organisation that Redmond 'neither willed nor approved'.[156] Allowed to exist independently and gradually expand their numbers, the Volunteers possessed their own identity – or, more accurately, a number of identities.[157] As it was, Redmond's support for the Volunteers was haphazard and reactionary, focused as he was on the parliamentary game. The politics of Home Rule were, however, radically transformed by the toil of the coming of the Great War; and Gwynn's wartime experiences encapsulated the crushing defeat of the Redmondite project.

Notes

1 Stephen Gwynn, *The history of Ireland* (London: Macmillan and Co., 1923), p. 503.
2 *Freeman's Journal*, 5 January 1909.
3 *Freeman's Journal*, 12 August 1909.
4 Stephen Gwynn (ed.), *What Home Rule means and other leaflets issued by the Irish Press Agency* (Dublin: Maunsel and Co., n.d. [1909]), p. 9.

5 *Ibid.*, pp. 10–13.
6 Stephen Gwynn to John Dillon, 4 September [1908], John Dillon papers, Trinity College Manuscript Department, Dublin (TCD), MS 6754/577.
7 Dated 31 August 1908, John Dillon papers, TCD, MS 6754/577.
8 John M. MacKenzie, *Propaganda and empire: the manipulation of British public opinion, 1880–1960* (Manchester: Manchester University Press, 1984), p. 258.
9 *Leader*, 15 August 1908.
10 *Daily Mail*, 12 May 1909.
11 Bruce K. Murray, *The People's Budget 1909/10: Lloyd George and Liberal politics* (Oxford: Oxford University Press, 1980), p. 177.
12 *Freeman's Journal*, 16 October 1909.
13 *Daily Chronicle*, 24 March 1910.
14 T. M. Healy, *Letters and leaders of my day* (London: Thornton Butterworth, two vols, 1928), vol. II, p. 486.
15 John Redmond to Lord Morley, n.d. [late November/early December 1909], H. H. Asquith papers, Bodleian Library, Oxford, MS 36.
16 *Times*, 11 December 1909.
17 *Freeman's Journal*, 16 December 1909.
18 Stephen Gwynn to Frederick Macmillan, 6 July [1908], Macmillan archive, British Library (BL), box M44.
19 Stephen Gwynn, *Experiences of a literary man* (London: Thornton Butterworth, 1926), p. 251.
20 Gwynn's *Highways and byways in Donegal and Antrim* is discussed in Chapter 2, p. 48.
21 Stephen Gwynn, *A holiday in Connemara* (London: Methuen and Co., 1909), pp. 4–5, 264.
22 Stephen Gwynn, 'Introductory memoir', in *Charlotte Grace O'Brien: selections from her writings and correspondence with a memoir by Stephen Gwynn* (Dublin: Maunsel and Co., 1909), p. 132.
23 *Freeman's Journal*, 18 December 1909.
24 Stephen Gwynn, *Robert Emmet: a historical romance* (London: Macmillan and Co., 1909), p. v.
25 See Chapter 3, p. 67.
26 Stephen Gwynn to Frederick Macmillan, 29 September [1908], Macmillan archive, BL, box M44; Miles Byrne, *Memoirs of Miles Byrne: a new edition with an introduction by Stephen Gwynn* (Dublin: Maunsel and Co., two vols, 1907).
27 Stephen Gwynn to George Brett, 2 June 1909, Macmillan Company records, New York Public Library (NYPL), box 52.
28 Frederick Macmillan to Stephen Gwynn, 30 September 1908, Macmillan archive, BL, MS 55492(1)/112; Frederick Macmillan to Stephen Gwynn, 9 December 1909, Macmillan archive, BL, MS 55496(4)/1870.
29 Aubrey Gwynn, 'Draft of an autobiography of Father Aubrey Gwynn', n.d. [1979], Aubrey Gwynn papers, Irish Jesuit Archive (IJA), J10/90 (80).
30 *Freeman's Journal*, 11 April 1910; Holloway quoted in Ruth Dudley Edwards, *Patrick Pearse: the triumph of failure* (Dublin: Irish Academic Press, 2006; first published 1977), p. 123.
31 *Irish Times*, 21 May 1983.
32 *Freeman's Journal*, 27 June 1910; Aubrey Gwynn to Stephen Gwynn, n.d. [June 1910], Aubrey Gwynn papers, IJA, J10/8 (1).
33 Stephen Gwynn to Aubrey Gwynn, 20 June [1910], Aubrey Gwynn papers, IJA, J10/8 (3).
34 Stephen Gwynn to J. O. Hannay, 14 October [1906], J. O. Hannay papers, TCD, MS 3455/337.

35 Alvin Jackson, *Home Rule: an Irish history 1800–2000* (London: Weidenfeld and Nicolson, 2003), pp. 107–8.
36 *Spectator*, 12 February 1910.
37 Stephen Gwynn, *The Irish situation* (London: Jonathan Cape, 1921), p. 15.
38 Paul Bew, *Conflict and conciliation in Ireland 1890–1910: Parnellites and radical agrarians* (Oxford: Oxford University Press, 1987), p. 200.
39 *Freeman's Journal*, 16 April 1910.
40 Stephen Gwynn to John Dillon, 7 March [1910], John Dillon papers, TCD, MS 6754/589.
41 G. K. Peatling, *British opinion and Irish self-government, 1865–1925: from unionism to liberal commonwealth* (Dublin: Irish Academic Press, 2001), p. 126.
42 'Pacificus', *Federalism and Home Rule* (London: John Murray, 1910).
43 *Times*, 31 October 1910; reprinted in 'Pacificus', *Federalism and Home Rule*, p. 55.
44 *Round Table*, 1 (November 1910–August 1911), p. 64.
45 Gwynn, *Experiences*, p. 223.
46 *Peasant*, 16 May 1908.
47 *Parliamentary Debates*, 5th series, 16, 11 April 1910, col. 929.
48 Peatling, *British opinion and Irish self-government*, p. 122.
49 Michael Wheatley, 'John Redmond and federalism in 1910', *Irish Historical Studies*, 32:127 (May 2001), pp. 354–6.
50 *Leader*, 22 October 1910.
51 *Leader*, 13 January 1911.
52 *Irish Times*, 2 December 1910.
53 *Freeman's Journal*, 5 and 8 December 1910.
54 Paul Bew, *Ideology and the Irish question: Ulster unionism and Irish nationalism, 1912–1916* (Oxford: Oxford University Press, 1994), pp. 29–34; A. T. Q. Stewart, *The Ulster crisis: resistance to Home Rule, 1912–14* (London: Faber and Faber, 1969; first published 1967), pp. 43–4.
55 The McCann case occurred after Alexander McCann, a Catholic, left his Protestant wife and took the children, and this was upheld by the clergy. The affair was the subject of a parliamentary debate and was used by unionists as evidence that Home Rule would mean 'Rome Rule', an argument which the Irish Party rejected.
56 Stephen Gwynn, *John Redmond's last years* (London: Edward Arnold, 1919), pp. 49–50.
57 *Freeman's Journal*, 9 May, 25 July and 24 October 1910.
58 *Times*, 24 December 1910.
59 Alvin Jackson, *The Ulster party: Irish Unionists in the House of Commons, 1884–1911* (Oxford: Oxford University Press, 1989), pp. 314–15.
60 Michael Wheatley, *Nationalism and the Irish Party: provincial Ireland 1910–1916* (Oxford: Oxford University Press, 2005), p. 160.
61 *Morning Post*, 29 December 1910. Reprinted in the *Freeman's Journal*, 30 December 1910.
62 Sean O'Faolain, *Vive moi! An autobiography* (London: Rupert Hart-David, 1965), p. 270.
63 W. B. Yeats to Lady Gregory, n.d. [5 February 1911], Lady Gregory papers, Henry W. and Albert A. Berg Collection (Berg), NYPL. I am indebted to Professor Warwick Gould for this reference.
64 Stephen Gwynn to Frederick Macmillan, 16 February [1911], Macmillan archive, BL, box M44.
65 Patricia Jalland, *The Liberals and Ireland: the Ulster question in British politics to 1914* (Brighton: Harvester Press, 1980), pp. 37–8.

66 Stephen Gwynn to Winston Churchill, 29 July 1910, Winston Churchill papers, Churchill College Archives, Cambridge, CHAR 2/46/29.
67 *Parliamentary Debates*, 5th series, 22, 27 February 1911, cols 87–8.
68 John Redmond claimed that 'We must get our constitution at once, and must not be asked to wait until the other portions of the United Kingdom have made up their minds to obtain Parliaments for themselves'. *Freeman's Journal*, 28 January 1911.
69 Jeremiah MacVeagh (ed.), *Religious intolerance under Home Rule: some opinions of leading Irish Protestants* (London: Irish Press Agency, 1911).
70 Jalland, *The Liberals and Ireland*, p. 56.
71 Stephen Gwynn to Violet Martin, 17 January [1912], Somerville and Ross papers, Queen's University Library, Belfast (QUB), MS 17/919; John. J. Horgan, *Parnell to Pearse: some recollections and reflections* (Dublin: Richview Press, 1948), p. 164; Patrick Maume, 'Introduction', in Harold Begbie, *The lady next door* (Dublin: University College Dublin Press, 2006; first published 1914), pp. xii–xiii.
72 Begbie, *Lady next door*, p. 12.
73 *Ibid.*, pp. 156, 158.
74 Stephen Gwynn, *The case for Home Rule: with an introduction by John E. Redmond* (Dublin: Maunsel and Co., n.d. [1911]), p. v.
75 T. M. Kettle, *Home Rule finance: an experiment in justice* (Dublin: Maunsel and Co., 1911).
76 Gwynn, *The case for Home Rule*, pp. 24, 59, 126.
77 *Ibid.*, p. 5.
78 P. Kerr-Smiley, *The peril of Home Rule* (London: Cassell and Co., 1911), pp. 15–16.
79 *Ibid.*, pp. 70–1.
80 Gwynn, *John Redmond's last years*, p. 62.
81 For Lord Randolph Churchill's visit to Belfast in 1886, see R. F. Foster, *Lord Randolph Churchill: a political life* (Oxford: Oxford University Press, 1981), pp. 255–7.
82 Stephen Gwynn to John Dillon, 4 January [1912], John Dillon papers, TCD, MS 6754/591.
83 Stephen Gwynn to John Dillon, 12 January [1912], John Dillon papers, TCD, MS 6754/592. Emphasis added.
84 John Redmond to John Dillon, 30 December 1911, John Dillon papers, TCD, MS 6748/481.
85 *Freeman's Journal*, 9 February 1912.
86 Bew, *Ideology and the Irish question*, p. 55.
87 See *Irish Independent*, 2 January 1912.
88 S. Rosenbaum (ed.), *Against Home Rule: the case for the Union* (London: Frederick Warne and Co., 1912), p. 27.
89 For a detailed summary of the Agar-Robartes amendment, see Jalland, *The Liberals and Ireland*, pp. 92–102.
90 *Parliamentary Debates*, 5th series, 37, 2 May 1912, col. 2171.
91 *Freeman's Journal*, 12 June 1912, emphasis added.
92 Alvin Jackson, *Sir Edward Carson* (Dundalk: Dundalgan Press, 1993), p. 31.
93 Alvin Jackson, *Home Rule: an Irish history 1800–2000* (London: Weidenfeld and Nicolson, 2003), p. 124.
94 Stephen Gwynn to George Brett, 31 December 1911, Macmillan Company records, NYPL, box 52.
95 Stephen Gwynn to George Brett, 12 December 1913, Macmillan Company records, NYPL, box 52.

96 John Murray to Gertrude Tuckwell, 18 October 1916, Sir Charles Dilke papers, BL, MS 43,967 f. 109; Stephen Gwynn and Gertrude Tuckwell, *The life of the Rt. Hon. Sir Charles W. Dilke* (London: John Murray, two vols, 1917), vol. I, p. vi.
97 Gertrude Tuckwell to Mr Thursfield, 4 August 1911, Sir Charles Dilke papers, BL, MS 49,612A, ff. 6–7. Tuckwell's commitment to Dilke's moral rehabilitation never wavered: see the comments on the matter in her obituary in the *Times*, 6 August 1951.
98 Daniel J. Murphy (ed.), *Lady Gregory's journals* (Gerrards Cross: Colin Smythe, two vols, 1978 and 1987), vol. I, p. 40.
99 Roy Jenkins, *Dilke: a Victorian tragedy* (London: Papermac, 1996; first published 1958), p. 5; David Nicholls, *The lost prime minister: a life of Sir Charles Dilke* (London: Hamble Continuum, 1995), p. ix.
100 John Murray Gertrude to Tuckwell, 18 October 1916, Sir Charles Dilke papers, BL, MS 43,967 f. 109.
101 *Freeman's Journal*, 13 October 1914.
102 *Irish Times*, 8 July 1912.
103 Bew, *Ideology and the Irish question*, p. 68.
104 *Parliamentary Debates*, 5th series, 43, 30 October 1912, col. 483. See also Stephen Gwynn, 'The Irish gentry', *The Nineteenth Century and After*, January 1914, pp. 171–9.
105 *Freeman's Journal*, 7 December 1912.
106 Stephen Gwynn to George Bernard Shaw, 2 November [1912], George Bernard Shaw papers, BL, add. 50,516, f. 264.
107 *Freeman's Journal*, 7 December 1912.
108 W. B. Yeats to Stephen Gwynn, 30 November [1912], W. B. Yeats papers, Harry Ransom Humanities Research Center, Texas (HRHRC), 6.3.
109 *Freeman's Journal*, 7 December 1912.
110 Stephen Gwynn, 'The positions of Protestants under Home Rule', *British Review*, November 1913, pp. 161–73.
111 *Freeman's Journal*, 8 November 1912.
112 James McConnel, 'The franchise factor in the defeat of the Irish Parliamentary Party, 1885–1918', *Historical Journal*, 47:2 (2004), p. 362.
113 Dillon's house was attacked by suffragettes days after the Bill was defeated, while an explosive device addressed to Redmond was intercepted at the General Post Office in Dublin a month later. See *Freeman's Journal*, 13 May and 11 July 1913.
114 *Irish Times*, 7 May 1913.
115 Gifford Lewis, *Edith Somerville: a biography* (Dublin: Four Courts Press, 2005), p. 262.
116 *Parliamentary Debates*, 5th series, 47, 24 January 1913, cols 924–6.
117 *Freeman's Journal*, 10 May 1913.
118 Cliona Murphy, *The women's suffrage movement and Irish society in the early twentieth century* (London: Harvester Wheatsheaf, 1989), p. 221; *Irish Times*, 7 February 1913.
119 *Galway Express*, 20 June 1914.
120 Murphy, *The women's suffragette movement*, pp. 141–2.
121 See, for example, May Gwynn to Hanna Sheehy Skeffington, 9 April [1915], Sheehy Skeffington papers, National Library of Ireland (NLI), MS 33, 603 (16) and 3 October [1915], MS 33, 604 (1).
122 Bew, *Ideology and the Irish question*, pp. 14–16, charts the substantial number of Irish MPs who had Land League pasts.
123 Francis Hackett, *Ireland: a study in nationalism* (New York: Huelsch Inc., 1920; first published 1918), p. 331.

124 James McConnel, 'The Irish Parliamentary Party, industrial relations and the 1913 Dublin lockout', *Saothar*, 28 (2003), p. 30.
125 Stephen Gwynn to William Walsh, 29 October [1913], William J. Walsh papers, Dublin Diocesan Archives (DDA), box 385.
126 *Leader*, 6 September 1913.
127 For Sheehy, see *Freeman's Journal*, 23 September 1913; for O'Malley, see *Freeman's Journal*, 10 November 1913. Also see McConnel, 'Dublin lockout', pp. 30–1.
128 *Irish Worker*, 20 September 1913.
129 Stephen Gwynn to W. B. Yeats, 8 October 1913, W. B. Yeats papers, Berg, NYPL.
130 *Ibid.*
131 Stephen Gwynn to John Redmond, n.d. [April 1907], John Redmond papers, NLI, 15,192/9.
132 Pádraig Yeates, *Lockout: Dublin 1913* (Dublin: Gill and Macmillan, 2001; first published 2000), pp. 216–19; also see R. F. Foster, *W. B. Yeats: a life. Vol. I: The apprentice mage 1865–1914* (Oxford: Oxford University Press, 1997), pp. 499–500.
133 Lucy McDiarmid, *The Irish art of controversy* (Dublin: Lilliput Press, 2005), pp. 124–5.
134 Stephen Gwynn to William Walsh, 29 October [1913], William J. Walsh papers, DDA, box 385.
135 Gwynn also privately dismissed the 'Dublin six' in a pithy fashion to Walsh: '[J. P.] Nannetti is moribund, [William] Abraham devoid of local connection, [William] Field too eccentric and [P. J.] Brady new to the work. [J. J.] Clancy is very good, but strongly conservative. [W. F.] Cotton no use politically and committed to the employers'. Stephen Gwynn to William Walsh, 29 October [1913], William J. Walsh papers, DDA, box 385. For useful background information on these Irish Party MPs, see Bew, *Ideology and the Irish question*, pp. 14, 16, 18, and Patrick Maume, *The long gestation: Irish nationalist life 1891–1918* (Dublin: Gill and Macmillan, 1999), pp. 223–5, 228, 237.
136 *Freeman's Journal*, 2 November 1913.
137 *Freeman's Journal*, 5 November 1913.
138 Alan Denson (ed.), *Letters from AE* (London: Abelard-Schuman, 1961), p. 91.
139 *Freeman's Journal*, 5 November 1913.
140 *Freeman's Journal*, 21, 22 and 24 November 1913.
141 Stephen Gwynn to William Walsh, 29 October [1913], William J. Walsh papers, DDA, box 385; *Freeman's Journal*, 5 November 1913.
142 *Freeman's Journal*, 22 April 1914; Stephen Gwynn, *Memories of enjoyment* (Tralee: Kerryman, 1946), p. 91.
143 Gwynn, *John Redmond's last years*, p. 90.
144 Charles Townshend, *Easter 1916: the Irish rebellion* (London: Allen Lane, 2005), p. 36.
145 Roy Jenkins, *Asquith* (London: Collins, 1969; first published 1964), pp. 288–92; R. J. Q. Adams, *Bonar Law* (London: John Murray, 1999), pp. 133–41.
146 Jalland, *The Liberals and Ireland*, pp. 168, 170–5, 200.
147 Jackson, *Sir Edward Carson*, p. 33.
148 Maud Gonne to John Quinn, 1 April 1914, in Janis Londraville and Richard Londraville (eds), *Too long a sacrifice: the letters of Maud Gonne and John Quinn* (London: Associated University Presses, 1999), p. 130: 'I got a letter from Stephen Gwynn yesterday saying Home Rule had never been in such a strong position before and that it was certain to go through now'.
149 Gwynn, *John Redmond's last years*, pp. 100–1.
150 *Ibid.*, p. 103.

151 See Chapter 7, pp. 180–1.
152 William O'Brien, *The Irish revolution and how it came about* (Dublin: Maunsel and Roberts, 1923), pp. 203–6; John Quinn to Maude Gonne, 12 April 1914, in Londraville and Londraville (eds), *Too long a sacrifice*, p. 133.
153 Inspector General, Royal Irish Constabulary (RIC), report, June 1914, Colonial Office papers, The National Archives (TNA), London, CO904/94/407.
154 On this, see Colin Reid, 'The Irish Party and the Volunteers: politics and the Home Rule army, 1913–1916', in Caoimhe Nic Dháibhéid and Colin Reid (eds), *From Parnell to Paisley: constitutional and revolutionary politics in modern Ireland* (Dublin: Irish Academic Press, 2010), pp. 33–55.
155 Stephen Gwynn to Eoin MacNeill, 19 May 1914, Eoin MacNeill papers, NLI, MS 10,833.
156 Gwynn, *John Redmond's last years*, p. 91.
157 M. J. Kelly, *The Fenian ideal and Irish nationalism, 1882–1916* (Woodbridge: Boydell Press, 2006), pp. 207–8.

5

Ireland's sacrifices

1914–17

> What [Patrick Pearse] embodies is the central strength of Irish nationalism – its disregard of the immediate event. (Stephen Gwynn, 1918)[1]

THE First World War was truly apocalyptic: the conflict claimed an average of 6,046 lives *every day* over its four bloody years.[2] In Ireland, it altered life irreconcilably, providing the essential backdrop for the immediate defusing of the unionist–nationalist conflict, the gradual disenchantment with John Redmond's pro-imperial sentiments, and the Irish Party's electoral obliteration (at the hands of the Sinn Féin movement) in 1918. One historian of the Great War has argued that in 'four years, the world went from 1870 to 1940'.[3] It is tempting to take this analogy and apply it to Irish nationalism: the First World War can be seen as the bridge that took Ireland from Isaac Butt to Éamon de Valera. But such a model of investigation does not reflect the intricacies of the time. Stephen Gwynn's experience of war was complex and profound, and resulted in the termination of his relationship with the Irish Party. Following the declaration of war, Gwynn became one of the most prominent nationalist recruitment campaigners and was among seven nationalist MPs who enlisted for active service.[4] As the war spiralled on relentlessly, Gwynn preached martial virtues, advocating the spilling of blood in Europe to heal Irish divisions; it was the spilling of blood *in Ireland* in 1916, however, that ushered in the destruction of Redmondism. Gwynn later wrote that Redmond's strategy from the commencement of war 'was not limited to Ireland's interest'[5] and this was perhaps to be the undoing of the Redmondite project, despite the confident assertion of a police report in November 1914 that 'the people generally appear to be loyal to the Empire'.[6]

War's choices

THE coming of war radically altered the Home Rule quagmire. The Home Rule Bill received its Royal Assent in September 1914, but was suspended for the duration of the conflict. In August, Redmond pressured Asquith to concede Home Rule immediately, arguing that this would promote more enthusiasm for the war in Ireland. The request was, however, politely declined.[7] This left Gwynn in a sombre mood in August 1914, as W. B. Yeats told Lady Gregory:

> I have just left Stephen Gwynn, we lunched together and I send you his gloomy prophecy as much in his own words as I can. '[Winston] Churchill and [Lord] Grey have won Asquith over to a postponement of the Home Rule question.... The position will become very difficult but if there is a cataclysm of some kind and a Conservative Government is elected it will become desperate. The Conservatives are pledged against Home Rule. Should that happen, Ireland will have been betrayed by the Liberals; and the Irish Party ... will cease to exist. It will leave all political power to the Volunteers and let them make what terms they can. The Ulster Volunteers will be formed into a yeomanry by the Unionists, and as they are bettered drilled and armed, they will be more than a match for the [Irish] National Volunteers'.[8]

Despite his political concerns, Gwynn was convinced about the righteousness of the war. He outlined his belief that Ireland was fundamentally tied to the British war effort on the grounds of realism and honour in two articles in the *Freeman's Journal* during the autumn of 1914. It was in Ireland's interest, Gwynn argued, to give men voluntarily to the Allies, as the alternative was conscription.[9] But Ireland must morally support the war to defend small nations: 'If we submit', Gwynn wrote, 'to see Belgium deprived of her liberties without sending her help ... we are not ourselves worthy of liberty as a nation'.[10] 'This is a just war', Gwynn enthused to his mistress, Mabel Dearmer, during the late summer of 1914; Dearmer was, however, alarmed at Gwynn's determination to serve in Europe's battlefields despite being over the British Army's age limit.[11] The war did terminate their relationship, but in an unforeseen manner: in 1915, Dearmer succumbed to a fever at a field hospital in Belgium, where she was stationed as a nurse. On her death, Gwynn became her literary executor, and used his Macmillan connection to publish a touching eulogy the following year.[12] The affair had been kept out of the public domain for its duration; despite its longevity, Stephen returned to the family home, showing little sign of mourning. The void in his life was filled by the imperatives of politics and war.

The extent to which politics were altered by the war became evident when John Redmond and John Dillon held talks with Lord Kitchener,

FIGURE 4. Mr Stephen Gwynn, 1914. From Max Beerbohm, *A survey* (London: William Heinemann, 1921).

the newly appointed Secretary of State for War, on 7 August to discuss regularising and arming the Irish Volunteers. Kitchener was hostile to the idea, as he regarded Irish nationalists as little more than rebels. He rejected the politicising of his new armies and was interested only in Irish recruits to regular divisions. Gwynn retrospectively argued that the failure of the British to officially recognise the Irish Volunteers fatally undermined the wartime Redmondite project.[13] It is questionable, though, how the Irish Volunteers, as they stood in August 1914, could have been transformed *en masse* into an 'Irish brigade', as they were a shabbily armed force with no military experience. So, while Kitchener and the War Office were tactless with regard to the political concerns of the Irish Party, it is equally true that Redmond and the Irish Party were insensitive to the military concerns of the War Office. The inflexibility of Kitchener on this issue, after all, was not confined to Irish nationalism: he was also unsympathetic to the demands of the Ulster Volunteer Force (UVF) as well as the Welsh Army Corps. Nationalist grievances came into sharper focus, however, after the UVF received concessions which the Irish Volunteers did not.

Despite Redmond's stated wish that the Volunteers be used to defend Ireland from invasion, the Irish Party's stance in relation to recruiting to the British Army remained hazy over August and September 1914.[14] Redmond's dramatic speech on 20 September at Woodenbridge, which called for Irishmen to serve not just in Ireland but 'wherever the firing-line extends', was therefore a pivotal moment.[15] Redmond's declaration split the Irish Volunteers, with a small faction led by MacNeill and the IRB element rejecting his advocacy of the British war effort. While, nationally, only 12,000 from a total of 170,000 Volunteers followed MacNeill, Gwynn noted in *John Redmond's last years* that in Dublin these numbered almost 2,000, including two of the stronger battalions. 'These battalions', he lamented, 'along with the Citizens' Army, were destined to alter the course of Irish history'.[16]

The challenges of encouraging Irish nationalists to enlist for service became quickly apparent to Gwynn. At the beginning of October, he was the keynote speaker at a recruiting meeting in Galway: he found himself repeatedly interrupted, before the electricity was cut off and a number of bottles containing an 'evil-smelling chemical' were thrown towards the platform, forcing those gathered to move outside.[17] Gwynn was quick to point out to the *Irish Independent* that the actions of 'two or three inter-rupters' should not be given credence when around a thousand people listened sympathetically to the pro-Allied rhetoric of the speakers.[18] The moral was perhaps correct, but these interruptions Gwynn experienced in his own constituency while attempting to encourage recruitment set a grim precedent for the future. During the course of the war, Galway City would maintain an ambiguous relationship with Redmondism: while the majority of the local Volunteers followed the Irish Party in the aftermath of the September 1914 split, many of these companies tended to become inactive and often ceased to exist soon afterwards. In contrast, the MacNeill Volunteers experienced a growth in membership after the spring of 1915.[19] Recruiting rallies in Galway found less sympathy as the war rumbled on, as Gwynn found out to his cost over the years to follow.

Gwynn retrospectively critiqued the government in *John Redmond's last years* for not providing the Irish Party with the tools to maximise recruiting in Ireland, concluding that the 'War Office crippled the Nationalist efforts' to raise Irish recruits.[20] But this did not undermine his zeal at the time. Attempting to touch a raw nerve of nationalism, Gwynn composed a battle song, which was published in November.[21] 'The Irish brigade, 1914', a verse 'to quicken the blood', according to one contemporary, was a popular feature at recruiting rallies across the country over the next year.[22] At its heart was a desperate plea for Irishmen to come forward to protect the national identity of the new Sixteenth (Irish) Division:

> Must English fill the Rangers' ranks? Welsh pad the Munsters' line?
> Where stood the Dublin Fusiliers, Scots give the countersign?
> Or when the Inniskillings faint, shall Sikhs the trench re-man?
> Pathan and Gurkha finish what the Irish Guards began?
>
> No shame for comrades' help to seek; but when the Irish fall,
> To Ireland for more Irishmen first comes the clarion call.
> Who says she cannot spare her sons to pay her honour's debt?
> Poor Ireland is poor Ireland still – but abject, never yet.

Gwynn took to a number of recruiting platforms around Galway before the close of the year, when he appealed to the courage and conscience of his audiences.[23] His vocal support for Irish enlistment, amplified by parliamentary colleagues such as Hugh Law and William O'Malley, ran somewhat counter the war apathy of the Irish Party as a whole, which was generally more cautious in calling for recruitment to the British Army.[24] But Gwynn now aimed to go one step beyond most in the Irish Party by enlisting for active service himself.

Enlistment and the recruitment drive

THE Sixteenth (Irish) Division was as close as Redmond got to his dream of a distinct 'Irish brigade'. Its commander, Sir Lawrence Parsons, urged the nationalist leader to refer to the new division as the 'Irish Division':[25] it was, after all, created explicitly to attract recruits from the Redmondite Volunteers. Despite this, Parsons, like Kitchener, had little time for political considerations in the Army. Citing the precedent of the Thirty-Sixth (Ulster) Division, which largely subsumed the Ulster Volunteers, Redmond lobbied the War Office to gain concessions for 'his' Division, such as the granting of special regimental colours and badges, and permitting Irishmen who had enlisted in Britain to transfer to it. Parsons was, however, opposed to such trappings and informed Redmond that he was not in favour of aping the Ulster Division in creating 'a silly badge' to replace 'the time honoured badges of the Regiments'.[26] Scanning over the correspondence between Parsons and Redmond when preparing his study of his late political chief in 1919, Gwynn felt that the antagonism between the two men boiled down to a question of status recognition:

> Running through [the Redmond–Parsons letters] is the tone of a soldier in authority who accepts assistance from a friendly, influential, well-meaning but imperfectly instructed civilian. There is no recognition of the fact that Redmond was the accepted leader of a Volunteer Force numbering over a hundred thousand men; no glimpse of any perception that morally, and almost officially, Redmond was the accredited head of the nation in whose name the division was being raised – a nation to which the statutory right of self-government had just been accorded.

Gwynn's conclusion was simply that 'The whole position was extraordinary'. His point was that although Redmond was powerless legislatively, he was the uncrowned 'Prime Minister of his country'.[27] For the concerns of the Irish leader to be ignored was deeply demoralising for nationalism.

It was time for Gwynn to throw himself into literal battle. On the morning of 12 November 1914, the *Irish Times* carried the news that Gwynn and his former parliamentary colleague Tom Kettle had applied for, and received, commissions in the Army.[28] Kettle's poor health, the result of chronic alcoholism, however, delayed the granting of his commission.[29] Gwynn, too, did not receive an immediate commission and the precise details of his entry into the British Army are clouded in confusion. Gwynn's son Denis was convinced that his father had applied for a commission and had been turned down by Parsons.[30] It seems, though, that Stephen Gwynn turned down a commission and instead joined the Seventh Leinster Regiment as a private. As the literary critic Gerald Griffin put it, 'Gwynn said that he would rather remain in the ranks for the time being, as he thought that he was thus doing better work in encouraging recruiting, whereupon General Parsons informed him that he could have a commission whenever he liked'.[31] This is confirmed by an entry in Parsons's diary. He discussed commissions with Kettle and Gwynn in February 1915 and was confronted with contrasting concerns. While Parsons recorded that Kettle did not take the news well that his officer application was being turned down, Gwynn, who enjoyed a friendly relationship with the commander, 'looked very ill, but would not take a commission'.[32]

On 13 January 1915, Gwynn underwent a medical test at the base of the Forty-Seventh Brigade in Fermoy, County Cork. Deceitfully declaring his age as thirty-seven (he was in fact almost fifty-one, over the permitted age for active service), the report found Gwynn to be five feet ten and a half inches in height, 168 pounds in weight and with good vision in both eyes.[33] Gwynn was posted to the Seventh Leinster Regiment. Soon to join Gwynn in Fermoy was his parliamentary colleague Willie Redmond, who was gazetted as a temporary captain of the Royal Irish Regiment. The morale of the Sixteenth (Irish) Division during its training at Fermoy over the winter of 1914–15 as 'total war' lurched onto the horizon seems to have been high. The *Freeman's Journal* sent a special correspondent to Cork to observe the progress of the Division. Despite atrocious weather, it was found that the trainee soldiers 'are generally eager and attentive in drill, and cheerfully bear the insistent, everyday work – one might almost say the drudgery – necessary to the training of an army within a limited period'.[34] Gwynn was based in Fermoy for only one month: due to overcrowding, his regiment was marched seven miles in freezing conditions, with full equipment and arms, to Kilworth.[35] The *Freeman's Journal* special correspondent followed the Leinsters to Kilworth: after complaining that heavy downpours had left much of the camp 'flooded out' and caked in slush, the reporter observed 'a cheery spirit of indifference to the discomforts induced' by the conditions.[36]

Gwynn did not buckle under the strain of separation from his creature comforts. If anything, war fever possessed him completely, as he threw himself into a gruelling schedule of training during the week, before taking to recruiting platforms around the country at weekends. Freedom, justice and the unity of Irishmen serving in the trenches were the major themes that Gwynn zealously articulated as he travelled from county to county.[37] Kettle, also now in the Seventh Leinster Regiment, frequently partnered Gwynn on the recruiting platforms: like Gwynn, Kettle was consumed by the righteousness of the Allied cause.[38] The energies of both men at this time were remarkable. Gwynn and Kettle collaborated on a short collection of war ballads, *Battle songs for the Irish brigades*, to which they made several original contributions. The verses were grounded in nationalist mythology, tracing the first 'Irish brigade' back to Patrick Sarsfield and the Williamite war: 'The past is in our blood', the book's preface asserted, 'and should be in our minds as we face the present'.[39] Included in the volume were lyrics by Emily Lawless, Arthur Conan Doyle and (inevitably) Thomas Davis.

Despite the earnest efforts of Gwynn and Kettle, recruitment levels from Ireland plunged rapidly from 1915, particularly after news of the horrors of Gallipoli – where 3,000 Irishmen died – reached Ireland.

Gwynn's high profile on the recruiting platforms of Ireland through 1915 inevitably provoked ire from more 'advanced' nationalist circles. He was, after all, a prominent example of what the *Leader* dubbed 'English recruiting sergeants' within the Irish Party.[40] The *Spark*, a new anti-war nationalist newspaper, issued a number of fictitious forthcoming books in July: included was *How I rose from the ranks*, by Stephen Gwynn, 'a thrilling story of the perils escaped by remaining in Ireland during the Great War'.[41] The often humorous tone of the wartime nationalist critics of the Irish Party belied a more serious issue: as the Redmondite Irish Volunteers shrank in number, the small breakaway MacNeillite Volunteer group was expanding and was deemed by April 1915 to be 'better organised' than its larger rival.[42] By November, the government was concerned that 'Sinn Féin and [the] Irish Volunteer Party was gaining strength and that the Parliamentary and National [Redmondite] Volunteer Party were losing'.[43] A lack of success on the Western Front and increasing fears of conscription slowly sapped the Redmondites through 1915.

In April, Gwynn received a commission and transferred to the Sixth Connaught Rangers as a lieutenant. He was promoted to captain in July.[44] It was perhaps fortunate for Gwynn that he did not serve in the ranks in Europe; as he told William Rothenstein in 1918, 'Being a private is a rotten job unless you are very young and strong and in the last resort enjoy killing'.[45] Coinciding with his promotion was the establishment of the wartime coalition government at Westminster, with senior Conservative politicians joining Asquith's administration. Asquith asked Redmond, as well as Edward Carson, to join the new government; but Redmond promptly rejected the offer on Irish nationalist principle and appealed to the Prime Minister to exclude Carson, as it would do 'infinite harm' from an Irish viewpoint if the 'leader of the Ulster revolters' was included.[46] Redmond had previously argued that once Home Rule was granted, Irish nationalists could conceivably take Cabinet postings in Westminster; even with the Home Rule Bill on the statute book in 1915, he decided that the time was not yet ripe for such a move. It was, perhaps, an unwise decision, leaving Redmond to face continued responsibility for the British war effort without any means to control its direction.[47] The former Under-Secretary for Ireland, Sir Antony MacDonnell, pleaded with Redmond to take his place inside the government: 'if you remain out your motives will be misunderstood and misrepresented.... You cannot doubt that if occasion occurs the Covenanting interest will not hesitate to take advantage of it to injure Home Rule'.[48] Redmond did not budge; and recruitment from Ireland notably dropped in the wake of the formation of the coalition.[49] In a subtle critique of Redmond, Gwynn, retrospectively, viewed the creation of a coalition government minus the Irish nationalist interest as 'the first stage in the history of Redmond's defeat and the victory of Sir Edward Carson and Sinn Féin'.[50]

'These are the damned circles Dante trod'[51]

STRANGELY for such an industrious man of letters, Gwynn did not publish any narrative account of his war experiences. His autobiography, *Experiences of a literary man*, leaves the reader at 1906: he did not follow in the 'war books' boom of the late 1920s and 1930s, most notably represented by Robert Graves' *Goodbye to all that* and Siegfried Sassoon's semi-fictional trilogy, *The complete memoirs of George Sherston*. Gwynn did, however, contribute introductory pieces to two war novels with Irish backgrounds: A. M. Cogswell's *Ermytage and the curate* and R. H. Kiernan's chilling *Little brother goes soldiering*.[52] Gwynn also left a trail of scattered references to the 1914–18 conflict throughout his post-war writings, particularly in his travel-cum-history books. These often drew on Redmond's dictum of a war to bind the soldiers of Ireland and Ulster together, illustrating Gwynn's continued adherence to that idea, but reveal little about his experiences of life in the trenches. What is clear, though, is that while Gwynn found active service a tough existence for a man of over fifty years of age with no previous military experience, it was also for him a profound adventure.[53]

The Sixteenth (Irish) Division left Cork for its final training in England in September 1915. John Redmond regularly visited the camp near Aldershot, staying with his brother.[54] Despite strained relations with the War Office over recruiting and nationalist recognition, Redmond remained wholeheartedly committed to the Allied cause, vividly demonstrated at the beginning of 1916 in his upbeat introduction to Michael MacDonagh's *The Irish at the front*: 'it is these soldiers of ours to whose keeping the Cause of Ireland has passed today'.[55] The Sixteenth (Irish) Division departed from Southampton harbour on 17 December, reaching France the following day. On 19 December, at Béthune railway station, the Sixth Connaught Rangers – consisting of thirty-six officers and 952 ordinary ranks – 'heard the sound of the guns in the firing line for the first time'.[56] The Division's new commander, General William Hickey, who replaced Parsons in the winter of 1915, cheerfully inspected the troops before Christmas. In one of the ironies of war, the Sixteenth became part of the IV Corps, which had recently come under the leadership of the staunch unionist Sir Henry Wilson. From December 1915 to August 1916, the Division was stationed 'on the troubled front between Loos and Hohenzollern Redoubt'.[57]

Gwynn's battalion, like the Sixteenth (Irish) Division more generally, did not engage in battle immediately after arrival in France. Instead, the men were 'broken in' gradually to the grim realities of life in the trenches.[58] From 26 January to 7 February 1916, the Sixth Connaught Rangers received trench warfare instruction for the first time. Despite the suspect qualities of their trenches and ammunition, coupled with an outbreak of diarrhoea caused by a bad water supply, the Rangers' war diary recorded that morale was high: 'the men showed a fine soldierly spirit, and bore up bravely under the heavy bombardments the Germans indulged in on the Loos salient'.[59] The battalion spent the remainder of February drilling and parading, with an inspection made by the I Corps commander, General Hubert Gough.[60] Gough, the army chief at the centre of the Curragh 'incident' in 1914, was later (in 1919) to join Gwynn in the Irish Centre Party: the war greatly mellowed his hard-line unionist sensibilities. In 1931, he wrote about the arrival of Gwynn and Willie Redmond on the front: 'Brought up, as I had been, in an atmosphere hostile to Home Rule and all who supported it, I found in these two – and in many other Irishmen of the division – a loyalty, a devoted sense of duty, and a gallant spirit, which won my esteem and affection'.[61] The conciliatory and imperially minded tones of wartime Redmondism, it seemed, could indeed break down old barriers.

Entering the trenches again in March during a spell of 'cold, wet and almost arctic weather', the Sixth Connaught Rangers nevertheless were found to be 'in excellent spirits' by their commander.[62] The battalion suffered a small number of casualties between January and March, but Gwynn had a first-hand taste of death when he buried a Donegal man whose legs had been shattered in a bombardment.[63] The Sixteenth (Irish) Division had its first experience of direct battle on 27 April 1916, when the Germans launched a large-scale attack under a blanket of chlorine gas. Killing clouds of gas struck again on 29 April: the Division suffered heavy casualties.[64] And while the Irish Division faced its first blooding, a small band of rebels, led by Gwynn's old friend Patrick Pearse, occupied the General Post Office in Dublin city centre.

The Rising and its aftermath

GWYNN sadly recalled in 1917 that 'News of the Easter Week Rising reached us just as the Brigade was going into the trenches'.[65] In *John Redmond's last years*, he described the horror that struck his regiment after the shocking news filtered through the frontline: 'I shall never forget the men's indignation. They felt they had been stabbed in the back'.[66] After learning of the Rising, Gwynn immediately sought the counsel of Willie Redmond, who was also stationed in Loos. Redmond was devastated by the news[67] and agreed to Gwynn's suggestion that the two of them, by virtue of their war records, could have a 'special influence' over the Irish situation and should apply for leave. But Redmond's reply to Gwynn was also darkly prophetic: 'Don't imagine that what you and I have done is going to make us popular with our people. On the contrary, we shall both be sent to the right about at the first General Election'.[68]

Redmond did not, however, apply for leave: Gwynn warmly recorded later that he 'could not bring himself to leave his post with his company'.[69]

The Easter Rising was, of course, a Great War event: it was the context of Britain's involvement in a foreign war which cemented the idea of insurrection in the mind of the rebels. In his 1919 analysis of the Rising, Gwynn placed it within the contemporary national and international milieu: 'Pearse, at a time when all the world was plunged in a prodigal welter of destruction, came forward, demanding from Irishmen nothing but a sacrifice – promising nothing but the chance for young men to shed their blood sacramentally in the cause of Ireland's freedom'. Was this any different from what Redmond was asking? Gwynn saw this parallel: 'Redmond also was calling for the extreme risk, but on a sane and sound calculation, to ensure the full development of something already gained. Pearse preached, mystically, the efficacious power simply of bloodshed in the name of Ireland'. The forces which guided the direction of the oncoming Irish revolution would ignore the Redmondite sacrifices, 'obscured in the chaos of war' as they were; it was the 'recklessness' of the Easter Rising, in Gwynn's retrospective view, that 'touched the popular imagination'.[70]

What of Gwynn's reaction to Patrick Pearse's central role in the drama that unfolded in Dublin in Easter week 1916? Pearse and Gwynn were, of course, contemporaries in the Gaelic League during the Edwardian period, with both men serving on its executive body, the Coiste Gnótha. Gwynn and his wife were early supporters of St Enda's, Pearse's bilingual school: their son Denis, who enlisted for active service in Europe in 1916, had been among its first intake of pupils. Pearse's rapid development from cultural activism to insurrection has been well documented by Ruth Dudley Edwards.[71] His martyrdom in 1916 was crucial in defining the tenor of the new nationalism that swept the Irish Party away at the 1918 election. Despite this, Gwynn's later reflections on Pearse were marked by a sober tone:

> I suppose that Pearse was a fanatic; but I met no suggestion of it in my dealings with him.... I liked him thoroughly and unreservedly.... Nobody has ever done more than Pearse to show how much clearer the mystic's vision is than that of the ordinary decent man. But that he should have got men to follow him into that desperate adventure is to me a marvel, for in the days when I knew him, he had none of the challenging magnetic quality. There was then no suggestion of the leader in him.[72]

Pearse was executed by the British for his part in the rebellion, the same fate his hero, Robert Emmet, met in 1803. Gwynn's poem from 1903, 'The song of defeat', drew on Emmet to put into verse the paradoxical spirit of radical Irish nationalism, which placed a higher premium on a romantic fight and inevitable defeat than straight military victory.

Now, in his own time, Gwynn looked on as the final lines of his poem were played out for real against the background of war, inspired by the martyrdom of Patrick Pearse during Easter week 1916: 'Of a land, where to fail is more than to triumph / And victory less than defeat'.[73]

Gwynn wrote to John Redmond after speaking to Willie, to tell his leader that he believed that 'we were more wanted at home'. Tellingly, Gwynn confided in Redmond that his age was catching up with him: 'both of us [Gwynn and Willie Redmond] are too old for the job. I probably have a month or so more than he, but it is only a question of time before we [are] off to the knacker's yard in any case'.[74] His deteriorating health was in fact another factor in his application for leave. His commanding officer, Lieutenant Colonel John Lenox-Conyngham, wrote a reference for Gwynn's application for leave on 14 May 1916:

> I regret to have to report that in my opinion Captain S. Gwynn, MP, will not be able to stand the work of a company commander in the trenches much longer.... He thinks also that at the present time his services would be of greater value to the country in Parliament than serving here.... Captain Gwynn has always done excellent work with the battalion and his departure will be a serious loss to it but it would be better for him to go now than to struggle on till he breaks down.[75]

J. H. M. Staniforth, a captain with the Seventh Leinsters, recorded that Gwynn was in the thick of action in early May, having had 'three dugouts blown in on him',[76] and the toll of five months of trench life was beginning to tell on the MP. Gwynn's age and health were as pressing in his application to leave the trenches as any notion of resuming his parliamentary duties. This, of course, makes his desire to recommence life in the trenches once again from autumn 1916 all the more remarkable.

The scale and disjointed pace of the executions that followed the Rising shocked nationalist opinion in Ireland. On 11 May, John Dillon took to the floor of the House of Commons to deliver a bitter speech condemning the executions and saluting the courage of the rebels, which outraged many English MPs and shocked several of his own colleagues. Gwynn was still in France when Dillon spoke out, but later wrote that 'Even in print the speech seethes with growing passion; and its delivery, I am told accentuated its bitterness and its anti-English tone'.[77] Gwynn did not pass judgement on Dillon's intervention in later accounts of the period, but his attitude at the time was very different. On his return to Britain, he dined with his friend F. S. Oliver, who pithily recorded the details of their conversation in his diary: 'S. G. just back from France.... No criticisms about the shooting of rebels. Denounced Dillon's speech'.[78] Given his absence from Ireland during April and May, Gwynn perhaps underestimated the emotional power of the executions. Worryingly for the Irish Party grandees, Dillon believed that 'the feeling is strong even amongst those who had no sympathy whatever with the Sinn Féiners or with the Rising'.[79] While the picture of Gwynn from Oliver's diary is of a man disconnected from these fears, his anger was not completely one-sided. After learning that the Attorney General, F. E. Smith, was calling for the hanging of Roger Casement in connection with the planning of the Rising, Gwynn sent a furious telegram to John Redmond: if Casement hangs, he asserted, 'so must the man who shot Skeffington'.[80] Francis Sheehy Skeffington was killed in cold blood by a British officer who, after much delay, was tried and found guilty but insane, and released in 1918: the affair was a public relations nightmare for the British forces in Ireland.[81] Underlying the political heartbreak of the Rising for Gwynn was the personal tragedy: Pearse, Casement and Sheehy Skeffington were all long-standing friends.[82]

The Irish Party needed to gain a substantial concession to offset the political damage that the Rising had inflicted on the Redmondite project. The Lloyd George initiative of May–June 1916 was intended to do just that: the Liberal minister found Redmond and Carson as eager to reach an agreement as he was. The content of the scheme – essentially the immediate enactment of Home Rule, with the exclusion of six northern counties for the duration of the war, after which time a more permanent settlement would be discussed – has been well documented.[83] The main barrier to a deal was the influential southern Irish unionist presence within the coalition Cabinet, particularly Walter Long and Lord Lansdowne, who, along with a number of backbench English Tories, opposed the concession of Home Rule, unravelling the deal.[84] As with previous negotiations, Gwynn was not party to these talks; but his retrospective account, inevitably coloured by the Irish Party's defeat in 1918, nevertheless remains striking. In 1919, he pinpointed the collapse of the initiative on 22 June 1916 as the most significant turning point in pushing the IPP towards electoral obliteration: 'That day really finished the constitutional party and overthrew Redmond's power. We had incurred the very great odium of accepting even temporary partition ... and now we were thrown over'. Hinting at his own troubled experiences from 1916 to 1919, Gwynn then reflected on how the public mood was changing following failure to secure the immediate enactment of Home Rule:

> Apart from the effect on Redmond's position, the result was to engender in Ireland a temper which made settlement almost impossible. No British Minister's word would in the future be accepted for anything; and any Irishman who attempted to improve relations between the countries was certain to arouse anger and contempt in his countrymen.[85]

The failure to enact Home Rule in 1916 was a devastating blow to the Irish Party's political fortunes. A commentary which Gwynn provided for the *Daily Mail* in August captures constitutional nationalism's frustrations of the summer of 1916: 'The failure to settle Ireland was a victory for the Germans ... and it is Lord Lansdowne and his associates who deserve the Iron Cross'.[86]

Soon after his return to Ireland, Gwynn applied for, and received, permission to take up temporary duty with the Tenth Royal Dublin Fusiliers. This gave him the scope he desired to sound out Irish opinion during the 'present crisis', while being of some use to the war effort 'employed as a soldier in Ireland' with the remit of training troops.[87] He agreed to serve on the Dardanelles commission at the end of July, but took little part in the enquiries, which led to bland reports on the Gallipoli defeat ('it is no place for an able bodied officer', he told Lloyd George before returning to France).[88] Remaining in Ireland from June until October 1916, Gwynn witnessed the collapse of the Lloyd George initiative at first hand, while news of the terrible sacrifices at the Somme by the Sixteenth (Irish) and Thirty-Sixth (Ulster) Divisions filtered back over the next few months. This provides the context for Gwynn's activities in support of a compromise Home Rule deal.

The tracks that would take Gwynn to a more sympathetic understanding of Ulster unionism were beginning to be put in place. As an invited speaker at a session of the Galway County Council one week before the Lloyd George initiative collapsed, Gwynn strongly supported the immediate enactment of a compromise as the first instalment of Home Rule, rather a new round of negotiations based on the Buckingham Palace formula of 1914. 'What they had to consider', Gwynn told the Council, 'was whether that might not be the best way to get a Home Rule measure which would be an expression of the demand, not of the Nationalists, but of the whole of Ireland'. Gwynn appealed to nationalists to enthusiastically operate a partitioned settlement, and to demonstrate to the Ulster unionists that it was in their interests to become part of a united political entity.[89] This plea was not made in a political vacuum: after the Rising, Sir Edward Carson made conciliatory noises to the Irish Party.[90] This was clearly not lost on Gwynn. Two months later, he went further in a startling speech in his constituency: 'As to the Ulster question, he believed there was no use in anticipating that Ulstermen would come back from the position they had taken up. He thought they would have to start with exclusion, but believed exclusion would only be a passing phase'.[91] While Redmond reluctantly conceded the principle of temporary partition in 1914, by August 1916 Gwynn was explicitly voicing the need for the IPP to accept Ulster exclusion – on unionist terms – from a Home Rule settlement as the party's starting position in any new round of negotiations. Unsurprisingly, such a declaration provoked ire from within the nationalist family. At a stormy UIL meeting in Sligo, Gwynn's parliamentary colleague and former associate in the IPA, Thomas Scanlan, was forced to issue a denial that the Irish Party consented to a 'final settlement' based on exclusion,[92] while the *Irish Independent* savaged the Galway MP's advocacy of the 'mutilation of Ireland'.[93] Gwynn's intervention was based on the need for compromise amid the extraordinary circumstances of 1916, but it may have inadvertently further demoralised constitutional nationalism.[94]

If Gwynn was gradually coming to the view that the political partition of Ireland was necessary as the first step in securing any form of Home Rule, he continued to romanticise the unifying powers of the Great War. Unionists inevitably contrasted the blood sacrifice for King and country of the Thirty-Sixth (Ulster) Division during the first week of the battle of the Somme, in which thousands of its men fell, with the treachery of the Rising.[95] Gwynn recognised the damaging potential of this contrast even before the Somme offensive, telling the *Irish Times* that the Rising had given credence to 'what we were used to describ[ing] as Ulster's imaginary fears'.[96] The Rising seemingly did not affect the fighting capabilities of the Sixteenth (Irish) Division, which distinguished itself on the Somme.[97] There was still a sense of the symbolic power of Irish sacrifices among the senior nationalist officers on the Western Front. In August, Tom Kettle made a poignant declaration: 'If it should come my way to die I shall sleep well in the France I always loved, and know that I have done something towards bringing to birth the Ireland one has dreamed of'.[98] Kettle died in action in Ginchy one month later, a 'glorious death' for Ireland, according to Major Willie Redmond (although not John Dillon).[99] 'It was the fate that he expected', Gwynn wrote of Kettle in 1919, 'So was lost to Ireland the most variously-gifted intelligence that I have ever known'.[100] Colonel John Lenox-Conyngham, the Officer Commanding of the Sixth Connaught Rangers, was killed one week before Kettle. Gwynn mourned the death of his military chief in an essay published in 1918: 'I have known no better Irishman than this son of an Ulster house, whose kindred were deep in the Ulster Covenant'.[101] That an Ulster Protestant with a long family connection to landlordism and the British Army could inspire such love and respect from Irish Catholic soldiers was a point not lost on Gwynn.[102] More immediately, though, the death of Lenox-Conyngham in action drew Gwynn closer to his comrades in the Sixth Connaught Rangers. With the *Irish Times* reporting in September 1916 that voluntary recruiting was 'virtually dead in Ireland', the MP for Galway immediately organised his own return to the frontline.[103]

The return to the front

'THE war is a vast, hideous, devastating tide kept back by dykes and barriers whose mainstay is the bodies of men'.[104] So Gwynn declared in 1918; but in September 1916 he threw himself quite willingly into the tide of death that had so recently taken his friend Tom Kettle. The loss of Lenox-Conyngham was not the only tragedy that the Sixth Connaught Rangers suffered in September 1916: in just over one week at the Somme, the battalion lost twenty-three officers and 407 men. After learning of the horrific scale of the slaughter, Gwynn requested to be sent to France again to resume duties with the Connaught Rangers.[105] War Office and army bureaucracy proved, however, a substantial obstacle, with his age and health coming into question: Gwynn spent a week from the end of September to the beginning of October in Étaples before being sent back to England, having been deemed unfit for active service.[106] He pleaded with the War Secretary, Lloyd George, to overrule the decision, stressing the potential recruitment boost that his return to active service could provide.[107] Despite his previous battle fatigue, Gwynn's appeal was pushed through and he was permitted to rejoin the depleted ranks of the Sixth Connaught Rangers.[108]

Gwynn arrived at the frontline on 26 October 1916, to find many new faces in his old battalion: the Galway MP was one of four officers who arrived at the Sixth Connaught Rangers' camp that day.[109] Following the death of Lenox-Conyngham, an English Catholic, Rowland Feilding, became the Officer Commanding of the Sixth Connaught Rangers.[110] Gwynn made an immediate impression on Feilding: on the day of his arrival, Feilding wrote to his wife that Gwynn 'is the very antithesis of the Irish politician as popularly represented by the Tory School'.[111] The following week, after some atrocious weather, Feilding picturesquely described the wartime Gwynn:

> We are in the front line till the day after tomorrow, and all is going well. How war alters one's preconceived ideas! You know the sort of impression one is apt to get in England of the Irish Nationalist MP. Well, ours here! – you should see him – a refined, polished, brave gentleman; adored by his Company, which he commanded before, earlier in the war. Knee-deep in mud and slush; enthusiastically doing the duty of a boy of twenty. I have seldom met a man who, on first acquaintance, took my fancy more.

Given the appalling autumn weather that the battalion endured, Feilding also expressed concerned for his senior captain: 'My only real fear is that the exactions of the trenches during the winter months may prove too much for him'.[112] This trepidation was very real: sustained exposure to the cold and wet during the war potentially did more damage to the resistance of troops than artillery fire.

Gwynn's enthusiasms for soldierly life, however, sustained him over the bitterly cold winter of 1916–17, which saw him take the role as commanding officer at an extraordinary outdoor mass on the Wytschaete Ridge on Christmas Day, with German shells dropping within a few hundred yards of the muddy gathering of several hundred men.[113] During

Gwynn's first months back at the front, the Sixth Connaught Rangers saw little action, with the battalion's war diary recording that most days passed relatively quietly, while the camp off the Messines Ridge was defensively reinforced.[114] Writing to his cousin Amelia McCaughlen in November 1916, Gwynn admitted that 'This part of the line is absurdly safe'. The lack of intense shelling made fraternisation with neighbouring divisions possible, and this had a special resonance for Gwynn: 'We are close neighbours of the Ulster division and get on admirably.... I hope that comradeships may establish themselves which will be of use in Ireland some day'.[115] When Redmond called for the Ulster and Irish Volunteers to defend the shores of Ireland at the immediate outbreak of war in 1914, he did so with the ambition of eliminating national differences in the face of a common enemy.[116] It was not until September 1916, though, that the Sixteenth (Irish) and Thirty-Sixth (Ulster) Divisions were stationed near each other, and they did not fight together until June 1917. Despite its major setbacks in Ireland, could wartime Redmondism yet be redeemed in the trenches of France?

Gwynn, for one, certainly believed so. His later writings repeatedly address the coming together of the Irish and Ulster Divisions, with soldierly camaraderie breaking down political barriers, and the ultimate destruction of this wartime *rapprochement* by those who initiated the revolutionary actions of 1919–21. In 1922 he declared that the Irish and Ulster Divisions were 'the best means of bringing together Irishmen of different creeds and factions in a common comradeship'.[117] More than a decade later, Gwynn referred to the friendly feeling between the Irish and Ulster Divisions born 'in the mud of Passchendaele': 'What was done there was undone later in Ireland'.[118] While there was perhaps an inevitable Redmondite romanticising of the healing powers of the Great War, seen through the lens of post-revolutionary Ireland, Gwynn's view from the trenches tallied with his later positive interpretations. In December, he happily told his cousin that 'we are alongside the Ulster division and making great friends with them, which is well'.[119] It is not clear, however, if Gwynn was referring to the officer classes or the wider ranks; he may have imposed an unduly rosy picture on the rapport between the Sixteenth and Thirty-Sixth Divisions from the excellent relations that both he and Willie Redmond developed with several senior Ulstermen over the winter of 1916–17.

The war was indeed creating strange bedfellows. General Oliver Nugent, commander of the Ulster Division, greatly enjoyed the company of the sociable Willie Redmond.[120] Despite his Ulster Protestant background, Nugent was not always sympathetic to the political and religious loyalism which many within his Division demonstrated, partly because he was emotionally closer to a more secular Irish unionist worldview.[121] On the final day of 1916 – a black year for constitutional nationalism in Ireland – Nugent and his aide, Somerset Saunderson, the son of the former leader of Irish unionism, dined with Redmond and Gwynn. Also present were Brigadier-General Charles Gwynn – Stephen's brother, who was a career soldier – and Alexander Godley, who left a vivid account of the meeting: 'The talk and argument between the two Unionist Orangemen of the Black North, and the two Southern Home Rulers, egged on by Charles Gwynn and myself, would at times become rather heated; but I need hardly say that they always finished by falling on each other's necks, and were in reality the best of friends'.[122] Feilding described a dinner organised by Stephen Gwynn, which found the two Connaught Rangers alongside Willie Redmond, General C. H. Powell (Nugent's predecessor as the Ulster Division's commander) and Peter Kerr-Smiley, the articulate unionist MP, who was also serving in France.[123] But it is pushing a point too far to argue that the Irish and Ulster Divisions sank their political differences in the face of a common enemy. For every instance of unionists and nationalists playing football together behind the frontline, one can find similar anecdotal evidence of violent disputes triggered by bottles labelled 'Boyne Water'.[124] Dying on the battlefield in the name of King and country on the one hand, and Ireland and freedom on the other, can hardly be said to have weakened political differences. Anyhow, from a national vantage point, what was happening in the trenches between Irishmen was ultimately of far less importance than what was happening in Ireland itself from 1917.

While the Sixteenth and Thirty-Sixth Divisions prepared for their offensive on the Messines Ridge, Gwynn was again struck down with health problems. At the beginning of February 1917, he suffered 'a spell of mild dysentery', which left him requiring several weeks' recuperation. He was also struggling with the extreme cold that locked the Messines area, described by Feilding as 'Arctic'.[125] While Gwynn was convalescing in hospital, the Irish Party lost the first of a string of by-election contests to Sinn Féin, with Count Plunkett, the father of three men who fought in the Rising, taking North Roscommon by a wide margin over the IPP candidate. The victory raised the enthusiasm within 'advanced' nationalist circles for a restructuring of the Sinn Féin organisation while simultaneously denting the already shaky confidence of the Irish Party. Gwynn put the loss in perspective in 1919: 'This was the first open defeat inflicted by the physical force men on the Constitutional party since the beginning of Parnell's day'.[126]

The immediate aftermath of the North Roscommon defeat represented the lowest point to date of wartime Redmondism. The seepage of nationalist support to Sinn Féin was destroying the morale of the constitutional movement: this was merely amplified by the lack of viable ideas to pull Irish opinion back. Despite his absence from Ireland, a sense of total depression struck Gwynn, as he gloomily related to F. S. Oliver:

I continue to serve here but without expectation that anything of what I hoped will result from the service of those whom we asked to join for the sake of Ireland. England has so managed the affair that Pearse and his handful of half armed men have affected more against the Allies than all the Irish troops together in all their fighting have affected against Germany; and at the end of the war we shall probably find ourselves (if we are not so already) part of an army, part of whose task is to hold Nationalist Ireland down, whilst Carson issues the order.[127]

That the sacrifices made by Irishmen in Europe could potentially be forgotten was clearly on Gwynn's mind as Sinn Féin continued to expand at the expense of the Irish Party. His sense of desperation was such that he refused to aid Maud Gonne's attempts to return to Ireland from Paris after the execution of her husband and Easter rebel, John MacBride, unless she voiced support for Redmond. Gonne, who faced the considerable barrier of British government opposition to her presence in Ireland, refused.[128]

The only positive aspect about Gwynn's comments to Oliver concerned his health, which he assured his old friend was better 'than any time since January'. Unfortunately for Gwynn, this did not last. At the beginning of April, with the snow still falling, the Sixteenth (Irish) Division left its sector in Locre for intensive training in preparation for the assault on Messines Ridge.[129] Simultaneously, though, Gwynn was struck down with malaise and symptoms of influenza.[130] He was granted a month's leave of absence to recuperate in a London hospital, but would never return to the front.[131] At this inopportune time, Gwynn received a tragic personal blow: his aged and beloved father, John, passed away in April 1917.[132] Still grieving, Gwynn returned to Ireland after his discharge from hospital, and wrote to the War Office to resign his commission on the grounds of his age and health, while expressing a desire to resume full-time parliamentary duties.[133] He received permission to resign in early May, gaining the honorary rank of captain, and was later awarded the Legion d'Honneur and 1914–15 Star.[134] Gwynn's war had stumbled to a close without participation in any major battles; despite his hopes of reconciliation between unionism and nationalism in the trenches, his own service was blighted by ill-health, his father's death and political worries. Dejected, he returned to Ireland to assess the changed mood within nationalism.

Notes

1 Stephen Gwynn, 'Yesterday in Ireland', in *Irish books and Irish people* (Dublin: Talbot Press, 1919), p. 116.
2 Niall Ferguson, *The pity of war* (London: Penguin, 1999; first published 1998), p. 436.

3 Norman Stone, *World War I: a short history* (London: Allen Lane, 2007), p. 29.
4 The other Irish MPs who enlisted were Willie Redmond, William Archer Redmond (John Redmond's son), John Esmonde and his son John Lymbrick Esmonde, Arthur Lynch and the O'Brienite D. D. Sheehan. See Patrick Maume, *The long gestation: Irish nationalist life 1891–1918* (Dublin: Gill and Macmillan, 1999), pp. 152–3.
5 Stephen Gwynn, *John Redmond's last years* (London: Edward Arnold, 1919), p. 153.
6 Inspector General, Royal Irish Constabulary (RIC), report, November 1914, Colonial Office papers, The National Archives, London (TNA), CO904/95.
7 Denis Gwynn, *The life of John Redmond* (London: George G. Harrap and Co., 1932), p. 362; H. H. Asquith to John Redmond, 6 August 1914, John Redmond papers, National Library of Ireland (NLI), MS 15,520; Redmond to Asquith, 8 August 1914, H. H. Asquith Papers, Bodleian Library, Oxford (Bodleian), MS Asquith 36.
8 W. B. Yeats to Lady Gregory, n.d. [28 August 1914], Lady Gregory papers, Henry W. and Albert A. Berg Collection, New York Public Library.
9 *Freeman's Journal*, 9 October 1914.
10 *Freeman's Journal*, 20 November 1914.
11 Mabel Dearmer, *Letters from a field hospital: with a memoir of the author by Stephen Gwynn* (London: Macmillan and Co., 1916), p. 51.
12 Dearmer, *Letters from a field hospital*; Stephen Gwynn to Frederick Macmillan, 17 August [1915], Macmillan archive, British Library (BL), box M44.
13 Gwynn, *John Redmond's last years*, p. 153.
14 James McConnel, 'Recruiting sergeants for John Bull? Irish nationalist MPs and enlistment during the early months of the Great War', *War in History*, 14:4 (2007), p. 412; Timothy Bowman, 'The Irish recruiting and anti-recruiting campaign, 1914–1918', in Bertrand Taithe and Tim Thornton (eds), *Propaganda: political rhetoric and identity 1300–2000* (Thrupp: Sutton Publishing, 1999), p. 224.
15 Gwynn, *Life of John Redmond*, pp. 391–2.
16 Gwynn, *John Redmond's last years*, p. 180.
17 *Galway Express*, 2 October 1914.
18 *Irish Independent*, 3 October 1914.
19 Fergus Campbell, *Land and revolution: nationalist politics in the west of Ireland 1891–1921* (Oxford: Oxford University Press, 2005), pp. 198–9.
20 Gwynn, *John Redmond's last years*, p. 167.
21 *Freeman's Journal*, 27 November 1914. 'The Irish brigade, 1914' was republished in Stephen Gwynn and T. M. Kettle, *Battle songs for the Irish brigades* (Dublin: Maunsell and Co., 1915), pp. 30–1.
22 Norreys Jephson O'Conor, *Changing Ireland: literary backgrounds of the Irish Free State 1889–1922* (Cambridge, MA: Harvard University Press, 1924), p. 123.
23 *Galway Express*, 5 December 1914; *Irish Independent*, 7 and 12 December 1914.
24 McConnel, 'Recruiting sergeants', p. 428.
25 Lawrence Parsons to John Redmond, 16 October 1914, John Redmond papers, NLI, MS 15,220/3.
26 Timothy Bowman, *Irish regiments in the Great War: discipline and morale* (Manchester: Manchester University Press, 2003), p. 78.
27 Gwynn, *John Redmond's last years*, pp. 171–2.
28 *Irish Times*, 12 November 1914.
29 Senia Pašeta, *Thomas Kettle* (Dublin: University College Dublin Press, 2008), p. 82.
30 Denis Gwynn, 'Thomas M. Kettle 1880–1916', *Studies* (1966), p. 384–91, and the same author's *Life of John Redmond*, p. 405.

31 Gerald Griffin, *The wild geese: pen portraits of famous Irish exiles* (London: Jarrolds, n.d. [1938]), pp. 146–7.
32 Diary entries for 12 January, 27 February and 23 October 1915, Sir Lawrence Parsons diaries, NLI, MS 32,634 (7). The discussion about the commission appears on 8 February 1915. Their friendship continued after Gwynn returned to Ireland – see Gwynn to Lady Parsons, 14 December [1917], and Gwynn to Sir Lawrence Parsons, 2 February [1918], Robertson papers, NLI, MS 24,286.
33 'Medical history of Stephen Lucius Gwynn', 13 January 1915, War Office papers, TNA, WO339/26731.
34 *Freeman's Journal*, 4 February 1915.
35 Frederick Ernest Whitton, *The history of the Prince of Wales's Leinster Regiment (Royal Canadian)* (Aldershot: Gale and Polden, n.d. [1924]), p. 196; also see Tom Johnstone, *Orange, green and khaki: the story of the Irish regiments in the Great War, 1914–18* (Dublin: Gill and Macmillan, 1992), p. 190.
36 *Freeman's Journal*, 8 February 1915.
37 *Meath Chronicle*, 6 February 1915; *Westmeath Examiner*, 20 March 1915; *Connacht Tribune*, 1 May 1915; *Irish Times*, 18 January and 6 July 1915; *Freeman's Journal*, 24 March 1915.
38 Pašeta, *Thomas Kettle*, p. 81.
39 Gwynn and Kettle, *Battle songs*, p. v.
40 *Leader*, 3 October 1914.
41 *Spark*, 18 July 1915.
42 Inspector general, RIC, report, April 1915, Colonial Office papers, TNA, CO904/96.
43 Memorandum of an interview with John Dillon, 12 November 1915, Augustine Birrell papers, Bodleian, MS Eng. C. 7033.
44 'Military service record during the Great War of Gwynn, Captain Stephen Lucius', War Office papers, TNA, WO339/26731.
45 Stephen Gwynn to William Rothenstein, n.d. [1918], Sir William Rothenstein papers, Houghton Library, Harvard University, bMS Eng. 1148 (134).
46 Gwynn, *Life of John Redmond*, pp. 423–4.
47 Paul Bew, *John Redmond* (Dundalk: Dundalgan Press, 1996), p. 39.
48 Sir Antony MacDonnell to John Redmond, 20 May 1915, John Redmond papers, NLI, MS 15,203/4.
49 David Fitzpatrick, 'The logic of collective sacrifice: Ireland and the British Army, 1914–1918', *Historical Journal*, 38:4 (1995), p. 1020.
50 Gwynn, *John Redmond's last years*, p. 193.
51 From 'Grotesque', by Frederick Manning, in George Walter (ed.), *The Penguin book of First World War poetry* (London: Penguin, 2006; first published 2004), p. 67.
52 A. M. Cogswell, *Ermytage and the curate* (London: Edward Arnold and Co., 1922), pp. 5–7; and R. H. Kiernan, *Little brother goes soldiering* (London: Constable and Co., 1930), pp. 9–20.
53 Stephen Gwynn, *Fond opinions* (London: Frederick Muller, 1938), p. 28.
54 Gwynn, *John Redmond's last years*, p. 200.
55 John Redmond, 'Introduction', in Michael MacDonagh, *The Irish at the front* (London: Hodder and Stoughton, 1916), p. 2.
56 Sixth Connaught Rangers war diary, 18 December 1915, War Office papers, TNA, WO95/1970.
57 Stephen Gwynn, 'Irish regiments', in Felix Lavery (ed.), *Great Irishmen in war and politics* (London: Andrew Melrose, 1920), p. 179.
58 Terence Denman, *Ireland's unknown soldiers: the Sixteenth (Irish) Division in the Great War, 1914–1918* (Dublin: Irish Academic Press, 1992), p. 65.

59 Sixth Connaught Rangers war diary, 8 February 1916, War Office papers, TNA, WO95/1970. An Irish reporter also found the men full of 'self confidence' after their first taste of trench warfare. See *Freeman's Journal*, 19 February 1916.
60 Sixth Connaught Rangers war diary, 21 February 1916, War Office papers, TNA, WO95/1970.
61 General Sir Hubert Gough, *The fifth army* (London: Hodder and Stoughton, 1931), p. 130.
62 Sixth Connaught Rangers war diary, 11 March 1916, War Office papers, TNA, WO95/1970.
63 *Irish Times*, 22 June 1916.
64 Denman, *Ireland's unknown soldiers*, p. 68.
65 *Freeman's Journal*, 19 June 1917.
66 Gwynn, *John Redmond's last years*, p. 230. Also see Gwynn's article in the *Observer*, 15 January 1922.
67 Terence Denman, *A lonely grave: the life and death of William Redmond* (Dublin: Irish Academic Press, 1995), p. 97.
68 Gwynn, *John Redmond's last years*, pp. 230–1. 'Sent to the right about' was a service expression meaning dismissed.
69 *Freeman's Journal*, 19 June 1917.
70 Gwynn, *John Redmond's last years*, pp. 222–3.
71 Ruth Dudley Edwards, *Patrick Pearse: the triumph of failure* (Dublin: Irish Academic Press, 2006; first published 1977).
72 Stephen Gwynn, *Experiences of a literary man* (London: Thornton Butterworth, 1926), pp. 284–5.
73 Stephen Gwynn, *Collected poems* (Edinburgh: William Blackwood and Sons, 1923), p. 38.
74 Stephen Gwynn to John Redmond, 13 May 1916, John Redmond Papers, NLI, MS 15,192/9.
75 Untitled confidential report, section dated 14 May 1916, War Office papers, TNA, WO339/26731.
76 Denman, *Ireland's unknown soldiers*, p. 146.
77 Gwynn, *John Redmond's last years*, p. 231.
78 F. S. Oliver diary, 19 May 1916, F. S. Oliver papers, National Library of Scotland (NLS), acc. 7726/216.
79 John Dillon to John Redmond, 7 May 1916, John Redmond papers, NLI, MS 15,182/22.
80 Stephen Gwynn to John Redmond, n.d. [May 1916], John Redmond papers, NLI MS 15,192/9. Gwynn signed a petition in July that attempted to reverse Casement's death sentence: see Séamas Ó Síocháin, *Roger Casement: imperialist, rebel, revolutionary* (Dublin: Lilliput Press, 2008), p. 464.
81 Charles Townshend, *Easter 1916: the Irish rebellion* (London: Allen Lane, 2005), pp. 193–5, 289–92.
82 Gwynn, *Experiences*, pp. 260–1, 284–5; Stephen Gwynn to Hanna Sheehy Skeffington, 26 November 1916, Sheehy Skeffington papers, NLI, MS 22,680.
83 Cornelius O'Leary and Patrick Maume, *Controversial issues in Anglo-Irish relations 1910–1921* (Dublin: Four Courts Press, 2004), pp. 48–55.
84 See the discussion in Patrick Buckland, *Irish unionism. Vol. I: The Anglo-Irish and the new Ireland 1885–1922* (Dublin: Gill and Macmillan, 1972), pp. 51–82. In Buckland's view (p. 82), the southern unionists were largely responsible 'for turning the 1916 negotiations into a crisis'.
85 Gwynn, *John Redmond's last years*, p. 239. Also see Gwynn's *The Irish situation* (London: Jonathan Cape, 1921), pp. 50–1.
86 *Daily Mail*, 7 August 1916.

87 Gwynn to HQ Irish command (John Maxwell), 5 June 1916, War Office papers, TNA, WO339/26731.
88 *Times*, 28 July 1916; Stephen Gwynn to David Lloyd George, 22 September [1916], War Office papers, TNA, WO339/26731.
89 *Connacht Tribune*, 17 June 1916.
90 Alvin Jackson, *Sir Edward Carson* (Dundalk: Dundalgan Press, 1993), p. 54.
91 *Irish Times*, 2 September 1916.
92 *Freeman's Journal*, 5 September 1916.
93 *Irish Independent*, 9 September 1916.
94 D. P. Moran's *Leader*, 29 October 1916, carried an article entitled 'The future of the constitutional movement', which declared that 'what is called the constitutional movement must either die or go along some amended lines'. Partition was probably not, however, what its writer had in mind.
95 Thomas Hennessey, *Dividing Ireland: World War I and partition* (London: Routledge, 1998), p. 200.
96 *Irish Times*, 22 June 1916.
97 Denman, *Ireland's unknown soldiers*, p. 144.
98 Thomas Kettle to Henry McLaughlin, 7 August 1916, Thomas Kettle papers, University College Dublin Library (UCD), MS LA34/397.
99 Denman, *A lonely grave*, p. 98. Dillon told the House of Commons that Kettle 'died gallantly fighting in *your* war': *Parliamentary Debates*, 5th series, 86, 18 October 1916, col. 686.
100 Gwynn, *John Redmond's last years*, p. 241.
101 Stephen Gwynn, 'A colonel of the Irish brigade', in *For second reading: attempts to please* (Dublin: Maunsel and Co., 1918), p. 160. Gwynn also wrote the Foreword to a Lenox-Conyngham family memoir: Mina Lenox-Conyngham, *An old Ulster house and the people who lived in it* (Dundalk: Dundalgan Press, 1946), pp. v–vi.
102 Gwynn, 'A colonel of the Irish brigade', pp. 160–1.
103 *Irish Times*, 30 September 1916.
104 Gwynn, 'The turn of the tide', in *For second reading*, p. 166.
105 Stephen Gwynn to David Lloyd George, 11 October [1916], War Office papers, TNA, WO339/26731.
106 The General Officer, Commander-in-Chief, the British Armies in France to the Secretary of the War Office, 2 October 1916, War Office papers, TNA, WO339/26731.
107 Stephen Gwynn to Lloyd George, 1 October [1916], David Lloyd George papers, Parliamentary Archives, London (PAL), LG/E/4/2/1; Stephen Gwynn to David Lloyd George, 11 October [1916], War Office papers, TNA, WO339/26731.
108 Stephen Gwynn to John Redmond, 13 May 1916, John Redmond papers, NLI, MS 15,192/9; Lieutenant-Colonel H. F. N. Jourdain and Edward Fraser, *The Connaught Rangers* (Cork: Schull Books, three vols, 1999; first published 1928), vol. III, p. 228.
109 Sixth Connaught Rangers war diary, 26 October 1916, War Office papers, TNA, WO95/1970.
110 Bowman, *Irish regiments*, p. 150.
111 Rowland Feilding, *War letters to a wife: France and Flanders 1915–1919* (London: Medici Society, 1929), p. 129 (26 October 1916).
112 *Ibid.*, p. 130.
113 Gwynn, 'Mass on the hillside', in *For second reading*, pp. 162–5; Feilding, *War letters to a wife*, p. 138 (25 December 1916).
114 Sixth Connaught Rangers war diary, November–December 1916, War Office papers, TNA, WO95/1970.

115 Stephen Gwynn to Amelia McCaughlen, 20 November 1916, McCaughlen family papers, Public Record Office of Northern Ireland (PRONI), D2912/1/18.
116 John E. Redmond, *The Irish nation and the war: extracts from speeches made in the House of Commons and in Ireland since the outbreak of the war* (Dublin: Sealy, Byers and Walker, 1915), pp. 3–4.
117 Stephen Gwynn, 'Irish soldiers and Irish brigades', *Cornhill Magazine* (1922), p. 737.
118 Stephen Gwynn, *Ireland in ten days* (London: George G. Harrap and Co., 1935), p. 237.
119 Stephen Gwynn to Amelia McCaughlen, 26 December 1916, McCaughlen family papers, PRONI, D2912/1/19.
120 Denman, *A lonely grave*, p. 101.
121 The complexities of Nugent's character are brought out in Nicholas Perry (ed.), *Major-General Oliver Nugent and the Ulster Division* (Stroud: Sutton Publishing, 2007).
122 Alexander Godley, *Life of an Irish soldier* (London: John Murray, 1939), pp. 214–15.
123 Feilding, *War letters to a wife*, p. 148 (17 January 1917).
124 For football, see *ibid.*, p. 169 (2 May 1917); for the 'Boyne Water' incident, see Deneys Reitz, *Trekking on* (London, 1933), p. 182.
125 Stephen Gwynn to Amelia McCaughlen, 2 February 1917, McCaughlen family papers, PRONI, D2912/1/20; Feilding, *War letters to a wife*, p. 148 (26 January 1917).
126 Gwynn, *John Redmond's last years*, p. 248.
127 Stephen Gwynn to F. S. Oliver, 24 March 1917 [wrongly dated 1918], Sir Edward Carson papers, PRONI, D1507/A/23/2. Oliver passed the letter on to Carson.
128 Maud Gonne to John Quinn, 11 March and 30 July 1917, in Janis Londraville and Richard Londraville (eds), *Too long a sacrifice: the letters of Maud Gonne and John Quinn* (London: Associated University Presses, 1999), pp. 186, 206.
129 Sixth Connaught Rangers war diary, 2 April 1917, War Office papers, TNA, WO95/1970.
130 Proceedings of a medical board for Captain Stephen Gwynn, 21 April 1917, War Office papers, TNA, WO339/26731.
131 Leave of absence notice for Captain Stephen Gwynn, 11 April–12 May 1917, War Office papers, TNA, WO339/26731.
132 *Irish Times*, 4 April 1917. See Gwynn's touching essay about his father, 'A scholar', in *Saints and scholars* (London: Thornton Butterworth, 1929), pp. 117–36.
133 Stephen Gwynn to the Adjutant, 26 April 1917, War Office papers, TNA, WO339/26731.
134 Military service record during the Great War of Gwynn, Captain Stephen Lucius', War Office papers, TNA, WO339/26731. Also see *London Gazette*, 9 June 1917.

6

Redmondism's last stand?
1917–18

Ever defeated, yet undefeated,
Of thy remembering race:
For their names are treasured apart,
And their memories green and sweet,
On every hillside and every mart
In every cabin, in every street,
Of a land, where to fail is more than to triumph,
And victory less than defeat.
(Stephen Gwynn, 'Song of defeat', 1903)[1]

AT the beginning of 1917, the writer Shane Leslie lamented that 'It is very disheartening work trying to hold the middle field in Irish affairs and yet there can be no peace except through "Middlemen"'.[2] Leslie was a supporter of the Irish Party, having unsuccessfully attempted in the past to enter Westminster under its banner; his lament encapsulated the difficulties that Gwynn faced over the next five years. As Redmondism was sacrificed at the altar of political freedom, Gwynn was one of the most prominent, and unwelcome, critics of the Sinn Féin project, attempting to hold the centre while the chaos of revolution forcibly altered the Irish political landscape.

Gwynn's return to Ireland in 1917 coincided with the establishment of the Irish Convention. In mid-May, David Lloyd George, who had replaced H. H. Asquith as Prime Minister the previous December, wrote to Redmond offering either immediate Home Rule with partition or the establishment of a national conference in Ireland to negotiate a settlement. Redmond plumped for the latter. The previous week, the Irish Party had suffered another by-election defeat, with South Longford falling into the hands of Sinn Féin, albeit with a narrow majority. This undoubtedly weakened Redmond's hand: accepting a partitioned form of the 1914 Home Rule Bill would not stop the electoral seepage to Sinn Féin. Even before the Longford by-election, C. P. Scott, after chatting to his ever-pessimistic friend John Dillon, recorded in his diary that enthusiasm for the third Home Rule Bill had vanished in Ireland: 'All the young forces were going over to Sinn Féin and the demand now was for Dominion Home Rule', which essentially equalled political independence.[3] A *Round Table* commentary in May expressed fears that the Irish Party possessed 'neither unity nor leadership':[4] a new framework to deal with the Irish difficulty was urgently needed, as much by Redmond as by the wartime government.

The Irish Convention

THE Irish Convention, to some at least within the Irish Party, offered a degree of hope that a settlement could still be reached on mutually beneficial lines. The government was keen to secure the involvement not only of Ulster and southern unionists and the Irish Party, but also of 'advanced' nationalists and representatives from civil society.[5] The scheme thus received a major blow when Sinn Féin not only refused to participate, but declared its outright hostility, granting the proceedings an air of unreality. Still, as Alvin Jackson has argued, this did not necessarily doom the Convention from the start: it is possible to view the absence of Sinn Féin as a help rather than a hindrance to the Irish Party, particularly if the proceedings had produced a rapid breakthrough.[6] The Irish Party, in truth, though, had no momentum going into the Convention. The string of by-election defeats destroyed morale; this was compounded by the death of Willie Redmond at the battle of Messines in June. Redmond was widely mourned: the *Irish Times* praised his gallantry, affirming that his memory 'deserves the highest honour that his King ... and his country can bestow'.[7] After learning of Redmond's fate in Messines, Stephen Gwynn's old Officer Commanding, Rowland Feilding, wrote frankly to his own wife:

> How one's ideas change! And how war makes one loathe the party politics that condone and even approve when his opponents revile such a man as this! I classify him with Stephen Gwynn and [Henry] Harrison – all three, MEN – Irish Nationalists, too, whom you and I, in our Tory schooling, have been brought up to regard as anathema! What effect will his death have in Ireland? I wonder. Will he be a saint or a traitor? I hope and pray it may teach all – North as well as South – something of the larger side of their duty to the Empire.[8]

Gwynn, for his part, was immensely fond of Willie Redmond and found the manner of his death on the battlefield – alongside the Ulster Division – intensely moving.[9] Addressing a meeting of the Irish Literary Society of London days after Redmond's fall, Gwynn claimed that 'no more gallant Irishman ever went out to fight for Ireland'. He then issued a blunt challenge: 'Perhaps in the face of Mr Redmond's death, the Irish people would now make up their minds as to their attitude towards the troops fighting in Ireland's name. Were the real heroes to be the people who stayed at home?'[10] Gwynn's words had a special resonance: only days before, while addressing a recruiting meeting in Castlegar, near Galway, he was struck in the mouth with a goose egg, before a volley of stones was hurled.[11] More profoundly, Sinn Féin's capture of Willie Redmond's East Clare seat was the most disheartening by-election defeat suffered by the Irish Party during the war.[12]

The death of Willie Redmond left a gap in the Irish Party's proposed Irish Convention team: his brother intended for Willie to represent the interests of nationalist soldiers. Gwynn, then, was the logical substitute and he took his place alongside John Redmond, Joseph Devlin, J. J. Clancy and Thomas Harbison in the Irish Party delegation.[13] John Dillon, suspicious of the intentions of the Lloyd George government, refused to serve. The first session of the Convention was fixed for mid-summer, amid conflicting hopes and expectations. George Russell, appointed by the government to represent 'advanced' nationalism, anticipated the meeting of minds of 'half a dozen intelligent men', who could overcome the rest through 'sheer force of argument';[14] the Chief Secretary for Ireland, H. E. Duke, was cautiously optimistic; but the Under-Secretary, Sir James B. Dougherty, believed that nothing could come of the Convention while Ulster unionism 'hankers after the clean cut'.[15]

Gwynn devotes a sizeable portion of *John Redmond's last years* – eighty-two pages – to the Irish Convention, which gives him space to set out details drawn from his insider's knowledge.[16] From his narrative, it is clear that he did not view the Convention as an experiment doomed to failure; rather, a settlement was, he argued, agonisingly within reach of the assembly. Gwynn's experiences of the Convention also inspired his post-war political project, the Irish Centre Party, which strived to represent moderate nationalism and unionism in an age when both were ostensibly defunct. This period marked the beginning of Gwynn's hypothesis that the Irish question was one which Irishmen themselves could resolve in order to halt the tide of extremism: moderate nationalism and unionism could yet haul Ireland back from the brink.

The first task facing the Convention was the election of a chair: Sir Horace Plunkett quickly emerged as the preferred candidate. As the leading centrist activist at the Convention, Plunkett may seem the natural choice, but he was a disappointment, combining bad judgements with a pedantic leadership.[17] The proceedings of the Convention were carried out in secret – newspapers were not given any information and carried only lists of those attending each session – but Plunkett took it upon himself to write 'confidential' reports for the King, which in actuality he sent to a range of correspondents, such as F. S. Oliver, John Dillon and George Bernard Shaw.[18] The leading southern unionist, Lord Midleton, believed that the choice of Plunkett as chair was the reason why the Convention failed.[19] Gwynn's account of the Convention does not overtly critique Plunkett's chairmanship, but this might reflect the fact that the two men were working together in the Irish Dominion League when *John Redmond's last years* was published. By September 1917, though, it is clear Gwynn believed that Plunkett's chairmanship was straining proceedings.[20] In Gwynn's narrative, however, others were to blame for the fall of the Convention ideal.

For the first few months of the Convention, all sides presented their arguments. Relations between the delegates seem to have been harmonious during the opening stages: Gwynn, for one, believed that the sessions were carried out in a 'very friendly atmosphere'.[21] He was co-opted to the grand committee of twenty members in August, the upper tier of the Convention's structure, and hopes were high of a breakthrough.[22] But the cordial environment was not immediately conducive to negotiating success: as the summer turned to autumn, little or no progress was made on any substantive (or even small) issue, despite the glimmers of hope that occasionally surfaced.

Gwynn was heavily involved in one such lost hope. As early as August 1917, Gwynn, after private talks with the southern unionist John Powell, reported to Redmond that the southern unionists were moving towards the Irish Party's position, but were not ready just yet publicly to advocate Home Rule.[23] All hopes for a deal lay with the Redmondites and southern unionists, the two endangered species of Irish politics. Such an agreement became even more of an imperative after the Ulster unionists made no suggestions for constitutional change during the first few months, with its delegates instead stressing economic arguments against Home Rule. Despite occasionally betraying a willingness to reach an agreement, the Ulster team were firm in maintaining both that a new Irish parliament should not have substantial fiscal powers (for fear of a trade war with Britain) and that exclusion for the north should be built into a settlement.[24] As Plunkett asserted in his final report, in 1918, 'The difficulties of the Irish Convention may be summed up in two words – Ulster and Customs'.[25]

The grand committee submitted seven proposals for a future government of Ireland to the Convention during the opening discussions.[26] Gwynn was immediately enthusiastic about the federalist scheme advocated by Joseph Alexander Moles, which would have established four provincial assemblies in Ireland working under a central parliament.[27] This radical proposal was rejected out of hand by most shades of nationalism in the Convention; Gwynn's attempts to convince Redmond of the merits of federalism were not successful.[28] Writing in 1919, when he was again pushing for a similar federalist scheme, Gwynn lamented that the Convention did not take the idea seriously: 'there was a strong feeling against anything that looked like partition or might in public be called partition'. It was something, he asserted, that should 'have been much more fully explored', a view with more than a ring of retrospective vindication.[29]

Despite the richness of the various proposals considered by the Convention, the grand committee remained deadlocked over the issue of control over customs and excise, even after an Ulster unionist revolt led to a more manageable nine-member committee, excluding Plunkett, to debate the main points of contention.[30] The crux was fiscal control. The Ulster unionists refused to concede an Irish parliament with powers to raise taxes; the nationalists angrily retorted that this was an insult to their integrity. Despair now descended on the Convention, which threatened to collapse in stalemate. The death of the Sinn Féin prisoner Thomas Ashe, through force-feeding during a hunger strike for political status, further heightened tensions at the least opportune moment in September. In mid-November, Plunkett told Henry Duke that 'Things, I am sorry to say, are not going well in the small Sub-Committee which is negotiating upon the real crux – fiscal autonomy *versus* fiscal union'.[31] Several days later, Gwynn spelled out to Redmond the choices the Irish Party ultimately faced in the Convention:

> There are two objectives which can be aimed at: one is to maintain Nationalist solidity by securing a report from the Convention which the majority, at all events, will accept as expressing their desires. The second is to secure a solution which Ulster will accept. This is impossible, without calling on Irish Nationalists to make great sacrifices of their susceptibility and even of their immediate legitimate interest.... Unfortunately, the second object cannot be attained without imminent risk of a breakdown. Unfortunately, also, only the second holds any value for Ireland.[32]

The logic of the situation was thus pushing nationalism into an ideological quandary; but Gwynn urged Redmond to work for an agreement with Ulster based on the establishment of Home Rule with extremely limited financial powers. Winning over unionism, it seems, was much more important to Gwynn than nationalism's right to a full measure of self-government.

Redmond's blushes were somewhat saved in late November when Lord Midleton announced a radical shift in the southern unionists' position: he proposed that Ireland be given a sweeping measure of Home Rule with tax-raising powers and generous minority safeguards, but that customs duties would remain with Westminster.[33] While Midleton later asserted that he tabled the motion as a 'consequence of there being no other hope of agreement', the Midletonite southern unionists had been seeking a new departure in political thinking from late 1916. This was sparked by their increasingly weakened position, the result of the seeming inevitability of partition and the growth of Sinn Féin.[34] Not all southern unionists backed this bold move, which contributed to a split in the movement in January 1919, but it provided the context for a potential agreement between nationalism and unionism – albeit only of the southern variety. It took three weeks for the Midleton scheme to come before a full sitting of the Convention. The torturously slow pace of the Convention – which Midleton blamed on Plunkett – would greatly contribute to the breakdown of the compromise. Yet from the vantage point of December 1917, a deal certainly was close. Immediately after Midleton presented his plan to the full sitting on 18 December, Plunkett immediately adjourned the Convention until the new year. 'The Convention is at a critical stage', Gwynn told Sir Lawrence Parsons's wife. 'We adjourned today until January 2nd. That week should be decisive'.[35]

There was plenty to concern the nationalist delegates over the Christmas recess. At a meeting soon after the adjournment, opposition was voiced to the scheme from Bishop Patrick O'Donnell, who pressed for fiscal autonomy. To this demand, Gwynn bluntly retorted, 'no agreement, no legislation'.[36] With illness incapacitating Redmond in late December, Gwynn emerged as nationalism's strongest advocate of the Midleton scheme. With a view to strengthening the foundations of the compromise plan, he sought to obtain a promise from the government to enact an agreement reached at the Convention; he received a non-committal reply which stressed that the government would need time to study any report before taking the appropriate parliamentary action.[37] When the Convention resumed its work in January, Midleton again tabled his Home Rule plan. Redmond then made what Gwynn later described as his finest speech to the Convention, when he admitted that while he had taken a risk in supporting the war effort in 1914, he would do so again. Then, in an extraordinary statement, Redmond let slip just how desperate he was for a settlement: 'I have had my surfeit of public life. My modest ambition would be to serve in some quite humble capacity under the first Unionist Prime Minister of Ireland'. Redmond then announced that he would back the Midleton scheme if the government legislated for it.[38] Midleton was confident that his compromise plan had widespread acceptance within the Convention, with only the Ulster unionist bloc opposing it.[39] The motion did not, however, go to an immediate division, and the delay killed the compromise.

Plunkett's most spectacular misjudgement of the Convention involved his decision to drop the constitutional debate for ten days in favour of one on land purchase: the momentum of the Midleton deal trickled away during the next week.[40] On the eve of the renewed constitutional debate, Redmond asked Gwynn to get one of the leading county councillor delegates to second his motion supporting the compromise scheme. The following morning, Gwynn caught up with his leader and informed him that he had succeeded in his task: 'When Redmond came in to his place, I said, "It's all right. Martin McDonogh will second your motion". He answered with a characteristic brusqueness, "He needn't trouble. I'm not going to move it; Devlin and the Bishops are voting against me"'.[41] A strong nationalist bloc had united around Bishop O'Donnell in advocating fiscal autonomy, which the Midleton scheme did not provide. Constitutional nationalists had now undermined Redmond's authority; to add to his woes, Dillon, from outside the Convention, voiced opposition to any failure to devolve customs unless there was an agreement with the Ulster unionists on a unitary settlement.

The Midleton scheme collapsed because Redmond was unwilling to split the nationalist delegates by putting it to a division. Gwynn attempted to act as an intermediary between Midleton and the nationalists to save the deal, but the southern unionists refused to make any further concessions.[42] By the end of January, Gwynn wearily conceded that the compromise was unworkable: as he told Midleton, O'Donnell and Devlin had 'succeeded in convincing the majority [of nationalist delegates] as to the best line to be taken'.[43] The fact that clerical influences defeated Redmond was not a point lost on Gwynn.[44] Politically, Gwynn was closer to the Midletonites than his own colleagues in his attitude to a deal: he was perfectly willing to dilute Irish national sovereignty to secure unionist support.

There was one more major attempt to reach a settlement at the Convention, with Gwynn at its heart. While the Convention was ostensibly an Irish body established to solve an Irish problem, the Prime Minister issued a set of proposals in February 1918 in an attempt to inject new direction into proceedings. These would have granted an Irish parliament powers over indirect taxation, leaving the control of customs and excise with Westminster for the duration of the war, with the establishment of a royal commission to examine the issue in peacetime. The nationalist delegates lacked Redmond's counsel at this critical moment, as his health rapidly deteriorated during what would be his final illness: Gwynn recalled that feeling 'was profoundly uneasy'.[45] With his leader absent, Gwynn took it upon himself to try to bring the bulk of the nationalist members along with the proposals by offering 'a compromise on a compromise': an amendment which accepted that customs and excise should rest with the imperial parliament for the period of the war, provided it was recognised that an Irish parliament would ultimately gain such powers.[46] The amendment aimed to manoeuvre nationalism towards southern unionism, but Lloyd George resisted the scheme, as Gwynn informed Midleton: 'The Prime Minister gave me a long time today. He says, as you thought, that any surrender of the Customs right to Ireland is impossible politically'. Lloyd George also expressed concern that an agreement between southern unionism and nationalism would drive the Ulster unionists out of the Convention; so while Gwynn conceded that his idea was politically 'barren', he appealed to Midleton to reject it in 'a friendly tone', to foster a spirit of agreement. The future could yet be bright for the moderate forces in the Convention, as Gwynn explained to the southern unionist leader: 'We cannot get an agreed report on all details. But we can lay the foundations of a Convention party – a constitutional self-government party.... I do not think we can reach any agreement with Ulster in the Convention: but we can avoid giving Ulster all the cards necessary to wreck Home Rule'.[47] In February 1918 the Ulster delegates re-introduced their demand for exclusion from a Home Rule settlement; but Gwynn clearly did not believe that this was a hindrance to agreement on a proposal for self-government between southern unionists and nationalists for the rest of Ireland. The amendment was moved on 5 March; it was respectfully criticised by the Midletonites and rejected by Bishop O'Donnell. Yet there seemed to be agreement between moderate nationalism and southern unionism on the general framework of the Prime Minister's proposals.

The following morning, John Redmond passed away, after suffering from heart failure, in a London nursing home where he had been recuperating from a recent operation. His son-in-law believed that Redmond died 'of a broken heart, broken by worry and disappointment'.[48] there was a sense of tragic drama to the moment of his death. Gwynn's entire political philosophy was encapsulated in the figure of Redmond. The scale of Redmond's ambitions – a self-governing Ireland with safeguards for unionism, friendly relations with the Crown and Empire and a continued, if more constructive, role for Irish MPs at Westminster[49] – would inspire Gwynn even after the Irish Party was wiped out by Sinn Féin at the general election in December 1918. The conciliatory philosophy of Redmondism would not die with Redmond.

Yet the Redmondite project had been all but broken by the late spring of 1918. John Dillon was elected chairman of the Irish Party immediately after Redmond's death; Gwynn took a position as party whip.[50] Dillon had had no faith in Redmond's political judgement since 1916 and was inclined to a more aggressive style of leadership, in a desperate bid to win back nationalist support from Sinn Féin. Dillon's elevation raised doubts about the Irish Party's continued participation at the Convention: the new leader had long considered it a waste of time.[51] The day before the new leader was crowned, the Convention accepted the first part of Lloyd George's compromise proposal – the crucial point regarding Westminster's retention of Irish customs – by thirty-eight votes to thirty-four. Gwynn and J. J. Clancy led this majority: they forcibly argued that it was imperative that an Irish parliament, even with limited powers, should be established immediately so that nationalist Ireland would gain something after the long months of deliberation.[52] But Gwynn, wary of his political distance from Dillon, felt that he had to confirm with his new leader that the Irish Party would stand by a settlement reached at the Convention.[53] Dillon's reply does not survive, but judging by the tone of his rejection of Plunkett's offer to take Redmond's Convention seat, it was most likely coldly ambiguous: 'I am not sure that you and I would find ourselves in agreement as to what would constitute success on the part of the Convention'.[54]

On 1 April, Gwynn addressed a meeting in Galway. Although he admitted that he was bound by the Convention's etiquette of secrecy, he let slip his confidence that Ireland would have a form of self-government within months.[55] The Convention had its final sitting several days later: despite the opposition of an unholy alliance of Ulster unionists who believed that the settlement went too far and nationalists who insisted it did not go far enough, a report with the Lloyd George scheme at its heart was carried by the Redmondites and Midletonites.[56] It was an unprecedented agreement; but in truth it came at least one year too late. By the spring of 1918 there was little scope for a constitutional project built around moderate nationalism and unionism in Ireland. Despite Gwynn's hopes for immediate Home Rule, the strength of Sinn Féin, Dillon's negative posturing and the opposition of Ulster unionism made such a scheme stillborn. These difficulties were only amplified by the government's decision to introduce conscription in Ireland after a substantial German advance on the Western Front in March. The impact of all this on the moderate forces which had reached a political consensus was starkly summed up by Gwynn:

> The troubles which Nationalists brought on themselves by supporting Lord Midleton were answered by the troubles which his group met for supporting Nationalist demands. The men who refused to make the compromise possible have the laugh of us. Neither section of us who voted for agreement achieved anything by facing the risk of unpopularity. We had followed Redmond's policy and we shared Redmond's fate. We had done our best to help the British Government and that Government itself defeated us.[57]

The conscription crisis and the Irish Recruiting Council

As the First World War dragged on – bloodily and seemingly endlessly – the Irish Party became discredited in the eyes of many nationalists. If the party had been dying a slow death since its failure to secure Home Rule in 1916, the conscription crisis effectively put it out of its misery. The decision to conscript the Irish was the result of a desperate manpower shortage resulting from the offensive of March 1918. It was made in great haste, with little analysis of its potential impact on domestic politics: the projected total of 200,000 recruits promised in theory seemingly was not counterbalanced by the realisation that compulsory service would be fiercely opposed in Ireland.[58] Conscription also threatened to destroy what remaining influence the forces of moderation possessed. The situation, then, made Gwynn acutely fearful. He wrote to the Prime Minister's secretariat on learning of the conscription plan, recording his dread that the government was accelerating the rise of Sinn Féin and the death of the Irish Party.[59] Nevertheless, the Military Service Bill, with its clause to conscript Irishmen, was introduced in the House of Commons on 9 April 1918. Gwynn joined with his parliamentary colleagues in attacking the Bill, while also condemning the government for treating the Convention's report as nothing more than 'waste paper'.[60] It was clear, though, that conscription would not be withdrawn; Gwynn tabled an amendment for a gradual introduction of compulsory service. He warned the government that it was creating a situation in Ireland that no British administration – or Irish authority – could control.[61] Dillon led the Irish Party out of Westminster at the conclusion of the debate. Gwynn's amendment, which was rejected, proved his last contribution to the business of the House of Commons, an institution he later described as 'the most civilising influence I have ever known'.[62]

The Irish Party returned to Ireland to join the campaign against conscription, which united all variations of Irish nationalism, constitutional, radical and clerical. Dillon joined representatives of Sinn Féin and the Roman Catholic Church at the Dublin Mansion House conference in April, which endowed republicanism with political respectability. Sinn Féin emerged as the body leading the campaign against conscription: the IPP had become, in a colourful expression used by the *Times*, the 'bond-slave' of the new nationalism.[63] Gwynn fretted over the Irish Party's apparent capitulation to Sinn Féin. Along with his fellow MPs Hugh Law and Sir Walter Nugent, he issued a statement opposing conscription while refusing to accept Sinn Féin's national leadership.[64] In Galway later in the month, while calling for 'passive resistance' to conscription, Gwynn appealed against any course 'that may give to the Government an excuse for taking violent action'.[65] A few days later, W. B. Yeats reported to Lady Gregory that Gwynn was 'heading a revolt against Dillon' and was preparing to lead a small number of Irish MPs back to Westminster.[66] It is not clear whether this was indeed Gwynn's intention, but certainly he was in rebellion against majority opinion in the Irish Party. He could do little but watch impotently as the government created further sympathy for Sinn Féin through the ill-conceived 'German plot' arrests of senior republican leaders in May. This forced a weary letter from the Galway MP to the press, asking for proof of a Sinn Féin–German link or the immediate release of the prisoners. To halt conscription, Gwynn called for recruits to come forward voluntarily.[67]

Gwynn's appeal for voluntary enlistment was not made in a vacuum: the government decided in May that conscription would be impossible to enforce given the current conditions in Ireland and instead, as a 'gesture of good will' towards moderate nationalism, made a fresh appeal for willing recruits from Ireland.[68] Gwynn reciprocated: the decision to shelve conscription – for now – was, he argued in the *Irish Independent*, an indication that 'British statesmen have made a terrible mistake and desire to escape from it'. Crucially, he added that 'It will be our wisdom to assist [the government]'.[69] With his pro-Allied sentiment still strongly intact, Gwynn was as committed as ever to the war effort and sympathised with the pressures on the British government. In 1919 he wrote that the sudden decision to impose conscription on Ireland should be seen in the context of a desperate struggle for survival against Germany; but he was at pains to argue that, had Redmond been alive in April 1918, he would have convinced Lloyd George to immediately adopt the voluntary recruitment course taken in June, hence saving Ireland from the chaos of the conscription crisis.[70] Such a view is questionable: Lloyd George, who was sceptical of the political and military value of introducing conscription in Ireland, but who faced major pressure from within his coalition government, did not in any case consult Irish opinion.

At the end of May, the government made a declaration that it wanted 50,000 new troops from Ireland by 1 October. Walter Long, the Secretary of State for the Colonies, had originally proposed that 20,000 volunteers was a possible target, but Lloyd George believed that this figure was too low and would imply that the government was not serious.[71] Recruiting 50,000 volunteers from Ireland in 1918 was an extraordinarily unrealistic goal: to put it into perspective, slightly over 50,000 Irishmen enlisted from August 1915 to May 1918 *in total*.[72] In June, the new Viceroy, Lord French, announced the formation of the Irish Recruiting Council (IRC), the public face of the government's new enlistment drive. Chaired by Serjeant Sullivan, the IRC's chief officers included Henry McLaughlin, Sir Maurice Dockrell, Arthur Lynch and Gwynn.[73] Much to Gwynn's delight, the IRC was not accountable to the War Office but to the Ministry of National Service. Nevertheless, if his correspondence with William Rothenstein around this time is a fair reflection of his mood, Gwynn did not relish the task ahead. Several days after the foundation of the IRC, he announced that 'I'm on the job now of trying to pick up recruiting here, and I'd sooner be fried on a gridiron'. The following week, he admitted that he would sooner 'be in France, or in the ranks, than on the Irish Recruiting Council, my present labour of despair'.[74]

In his 1927 memoir, serjeant at law A. M. Sullivan confidently spelled out his interpretation of the IRC's remit: 'Our first step, and the one great thing that we did accomplish, was to quench rebellious treachery, to quiet the minds of well-meaning men, to allay excitement and to get the nation to think calmly of its own honour pledged to the boys in the trenches'.[75] This somewhat exaggerated the responsibilities and effectiveness of the IRC. It was badly organised and under-funded, and operated in a very hostile environment; its recruitment campaign became fully operational only in September, due to financial wrangling and bureaucratic delay.[76] In this context, it is a wonder that the IRC managed to boost Irish enlistment figures at all. That it did is due in no small part to Gwynn's pro-active role on the Council as its most recognisable public figure: he was a constant presence on recruiting platforms over the summer months. The crux of his argument why Irishmen should enlist was simply that it was the right thing to do, as he told a meeting of the Dublin chamber of commerce: 'If we had an Irish Parliament today he [Gwynn] should be an advocate for finding, by the authority of the State, the men whom Ireland was in duty bound to find. That authority does not exist, but the lack of it does not exempt Ireland from its duty'.[77] But if the cause remained a just one, Gwynn was unafraid to resort to language laden with threat: 'If Irishmen did not do their share voluntarily', he told the Galway Urban Council, 'then conscription would come'.[78]

While the unionist *Irish Times* was enthused by the IRC's resolve,[79] it attracted a great deal of hostility from a nationalist Ireland which Sinn Féin was coming to dominate, organisationally and ideologically. Arthur Griffith's weekly, *Nationality*, characteristically despised what it dubbed Gwynn's 'schoolmaster to the Irish people' routine, but the Council faced more profound problems than snappy journalism as it struggled to gain a hearing.[80] As Sinn Féiners regularly broke up public recruiting meetings, the IRC was pushed into touring workplaces and council premises. Even behind closed doors, the reception which greeted the recruiters was occasionally distinctly frosty. Galway County Council rejected a request from the IRC to address its members. Drawing loud applause from the gallery, the chairman – a UIL man – gave notice that 'they would not listen to the speeches or give any recruits until they got their own Parliament. The Irish people offered their assistance before and sent their sons, and were offered Home Rule by the Government, but were humbugged by Lloyd George and Carson, and in the end their leader was killed'.[81] The following week, the *Connacht Tribune*, which still remained sympathetic to the Irish Party, declared that the attitude adopted by Galway County Council 'may be accepted as a fairly accurate index to the mind of the overwhelming majority of the representatives of the rural and town population in this country',[82] a deliberate snub to the MP for Galway City. Gwynn did not, however, pander to the grievances of the County Council: while he understood the bitterness of nationalist Ireland, he proclaimed in Meath that 'they had not the time necessary now to get Home Rule'.[83]

Such rhetoric inevitably enraged members of the Irish Party. Under Dillon's leadership, the IPP abandoned Redmond's consensual wartime strategy in favour of a more forceful policy in an attempt to recapture ground from Sinn Féin.[84] But this was as vague as it was unsuccessful, and despite returning to Westminster over the summer, a sense of despair was rotting the party machine from the inside. Party unity was also rapidly disintegrating. In August, Dillon received an angry letter from Gwynn, complaining that Hugh Law, a fellow MP and recruiting advocate, had told him that 'exceptions had been taken in party meetings to the actions he and I were engaged in'. Gwynn's response was to resign his office as whip.[85] Also in the summer of 1918, the IRC became embroiled in a foul-tempered exchange with John Horgan, Gwynn's friend and the leading Cork constitutional nationalist. Horgan was approached by Serjeant Sullivan to aid the Irish war effort, but the IRC chairman received a pointed reply refusing assistance in the absence of self-government in Ireland.[86] Horgan's argument provoked a scathing attack from Gwynn, who used the opportunity of reply to vent his anger with contemporary Irish nationalism:

> We have repeatedly been offered Home Rule on the spot on terms of leaving out the six counties. Freedom in Ireland has to come to mean freedom to coerce Ulster or freedom to accept Home Rule. Now I think that from the moment that large bodies of Irishmen endorsed the action of those who rebelled in Easter week – and de Valera's election was only the most conspicuous instance of this – Ulster's case was made unanswerable. I think it would be gross tyranny to force Ulster to accept a Parliament which might be predominantly Sinn Féin. If Ireland as a nation means what de Valera means by it, then Ulster is not part of that nation. If Ireland a nation meant what John Redmond meant by it, then the case was very different.[87]

It was a striking statement which encapsulated just how far Gwynn had travelled politically since the first rumblings of war in 1914. His concern was how to reconcile Ulster and promote national unity, and he believed that Ireland's continued involvement in the war was crucial to this process. Post-Rising nationalism, which was becoming more saturated with Sinn Féin's isolationist and anti-imperial doctrines, was, for him, politically and morally bankrupt; that he was forced to take such a tone with his constitutional colleagues did not bode well for his future, as he was wildly out of step with Dillonism on the question of partition. Horgan, for one, was unrepentant: 'Your whole scheme is designed to make straight the path for conscription, to divide the country, and to drug us into passive acceptance of the inevitable'.[88]

Armistice and the death of constitutionalism

THROUGH the summer of 1918, the Allies, reinforced with American troops, pushed through the German lines, dramatically transforming the dynamics of the Great War. The German army began to crack; the war at last had an end in sight. Despite the breakthrough on the Western Front, though, recruiting – and the tacit threat of conscription – remained pressing concerns in Ireland. In September, the IRC finally received the finances to open regional offices and design recruiting posters. From the IRC's establishment to the first week of September, just 4,110 volunteers had come forward, with over half of these from Belfast and Dublin.[89] Despite praising the IRC's 'zeal', the *Irish Times* could not see how the target of 50,000 could be reached by October.[90] Judging by the Council members' speeches throughout the country in September, they were certainly feeling the strain of the task. Again and again, the need for Irishmen to volunteer to avoid the imposition of conscription was stressed: so much so that Sir Maurice Dockrell wearily told the clerks of the Irish land commission in Dublin that 'if the conscription trouble should come, the last men upon whose shoulders responsibility for it could be laid were the five members of the Recruiting Council'.[91]

By the eve of the 1 October deadline, the IRC had cost the government almost £22,000 and had raised just over 7,500 recruits, a notable increase from previous periods.[92] The IRC issued a number of newspaper advertisements and sponsored films through picture houses during September. Thirty-four posters had been designed by the IRC by the first week of October; tellingly, a memorandum to the government conceded that 'Very large numbers are required because they are frequently destroyed by malice or design if not by weather and must be renewed'.[93] Gwynn also exploited his literary links by securing public backing for the recruiting campaign from George Bernard Shaw and G. K. Chesterton ('It was too late', Chesterton lamented several years later).[94]

Given the delay in bedding in the IRC, the government agreed to extend the deadline to 1 December: if the Irish quota was not filled by then, conscription would be introduced.[95] Shortly after this announcement, the IRC drafted a memorandum on behalf of the Ministry of National Service to Edward Shortt, the Irish Chief Secretary, stressing that the conscription order should be enforced in the areas of Ireland which had 'most notably failed to respond to the recruiting appeal' – in other words, the regions most hostile to the war effort.[96] Conscription under this scheme would have commenced in November, in Galway, Mayo, Limerick, Clare and Kerry, all of which were still significantly below their quotas. At the end of October, the IRC met with Shortt: Sullivan and Gwynn informed him that 'voluntary recruitment was dead' in Ireland.[97] The Council now reluctantly acknowledged that conscription was inevitable and prepared to dissolve itself on 1 December. At a private meeting of the IRC on 10 October, Gwynn conceded that conscription was the 'proper course' for the government to adopt.[98]

Had the war rumbled on for another month and conscription been introduced, chaos would have undoubtedly been unleashed in Ireland. As it was, the IRC sent Lord French, the Lord Lieutenant for Ireland, a warm note of congratulations on Armistice Day, which the Viceroy publicly acknowledged by praising the 'gallant efforts' of those behind the recruiting campaign.[99] Under the leadership of the IRC, some 10,000 recruits voluntarily enlisted in Ireland from July to November, a massive increase compared with previous figures.[100] Given that the quota of 50,000 recruits was wholly unrealistic, the discrepancy should not distort the achievement of Sullivan's body. It was not the case, however, that all 10,000 volunteers served on the front. The IRC recruited not just for the British Army but also for the Royal Navy and the Royal Air Force: a substantial number of the volunteers enlisted for service in the latter services, perhaps to gain a technical education.[101] Yet these men were still joining the British war effort: in the extremely hostile political and ideological conditions of Ireland in the latter half of 1918, the achievement of the IRC should not be understated.

With the close of the war came the promise of the first general election in the United Kingdom since 1910. At this crucial moment, the Irish Party's electoral machine was in a truly dire condition, a state of affairs Dillon conveniently blamed on Redmond.[102] With morale completely sapped, the party struggled to find candidates to contest a number of constituencies for the December poll. Even before the contest, Gwynn was going to lose his Galway seat: changes in the constituency boundaries meant that it was to be integrated into William O'Malley's Connemara constituency.[103] In the run-up to the election, Gwynn's work with the IRC clashed with the mood within the Irish Party: at a party meeting in September, Gwynn dissented from a motion condemning the threat of conscription.[104] It proved to be his last action in Dillon's party. Unable to balance the IRC's implied threat of compulsory service with the anti-conscription posturing of the Irish Party, Gwynn renounced his party pledge.[105] His attitude to conscription was wildly out of step with the Irish Party, but conscription was in truth just one of a number of issues that had divided him from mainstream nationalist opinion since his election in 1906: his opposition to compulsory Irish, and support for women's suffrage, the working class in their struggle against Dublin capitalists and, most importantly, partition at times pushed him awkwardly to the fringes of the constitutional movement.

With the Galway constituency disappearing and his retirement from the Irish Party, Gwynn could be forgiven for bowing out of electoral politics quietly; but as long as he believed in a cause, that was never on the cards. In December, he put his name forward to contest the Trinity College Dublin seat as an independent nationalist.[106] With his substantial family connections to Trinity and the respect that the Gwynn name commanded in the College, it seemed the logical constituency, bar one fatal flaw: the seat was solidly unionist. While he never had a chance of winning the seat, Gwynn's address to the College's electors ultimately served as a manifesto for his political programme for the coming year. National reconciliation was at the heart of his campaign, as he spoke of his pride in serving alongside the Ulster Division during the war: 'It is in the spirit of a comradeship established on the Wytschaete Ridge that I desire to approach all Irish affairs'. In policy terms, for Gwynn this implied a measure of federalism to reconcile the competing demands for Irish self-governance and Ulster separatism: 'I see no other policy by which moderate thinkers in all Irish parties can be brought into agreement. Moderate thinkers have been fighting abroad instead of quarrelling at home; it is time now that they should assert themselves in politics for the work of peace'.[107] Gwynn announced during the hustings that he was working with an unnamed federalist enthusiast from Ulster – who was in fact Joseph Alexander Moles, who had tabled to the Irish Convention the four-province assembly scheme – to assess whether a solid nucleus of moderate men could form a new political party to work towards a settlement.[108]

As expected, Gwynn, the only nationalist candidate contesting the seat, finished last, with just 257 votes, with the successful unionist candidate, Arthur Samuels, winning 1,273 votes.[109] Sinn Féin annihilated the Irish Party nationally, while Ulster unionism consolidated its position with a strong vote. Dillon, who angrily blamed Lloyd George for the IPP's massive defeat, now stood aside to let Sinn Féin and the government 'fight it out'.[110] Gwynn, however, had no such intention: his political career would have an afterlife. Following the death of John Redmond in March, Gwynn had written a touching obituary for the *Observer*. While a personal dedication to Redmond permeated the eulogy, it also acted as a statement of intent, signalling Gwynn's unwillingness to accept the victory of radical nationalism: 'I shall continue', he declared, 'to work for his ideals now he is dead'.[111] Redmondism without Redmond now faced up to an Irish populace largely backing the ambitious – and ambiguous – programme advocated by Sinn Féin.

Notes

1 *Collected poems* (Edinburgh: William Blackwood and Sons, 1923), p. 38.
2 Shane Leslie to William R. Castle, 16 January 1917, Shane Leslie papers, Burns Library, Boston College, box 1, folder 5, MS96-30.

3 C. P. Scott, *The political diaries of C. P. Scott 1911–1928*, ed. Trevor Wilson (London: Collins, 1970), p. 282 (1 May 1917).
4 *Round Table*, 7 (December 1916–September 1917), p. 561.
5 R. B. McDowell, *The Irish Convention 1917–18* (London: Routledge and Kegan Paul, 1970), p. 82.
6 Alvin Jackson, *Home Rule: an Irish history 1800–2000* (London: Weidenfeld and Nicolson, 2003), p. 179.
7 *Irish Times*, 11 June 1917.
8 Rowland Feilding, *War letters to a wife: France and Flanders 1915–1919* (London: Medici Society, 1929), pp. 191–2.
9 Gwynn penned an article in tribute to Willie Redmond in the *Freeman's Journal*, 19 June 1917. See Terence Denman, *A lonely grave: The life and death of William Redmond* (Dublin: Irish Academic Press, 1995), pp. 117–36, for the best account of Redmond's death in action.
10 *Irish Independent*, 11 June 1917.
11 *Connaught Tribune*, 20 June 1917.
12 David Fitzpatrick, *Politics and Irish life 1913–1921: provincial experience of war and revolution* (Dublin: Gill and Macmillan, 1977), p. 116.
13 Stephen Gwynn, *John Redmond's last years* (London: Edward Arnold, 1919), pp. 269–70.
14 George Russell to John Quinn, 4 July 1917, John Quinn papers, New York Public Library (NYPL), box 36.
15 Sir James B. Dougherty to Rev. J. B. Armour, Rev. J. B. Armour papers, Public Record Office of Northern Ireland (PRONI), D1792/A1/1/20.
16 Gwynn, *John Redmond's last years*, pp. 259–341.
17 Jackson, *Home Rule*, pp. 183–5.
18 Trevor West, *Horace Plunkett: co-operation and politics, an Irish biography* (Gerrards Cross: Colin Smythe, 1986), p. 167.
19 Lord Midleton, *Records and reactions 1856–1939* (New York: E. P. Dutton and Co., 1939), p. 237.
20 F. S. Oliver to Lord Selborne, 6 September 1917, in D. George Boyce (ed.), *The crisis of British unionism: Lord Selborne's domestic political papers, 1885–1922* (London: Historians' Press, 1987), p. 209.
21 Stephen Gwynn to William Rothenstein, 10 September [1917], William Rothenstein papers, Houghton Library, Harvard University, bMS Eng. 1148 (134).
22 *Report of the proceedings of the Irish Convention* (1918), p. 55.
23 Stephen Gwynn to John Redmond, 3 August [1917], John Redmond papers, National Library of Ireland (NLI), MS 15,192/9.
24 Jackson, *Home Rule*, p. 180.
25 *Report of the proceedings of the Irish Convention*, p. 5.
26 For these schemes, see McDowell, *The Irish Convention*, pp. 107–11.
27 Stephen Gwynn to John Redmond, 6 August [1917], John Redmond papers, NLI, MS 15,192/9. A copy of Moles's scheme can be found in the H. E. Duke papers, Bodleian Library, Oxford (Bodleian), dep. C. 715 (115–41).
28 Stephen Gwynn to John Redmond, 24 October [1917], John Redmond papers, NLI, MS 15,192/9.
29 Gwynn, *John Redmond's last years*, p. 286.
30 McDowell, *The Irish Convention*, pp. 119–20. Gwynn had been long sympathetic to this idea: see Stephen Gwynn to Horace Plunkett, 29 September 1917, John Redmond papers, NLI, MS 15,221.
31 Horace Plunkett to H. E. Duke, 13 November 1917, H. E. Duke papers, Bodleian, dep. C. 717 (54).

32 Stephen Gwynn to John Redmond, 17 November 1917, John Redmond papers, NLI, MS 15,192/9.
33 McDowell, *The Irish Convention*, p. 129.
34 Midleton, *Records and reactions*, p. 240.
35 Stephen Gwynn to Lady Florence Parsons, 19 December [1917], Robertson papers, NLI, MS 24,286.
36 McDowell, *The Irish Convention*, p. 135.
37 Stephen Gwynn to W. G. S. Adams, 22 December [1917]; W. G. S. Adams to Stephen Gwynn, 27 December 1917, David Lloyd George papers, Parliamentary Archives, London (PAL), LG/F/66/1/56-7. Also see John Turner, *Lloyd George's secretariat* (Cambridge: Cambridge University Press, 1980), p. 105.
38 Gwynn, *John Redmond's last years*, pp. 319–21.
39 Lord Midleton to 'My dear Lord Bishop', 7 January 1918, H. H. Asquith papers, Bodleian, MS Asquith 37.
40 Jackson, *Home Rule*, p. 182.
41 Gwynn, *John Redmond's last years*, p. 322.
42 Stephen Gwynn to Lord Midleton, 23 January [1918], Lord Midleton papers, The National Archives, London (TNA), PRO30/67/36/2050.
43 Stephen Gwynn to Lord Midleton, 27 January [1918], Lord Midleton papers, TNA, PRO30/67/36/2052.
44 Gwynn, *John Redmond's last years*, p. 323.
45 *Ibid.*, p. 328.
46 McDowell, *The Irish Convention*, p. 169.
47 Stephen Gwynn to Lord Midleton, 1 March 1918, J. H. Bernard papers, British Library (BL), add. 52,781 f 65–6.
48 Max S. Green to Lord Aberdeen, 28 May 1918, papers in the possession of Lord Aberdeen, Haddo House, Aberdeenshire, box 1/5.
49 Paul Bew, *John Redmond* (Dundalk: Dundalgan Press, 1996), pp. 50–1.
50 *Irish Independent*, 13 March 1918.
51 Patrick Maume, *The long gestation: Irish nationalist life 1891–1918* (Dublin: Gill and Macmillan, 1999), pp. 196–7.
52 *Report of the proceedings of the Irish Convention*, pp. 28, 140; McDowell, *The Irish Convention*, p. 174.
53 Stephen Gwynn to John Dillon, 17 March [1918], John Dillon papers, Trinity College Manuscript Department, Dublin (TCD), MS 6754/598.
54 F. S. L. Lyons, *John Dillon: a biography* (London: Routledge and Kegan Paul, 1968), p. 432.
55 *Connacht Tribune*, 6 April 1918.
56 *Report of the proceedings of the Irish Convention*, p. 29.
57 Gwynn, *John Redmond's last years*, p. 333.
58 Alan J. Ward, 'Lloyd George and the 1918 Irish conscription crisis', *Historical Journal*, 17:1 (1974), p. 110.
59 Stephen Gwynn to W. G. S. Adams, 8 April 1918, David Lloyd George papers, PAL, LG/F/63/2/25.
60 *Parliamentary Debates*, 5th series, 104, 9 April 1918, cols 1375–6.
61 *Parliamentary Debates*, 5th series, 105, 15 April 1918, cols 114–15.
62 Stephen Gwynn, *Fond opinions* (London: Frederick Muller, 1938), p. 38.
63 *Times*, 20 May 1918.
64 Maume, *The long gestation*, p. 206.
65 *Connacht Tribune*, 27 April 1918.
66 W. B. Yeats to Lady Gregory, 29 April 1918, in John Kelly (ed.), *The collected letters of W. B. Yeats* (Oxford: Oxford University Press, InteLex Electronic edition, 2002).

67 *Irish Independent*, 20 May 1918.
68 Ward, 'Lloyd George', p. 120; also see Turner, *Lloyd George's secretariat*, p. 118.
69 *Irish Independent*, 20 May 1918.
70 Gwynn, *John Redmond's last years*, pp. 334–5.
71 Ward, 'Lloyd George', p. 121.
72 Patrick Callan, 'Recruiting for the British Army in Ireland during the First World War', *Irish Sword*, 17 (1987), p. 42.
73 *Manchester Guardian*, 20 June 1918.
74 Stephen Gwynn to William Rothenstein, 23 and 30 June [1918], William Rothenstein papers, Houghton Library, Harvard University, bMS Eng. 1148 (134).
75 A. M. Sullivan, *Old Ireland: reminiscences of an Irish KC* (London: Thornton Butterworth, 1927), p. 220.
76 Ward, 'Lloyd George', p. 125; also see Timothy Bowman, 'The Irish recruiting and anti-recruiting campaigns, 1914–1918', in Bertrand Taithe and Tim Thornton (eds), *Propaganda: political rhetoric and identity 1300–2000* (Thrupp: Sutton Publishing, 1999), p. 232.
77 *Freeman's Journal*, 12 July 1918.
78 *Connacht Tribune*, 20 July 1918.
79 *Irish Times*, 12 July 1918.
80 *Nationality*, 27 July 1918.
81 *Connacht Tribune*, 3 August 1918.
82 *Connacht Tribune*, 10 August 1918.
83 *Irish Independent*, 13 August 1918.
84 Maume, *The long gestation*, p. 203.
85 Stephen Gwynn to John Dillon, 13 August [1918], John Dillon papers, TCD, MS 6754/600.
86 Serjeant [A. M.] Sullivan to John J. Horgan, 14 July 1918; John J. Horgan to Serjeant Sullivan, 19 July 1918; Serjeant Sullivan to John J. Horgan, 26 July 1918, J. J. Horgan papers (microfilm), NLI, P4645.
87 Stephen Gwynn to John J. Horgan, 20 August 1918, J. J. Horgan papers (microfilm), NLI, P4645.
88 John J. Horgan to Stephen Gwynn, 22 August 1918, J. J. Horgan papers (microfilm), NLI, P4645.
89 *Irish Independent*, 6 September 1918.
90 *Irish Times*, 7 September 1918.
91 *Freeman's Journal*, 20 September 1918. Also see the Dublin press (*Irish Independent*, *Irish Times* and others) on 6, 14, 25 and 27 September 1918 for IRC recruiting speeches.
92 'Statement of estimated cost of propaganda to date by C. M. Matthews, Accounting Official', 30 September 1918, Ministry of National Service papers, TNA, NATS1/248
93 Memorandum by Col. Reid-Hyde on the costs of the Irish Recruiting Council, 5 October 1918, Ministry of National Service papers, TNA, NATS1/248.
94 George Bernard Shaw, *The matter with Ireland*, ed. David H. Greene and Dan H. Laurence (London: Rupert Hart-Davis, 1962), p. 167; G. K. Chesterton, *Irish impressions* (New York: John Lane Co., 1920), p. 90.
95 Ward, 'Lloyd George', p. 125.
96 Memorandum from the Irish Recruiting Council, Ministry of National Service, to the Chief Secretary of Ireland, 10 October 1918, Ministry of National Service papers, TNA, NATS1/251.
97 Précis of a conference with the Chief Secretary for Ireland and the Irish Recruiting Council, 28 October 1918, Ministry of National Service papers, TNA, NATS1/251.

98 Notes of a conference held by the Irish Recruiting Council, 10 October 1918 [wrongly dated 10 November 1918], Ministry of National Service papers, TNA, NATS1/251.
99 *Irish Times*, 14 November 1918.
100 Callan, 'Recruiting for the British Army', p. 42.
101 Terence Denman, *Ireland's unknown soldiers: the Sixteenth (Irish) Division in the Great War, 1914–1918* (Dublin: Irish Academic Press, 1992), p. 174. The IRC was keen to stress the educational point: see its advertisement in the *Connacht Tribune*, 14 September 1918.
102 John Dillon to C. P. Scott, n.d. [December 1918], in Scott, *Political diaries of C. P. Scott*, pp. 362–3.
103 *Irish Times*, 11 September 1918.
104 *Irish Independent*, 26 September 1918.
105 *Irish Times*, 22 November 1918.
106 *Freeman's Journal*, 7 December 1918.
107 Stephen Gwynn, *To the electors of the University of Dublin* (pamphlet, 1918, copy held in the NLI, ILB300P4 (100)).
108 *Irish Times*, 7 December 1918.
109 *Irish Times*, 23 December 1918.
110 Lyons, *John Dillon*, p. 455.
111 *Observer*, 10 March 1918.

7

Holding the centre
1919–22

And it may be that Ireland
Crying it so, will take courage
To tread on the forward track.
(Stephen Gwynn, 'A song of victory', 1923)[1]

IF forced retirement from the House of Commons dampened Gwynn's political enthusiasm, it was not immediately apparent. If anything, he was more active in the political sphere, as an actor, propagandist and writer, over the next few years than at any point of his Commons career. Leisure time was found, however, for new interests such as gardening, a growing passion he shared with his daughter, Shelia, a horticulturist of note. Even in the garden, though, politics was to be found: as Gwynn jovially put it in 1921, 'Under any form of government there will be a demand for cabbages, and cabbages will not grow themselves'.[2] Leaving aside the demand for cabbages, the question of what form self-government would take in Ireland in the aftermath of the war was one without an obvious answer. Home Rule was on the statue book, pending the conclusion of the peace negotiations of 1919, but the Home Rule party was broken and Redmondism sidelined. Sinn Féin stood for separation from the Union, an inconceivable constitutional move from the vantage point of British statesmen of all political shades. Then there was the problem of Ulster, the loose piece of the Irish jigsaw.

While the last generation of Westminster-based Home Rulers were sidelined by the sheer scale of the Sinn Féin victory in December 1918, Gwynn did not accept that it represented a total defeat of constitutional nationalism. Unlike the vast majority of his former parliamentary colleagues, he was determined to carve out a public role for himself and had ambitious plans to construct a new constitutional nationalist party, running against the grain of the new republican dispensation. This would be based on the formula that had almost delivered a deal at the Irish Convention: consensus between moderate unionism and nationalism. But with the close of war also came the issue of returning Irish servicemen: Gwynn was immediately alert to their concerns and would remain their (self-styled) champion.

Demobilisation

WHILE the coalition government was wholly unprepared for the waves of conscript and volunteer soldiers returning to Britain, the unique political difficulties posed by the standing down of Irish troops was recognised by senior figures.[3] This is not to imply, however, that a long-term strategy was formulated to deal adequately with the issue. Gwynn, on the other hand, was alert to the potential difficulties of demobilisation in Ireland at an early stage. Shortly after Armistice Day, he sent a detailed memorandum to the Secretary of State for the Colonies, Walter Long, with his thoughts about the return to Ireland of thousands of discharged soldiers. The note, which was forwarded to the Lord Lieutenant, Lord French, stated Gwynn's belief that failure to secure speedy employment for the returning men would drive them into the waiting arms of Sinn Féin. Gwynn argued that the Easter Rising could not have happened without 'the smouldering industrial discontent of Dublin', which was 'embodied in the Citizens' Army': 'This same element will undoubtedly seek to recruit its strength among the discharged soldiers who fail to obtain situations to their likings'. To prevent this, Gwynn proposed that a new commission, with a massive budget, be established to oversee the task of creating thousands of new manual labour jobs in areas such as road building and foreshore reclamation. A propaganda drive should accompany the commission's work, 'to represent the importance to the nation of this work'. He proposed that the chairman of the new commission be Sir Henry Robinson, the Vice-President of the Local Government Board; the remainder would be members of the IRC. Gwynn saw himself as the leading propagandist in the new commission.[4]

The government's answer came at an IRC dinner on 16 December, where Lord French was the guest of honour. Rather than convening a new commission along the lines that Gwynn had urged, French advocated the continuation of the Recruitment Council, with it taking the responsibility of aiding returning soldiers in matters of employment, housing and health. Accepting this proposition on behalf of the IRC, Gwynn drew applause and laughter when he raised his glass to the real 'brave men in Ireland': 'the men who went out of Ireland, not those who stayed at home and sang "The Soldiers' Song"'.[5]

As it had displayed throughout 1918, the IRC was not a body to back down from a challenge. But entering 1919, the sheer scale of its task was overwhelming: Gwynn believed that some 80,000–100,000 demobilised

Irish soldiers would be seeking its assistance, and the Council was hindered by intra-governmental disputes about its exact responsibilities.[6] A mere two weeks after French asked the IRC to expand its role, Gwynn voiced his despair to Long that British delays in implementing a resettlement scheme in Ireland would drive the ex-soldiers into the waiting arms of Sinn Féin, undermining the government and all connected with it, including himself.

> It is even worthwhile to consider when Government has so few friends in the country whether it is sound policy to make a man like myself feel that efforts which he makes, in defiance of all party traditions and personal interests, to assist the existing Government, are simply thrown away and that he becomes a laughing stock.[7]

Gwynn was angry that French's words did not carry material or legislative weight. In particular, he was concerned that a lack of money would kill the renewed Council before it even started. On 10 January, Gwynn and Henry McLaughlin wrote to French to inform him that the IRC – now rechristened the Irish Demobilisation Committee – required £250,000 for immediate use as, 'owing to delays that have occurred, a mass of unemployed discharged men has already accumulated'.[8] Gwynn was less formal in his correspondence with Long: the Committee's lack of resources meant that 'We are going to be let into the fire when the house is well in flames'.[9]

Gwynn's energies were not, however, fully dedicated to the Demobilisation Committee. Shortly after his election defeat in December, Gwynn wrote to Lord Midleton, informing the southern unionist chief that he was determined to avoid retirement: 'I personally am not content to go out of public life without an effort to rally the forces of sane patriotism which are available in this country'.[10] The vehicle to settle Irish differences, Gwynn explained to Midleton, was a new federal organisation to promote Irish self-rule while recognising the distinctiveness of Ulster. On the final day of 1918, the *Freeman's Journal* published a letter from Gwynn calling for the formation of a federalist party. This asserted that the recent electoral successes of both Sinn Féin and the Ulster unionists threatened to bring anarchy to Ireland, with the two sides irreconcilably believing that they had achieved mandates for their hardline positions. What was now needed was a new moderate organisation to attract nationalists and unionists under a federal banner, imbued with the spirit of the Irish Convention.[11] But the grandeur of Gwynn's ideal was deflated almost immediately with Midleton's rejection of his terms; instead, Midleton led a split within unionism and established the Anti-Partition League.[12]

Gwynn, however, remained undeterred. On 24 January, three days after what historians have traditionally viewed as the start of the War of Independence – the day when republicans killed two RIC constables in Soloheadbed, County Tipperary, while Sinn Féin MPs not in British gaols gathered in Dublin for the first meeting of the underground Dáil Éireann – Gwynn launched the Irish Centre Party.[13] This was coincidently the final day of Gwynn's youngest son, Owen, who died at the age of seventeen.[14] Owen's young life was tragically cut short by tuberculosis, which had left him bed-ridden since March 1918.[15] His death went unreported in the Dublin press and his father did not mention his youngest son in later books and articles, most notably his 1926 memoir. The revolutionary period in Ireland coincided with revolutionary upheavals in Gwynn's life, beginning, but not ending, with Owen's death.

The Irish Centre Party and the Irish Dominion League

THE grief of losing his youngest child did not halt Gwynn's political ambitions. He was named as the chair of the Centre Party's provisional general committee at its first meeting. This body was heavily dominated by a number of professional men and women, several of whom were well known, but most had little experience of public life. Among the better-known members of the new party were the barrister W. E. Wylie, the academic Charles Oldham and, most prominently, the Army general Sir Hubert Gough.[16] Gough was the Brigadier-General who had voiced concerns about being sent to suppress Ulster unionism in 1914, which sparked the Curragh 'incident'. The war, however, changed his outlook on Irish politics: after serving with Gwynn, Willie Redmond and other nationalists, Gough believed that the north and south of Ireland could be reconciled under Home Rule.[17] In essence, the officers of the Centre Party (unfortunately, no evidence has survived to suggest the number or makeup of its overall membership) came from the Irish intellectual and professional elites alienated by the radical populism of both Sinn Féin and Ulster unionism. The party aimed to fill the political vacuum following the polarising 1918 election, which had cemented the Conservative-dominated coalition in Britain without a logical Irish nationalist partner. In this context, Gwynn hoped that the Centre Party could bridge the chasm separating Sinn Féin from the government, and promote a real and meaningful constitutional debate. The stated aim of the new party was firmly federal: the creation of self-government for Ireland within the Empire, under a central parliament for national affairs and four provincial assemblies to deal with local issues. It could be suggested that Gwynn was glossing over the intractable nature of the Ulster problem with his federal abstractions, but this is to miss his point. He argued in the summer of 1919 that 'Ireland, if it includes Ulster, is today not a nation in being. It is only the makings of a nation'.[18] Given that he so stridently stated Ulster's case, Gwynn's emphasis on the need for *four* provincial parliaments may seem superfluous; but he envisaged a federal framework for Ireland's constitutional design as providing the means for the provinces to meet on an equal footing, thereby weakening Ulster's sense of 'difference' and fostering an all-island unity.[19]

Unfortunately for Gwynn, the Centre Party did not inspire nationalist Ireland to raise the federalist banner. Numbers did not flock to the cause and its programme did not even find favour with Gwynn's allies in British constitutional circles, such as F. S. Oliver or the Round Table movement, who largely ignored its efforts.[20] More critically, Gwynn identified a misinformed and dangerously out-of-touch British policy in Ireland as the major obstacle in the path of both the Centre Party and the Irish Demobilisation Committee. Walter Long was a key figure within the Irish executive and he courted a belief that Sinn Féin's resolve would crumble in the absence of British concessions, much to Gwynn's chagrin.[21] The lack of constructive political policy was matched by a lack of interest in the Demobilisation Committee. Lord French caught influenza in the spring of 1919; in his absence the Cabinet abolished the Demobilisation Committee, on the grounds that 'it introduced unnecessary complications and expense'. It did, however, accept the Committee's recommendation that £250,000 be devoted to aid ex-soldiers in Ireland.[22] Gwynn was reflective in his response:

> We considered that action ought to have begun in December, and now no action can begin till March. For that reason I am very glad to be clear of the responsibility, for I believe that any action taken now will be too late. A great deal of invaluable time has been lost, and a great deal of harm has been done by the delay.[23]

Gwynn, who was wholeheartedly devoted to the cause of the Demobilisation Committee, was profoundly disappointed at the reluctance shown by the government to meet the 'special and shameful difficulties which beset the reparation of soldiers in Ireland'.[24] Ex-servicemen had little to celebrate in the unique Irish context to which they returned, as Gwynn rued the following year:

> And when the time came to rejoice over the war's ending, was there anything more tragic than the position of the men who had gone out by thousands for the sake of Ireland to confront the greatest military power ever known in history, who had fought the war and won the war, and who now looked at their friends and at each other with doubtful eyes?[25]

He himself, of course, was included in this tragedy.

Gwynn's involvement with former Irish soldiers did not end with the abolition of the Demobilisation Committee. While he formally relinquished his Army commission in January 1919, the following March

Gwynn helped Henry Harrison, a former Parnellite MP and British Army officer, to draw up a petition to the King on behalf of former Irish officers which called for Ireland's constitutional future to be discussed at the Peace Conference in Paris.[26] In a letter to the London *Times*, Gwynn argued that the petition's recommendation was the best option open to the government, which strongly hinted at a loss of faith in British policy-makers following the demise of the Demobilisation Committee. Crucially, though, Gwynn was careful to argue that 'the claims of Ireland *and* the claims of Ulster' should be presented to the Peace Conference,[27] a marked difference from the actual text of the petition, which made no such gesture to unionism in the north. While Gwynn's caveat was conditional – he argued that Ulster alone could not define its own 'rights'[28] – it subtly highlighted the gulf between his politics in 1919 and those of other war-generation Home Rulers. This chasm became more acute after Gwynn accepted the post of special Irish correspondent of the London-based *Observer* in March. Appearing weekly until the first half of 1925 and more sporadically afterwards, Gwynn's crisp *Observer* articles offer a piercing commentary on the subsequent course of politics in Ireland, north and south, illuminating his evolving political thought. More immediately, though, Gwynn's appointment to the *Observer* in 1919 reflected his continued detachment from the new nationalist politics in Ireland: the paper's editor was J. L. Garvin, a well known unionist (if former Parnellite).[29]

Gwynn's first few articles for the *Observer* were wide ranging: the plight of the ex-soldiers; John Redmond's vision of Irish unity; and social policy in Ireland. These diffuse preoccupations reflected, as he recognised, the disquieting lack of political activity in the spring of 1919.[30] What Gwynn *did not* write about is also of note: he did not comment on the Egyptian nationalist uprising that broke out in March. His *Observer* articles, in fact, steered clear of the emerging troubles within the British Empire, particularly in India and Persia, and he did not draw any contemporary colonial parallels throughout Ireland's War of Independence. It should be remembered, though, that Gwynn's conception of imperialism envisaged white self-ruling colonies: as his Irish Party propaganda showed, he believed that Ireland was comparable only to other parts of the Empire such as Australia and Canada. He had little to say about the non-white population who comprised the majority of the Empire, and did not frame the granting of dominion status to Ireland in 1921 as part of a larger de-colonialising process following the Great War.

The Irish problem, Gwynn argued until the summer of 1919, could be defused through the granting of a federal settlement, which had the potential to undermine Sinn Féin's radicalism. But if militant republicanism was sustained by the withholding of self-government from Ireland, Gwynn also identified a powerful cultural component within the new nationalism, one with which he was familiar from many years before: the Gaelic language revival. In the striking introduction to his *Irish books and Irish people* (1919), Gwynn's post-war frustrations boil over in a discussion of the Gaelic League:

> I cannot pretend to assess impartially the value of this movement. It asserted itself in passionate deeds at a moment when many thousands of us Nationalists were taking equally vigorous action in pursuit of a less tribal ideal. Thousands of us lost our lives, all of us risked our lives, with the hope of achieving a national unity which could never be built on the basis of regarding no man as an Irishman who did not speak, or at least desire to speak, Gaelic for his mother tongue. The action of Irish soldiers was thwarted and frustrated by the action of a very few separatists, with a very small expense to themselves in bloodshed. But the tribute to the work of the Gaelic League is that Ireland accepted them and rejected us.[31]

When the Gaelic League embarked on compulsion as a strategy to promote the Irish language in 1909, Gwynn had severed his ties with the body;[32] now, ten years later, he returned to the politics of language. One review recorded that Gwynn's introduction to *Irish books and Irish people* 'strikes a somewhat personal note, exhibiting his cosmopolitanism, and vindicating his attitude in regard to the compulsory teaching of Gaelic in the National University'.[33] Gwynn might have felt vindicated, on this issue and others, but it was a painful and alienating experience.

Although his break with the Gaelic League conditioned his viewpoint, Gwynn's assessment also shows how little his cultural thought had changed since the foundation of the National University, despite the massive alterations in his political thought fostered by the Great War. The League's 'tribal idealism', argued Gwynn in 1919, had divided Ireland, a consequence that he predicted ten years earlier in the debate over compulsory Irish for entrance to the National University. In stark contrast to the Gaelic chauvinism of Irish-Ireland, Gwynn praised the inclusive and pluralistic cultural activism of the Anglo-Irish literary and dramatic movements: 'Yeats and Synge have shown how completely it is possible to be Irish while using the English language'.[34] This was a theme that Gwynn articulated further in the *Observer*, when he accused the Gaelic League of distorting the concept of nationality, holding that 'it was possible to be very Irish in English speech and very un-Irish in Gaelic'.[35] The 'language equals nationality' juxtaposition forwarded by the Gaelic League was forced by the 'tyranny of the crowd', which Gwynn alleged the League blindly followed in demanding compulsory Irish for entrance to the National University. Yeats, on the other hand, stood up to 'mob-dictatorship' in the aftermath of the *Playboy of the western world* riots in 1907, risking the Abbey Theatre's popularity within nationalist Ireland. Thanks to Yeats, 'Ireland's thought is freer and more outspoken', valuable national characteristics for which Gwynn believed the poet never received credit.[36]

'Centre' politics were given a dramatic boost in June 1919 with the foundation of the Irish Dominion League by Sir Horace Plunkett. Plunkett claimed he had contacts inside the moderate wing of Sinn Féin: from these, he believed that a majority within the new nationalism would accept a dominion settlement – in other words, a full measure of self-government within the Empire rather than a republic – which encompassed the entire island.[37] Gwynn warmly greeted Plunkett's ideas, particularly after Plunkett conceded that 'there would be ample room for provincial rights' within a dominion-status Ireland. 'The idea of a settlement which would give to Ulster what Quebec has in Canada', Gwynn enthused, 'appears to be gaining ground'.[38] Gwynn's public support for Plunkett's dominion scheme followed private negotiations between the three moderate political movements in Ireland – Plunkett and his followers, Lord Midleton's Anti-Partition League and Gwynn's Centre Party – with the view of constructing unity of purpose. Midleton decided to remain aloof; but Gwynn reached agreement with Plunkett to merge the Centre Party with the League (whose name was retained). As Warre B. Wells, the editor of the *Irish Statesman* and participant at the negotiations, later observed, however, Plunkett was uneasy with Gwynn's insistence that Ulster should be afforded special constitutional conditions within an all-Ireland settlement.[39] The difficulties posed by the Ulster question threatened the harmony between Gwynn and Plunkett from the beginning of their joint venture.

The first edition of the Dominion League's newspaper, the *Irish Statesman*, carried its call to arms. The League's primary aim was to establish self-government for Ireland within the Empire; once this was achieved, Irish representation at Westminster would cease and Ireland would take its place alongside the other dominions in the newly created League of Nations. Minority rights would be protected within the dominion settlement, and the manifesto made a direct appeal to Ulster unionists to articulate what 'special safeguards they demand'.[40] Boasting an impressive and diverse cast of supporters, such as Lords Monteagle and Fingall, Henry Harrison and Francis Cruise O'Brien, the Dominion League, Gwynn believed, had become 'the rallying point of a new constitutional movement in Ireland'.[41]

Reaction to the Dominion League's programme was, however, uniformly negative. Plunkett's initiative, which aimed to bridge the philosophies of unionism and nationalism, succeeded in uniting them only in their disdain for the League. Not surprised at the less-than-generous response which greeted the Dominion League, Gwynn suggested in the *Observer* that many Irish people believed the British government would soon have to deal constructively with Ireland: it would, hence, offer more concessions if confronted with Sinn Féin's demand for a republic than with the League's more pragmatic approach.[42] Gwynn offered no ideas as to how to alter this scenario, which perhaps contained more than a hint of truth. In terms of bargaining positions, the Dominion League had left itself with little room for manoeuvre after publicly declaring that its programme represented 'the irreducible *minimum* of the Irish demand'.[43] The League also faced a challenge to be taken seriously by both the British government and the Irish electorate following an upsurge of revolutionary violence in the summer of 1919. Several days after the Centre Party merged with the Dominion League, an RIC district inspector was shot in the head in broad daylight in Thurles, County Tipperary. Such attacks thereafter became more widespread; the constitutional thinking propounded by the Dominion League lost much of its energy in the face of a violent alternative.

Preparing for partition

AT the end of September 1919, the British Cabinet was informed that the Home Rule Bill of 1914 would come into force following ratification of the last peace treaties in Europe. Irish opinion had mutated so much since the outbreak of the Great War that the 1914 Bill would have been a wholly inadequate measure to deal with the problems of establishing Irish self-rule in 1919. Moderate opinion now was campaigning for dominion status for Ireland, which was a substantial departure from the framework of the Asquithian Bill; the question of Ulster still had to be addressed. After a year of inactivity, then, the government was confronted with the immediate need to tackle the question head on, despite the unfavourable conditions brewing in Ireland – more so than ever after the British Army carried out a reprisal assault in September following a Volunteer attack in Fermoy, County Cork, setting in motion a grim pattern for the future.[44]

Sadly, on the same day as the Fermoy violence, Gwynn's eldest son, Edward Lucius (who was always known by his second name), died at the age of twenty-nine, after a long struggle with tuberculosis.[45] Like most of his family, Lucius was a promising scholar, an expert in the field of the Irish language; Gwynn described the special bond that Lucius enjoyed with his grandfather, the Reverend John Gwynn, both of whom were compelled by the passionate impulses of academic work.[46] Lucius emigrated to Australia after completing a master's degree in University College Dublin in 1915; as his brother Aubrey lamented, he died a lonely man in Sydney.[47] Coming only eight months after the death of the Gwynn's youngest son, Lucius's passing was heartbreaking. Like Owen, Lucius was not mentioned in his father's autobiographical writings which followed.[48] The double tragedy was one from which, perhaps, he never fully recovered.

Despite the mourning, politics inevitably continued. Sinn Féin and the Dáil Éireann were suppressed several days after the Fermoy attacks, a decision which Gwynn fiercely condemned. The banning of an assembly of legally elected members of parliament threatened, he contended, to bankrupt politics in Ireland, 'and there will be murders in plenty'.[49] But a potential way out became apparent to Gwynn with the establishment of Walter Long's parliamentary committee, which was given the task of investigating suitable forms of governance for Ireland to supersede the Home Rule Bill of 1914. Long's support for federalism was well known and his standing in the high political circles of London made him the natural choice to chair the new committee – at least from a British perspective. The selection of Long, a former leader of the Unionist Party and vocal opponent of Irish nationalism, to head such a committee was not, however, welcomed in Ireland. Gwynn nonetheless expressed his satisfaction with the committee's chair in a calmly rational way. As he informed the readers of the *Observer*, 'to have Mr Long committed to the support of a Home Rule scheme is the best possible proof of how far and how permanently public opinion in Great Britain has advanced on the whole matter. This Ireland does not realise'.[50] The nuances of this judgement were lost in the aftermath of the committee's report, delivered in December 1919: Home Rule would be the constitutional concession to Ireland, but in a partitioned form, recognising the political weightings of Ulster unionism and Irish nationalism. The scheme provided the framework for the Government of Ireland Bill of the following year.

The prospect of dividing Ireland was fiercely condemned by all wings of Irish nationalism, not least the Dominion League. Gwynn, though, was attracted to the idea as potentially the only available method to reconcile Ulster unionism with Irish self-government, and he emerged as the most vocal supporter of the scheme from within nationalism. Replying to criticisms of his pro-partitionist thinking made by the *Irish Independent*, Gwynn argued that the north-eastern counties could never be assimilated by the rest of Ireland 'any more than Quebec' could be by 'the rest of Canada'. The logic of this stance implied that Ulster should be granted its own institutions: this was, in the words of Gwynn, 'a necessary stepping-stone to securing Ulster's full concurrence and assistance in the general control and direction of Irish nationalist affairs'.[51] There was also another dimension to Gwynn's advocacy of partition, namely the nature of republican coercion. The IRA's violent campaign merely confirmed Protestant Ulster's sense of difference from the rest of the island: the excesses of republicanism, Gwynn insisted, had 'made Ulster's case for them as they could never have made it for themselves'.[52] Such partitionist thinking was, however, antithetical to the Dominion League.

Plunkett chaired a meeting of the League in November to discuss Long's report; although Gwynn was unable to attend, he indicated that he supported the creation of two parliaments in Ireland, which would at least place government on the island into Irish hands. 'If this proposal is put forward', Gwynn told Plunkett, 'I shall support it by all means in my power'.[53] Yet the chances that the Dominion League would also support such a scheme were slim: Plunkett fiercely rejected partition, believing that 'it would plunge Ireland into rebellion'.[54]

Somewhat fittingly, amid these emerging disputes within moderate nationalism over partition, Gwynn's *John Redmond's last years* was published. This has become his classic text, a vivid and analytical study of Irish politics from the third Home Rule Bill to Redmond's death in 1918, and has become a foundation stone in modern attempts to reassess Redmondism within Irish intellectual life.[55] *John Redmond's last years* established the former Irish leader as a totemic figure for Gwynn's own post-war brand of pluralist and conciliatory politics: Redmond's imperialism and sincere tolerance, two traits close to Gwynn's heart, were emphasised throughout. The book saw nothing inevitable in the fall of Redmond: it was the combination of the 1916 Rising and British policy that largely, in Gwynn's eyes, destroyed the Irish Party.[56] This was an uncontroversial argument for a defeated constitutional nationalist to make in 1919, but *John Redmond's last years* did not stop there. Gwynn used the book to critique the Irish Party at critical moments during the Ulster crisis, subtly arguing that Redmond's strategies during his final years also played a part in the downfall of the IPP in 1918. The Irish Party was therefore not held to be entirely blameless, a form of historical revisionism notably lacking in subsequent accounts from other former Redmondites, such as William O'Malley and John Valentine, who meekly pointed to external factors in explaining the outcome of the general election of 1918.[57] The book's most controversial passage concerned the temporary partition proposals mooted on the eve of the Great War: this, however, unmistakably reflected the political situation of 1919 more than that of 1914. Gwynn argued that the Irish Party should have conceded to Ulster unionism's demand for a permanent division, in the hope that it would attract moderate opinion in the north and further the long-term cause of reconciliation within Ireland.[58] The logic of this reassessment, however, needs to be weighed against contemporary political possibilities. Gwynn's retrospective analysis has been deemed a 'serious argument, coming as it does from the pen of one of Redmond's most trusted and talented colleagues'.[59] It was; but it should not be overplayed. Gwynn's hypothetical assessment was more a reflection of his post-1916 thinking on the Ulster question than a constructive criticism of IPP policy in 1914. Still, the book is one of the most important studies of the Irish Party published by a contemporary. The

Freeman's Journal described *John Redmond's last years* as 'the best piece of political biography which has been written in Ireland for a generation'; the *Spectator* claimed, characteristically, that 'Captain Gwynn has made the best possible case for his old chief, but his very readable book is essentially a record of wasted opportunities'.[60]

Around the time of the publication of *John Redmond's last years*, Gwynn opened a correspondence with a key member of the British government's inner circle, Lloyd George's private secretary, Philip Kerr (the future Lord Lothian). Kerr was a long-standing member of the Round Table group and a key influence on the Prime Minister on imperial and foreign affairs. Seeking Irish contacts in the winter of 1919, Kerr perhaps encountered Gwynn through a shared commitment to federalism and the war effort. Certainly, the two men had similar traits. Lord Riddell's description of Kerr – 'a clever, honourable, high-minded man, although rather fantastic in some of his ideas' – could also be applied to Gwynn.[61] Kerr hoped that moderate politics in Ireland could be rebuilt to accommodate a Home Rule settlement and undermine Sinn Féin's radicalism.[62] To this end, Gwynn reported to Kerr that several prominent – if not exactly representative – public figures would support the government should it decide to embark on Long's partition scheme: these included the Trinity College Provost, J. H. Bernard, and a Maynooth academic, Walter McDonald. Gwynn also prompted Kerr to send a copy of McDonald's new book, *Some ethical questions of peace and war*, to the Prime Minister, as, he claimed, it 'makes the case for partition out of Celtic history'.[63] This was a bold claim but *Some ethical questions* was an intrepid book, and the Prime Minister did take an interest in McDonald's work. Introducing the government's partition proposals in the House of Commons, Lloyd George quoted McDonald's key argument:

> The Protestants of Ulster differ from the majority in the rest of the island, not only in religion, but in race, mentality, culture generally.... A minority in Ireland, they are a majority in the north-east corner; and therefore, on the principles which we have been advocating, are entitled to Home Rule.[64]

Through Kerr, Gwynn obtained a line of communication with the Prime Minister; but whether Lloyd George would always listen was another matter. Kerr, however, was a significant figure in his own right, being heavily involved in drafting the Government of Ireland Bill in 1920.

Sinn Féin ignored the government's scheme, while the Dominion League rejected it: within nationalist Ireland, Gwynn was isolated on the issue. His support for partition should not be seen as a sudden conversion to unionism, or even to a 'two nations' theory. Rather, it was a heavy dose of *realpolitik*, a realisation that the proposals were simply the best that could be gained from the Conservative-dominated coalition. Gwynn recognised that unionist–nationalist relations had been severely damaged by the pre-war Home Rule crisis (partly due to the Irish Party's unwillingness to concede to unionist demands); republican extremism exacerbated and entrenched Irish divisions in the post-war period. In this atmosphere, an immediate measure of self-government in Ireland was imperative to rebuild the centre ground and to find a common unity of purpose among moderate people, north and south. Throughout his political career, Gwynn was committed to the cause of Irish self-rule; but it mattered less to him how it was framed. Analogies with the near-complete independence that Canada and other (white) self-governing British colonies enjoyed were employed in the drive for Irish Home Rule before the Great War, as were more modest notions of devolution and federalism. He desired as much political power as was possible to be in the hands of the Irish; but as a republic was an impossible dream and deeply repugnant to Ulster unionism, and while the government's lack of interest in conceding dominion status to Ireland left the Irish Dominion League politically bankrupt, a revised form of Home Rule seemed the logical compromise. The shifts in political positions that Gwynn made through 1919 were not down to lack of principle, but rather to a realisation of the limitations of British statesmanship *and* Irish nationalism.

The stepping-up of war

THE year 1920 was a pivotal one in the republican campaign against the British state in Ireland. There was an upsurge of revolutionary violence, which was sustained until the truce of July 1921; alongside the bloodshed was the evolution of the idealised 'Republic' into an underground state, which, although uneven in its geographical spread, seriously breached British rule in Ireland. A rebel administration of sorts was established in 1920, with the Dáil at the top of an apparatus which included republican courts and policing, leaving the British government's planned Home Rule settlement stillborn. It was a dangerous and bleak political environment for moderates such as Gwynn.

The human cost and day-to-day realities of the republican campaign were among the themes that Gwynn wrote about in the *Observer* in the new year. He noted that the IRA was beginning to become involved in 'ordinary' criminal behaviour, such as looting, in January; its assassination campaign, which almost claimed the life of Gwynn's former IRC comrade Serjeant Sullivan, was nothing more than 'murderous', despite republicans' pleas that they were engaged in legitimate warfare.[65] The IRA's decision to besiege police barracks around the country and the resultant stepping-up of the British military effort in February altered the dynamics of the conflict, forcing Gwynn to concede that there 'is now quite definitely a war in Ireland'.[66] Against this deteriorating security backdrop, the Cabinet decided to accept the Ulster unionists' preference for a six-county, rather than Long's proposed nine-county, arrangement for the northern administrative area to be established by the Government of Ireland Bill. This was greeted with horror by the Dominion League. Despite reservations about the partitioning of Ulster (he believed that a six-county 'Ulster' was less likely to work for *all* its inhabitants), Gwynn strongly backed the Bill; 'On the question of Irish unity', he asserted, 'it gets England out of the way'.[67]

After this declaration, Plunkett scribbled sardonically in his diary that Gwynn's support for the Bill was 'a great help to the Coalition Government'.[68] Plunkett, though, knew only half of the 'great help'. As well as his propaganda work, Gwynn was also supplying Philip Kerr with information and advice on the Irish situation. Like Gwynn, Kerr believed that the limited terms on offer were the best that could be gained from the coalition government, but he hoped that the Bill would appeal to republican pragmatists.[69] In a more Machiavellian vein, Kerr also saw the Bill as the means to 'take Ulster out of the Irish question which it had blocked for a generation and it would take Ireland out of English party controversies'.[70] Kerr was also aware of the criticisms that the Bill was attracting in Ireland and looked to Gwynn for moral support as the legislative details were being smoothed out. Gwynn confidently informed Kerr that the Bill represented the best way to secure self-government throughout Ireland:

> No body likes partition. But if self-government is to be started it can be only on a dual basis. The real alternative to this Bill is the retention of part of Ireland under rule from Westminster. The choice made is dictated by a desire to forward Irish unity. Irishmen are more likely to come together if dealing direct with one another and if self-government exists both in Ulster and the rest.[71]

Amid the sobering reality of Irish life, this was an extremely optimistic analysis; the great handicap in Gwynn's logic was the lack of Irish support for the Bill. This was the point which the *Irish Statesman* emphasised in its portrayal of Gwynn as a 'minority of one' within nationalist Ireland in supporting the 'detestable sham' that was the partition legislation.[72]

Gwynn was, however, unfazed by the *Statesman*'s criticism. He tied himself further to government policy by accepting the chairmanship of a small constitutional committee tasked with the unenviable challenge of suggesting amendments to render the Bill more palatable to Irish opinion. The *Statesman* scathingly attacked this amendment committee – 'Captain Stephen Gwynn's little group of time-servers' – which, it argued, threatened to give the false impression that Irish nationalism was behind the proposed plan, bar several minor amendments.[73] A short-lived war of words between Gwynn and the Dominion League's Henry

Harrison erupted in the pages of various newspapers. Harrison, an old Parnellite, informed the *Irish Times* that the Dominion League would have 'no truck with a bill designed to administer the *coup de grâce* to the indivisible nationhood of Ireland'.[74] Gwynn conceded that the amendment committee lacked the support of nationalist Ireland, but hoped to use his status to change public opinion.[75] The Bill, he asserted, should be taken seriously in Ireland, as it could lead to eventual dominion status: working against the Bill would undermine this ambition.[76]

Gwynn did attempt to make the Bill more satisfactory for Irish nationalist opinion. He led a deputation which met Long at Westminster in May: among the amendments Long received were an imaginative one to establish a parliament of Ireland consisting of northern and southern bi-cameral legislatures instead of the two separate entities, and another giving increased financial powers to the devolved institutions. These ideas were, however, politely rebuffed.[77] The amendment committee also looked at the existing civil administration, which was rapidly collapsing throughout the south of Ireland. In late May, Gwynn had a long conversation with Brigadier-General Cyril Prescott-Decie – who described Gwynn as 'rather a dreamer and idealist' to senior civil servant Sir John Anderson – emphasising to him that the problem of policing in Ireland was hindering those seeking the implementation of the Government of Ireland Bill.[78] Gwynn publicly blamed the government for the lack of Irish interest in the Bill and gave a stinging criticism of the policy to arm the RIC, which he regarded as symbolically disastrous and practically useless. Placing guns into the hands of the police, Gwynn argued in the *Observer*, made the RIC the 'chief-sufferers', as it transformed them into soldiers, putting their lives in danger and alienating them from even moderate Sinn Féiners.[79] By mid-summer 1920, recruitment to the RIC had all but dried up; throughout June and July, Gwynn called for the standing-down of the RIC on the grounds of expense and lack of public support.[80]

It was clear, though, that moral authority lay not in any committee room in Westminster but with Sinn Féin. By May 1920 the IRA had taken the place of the RIC in several parts of the country in dealing with crime and by that summer many Irish people had come to see the Dáil Éireann as the *de facto* government of Ireland.[81] But it was the phenomenon of the republican courts that most effectively challenged British administration in Ireland. Contrary to his anti-revolutionary stance, Gwynn praised the formation of the courts, describing them as the 'best feature to my thinking which Sinn Féin has yet developed'; he also argued that the government had tacitly accepted the courts to stave off anarchy in Ireland.[82] Certainly the 'people's courts' were far from radical: they were part of an alternative *conservative* establishment, seen most strikingly in their defusing of agrarian tensions.[83] The republican courts operated to quash land agitation, which the national leadership of Sinn Féin feared could undermine nationalist unity and distract from the struggle against British forces.[84] Gwynn's praise for this alternative establishment is significant: his days of reluctantly supporting cattle-driving, as he did during the Edwardian period, were long gone. But the significance of the courts went further than keeping a lid on agrarian tensions; as Gwynn concluded in the *Observer*, with the successful operation of an underground judicial system, 'nothing goes so far to give reality to the claim that there is an Irish Republic in being'.[85]

If the courts were one form of revolutionary expression, another was violence, the persistence of which overshadowed the efforts made by political moderates to present a viable Irish settlement. In addition, the moderate camp was deeply divided over the partition proposals, further weakening constitutional nationalism during the War of Independence. This was manifestly demonstrated at a peace conference in Dublin sponsored by the Dominion League in August. Attended by the leading moderate political figures and business people from around Ireland (Gwynn put the attendance at an impressive 800), the conference merely highlighted the depth of the divisions: Gwynn and the Earl of Shaftesbury accepted the need for a division of Ireland to kick-start self-government, while Plunkett and a former Irish Party MP, Sir Thomas Esmonde, strenuously opposed partition and called for nothing less than dominion status for the whole island.[86] Even the *Freeman's Journal* – the last bastion of constitutional nationalism – was decidedly unimpressed.[87] The historical value of the quickly forgotten peace conference initiative lies in revealing just how isolated and divided moderate opinion in Ireland had become.

Life in Ireland became grimmer in the summer of 1920. 'This business of reviewing the Irish situation gets more depressing week by week', a commentary by a dejected Gwynn read, just one week after the first mention in his column of a new force in Ireland – the Black and Tans.[88] The recruitment of the Black and Tans and the restructuring of the RIC to produce a new Auxiliary Division significantly militarised policing in Ireland, and was designed to wear down the IRA. The Black and Tans, who came under the control of General Hugh Tudor, Britain's 'police advisor' in Ireland, carried out reprisal attacks against presumed republicans, fuelling tit-for-tat violence to such a level that it worried even the commander-in-chief of the Army in Ireland, Sir Nevil Macready.[89] The reprisal campaign was a public relations disaster for the British state in Ireland, as Gwynn pointed out in 1921:

> There were now two terrors in Ireland. It would be difficult to say whether the community at large was more afraid of the police or the gunmen. But it was, and is, clear that the rebel organisation had a considerable measure of moral support and sympathy, whereas the police were the objects of universal detestation.[90]

The Crown forces' reprisals made headline news in Britain with the Black and Tan 'sack' of Balbriggan: responding to the assassination of an RIC officer, Black and Tans killed several men and destroyed a number of properties in the small town near Dublin. The British press was universally condemnatory of the Black and Tans, reporting on their misdeeds with startling detail.[91] Writing for the *Observer* shortly after, Gwynn's perspective was less sensationalist but actually more chilling. He included a section with the sub-heading 'The week's reprisals', citing Balbriggan as merely one among others in a ghastly list, which also included Galway, Limerick and Clare.[92] Plainly, Gwynn wanted the *Observer*'s readership to understand that Balbriggan was not an isolated incident.

Through the autumn and winter of 1920, Gwynn pressed in the *Observer* for the introduction of martial law, as reprisals followed IRA violence in a vicious cycle. He also keenly stressed the underlying catalyst for a new military policy: the lack of self-government in Ireland.[93] This claim was made with an eye on Westminster, where the Government of Ireland Bill was reaching the end of its legislative journey. Despite the further breakdown in Irish security from the late summer of 1920, Gwynn was still unrepentant in his advocacy of the Home Rule Bill and appealed to Irish nationalists to 'make the best and not the worst of it'.[94] Nationalist Ireland did not, however, have any incentive to work either of the two Home Rule parliaments which the Bill aimed to establish, a point reinforced by Lloyd George's increasing attempts to woo Sinn Féin as 1921 opened.

Searching for a compromise

DESPITE Gwynn's fears that the government was undermining its own legislation, the return of Éamon de Valera to Ireland in December, after eighteen months in the United States, opened a potential avenue of compromise, which he encouraged. At a Cabinet meeting on the day that de Valera arrived at Liverpool, Lloyd George asked his colleagues to read Gwynn's *Observer* article from the previous day.[95] This made the case that de Valera 'ought to be in Ireland' and that if he attempted to return 'the last thing the Government should do is to try to stop him'.[96] This view reflected a hope that de Valera was a man with whom government could do business: the Cabinet quickly accepted Gwynn's line and their commitment to it was shown when de Valera was arrested by chance and promptly released.[97] De Valera reached Dublin on 23 December, coincidentally the same day that the Government of Ireland Act received its Royal Assent. This fact was not lost on Gwynn: he met Lloyd George at the end of December, when he robustly told the Prime Minister that the government was 'neglecting to advertise' the new Act.⁹⁸ The first issue of the *Observer* in 1921 carried Gwynn's analysis of the post-Act situation in Ireland: the north's willingness to operate the new legislation could, he hoped, initiate a similar feeling in the south. This message was, however, somewhat muddled when placed alongside his assessment of de Valera's return: Gwynn commented that the presence of the 'Chief' in Ireland was likely to trigger negotiations.⁹⁹

Gwynn was also working behind the scenes with the government on the de Valera question, by suggesting how his return might lead to constructive talks. Both Gwynn and the government, not unreasonably, viewed de Valera as a moderate within Sinn Féin. On his return to Ireland, de Valera advocated making the IRA responsible to the Dáil, which would strengthen, publicly at least, the unity of the republican movement. But the IRA clearly did not come under the control of Sinn Féin's civil administration. In December, de Valera made a speech suggesting that the IRA should 'ease off' its campaign; the local army units, however, ignored his advice.¹⁰⁰ Tying the IRA to the Dáil, however, served to boost de Valera's profile within British circles, as he was seen as a potential negotiator on behalf of militant republicanism. One Dublin Castle official believed that pressure from the Dáil could end IRA violence;¹⁰¹ Gwynn, on the other hand, saw beyond public appearances of republican unity. As he bashfully told another Dublin Castle civil servant, Mark Sturgis, 'Dáil Éireann no more controls the gunman than you control the police'.¹⁰²

Gwynn sent a note to Philip Kerr in January with some thoughts on how the government should respond to de Valera's return to Ireland, which Kerr passed on to the Prime Minister. The theme of Gwynn's note is clear from one of its opening lines: 'Presumably it will be desired to make things as easy as possible for de Valera subject to maintaining the agreement reached with Ulster'.¹⁰³ Gwynn advocated a range of measures, including an amnesty for senior republican leaders and the abandonment of the RIC, in a bid to strengthen de Valera's hand over his more militant colleagues. He made it clear, though, that anything that would undermine the administrative unit now deemed 'Northern Ireland' must be avoided: as Gwynn asserted in the *Observer* on 9 January, 'If Mr de Valera cannot accept autonomy of Ulster then I fear peace will not come'.¹⁰⁴ The politics of the coalition, however, made progress on this point impossible: while Lloyd George strongly favoured meeting with de Valera, Andrew Bonar Law was equally strongly opposed, and no action was taken.

The only constitutional initiative taken over the winter of 1920–21 was the fixing of the first election under the Government of Ireland Act for May. Gwynn's *Observer* articles through the first few months of 1921 were sombre in tone, as he increasingly accepted that although Ireland had finally won Home Rule, after decades of nationalist struggle, it was a pyrrhic victory. He maintained that despite its financial and partitionist flaws, the new southern parliament should be supported by nationalists: as he put it, 'satisfactory Home Rule will in effect have to be won through unsatisfactory Home Rule'.[105] Linking the establishment of Home Rule in Ireland with disbandment of the hated Black and Tans was the last practical policy that Gwynn encouraged the government to adopt, in a desperate effort to energise moderate opinion alienated by the paramilitary policing of the Crown forces.[106] The Black and Tans must go, Gwynn told Kerr, as 'the Act cannot conceivably be worked without that riddance. With this inducement, a majority for working the Act *might* conceivably be obtained. Without it, it is ridiculous to expect it'.[107]

Ireland's political upheavals were mirrored by personal turmoil in Gwynn's life throughout 1921. During the first few months of that year, Gwynn became embroiled in an affair with Grace Henry, the wife of the landscape artist Paul.[108] The Henrys were guests at Gwynn's home in Terenure, a suburb of Dublin, for the best part of January and February; in the absence of May Gwynn, who appears to have been abroad, Stephen and Grace commenced a relationship which would contribute to both the Henrys' and the Gwynns' later separations. While Paul Henry is the better remembered by art historians, Grace was a formidable artist in her own right: she was possibly the first Irish artist to experiment with modernism in creating abstractions of landscapes in her early work.[109] Little direct evidence of the affair has survived, but it seems that Stephen and Grace travelled around Europe together several times during the spring and early summer of 1922 before the liaison petered out.[110] If their respective arts – literature and painting – are taken as insights into their relationship, though, they must have been close for a time. Grace's wonderful oil painting of Gwynn – entitled *The orange man* due to the vibrant tint used to colour his suit – dates from 1921; Gwynn's collection of essays from that year, *Garden wisdom*, has a frontispiece of his daughter, Shelia, by Grace, while his *Collected poems* from 1923 contains a verse dedicated to his mistress.[111]

It is not clear when May found out about the affair, but she remained with Stephen in Dublin for several years before separating from him.[112] Unlike the Henrys' legal separation, which was long, protracted and left a substantial paper trail, details of the Gwynns' parting are elusive. In 1981, a Jesuit priest, Michael Hurley, made some notes on the Gwynns' family history, with his information seemingly coming from his colleague Aubrey Gwynn. Aubrey, doubtlessly anxious to cover up any scandal, told Hurley that his 'father fell out of love with [his] mother'.[113] This does not, however, tell the whole story. Gwynn had two affairs with bohemian (and married) women, first Mabel Dearmer and then Grace Henry. This trait was perhaps sustained by a need for intellectual fulfilment as much as sexual desire. While these affairs were hidden from the public, they fundamentally undermined May Gwynn's trust in her husband. The two separated and reunited several times between 1921 and May's death in 1941. There was, however, another conflicting dynamic within the Gwynn household in 1921. Gwynn's friend the artist William Rothenstein spent some time in Dublin in 1921. Rothenstein later recorded that Stephen looked 'anxious and perturbed': family circumstances were perhaps behind his jaded appearance, as by this stage May had declared her support for Sinn Féin.[114] Stephen's old literary acquaintance from late-Victorian London, Evelyn Sharp, stayed with the Gwynns in the summer of that year. What she found was 'a house divided against itself in political opinions', although it was 'divided in no other respect', which implies that either May was not aware of her husband's involvement with Grace Henry at that time or she was putting a brave face on it.[115] The Gwynns' marriage was as complex as it was long lasting.

One of the stranger angles of this particular episode is Gwynn's public criticism of both the Henrys' works following the Dublin Painters' Exhibition, several months after the affair began. In a lengthy letter to the *Irish Times*, Gwynn stingingly attacked Paul's *Red earth*, a modernist interpretation of a peasant woman in Connemara:

> To me the woman seemed like an animated lump of potato patch.... There is nothing red about her but her petticoat: she is tanned black, and if Mr Henry drew what he saw, and not some vision in which that peaty soil threw up an incarnation, he must have met one of the rare types in which survives a stock older than the Gael.... Is it naturalism that these modern artists are after, or is it wild fantasy?

Without a hint of irony, Gwynn's mistress also became a victim of confused criticism, with Grace's landscape painting of Cushendall, *Country of amethyst*, coming under fire: 'Cushendall I know, but never at Cushendall or anywhere else did I see mountains of that colour.... The method is so novel that it almost shocks by its lack of verisimilitude; but probably Mrs Henry would answer that she wants to produce beauty, not a likeness'.[116] With these commentaries, Gwynn betrayed his late-Victorian artistic sensibilities, a sentiment identified by the poet Richard Rowland in a sarcastic reply to the *Irish Times*: 'If Captain Gwynn desires to see nature represented exactly as he sees it, let him take to photography'.[117] Gwynn, though, was versatile in his tastes and quickly adapted. A few years after his affair with Grace fizzled out, he wrote to John Quinn in New York to encourage an exhibition of the Henrys' work in America. Both Henrys, Gwynn told Quinn, were wonderful landscape artists with great marketing potential in the United States; he also added that 'personally, I have got more pleasure out of her work than his'.[118] Again, writing later, Gwynn hinted at the intimacy he shared with Grace by declaring that from all his possessions, two paintings by her were among the greatest of his 'luxuries'.[119]

If his romance with Grace provided a domestic distraction, it did not slow Gwynn's other activities through the spring of 1921. The tone of his *Observer* column, however, became increasingly bleak as he spoke out against the IRA's targeting of ex-servicemen and the British forces' disregard for the safety of non-combatants.[120] Once more, Gwynn decided that it was time for action. With his focus solely on the May elections to the Government of Ireland Act institutions, Gwynn wrote to Lord Midleton, as he had done after the December 1918 election, to gain a hearing for a new political party.[121] At a meeting between the two men, Gwynn pleaded that they should pool their combined resources. 'The time had come', Gwynn appealed to the unionist chief, 'when moderate men in Ireland of various shades of religious and political belief ought to come together and organise in order to be able to put forward candidates at the coming Election for a Parliament in Southern Ireland'. Gwynn believed that the moderate silent majority would rally to this call; what was needed was leadership. A new 'Centre Party', with Midleton at the head ('his name as leader would carry great weight'), was the formula Gwynn proposed. While Midleton listened sympathetically, he rejected the proposal, just as he had discarded Gwynn's original invitation to play a leading role in the first incarnation of the Centre Party. Midleton told Gwynn that a new organisation would be stillborn without overt support from the Roman Catholic Church.[122] This was southern unionism rejecting the thesis that the political centre could be reclaimed: instead, the theory was that a settlement could come about only with Sinn Féin's participation. Deflated, Gwynn left the meeting with no organisation to contest the election. A further blow came in March, when Philip Kerr stood down as Lloyd George's private secretary, thereby severing Gwynn's informal line to the inner circle of the British government.[123] Journalism was now Gwynn's only political outlet, as Ireland moved from revolution to settlement.

Towards the Treaty

THE May 1921 election was contested by Sinn Féin, but not in support of the new institutions; rather, a new underground Dáil was returned. Sinn Féin swept the board across Southern Ireland, winning every seat (bar the four university seats, which went to unionists) unopposed. The first election to Northern Ireland's parliament brought an impressive display of unionist unity, with the Ulster Unionist Party capturing forty of the fifty-two seats on offer. The constitutional machinery provided by the Government of Ireland Act thus starkly highlighted the demographic polarisation within Ireland. For Gwynn, the political division was not, in itself, the problem; rather, it was Sinn Féin's refusal to recognise Ulster unionism's right of self-determination which had 'made partition horribly real'.[124] The division of Ireland was more than a line across a territory: it was a visible expression of the psychological disparities between Ulster unionism and Irish nationalism. 'In Ireland we live ... under illusions', Gwynn lamented shortly before the election. 'The more complete the faith the more dangerous the illusion'.[125]

It is at this point in the narrative that Gwynn's *The Irish situation* draws to a close. Released in the summer of 1921, just after the July truce between the IRA and Crown forces, the publisher's blurb proclaimed that the book was a 'reasoned survey of the situation in Ireland' up to the 1921 elections, and (astonishingly) was 'Written without party bias'. The book was, in fact, a sustained attack on Ulster unionist militancy before the Great War, and Sinn Féin and British aggression afterwards. Gwynn's treatment of the post-1918 period, which makes up a third of the book, features many analyses which had been previously aired in the *Observer*: the book serves as a useful introduction to his political thought during 1919–21. This was enough for an *Irish Independent* reviewer to take issue with the book's design: it was pointed out that Gwynn's anti-Sinn Féin stance made a mockery of his publisher's claim that the book is a 'reasoned survey'.[126]

As the downbeat tone of *The Irish situation* makes clear, Gwynn did not foresee the truce of July 1921. The cessation of violence between the IRA and the Crown forces caught Gwynn, and many republicans, by surprise.[127] The potential for national reconciliation between north and south in an era of peace became the focus of his commentary in the *Observer* during the second half of the year; in this he followed a broader pattern, with most newspaper accounts after the truce stressing the centrality of the Ulster question within the larger Irish equation. Disappointingly for Gwynn, the crux of the Anglo-Irish negotiations which followed the truce did not concern Ulster, but rather Sinn Féin's demand for the recognition of Irish national sovereignty and Lloyd George's refusal to concede it.[128] While the republican leadership aspired to the ideal of Irish unity, southern independence was clearly the priority as de Valera and the leaders of Sinn Féin tentatively parleyed with the British government through the second half of 1921.

A curious aspect of Gwynn's analysis in his *Observer* column of events which led to the Anglo-Irish Treaty of December 1921 was his failure to comment on de Valera's controversial decision not to head the Irish negotiating team that held formal talks with the government in London. Gwynn's weekly commentaries kept a wide focus, but the potential for the negotiations to thaw north–south relations remained his prime topic. 'The real question for Ireland', he argued at the end of October, 'is how to create a healthy normal Irish nation, in which Protestant Ulster will be a willing integral unit. No such nation exists'.[129] The Lloyd George administration should make this goal the priority, Gwynn argued the following week; brokering an agreement between Sir James Craig's Northern Irish government and the Dáil Éireann would go far in furthering this ambition. The difficulty with this assessment was that the Government of Ireland Act provided Northern Ireland with constitutional protection: the Ulster question, from a unionist point of view, was settled. Craig and the Ulster unionists decided to remain outside the negotiations; Gwynn believed that this was ill-advised, as it gave the impression they were uninterested in Ireland's wider role in the Empire.[130]

On 6 December, faced with the threat of immediate war, the Irish delegation concluded their negotiations with the British government. The Anglo-Irish Treaty granted Ireland dominion status but granted Northern Ireland an opt-out, which was immediately enacted. The Treaty also established a Boundary Commission to decide the position of the border at a later date. The compromise clearly reflected Britain's strategic concerns more than Ireland's aspirations. As a result, the Treaty, as Fearghal McGarry has pointed out, split every republican body in Ireland: the Cabinet, Dáil, Sinn Féin, IRA and IRB.[131] Gwynn's first commentary following the Treaty's signing – and de Valera's rejection of it – repeated his claim that the 'Republic' was only 'bargaining rhetoric'. He strongly believed that Ireland would accept the terms offered, although conceded that the forces lining up against the Treaty were impressive in stature, making the mood 'grave'.[132]

Gwynn offered many valuable insights into the debates surrounding the Treaty in the *Observer*, as he advocated its acceptance while describing the poisonous split it was causing within republicanism. The agreement was seen as far from ideal even within the pro-Treaty wing of Sinn Féin: what made the difference in terms of acceptance was the threat of war made by the British. Treatyite pragmatism – notably led by the military men Michael Collins and Richard Mulcahy – accepted Irish nationalism's unequal relationship with the British state and Empire. Some anti-Treaty Sinn Féiners believed that the threat of war was a bluff, while others argued that the politics of coercion should not be given preference over the right of national self-determination. Harry Boland, a prominent anti-Treatyite, articulated both these themes in his contribution in the Treaty debate in the Dáil: 'If we reject that Treaty England will not make war on us; if she does we will be able to defend ourselves as we have always done'.[133] Gwynn was intrigued at how the split was playing out within Sinn Féin, and he focused on the military dynamic of the situation: 'Mr Collins and Mr Mulcahy evidently both reckon automatically that they must cut their coat according to their cloth, and the cloth is the amount of military force at their disposal. It does not appear to shock them that England should make a similar calculation'.[134] As he added on New Year's Day 1922: 'The fighting men in this instance appear to be for peace'.[135] The following week, the Dáil narrowly voted in favour of the Treaty; nationalist opinion as a whole was much more welcoming of the deal, which gave it a sturdy foundation. De Valera's withdrawal from the Dáil following the Treaty's acceptance, Gwynn lamented, made him an asset to extremists and a real danger to the new Irish Free State.[136] What form this would take, however, would become apparent only with the fullness of time.

Notes

1 *Collected poems* (Edinburgh: William Blackwood and Sons, 1923), p. 47.
2 Stephen Gwynn, 'The ageing of a poet', in *Garden wisdom: or from one generation to another* (Dublin: Talbot Press, 1921), p. 10.
3 Memorandum on demobilisation and resettlement in Ireland, 19 December 1918, Ian Macpherson papers, Bodleian Library, Oxford (Bodleian), MS Eng. Hist. C.490 (36).
4 Stephen Gwynn to Walter Long, 19 November [1918]; untitled memorandum by Stephen Gwynn, Walter Long papers, Wiltshire and Swindon Record Office (WSRO), 947/245.
5 *Freeman's Journal*, 17 December 1918.
6 *Irish Independent*, 26 February 1919.
7 Stephen Gwynn to Walter Long, 2 January 1919, Walter Long papers, WSRO, 947/245.
8 Stephen Gwynn and Henry McLaughlin to Lord French, 10 January 1919, Lord French papers, Imperial War Museum Library (IWML), JDPF/8/1C.
9 Stephen Gwynn to Walter Long, 6 January 1919, Walter Long papers, WSRO, 947/245.
10 Stephen Gwynn to Lord Midleton, n.d. [December 1918], Lord Midleton papers, The National Archives, London (TNA), PRO 30/67/39.
11 *Freeman's Journal*, 31 December 1918.
12 Lord Midleton to Stephen Gwynn, 30 December 1918, Lord Midleton papers, TNA, PRO 30/67/39.
13 Michael Hopkinson, *The Irish War of Independence* (Dublin: Gill and Macmillan, 2004; first published 2002), p. 25.
14 Memorial card of Owen John Gwynn, Aubrey Gwynn papers, Irish Jesuit Archive (IJA), J10/41(1).
15 Stephen Gwynn to William Rothenstein, 29 May [1918], William Rothenstein papers, Houghton Library, Harvard University, bMS 1148 (631).
16 *Irish Independent*, 24 January 1919.
17 General Sir Hubert Gough, *Soldiering on* (London: Arthur Barker, 1954), p. 182.
18 *Observer*, 27 July 1919.
19 *Observer*, 31 August 1919.
20 *Round Table*, 9 (1918–19), p. 583.
21 Stephen Gwynn to Walter Long, 5 February [1919], Walter Long papers, WSRO, 947/245.
22 *Irish Times*, 26 February 1919.
23 *Irish Independent*, 26 February 1919.
24 *Observer*, 2 March 1919.
25 Stephen Gwynn, 'Irish regiments', in Felix Lavery (ed.), *Great Irishmen in war and politics* (London: Andrew Melrose, 1920), p. 186.

26 *London Gazette*, 12 June 1923; Gerald Griffin, *The wild geese: pen portraits of famous Irish exiles* (London: Jarrolds, n.d. [1938]), p. 149. There is a copy of the petition in the Stansgate papers, Parliamentary Archives, London (PAL), ST/207/17/817a. Some 140 former Irish officers signed it, including Gwynn's son Denis.
27 *Times*, 25 March 1919, emphasis added.
28 *Irish Times*, 11 March 1919.
29 On Garvin, see John Stubbs, 'Appearance and reality: a case study of *The Observer* and J. L. Garvin, 1914–42', in D. George Boyce, James Curran and Pauline Wingate (eds), *Newspaper history: from the seventeenth century to the present day* (London: Constable, 1978), pp. 328–9.
30 *Observer*, 2, 9, 16 and 23 March 1919.
31 Stephen Gwynn, *Irish books and Irish people* (Dublin: Talbot Press, 1919), pp. 2–3.
32 See Chapter 3, p. 89.
33 *Irish Book Lover*, January–February 1920, pp. 59–60.
34 Gwynn, *Irish books and Irish people*, p. 4.
35 *Observer*, 1 June 1919.
36 Gwynn, *Irish books and Irish people*, p. 5.
37 Trevor West, *Horace Plunkett: co-operation and politics, an Irish biography* (Gerrards Cross: Colin Smythe, 1986), p. 182. Also see Senia Pašeta, 'Ireland's last Home Rule generation: the decline of constitutional nationalism in Ireland, 1916–1930', in Mike Cronin and John M. Regan (eds), *Ireland: the politics of independence, 1922–49* (Basingstoke: Macmillan, 2000), p. 24.
38 *Observer*, 20 April 1919.
39 Warre B. Wells, *Irish indiscretions* (London: George Allen and Unwin, 1922), pp. 90–1.
40 *Irish Statesman*, 28 June 1919.
41 *Observer*, 29 June 1919.
42 *Observer*, 6 July 1919.
43 *Irish Statesman*, 12 July 1919. To further this point, the emphasis is found in the original.
44 Charles Townshend, *The British campaign in Ireland 1919–21: the development of political and military policies* (Oxford: Oxford University Press, 1975), p. 30.
45 *Irish Provincial News*, 20:11 (July 1983), p. 367 (anonymous article commenting on the family tree of Aubrey Gwynn).
46 Gwynn, *Garden wisdom*, p. 121.
47 Aubrey Gwynn, 'Draft of an autobiography of Father Aubrey Gwynn', n.d. [1979], Aubrey Gwynn papers, IJA, J10/90 (65). Stephen Gwynn's niece, Mrs Rose Gayner, informed the present author that Stephen and May were unable to travel to Australia during Lucius's illness or after his death. He was buried in Sydney in a funeral service without any of his family present.
48 This is probably the cause of the error which a number of short entries on Gwynn's life in biographical dictionaries have made: most indicate that he had four children rather than six.
49 *Observer*, 21 September 1919.
50 *Observer*, 19 October 1919.
51 *Irish Independent*, 15 October 1919. The *Independent*'s attack on Gwynn was made the previous day.
52 *Observer*, 2 November 1919.
53 Stephen Gwynn to Horace Plunkett, 18 November 1919, Lord Lothian papers, National Archives of Scotland (NAS), GD/40/17/610/2 (i).
54 Sir Horace Plunkett diaries (microfilm), 20 November 1919, Belfast Central Library (BCL).

55 *John Redmond's last years* has been used most skilfully by Paul Bew in a number of publications: *Ideology and the Irish question: Ulster unionism and Irish nationalism, 1912–1916* (Oxford: Oxford University Press, 1994); *John Redmond* (Dundalk: Dundalgan Press, 1996); and 'Moderate nationalism and the Irish revolution, 1916–1923', *Historical Journal*, 93:3 (1999), pp. 729–49.
56 Best expressed when Gwynn discusses the formation of the Irish Volunteers: 'Government action – and this sentence will run like a refrain through the rest of this book – contributed largely to strengthen the extremists and to weaken Redmond's hold on the people'. Stephen Gwynn, *John Redmond's last years* (London: Edward Arnold, 1919), p. 94.
57 William O'Malley, *Glancing back: 70 years' experiences and reminiscences of press man, sportsman and member of parliament* (London: Wright and Brown, n.d. [1933]), p. 137; John Valentine, *Irish memories* (Bristol: St Stephen's Press, n.d. [c. 1928]), p. 58.
58 Gwynn, *John Redmond's last years*, p. 103.
59 Bew, *John Redmond*, p. 35.
60 *Freeman's Journal*, 8 December 1919; *Spectator*, 29 November 1919.
61 Lord Riddell, *Lord Riddell's intimate diary of the Peace Conference and after 1918–1923* (London: Victor Gollancz, 1933), p. 295.
62 G. K. Peatling, *British opinion and Irish self-government, 1865–1925: from unionism to commonwealth* (Dublin: Irish Academic Press, 2001), p. 154.
63 Stephen Gwynn to Philip Kerr, 5 December 1919, Lord Lothian papers, NAS, GD40/17/78.
64 *Parliamentary Debates*, 5th series, 123, 22 December 1919, col. 1173; Walter McDonald, *Some ethical questions of peace and war: with special reference to Ireland* (Dublin: University College Dublin Press, 1998; first published 1919), p. 70.
65 *Observer*, 11 and 18 January 1920.
66 *Observer*, 29 February 1920.
67 *Irish Times*, 5 March 1920.
68 Sir Horace Plunkett diaries (microfilm), 5 March 1920, BCL.
69 G. K. Peatling, 'The last defence of the Union? The Round Table and Ireland, 1910–1925', in Andrea Bosco and Alex May (eds), *The Round Table: the Empire/Commonwealth and British foreign policy* (London: Lothian Foundation Press, 1997), pp. 292.
70 C. P. Scott, *The political diaries of C. P. Scott 1911–1928*, ed. Trevor Wilson (London: Collins, 1970), p. 382 (16–17 March 1920).
71 Stephen Gwynn to Philip Kerr, 24 March [1920], Lord Lothian papers, NAS, GD40/17/78.
72 *Irish Statesman*, 27 March 1920.
73 *Irish Statesman*, 1 and 8 May 1920.
74 *Irish Times*, 6 May 1920.
75 *Irish Independent*, 7 May 1920.
76 *Manchester Guardian*, 5 May 1920.
77 *Irish Times*, 25 May 1920.
78 Brigadier-General Cyril Prescott-Decie to John Anderson, 28 May 1920, Sir John Anderson papers, TNA, CO904/188/1/579.
79 *Observer*, 9 May 1920.
80 *Observer*, 13 June and 25 July 1920.
81 Arthur Mitchell, *Revolutionary government in Ireland: Dáil Éireann 1919–22* (Dublin: Gill and Macmillan, 1995), pp. 151, 154.
82 *Observer*, 23 May and 11 June 1920.
83 Mary Kotsonouris, *Retreat from revolution: the Dáil courts, 1920–24* (Dublin: Irish Academic Press, 1994), p. 19.

84 Fergus Campbell, *Land and revolution: nationalist politics in the west of Ireland 1891–1921* (Oxford: Oxford University Press, 2005), pp. 254–5.
85 *Observer*, 11 July 1920.
86 *Observer*, 29 August 1920; *Irish Times*, 25 August 1920.
87 *Freeman's Journal*, 25 August 1920.
88 *Observer*, 19 September 1920.
89 Nevil Macready to Sir Henry Wilson, 28 August 1920, cited in Keith Jeffery, *Field Marshal Sir Henry Wilson: a political soldier* (Oxford: Oxford University Press, 2006), pp. 265–6.
90 Stephen Gwynn, *The Irish situation* (London: Jonathan Cape, 1921), pp. 84–5.
91 D. George Boyce, *Englishmen and Irish troubles: British public opinion and the making of Irish policy 1918–1922* (London: Jonathan Cape, 1972), pp. 52–3.
92 *Observer*, 26 September 1920.
93 *Observer*, 7 November 1920.
94 *Observer*, 14 November 1920.
95 Thomas Jones, *Whitehall diary, vol. III: Ireland 1918–1925*, ed. Keith Middlemass (London: Oxford University Press, 1971), p. 46.
96 *Observer*, 19 December 1920.
97 Michael Laffan, *The resurrection of Ireland: the Sinn Féin party, 1916–1923* (Cambridge: Cambridge University Press, 2005; first published 1999), p. 277.
98 Mark Sturgis, *The last days of Dublin Castle: the Mark Sturgis diaries*, ed. Michael Hopkinson (Dublin: Irish Academic Press, 1999), p. 102 (31 December 1920).
99 *Observer*, 2 January 1921.
100 Laffan, *The resurrection of Ireland*, p. 295.
101 C. J. C. Street, *The administration of Ireland, 1920* (London: Philip Allan and Co., 1921).
102 Sturgis, *The last days of Dublin Castle*, p. 88, 9 December 1920.
103 Copy of memorandum by Mr Stephen Gwynn, 4 January 1921, David Lloyd George papers, PAL, LG/F/90/1/31.
104 *Observer*, 9 January 1921.
105 *Observer*, 6 February 1921.
106 *Observer*, 13 February 1921.
107 Stephen Gwynn to Philip Kerr, 11 February 1921, Lord Lothian papers, NAS, GD40/17/78. Original emphasis.
108 S. B. Kennedy, *Paul Henry* (New Haven: Yale University Press, 2000), p. 84.
109 J. G. Cruickshank, 'Grace Henry', *Irish Arts Review*, 9 (1993), p. 178.
110 Kennedy, *Paul Henry*, p. 90.
111 Stephen Gwynn, 'Portrait of a painter', in *Collected poems*, pp. 107–9.
112 Private information from Mrs Rose Gayner (née Gwynn).
113 Rough typescript notes on Aubrey Gwynn's family by Father Michael Hurley, 16 December 1981, Aubrey Gwynn papers, IJA, J10/55.
114 William Rothenstein, *Men and memories: recollections of William Rothenstein* (London: Faber and Faber, two vols, 1932), vol. II, p. 373.
115 Evelyn Sharp, *Unfinished adventure: selected reminiscences from an Englishwoman's life* (London: John Lane the Bodley Head, 1933), pp. 226–7.
116 *Irish Times*, 4 April 1921.
117 *Irish Times*, 12 April 1921.
118 Stephen Gwynn to John Quinn, 29 April [1924], John Quinn papers, New York Public Library (NYPL), box 15.
119 Stephen Gwynn, *Fond opinions* (London: Frederick Miller, 1938), pp. 81–2.
120 *Observer*, 27 February and 20 March 1921.
121 Stephen Gwynn to Lord Midleton, 2 March [1921], Lord Midleton papers, TNA, PRO 30/67/44/2560.

122 Resumé of a meeting at 103 Grafton Street, Dublin, on 5 March 1921 at 12 noon between Lord M. and Lord O., and General O'G. and Captain G., Lord Midleton papers, TNA, PRO 30/67/44/2561-2.
123 Riddell, *Lord Riddell's intimate diary*, p. 295 (24 April 1921).
124 *Observer*, 10 April 1921.
125 *Observer*, 24 April 1921.
126 *Irish Independent*, 25 July 1921.
127 *Observer*, 10 July 1921.
128 Kevin Matthews, *Fatal influence: the impact of Ireland on British politics 1920–1925* (Dublin: University College Dublin Press, 2004), p. 36.
129 *Observer*, 30 October 1921.
130 *Observer*, 20 November 1921.
131 Fearghal McGarry, *Eoin O'Duffy: a self-made hero* (Oxford: Oxford University Press, 2005), p. 90.
132 *Observer*, 11 December 1921.
133 Quoted in David Fitzpatrick, *Harry Boland's Irish revolution* (Cork: Cork University Press, 2003), p. 268.
134 *Observer*, 25 December 1921.
135 *Observer*, 1 January 1922.
136 *Observer*, 15 January 1922.

8

Spiritually hyphenated

1922–26

If the victory is a just one, if the revolution has been really due, the last and worst of injustices is that the victors come out demoralised by their victory. (Stephen Gwynn, 1938)[1]

THE provisional government of the Irish Free State was installed in January 1922 without pomp or ceremony. Addressing the inaugural meeting, Arthur Griffith – now President of the Irish Republic after the resignation of Éamon de Valera, creating a confusing hierarchy of political structures – appealed for the old divisions of Ireland to be banished forever.[2] Ireland's newer divisions – those forced by the Anglo-Irish Treaty – would, however, occupy the Irish government until 1923. The major theme of Gwynn's weekly commentary on Irish politics in the *Observer* through the Civil War period was the need for strong government to tackle the anti-Treatyite IRA, as nationalism suffered its most venomous estrangement since the disfiguring fallout of the Parnell split in 1890.

In his piercing study *Ireland*, published in 1924, Gwynn claimed the 'first thing that the Free State had to do was to establish the idea of liberty'. The context indicates that this had nothing to do with IRA violence; rather, the lack of 'liberty' in this analysis was connected with the 'thoroughly bad electoral tradition in Ireland'. 'Up to a time within living memory', Gwynn argued, 'voters were driven to the poll by their landlords' bailiffs under threat of eviction'. During his own political career within the Irish Party, he noted, there was not serious opposition to Home Rule outside of Ulster and Dublin.[3] Electoral competition within the nationalist bloc was, therefore, a relatively new phenomenon within Ireland.[4] The terms of the Treaty committed the new dominion state to holding an election in 1922, but the Sinn Féin Ard-Fheis of February postponed what would inevitably have been a divisive contest. It was a decision that Gwynn bitterly lamented: he strongly asserted that the Treaty must be put to a public vote as soon as possible.[5] The democratic voice of Ireland, which Gwynn believed was resolutely pro-Treaty, should be heard in order to grant the Treatyite elite effective responsibility for the country. While preparing to vacate Dublin Castle, a senior civil servant, Mark Sturgis, noted in his diary 'It is clearly now up to Ireland to make a success of [the settlement] or not'.[6] This was a sentiment shared by Gwynn. 'It may be truthfully said', he declared a few years later, 'that Ireland's education in the practical side of politics began in 1922'.[7]

The clash between the practical and the ideal was one never likely to be adequately resolved within Irish nationalism in the spring of 1922. The only unifying thread between the pro- and anti-Treaty forces was their opposition to partition: this was manipulated by Michael Collins, President of the provisional government, who authorised IRA raids into Northern Ireland in a bid to destabilise Sir James Craig's regime and distract republicanism from its internal problems. This only added impetus to the spiralling sectarian violence within the six counties. The northern bloodshed reached a hideous low with the murder of the entire male line of the McMahon family in Belfast in March, a massacre which was connected to the rogue police district inspector, John Nixon.[8] 'Belfast sends its daily tale of butchery', Gwynn recorded sorrowfully several days later; he believed that the 'need to keep the IRA solid in the North' would prevent Collins from making 'any serious concession to the Northern Parliament'.[9] A dramatic development the following week, however, proved him wrong.

The Craig–Collins pact of 30 March 1922, in the circumstances, was a remarkable achievement. The pact, negotiated under the watchful eye of Winston Churchill, represented a trade-off: Collins would rein in the IRA, while Craig consented to reform the police force in Northern Ireland to make it more representative of northern demographics. Gwynn warmly greeted the pact, which contained what he believed was the *modus operandi* that might yet save both north and south from self-destruction: 'Generous recognition for differing interests without regard to their numerical strength is the saving formula for Ireland'.[10] Gwynn's optimism did not last long, as de Valera and other anti-Treatyites mocked the provisional government's new northern policy, further restricting Collins's room for manoeuvre: taking more direct action, as his biographer notes, would have gained him allies within republicanism, but at the price of breaking the pact.[11] Ultimately, the Craig–Collins pact would be cast aside, with neither side in reality able to deliver on it. But the breakdown of the pact did not stop republican haemorrhaging over the Treaty. On 9 April, Gwynn angrily wrote of his impatience with the new political order: 'All whom I meet – old Nationalists, old Unionists – want evidence that there is a Government in the country, and we have not yet had that evidence'. Confronted with sporadic violence in the south, Gwynn warned that the forces of revolution had not yet finished with Ireland: 'acts of war, acts of civil war, acts of revolution, and acts of murder shade delicately into each other, and once the habit of arguing about cases is established, it is very hard to get lines drawn'.[12] The demarcation of political action became further blurred two weeks later, when anti-Treatyite elements of the IRA, led by Rory O'Connor, occupied the Four Courts in Dublin – in shades of the defensive, and ultimately self-defeating, tactics of the Easter Rising. Gwynn's response set the tone for his *Observer* column for the next year: 'Does the Provisional Government want to cover Ireland with trickling fights between small parties, or is it going to organise a real striking force?' He called on Collins to take over the Irish battalions made redundant by the dissolving of the Union in order to build an experienced and disciplined Free State army – a proposal never likely to be implemented, but one which showed that Gwynn was keen to bring a portion of the old order to which he belonged into the new dispensation.[13]

This also had a special contemporary resonance for Gwynn. In June 1920, 350 soldiers from his old regiment, the Connaught Rangers, staged a rebellion in India in protest against British actions in Ireland. By the time of Gwynn's recommendation, over forty mutineers were still in prison. In the autumn of 1922, Gwynn opened a correspondence with the new Prime Minister, Andrew Bonar Law, in the hope of obtaining the soldiers' freedom. While Bonar Law encountered some resistance within his Cabinet – Lord Derby argued that the Rangers 'were guilty of the most serious form of military offence' – he persevered, and the remaining men were granted an amnesty at the beginning of 1923.[14] 'And so ends the history of the Connaught Rangers', Gwynn wrote affectionately in the *Observer* after their release; 'I am glad anyhow that it ended in a reconciling action'.[15] Reconciling actions were, however, few and far between as Ireland stumbled into the haze of the summer of 1922.

The Civil War

THE first election within the Free State was held in June 1922, granting the electorate of the twenty-six counties an opportunity to pass judgement on the Treaty settlement. They did so strongly in support of the Collins/Griffith administration. Fifty-six pro-Treatyites and thirty-five anti-Treatyites were elected from within Sinn Féin, while the burly re-emergence of sectional interests, such as Labour and the Farmers' Party, was reflected in the return of a number of their candidates – all of whom were fundamentally pro-Treaty. But the tensions over the Treaty now began to produce a deadly fruit. O'Connor led his band of anti-Treatyite IRA men into the Four Courts on 13 April. This act was largely ignored by the provisional government; but the assassination of Field Marshal Henry Wilson, who had been advising the Ulster unionist regime on security matters, by the IRA in London on 22 June fundamentally altered the dynamics of Irish politics. Gwynn decried the killing of Wilson as 'a crime against Ireland' and stoutly called for the provisional government to 'deal at once with the forces of anarchy which exist'.[16] The British government was appalled at the circumstances of Wilson's violent death and demanded action against the anti-Treatyite IRA: the day after the assassination, Sir Nevil Macready, Commander-in-Chief of the British forces in Ireland, was asked by the Prime Minister whether the Four Courts could be recaptured by British troops in retaliation. Macready reasoned that such an action would serve only to unite a large portion of Collins's men with the anti-Treatyites and the loss of civilian life would be blamed on the British.[17] Defying sensitivities in this explosive environment, the anti-Treaty IRA members in the Four Courts proceeded to kidnap the Deputy Chief of Staff of the Free State Army, Ginger O'Connell: Collins's reply was swift and firm. After issuing a demand that the anti-Treatyites vacate the Four Courts and surrender – an order which was, of course, ignored – Collins and Griffith ordered the bombardment of the building with borrowed British field guns. The Civil War had begun.

Gwynn vividly described the scene of the first day of the 'fight for the Four Courts' in the *Observer*, highlighting in particular the incalculable damage to the nation's heritage with destruction of the adjoining Public Record Office:

> On Wednesday afternoon a great multitude of Dublin citizens stood on the quays and watched while a gun, directed by an Irish Government, got its range on the dome of a most beautiful building, in which are piled up irreplaceable materials of our national history, as well as documents, the loss of which will make confusion in every Irish estate. It was disgusting to see – none the less disgusting because the Irish Government had then really no alternative.[18]

Despite the moral support of de Valera, the anti-Treaty IRA did not withstand the artillery assault for long and the Four Courts fell within days. The conflict quickly spread, however, with the counties of Cork, Kerry and Limerick experiencing the highest levels of IRA violence between June 1922 and April 1923. For Gwynn, the 'Irregulars' (as he and many others dubbed the anti-Treatyite IRA) left a trail of destruction more devastating than the hated Black and Tans.[19]

The Free State lost its two most important leaders in August, as Arthur Griffith died of a brain haemorrhage and Michael Collins became the highest-profile victim of the Civil War. Griffith's transformation from fringe journalist to mainstream political figure was one of the more extraordinary personal tales of the Irish revolution. In the days of

Redmond and the Irish Party, Gwynn was frequently a target of Griffith's 'advanced' nationalist journalism, particularly during the debate over compulsory Irish at the founding of the National University. But the revolution turned the Irish political world upside down: Gwynn was now the journalist commenting on Griffith the politician. Unsurprisingly, the Gwynn's eulogy in the pages of the *Observer* carried a mixed message: he praised Griffith's work towards the end of his life while holding no personal liking for him. Gwynn believed that Griffith's death would not affect Ireland politically or militarily: 'His work was done'.[20] The same could not be said of the death of Collins, killed by anti-Treayites in an ambush at Béal-na-Bláth in his native Cork on 22 August 1922. In July, Collins had assumed the title Commander-in-Chief, a move not without controversy, as it was seemingly left to him to define what powers came with the post.[21] John Regan has argued that historians have been slow to identify a short-lived military dictatorship under Collins as the unaccountable Commander-in-Chief, and the reason why Ireland did not suffer a destabilising crisis following his death was that 'Collins was the crisis'.[22] This perhaps places too much of an emphasis on Collins, at the expense of able politicians around the 'Big Fellow', such as William Cosgrave and Kevin O'Higgins, who emerged from his shadow and ultimately steered Ireland to peace while, crucially, anchoring democracy in the political system. Yet the dictatorship charge was one with a level of contemporary currency. 'We have not yet passed out of the revolutionary period', Gwynn wrote five days after Collins's assassination,

> and in all such periods power, held at first by a group, passes to a section of that group, which again often discards a part of itself. The usual end is a dictatorship – actual or virtual. Virtually, when the death of Mr Griffith occurred, we had got to dictatorship of the right kind – that is, a generally and willingly accepted supremacy of one man.[23]

Collins, in this reading, was a 'virtual' if not 'actual' dictator. The essence of Gwynn's immediate reaction to the events at Béal-na-Bláth captured something about the unusual structure of the provisional government – or, at least, the *perception* of the structure.

The government swiftly introduced a programme to crush the rebellious anti-Treatyites. Military courts with the power of execution were established, marking an irreversible turning point of the conflict.[24] Gwynn fully backed the government in its efforts to establish order: he pointed to the example of Northern Ireland, where, as he saw it, a firm security policy had re-introduced relative peace.[25] The execution of five relatively unknown IRA men in November branded a harshness which carried a degree of continuity with the Union administration; after the death of Collins, the new state largely took up from where the British left off in 1921, the only security policy the young heads of the Free State government understood.²⁶ One week later, the stakes were raised by Erskine Childers's appearance before the firing squad, a notable step up from the 'small fry' of the first executions. Childers's sentence shocked the Irish public, as Gwynn noted in the *Observer*. Yet Gwynn believed such an extreme measure was necessary: there was a lethargic spirit within the people, he lamented, which fed into the prolongation of violence.²⁷

With the new Irish administration fighting for its legitimacy – and very survival – the provisional government came to an end one year to the day of the signing of the Treaty, and the Free State enjoyed its official inauguration. Gwynn watched the Free State's first parliamentary meeting from the press box. While observing the unfolding activities of the day, his mind wandered 'to the modest family vault in Wexford, where we left John Redmond'.²⁸ In a Home Rule parliament, with Redmond as Prime Minister, Gwynn could have expected to play a senior role in the first Irish government since the Act of Union; now, following the defeat of Redmondism, the new generation of Irish politicians celebrated their success in achieving self-government without acknowledging the groundwork laid by constitutional nationalism, since the days of Isaac Butt. Gwynn could only look on meekly, a feeling heightened by the naming of the Irish Party's old enemy, Tim Healy, as Governor-General of the Free State. 'Do the ironies of this hour reach the dead, I wonder?', Gwynn mournfully asked.²⁹

Despite the ironies and confusions of life in the Free State, Gwynn did not slacken his tough resolve as the year closed, even after the Irregulars introduced a new dynamic which enlarged the definition of 'legitimate target'. At the end of November 1922, following the first executions carried out by the Free State, the anti-Treatyite IRA commander, Liam Lynch, issued orders that persons in fourteen categories were to be shot on sight and their properties destroyed. The categories included all Dáil deputies who voted for the establishment of military courts, certain members of the upper house of the Irish parliament, and newspaper journalists and publishers who were deemed hostile to the Irregular campaign.³⁰ The Irregulars soon made good on their threat by burning the homes of mostly 'soft' pro-Treatyite targets. On 14 January 1923, Gwynn reported in the *Observer* that Irregulars had destroyed the home of Senator John Bagwell in Tipperary.³¹ The next week he told his readers of the remarkable escape from gunmen of his friend Senator Oliver St John Gogarty. Gwynn's response to these new strategies was uncompromising: what was needed to deliver the deathblow to the Irregulars was a 'hard hand'.³² The Irregulars decided to issue their own rebuke to Gwynn the following week. On the afternoon of 31 January, three young IRA men entered Gwynn's spacious house in Terenure, in the suburbs of Dublin. After ordering the Gwynns' cook and housemaid, the only occupants at the time, out of the property, the Irregulars planted a mine at the heart of the house. Minutes later, the building was destroyed, leaving only a scene of 'utter desolation and ruin'.[33] A claim in the name of May Gwynn was submitted to Dublin County Council in February: in lieu of the ruin of their home, furniture and household goods, the Gwynns sought £6,360 in damages. Disappointingly, they received just over £3,000 the following year.[34]

It could, of course, have been much worse. Father John Ryan, a friend of Gwynn's son Aubrey, believed the *Observer*'s Irish correspondent was perhaps fortunate that he did not receive 'rougher treatment' from the IRA during its earlier campaign against the Crown forces. While teaching philosophy in Louvain in 1920, Aubrey, Ryan told Myles Dillon, 'was expecting to hear of his [Stephen's] murder any moment'.[35] The destruction of his home did little to sway Gwynn's stinging criticisms of the anti-Treatyites; if anything, it heightened his public loathing for their campaign. In his first article after the drama, Gwynn revealed that one of the Irregulars who targeted his property told his maid the attack was a 'reprisal for the execution of some particular man whose name escaped her, and also for "non-sympathy in my articles"'. He remained unrepentant: 'I admit non-sympathy, except with a probably decent little boy who is ordered out to do dirty jobs'. While he took the blow in his stride – 'books suffer very little', he wrote philosophically about the destruction of his library – there was also a latent menace in his words; he pointed to the existence of relative peace in Northern Ireland, and highlighted the Ulster Special Constabulary's role in achieving (or, rather, enforcing) it, and argued that the time had come in the Free State for its 'supporters' to be armed.[36] Two weeks later, he staunchly asserted that there could be 'no surrender to mines or murder'.[37]

The destruction of Gwynn's house was part of a larger campaign aimed mostly, but not exclusively, at well known Anglo-Irish families.[38] In the same week that Gwynn lost his house, the property of Sir Horace Plunkett was targeted; the historic ancestral homes of George Moore and the Desarts were also wrecked. Gwynn was concerned about the sectarian implications of the Irregulars' tactics and the apparent apathy in Ireland to the fate of the 'old gentry'.[39] Yet the sight of burning buildings merely emphasised the Irregulars' military hopelessness, and reliance on terror tactics was never likely to win hearts and minds.

With the republican campaign brutally spluttering to its conclusion, Gwynn debuted a new poem in the *Observer*. Given the ironic title 'A song of victory', the poem was dedicated to the memory of John and Willie Redmond: it marked the beginning of a ruminative exercise for Gwynn, as Ireland neared a sense of normality. The themes of the poem – the tragic loss of the courage and honour of Redmondism, the unnecessary bloodletting commenced by republicanism – ran through his published work during the next few years. The opening of 'A song of victory' is categorically 1916, the setting France:

> Ditches of mud
> Where the boot clung till it tore,
> Snow-cold water thigh-deep,
> Holes in the ground for shelter
> It was not well to be there.

After exalting soldierly virtues and the coming together of the Ulster and Irish brigades, Gwynn recalled the moment when news from Ireland in Easter week filtered through to the front:

> We trod our way to the end;
> We were part of victory:
> And in the face of the world
> Ireland disowned us.
>
> Ditches of blood in Ireland.
> Hate speeding the bullet
> Where man stalked like a beast,
> Aimed, brought down in his quarry,
> Saw him writhing:
> Ditches of blood in Ireland
>
> So in the end they won,
> Won for Ireland.[40]

George Russell wrote later in the year that 'A song of victory' moved him profoundly: Gwynn 'writes on behalf of the generation preceding this who loved Ireland as truly as those who followed after, but with less hatred of enemies'.[41] It was not a great poem in a technical sense, but the lugubrious emotion summoned by 'A song of victory' struck a raw nerve, with its lines mournfully recalling an Ireland lost in the killing fields of Europe. Its composition was stimulated by the need for a therapeutic release as much as the dynamics of artistic creativity.

The Civil War petered out in April 1923 following the death of the anti-Treatyite IRA leader Liam Lynch, and a ceasefire order from de Valera, who somewhat sheepishly sought to reposition himself at the centre of constitutionalism. While Gwynn rather glibly commented that 'Some people miss the murders, I think: the paper seems dull', the conclusion of the anti-Treatyite IRA's campaign against the Free State was universally welcomed.[42] The damage inflicted by national infighting on Ireland's infrastructure and economy was immense; while the human cost of the Irish Civil War was low when compared to other conflicts, the psychological scarring cut deep on all sides.

The burden of history

THE collapse of the republican campaign against the Free State and the relaxing of the security situation opened up a wave of opportunities for national debates on political, civil and cultural issues. Revolution had shaken the foundations of Ireland: it had destroyed the old political elite, weakened the position of the Anglo-Irish element in the south and entrenched partition. It is not a coincidence that this was the period which confirmed Gwynn's marginalisation, as he struggled to find a role in the new dispensation. Gwynn entered his fifty-ninth year in 1923; he spent his remaining twenty-seven years moving restlessly between England and Ireland. The Cosgrave administration keenly appointed leading cultural and literary figures – with a heavy weighting of southern Protestants – to the upper house of the Irish parliament: among the first batch of Senators were W. B. Yeats, Alice Stopford Green and Oliver St John Gogarty. Douglas Hyde soon followed; Gwynn apparently was never considered for nomination. While his past in Redmond's Irish Party was a likely hindrance, the new administration could not have overlooked his sustained critique of Sinn Féin during the War of Independence. For the new generation of politicians, Ireland's foundations were laid in 1916: Irish nationalism before the Rising was largely swept away from the political consciousness, much to Gwynn's chagrin.[43] The memory of the nationalist 'long nineteenth century' – the constitutional struggle that began with Daniel O'Connell and ended with Redmond – was forgotten by the Free State elite; this collective amnesia took decades to wear off.[44]

The *Observer* retained Gwynn's services as its special Ireland correspondent, with his column remaining a weekly fixture until the first half of 1925; it appeared more sporadically thereafter. This was a reflection of both Gwynn's activities – he travelled extensively throughout Ireland and France at different times after 1923 – and the waning interest in Irish affairs in Britain. The sources Gwynn used for information for his commentaries on Free State politics remain unknown, but he appears to have enjoyed a warm relationship with the Minister for Home Affairs, Kevin O'Higgins.[45] Three of Gwynn's most important books were also published during the next few years: *The history of Ireland* (1923), *Ireland* (1924) and his memoir, *Experiences of a literary man* (1926). While this was a literarily productive time for Gwynn, of equal importance in assessing his place in independent Ireland was what he did *not* do. Gwynn carried the mantle of unabashed Redmondism into the post-revolutionary epoch through the medium of his published output; he did not, however, involve himself in a new political party formed in 1926 by Captain William Archer Redmond and Thomas O'Donnell, which harked back to the values of the old Irish Party.

This, though, was in the distant future as the Civil War spluttered to an end. Gwynn was in a hopeful mood over the summer of 1923. Writing about Dublin at the end of June, he noted that the city was at its most cheerful in eighteen months; after spending time in Belfast over the following few weeks, Gwynn gratefully recorded that the annual Twelfth of July festivities passed off peacefully.[46] The sense of normality which was returning to day-to-day life in Ireland represented an intriguing test for the governing party (now rechristened Cumann na nGaedheal) with the dissolution of the Dáil at the end of July. Gwynn pinned his colours to the mast when he publicly backed Major Bryan Cooper, the former unionist MP for South Dublin and a war veteran, who stood (successfully) for the Dáil as an independent. Joining perhaps the most eclectic political platform assembled for some time – Cooper, Yeats and the former unionist Andrew Jameson – Gwynn spoke in glowing terms of his service with the Major in the Connaught Rangers, and his hopes that Cooper could secure election to the Dáil to represent the interests of ex-servicemen and Irish unity.[47] The implication was that Cumann na nGaedheal did not, and could not, represent these interests.

The publication of Gwynn's *Collected poems* in the autumn of 1923 brought a representative sample of his long out-of-print verse back into the public domain, to general acclaim.[48] Gwynn's poetry, dominated by Irish images, is an understated side to his literary profile. While his poetry does not come close to the profundity of his sharply written historical works or literary commentaries, he composed a few verses of merit. These have been largely forgotten, partly because they pale in the shadow of Gwynn's great contemporaries, and the collections tended to have short print runs. 'The ash walk', with its delicate depiction of a Donegal scene, is one such poem which has been undeservedly neglected. One stanza runs:

> A pointed arch in the grey wall
> Leads where the slanting sunbeams fall
> On the white path of river sand,
> And, range in rank, great ash trees stand.
> Not theirs the oak's round massive lines,
> Nor measured symmetry of pines,
> Each, vast yet limber, in his place
> Grows with an undictated grace.
> High soars the feathery cloud of green,
> Light, fluttering, touched with wavering sheen,
> And rifted, where the sky shows through
> In jewelled fretwork, lucent blue.[49]

Gwynn's poetry attracted a diverse audience in his day. For George Russell, Gwynn's power of creative expression was a victim of his dedication to politics: 'in his reveries over gardens we find the real Stephen Gwynn, the man behind the political'.[50] Gwynn also received warm praise for his verse from Edith Somerville, who especially admired 'The ash walk'.[51] At the other end of the political, social and religious scale was Kevin O'Higgins: his biographer recounts that, while in government, O'Higgins spent a restless night searching his house for his copy of *Collected poems*, refusing to go to bed until he had found it and recited the Davis-esque 'A song of defeat' ('Lone, yet unforsaken / Out of no far dim past / Call I the names of the last / Who strove and suffered for Eire'), his particular favourite.[52]

Gwynn travelled through France on a number of occasions from the spring of 1922 to the autumn of 1926, partly to research what became *In praise of France*, published in 1927, and partly to escape Ireland's troubles. He was in France when the *Irish Statesman*, the Dominion League's old journal, was resurrected under the confident editorship of George Russell in September 1923. Gwynn occasionally contributed to its pages, although he avoided the large debates seeking to define a pluralist national culture which saturated its pages. Gwynn's main output remained his *Observer* column, through which he continued to offer thoughtful and, at times, audacious commentaries. When he returned from France in the autumn of 1923, for instance, he waded into a major controversy centred on Northern Ireland. Gwynn issued a harsh rebuttal to Cardinal Logue and the northern Hierarchy, who had condemned the treatment of Catholics under Sir James Craig's administration. Logue's protest listed a number of grievances felt by Catholics in the north: the abolition of proportional representation in local government elections, gerrymandering, discrimination in educational policy and the imposition of an oath of allegiance to the Northern Irish government as well as the King.[53] Gwynn was unsympathetic: 'if it was desired to fight' these issues, 'the proper place to do that was in the Northern Parliament'. Northern nationalism was still boycotting the institution in Belfast established under the Government of Ireland Act; Gwynn believed that this was underpinned by the 'Bishops'. Ireland's recent violent past was also fished for explanations of contemporary troubles in his analysis:

> And as to the oath of allegiance, Sinn Féin honeycombed the British Service in Ireland with persons who thought it honest to conspire actively against the Government which paid them. One cannot expect Sir James Craig and his Ministers to have forgotten that, nor blame them for acting on their memory.[54]

This was an astonishing commentary from a writer with a background in nationalist politics; but if Gwynn's political trajectory is examined over the course of the Irish revolution, it is hardly surprising that he adopted these views in support of the unionist administration which chose to support the Government of Ireland Act. Even later, Gwynn never doubted Craig's sense of 'fair play', despite Craig's clear desire to maintain Unionist Party control over Northern Ireland.[55]

If Gwynn was willing to challenge nationalist orthodoxies in relation to Northern Ireland, the same was also true in the cultural sphere. The conferring of the Nobel Prize for Literature on W. B. Yeats in November 1923 recognised the unique talent of the master poet; the symbolism of an Irish winner so soon after Ireland had achieved independence, as Yeats was fully aware, was also immense.[56] Yeats's famous acceptance speech eliminated the Redmondite tradition of constitutional nationalism from history: Yeats suggested that the cultural, rather than the political, activities of his generation had stirred the soul of Ireland after the fall of Parnell, which created the conditions under which independence could be achieved.[57] Gwynn welcomed his old friend's international recognition with words that cautiously glossed over the Yeatsian rewriting of the past:

> A fine solidarity of comradeship links [Yeats's] work to that of Synge and of Lady Gregory; and he associates with these a younger writer, Mr Lennox Robinson. These people have done more to make Ireland really a nation in Europe than all the organised gunmen – if, indeed, the gunmen have done anything but disunite us.

He challenged Ireland to recognise Yeats as *the* national poet: 'Mr Yeats and those whom he associates with are none the less Irish because they belong to the Anglo-Irish stock. Irish nationality is a real thing, none the less real because it defies definition'.[58] This would become a central theme of Gwynn's post-revolution writings, as ideas of what constituted the 'nation' tussled with the realities of partitioned statehood.

The moderate tone of Gwynn's *History of Ireland*, published at the end of the year, encapsulated the complexities of what 'Irishness' represented in independent Ireland. The book explored a vast territory – over 1,000 years of Irish history – while maintaining a dogged desire to break away from the traditional nationalist interpretation of the past. This permitted a rational discussion of the Cromwellian settlement and a critical analysis of 'Grattan's Parliament'; but the central thrust of Gwynn's *History* stressed the plurality of identities on the island since legendary times and subsequent attempts to reconcile them. While Gwynn came to view his *History* after its publication as 'too stiff for the general reader' (prompting a more accessible abridged version which appeared in 1925 entitled *The student's history of Ireland*), reviews were largely positive.[59] The restrained tone throughout the work was praised, particularly Gwynn's detached handling of those episodes of recent history in which he had been an active participant.[60] The historian Edmund Curtis reviewed the book for the *Irish Statesman*: while he argued that the work was not a 'historian's

FIGURE 5. Nobel laureate, W. B. Yeats, *c.* 1931.

history', as it lacked a full scholarly apparatus and original research, he commended Gwynn's 'well-weighted and dispassionate judgements'.[61] But such a history did not appeal to P. S. O'Hegarty, who queried the book's refusal to define an Irish nation and accused Gwynn of politicising his history.[62] This Gwynn did not deny: as he put it in the book's preface, 'I have studied Irish history as a means to understand my own country, in which I have lived long and travelled much, about which I have written much, and for which I have worked; and in so far as I have felt able to interpret the past, it has always been in the light of the present which I knew'.[63] With his focus on the end result of history, the tenor of Gwynn's *The history of Ireland* should be clear: it was a text which exonerated the constitutional nationalist tradition in Ireland from the failures of the republican political revolution. It is unsurprising, then, that the book was savaged in more extreme nationalist circles. The *Catholic Bulletin*, the *über*-zealous monthly, commissioned a two-part assault on *The history of Ireland*, in which Gwynn was accused of employing a 'suave' writing style to produce a piece of 'racial propaganda' which subtly affirmed the inferiority of the Catholic 'Gael' against the more 'civilised' Anglicising elements of Ireland and England.[64] While the *Catholic Bulletin* was hardly a representative mainstream journal, the ferocity of its attacks on Gwynn as well as other public Irish Protestant figures came at a sensitive time in national explorations of identity and culture, and ultimately reinforced post-revolutionary differences.[65]

Insecurity defined the cultural politics of the Free State's first decade: Cumann na nGaedheal was sensitive to charges of compromising the Irish republican political programme and so reflexively pushed the Gaelicisation programme. Compulsory Irish was soon introduced in the school curriculum; but the ideals of the Gaelic League were not realised, as enthusiasm for the language was not ignited by forced learning and Gaeltacht areas suffered from dwindling numbers. Compulsory Irish was perhaps the issue which most estranged Protestants in southern Ireland, particularly those of an intellectual hue, as the eminent Trinity College Dublin historian R. B. McDowell and the journalist and writer Brian Inglis later testified.[66] Gwynn, who lost the argument against compulsory Irish in the National University in 1909, was not surprised that such a policy was adopted by the government, but he focused more on attacking the excesses of the language zeal than critiquing the principles behind it. In July 1924, he struck out at an amendment placed in the Railway Bill, which forced all stations to put up bilingual name signs and required all tickets to be printed in Irish. As the majority of Irish people could not speak or read Irish, Gwynn argued, this proposal was 'silly and wasteful'. The language should be revived, he argued, only 'for reasons of sentiment and cultural value': the resources needed to change the signs in every station in Ireland would be better spent in promoting meaningful educational and research uses of Irish.[67] The lack of a meaningful language programme fed into Gwynn's critique of Irish intellectual life – or the lack of it – more generally during the first decade of independence.

This critique of Free State policy received another airing later in 1924 with the publication of Gwynn's major snap-shot study *Ireland*. The book provided the first truly in-depth study of Ireland since the revolution: arranged thematically, each chapter gave Gwynn scope to write at length about such topics as the Irish nation, education, the churches and the language movement. The heart of the book, though, was the loss of national unity, territorially and culturally: 'as a nation, Ireland stands incomplete. The division which mars her unity has on the map a geographical aspect; but its causes are not geographical, and the real division is not limited by any territorial boundary'.[68] Readers who followed Gwynn's weekly *Observer* articles would have been familiar with much of the material in *Ireland*. The crudeness of compulsory Irish, the divisive nature of the revolution: these were well established themes of Gwynn's modern canon. What was particularly striking about the book was, however, the resurrection of the old Irish Party tradition.

Gwynn rejected any notion that Irish freedom gestated between 1916 and 1921: it was the Irish Party, over forty years of constitutional struggle, which paved the path that the IRA would ultimately spatter in blood. It was Parnell who 'did more than any one man to carry the Irish people to freedom'; Redmond 'represented the sane and normal mind of Ireland better than any man in her public life today'.[69] In Gwynn's reading, the revolution started with the founding of the Land League;[70] the violent upheavals that preceded the birth of the Free State would forever tarnish nationalism, representing nothing more than an ugly blip on Ireland's journey to self-rule. Bringing the book to a conclusion, Gwynn issued a thunderous critique of modern Irish nationalism:

> Forty-five years ago, when the revolution began, we in Ireland did not know where the real heart of the difficulty lay.... Some thought the essential was to be rid of landlordism: landlordism has gone, and the problem remains. Some thought it was British rule, and some still think so yet; yet the Irish Free State exists, it is Irish, and it is free, and it has, with Great Britain's full concurrence, the rank of a nation. Stripped down to its ultimate elements, the problem stands clear: how to reconcile the ideals, the traditions, and the purposes of two races and blend them into one, so that 'Irish' shall be no longer a word of ambiguous meaning, but equally applicable to all citizens of a free and united country.[71]

Criticism came from a predictable quarter: the *Catholic Bulletin* again dedicated two articles to a Gwynn text.[72] Like its treatment of *The history of Ireland*, the *Bulletin* angrily focused on what it read as the subtext to Gwynn's new work, accusing him of foisting a benign respectability on the Anglo-Irish presence in Ireland over the centuries and diminishing the virtues of the Gael. 'His method of historical doping is carried out by means of a hypodermic needle', ranted the *Bulletin*: 'Doctrinal injection brings out all his suave dexterity'.[73]

Self-reflections

IN July 1926, Shan Bullock wrote to the Ulster poet Richard Rowley to complain about what he saw as Gwynn's lack of direction: 'I am not satisfied about Gwynn. He wastes himself and his gifts. Always on the rush.... He is a born literary man. Yet he is always after other things – and he has one obsession that hinders him greatly. However, it is his life and no doubt he enjoys it'.[74] The 'obsession' was politics; the irony was that when Bullock wrote these words, Gwynn was slowing his involvement in this sphere and restyling himself as a man of letters once more. This was as much from necessity as choice. The space the *Observer* gave to Irish affairs from 1926 was seriously curtailed: Gwynn contributed just ten articles to the paper during the year. Kevin O'Higgins was perhaps on the mark when he suggested to Gwynn that 'the closing down of the *Observer* column indicates that we are becoming less morbidly interesting to English readers'.[75] But Gwynn also chose not to re-involve himself in active politics when former members of the Irish Party launched a new movement in September. By the end of the year, he published his memoir: its title, *Experiences of a literary man*, spoke volumes.

Gwynn's move away from the purely political coincided with the new state's consolidation after its first few difficult years. While the conservative Boundary Commission report of 1925 did not satisfy nationalist opinion, the Free State's decision tacitly to accept the existing border put the issue to rest for the time being. Gwynn was quick to point out the advantages of this solution. With the Irish boundary accepted by both sides, the Free State could, in his view, get on with governing without the distraction of the north, while northern nationalists would not be weakened by a loss of heartlands to the south. This boded well, he hypothesised, for the development of parliamentary democracy in the two Irelands, and for the prospects for their coming together in the future.[76] Until that day, Gwynn was content to give his support to Cumann na nGaedheal. He supported the government in the aftermath of the Army Mutiny in 1924, which ended the IRB's dominance of the officer classes of the National Army – 'a relic of revolution', as Gwynn put it.[77] He corresponded with Kevin O'Higgins on this matter, agreeing with the Minister of Home Affairs' argument that the National Army needed to root out the secret society in its midst.[78]

At the beginning of 1926, Gwynn addressed the Oxford Luncheon Club on the topic of 'present-day Ireland', where he extolled the stabilising virtues of the Cumann na nGaedheal government.[79] The following week, though, his name was connected with a parliamentary vacancy in Dublin caused by the death of Darrell Figgis.[80] The rumours came to nothing, but Gwynn's political appetite seemed high as he issued an energetic attack on the ethos of the Easter Rising on its tenth anniversary. It was his most dramatic commentary since the signing of the Treaty: while Gwynn praised Cumann na nGaedheal, he remained a savage critic of the process which had brought the party to power. The leaders of the Rising, in his pensive observation, blended the explosively divisive combination of hatred and politics:

> perhaps there is no use in speculating on what might have come about, had they not unchained old hates. Only it is well to remember that the right of self-government had been conceded in principle.... The main objection taken to it [Home Rule] was a pledge given that Ulster should not be forced under a Dublin Government. By the methods which flowed from the Rising, Ulster has been more completely separated than was ever contemplated when Ulster demanded the pledge.

Echoing the self-critical motif of *John Redmond's last years*, Gwynn admitted that 'the fault was partly our own': the Irish Party should have conceded the right of self-determination to Ulster unionism. Partition will last forever, Gwynn warned, 'if Ireland is to be pinned to the Republican aim set out by that handful in 1916'. The War of Independence dragged Ireland through 'Hell', and the violent excesses of the revolutionary period left the country dejected and ungrateful to the party which restored order. Ireland did not possess heroes anymore.[81]

Gwynn's Easter message coincidently pre-empted a rallying call to nationalism's old guard by Captain William Archer Redmond. Speaking at a memorial service to his uncle, Redmond appealed to the crowd to 'come with me and we will fight as we fought before'. The Irish National League was founded in September 1926, styling itself as an alternative to Cumann na nGaedheal. While Redmond was the League's nominal head, another former Irish Party MP, Thomas O'Donnell, did much of its organisational legwork. During the first few months of 1926, O'Donnell canvassed the opinion of his former comrades with regard to the foundation of a new political party.[82] Despite John Dillon's characteristic pessimism, O'Donnell received encouraging support.[83] Most prominently, Henry Harrison, the perennial Irish journeyman, defected from Cumann na nGaedheal to the National League at its foundation.[84] Gwynn's attitude to these developments remains ambiguous: he certainly was not as forthcoming in active support for the National League as Redmond and O'Donnell would have perhaps predicted. His name was attached to a list of supporters prior to the League's official launch, but he did not involve himself in any organisational sense.[85] He was asked by the League to address a meeting in the winter: the reply, if there was one, has not survived, but Gwynn did not attend.[86] His contribution to the cause was one article in the *Observer*. 'It is necessary to give these discontented voters a reasonable alternative'. Gwynn made no attempt to communicate the party's ideas beyond the gnomic phrase 'the existing policy can be better administered'.[87]

Gwynn seemingly lacked the appetite for a return to frontline politics in 1926. Besides emitting a palpable indifference to the National League, he also did not involve himself in Yeats's boldly ambitious plan to establish a 'National Unionist Party' in the wake of the poet's notorious divorce speech to the Irish Senate in 1925.[88] The most politically active of the Irish Party's final generation, Gwynn was the man who founded the Irish Centre Party immediately after the 1918 general election, and attempted to create another moderate organisation in 1921 to contest the Government of Ireland Act elections. But Ireland now had self-rule, both sides of the border; a new political elite, much younger than the remnants of the Irish Party, had solidified the new independent state and ensured its constitutional position was protected against republicanism. Despite his sustained critique of how the Irish revolution had unfolded, Gwynn recognised that the task of Irish nationalism was almost complete. Ireland had won the institutions of self-government, but needed to unite the territory – and people – of the island to achieve full nationhood.[89] He realised that this was not his task: ending partition was for later generations.

There were, however, things still to be said. Gwynn's memoir, *Experiences of a literary man*, was published towards the end of 1926. Its opening gambit is characteristically endearing:

> I was brought up to think myself Irish, without question or qualification; but the new nationalism prefers to describe me and the like of me as Anglo-Irish.... So all my life I have been spiritually hyphenated without knowing it: and since there are a good many like me I shall try and explain how much and how little that means.[90]

P. S. O'Hegarty later told Gwynn that the term 'Anglo-Irish' did not imply a racial difference, but was used to differentiate works of literature.[91] But Gwynn was unconvinced, believing that modern Irishness, with its Gaelic and Catholic ethos, excluded Protestants from the nation. His memoir rejoiced in his family connection with Irish high kings and his mix of Gaelic and planter blood.[92] His essential point was that there was no uniform profile of Irishness: the country should cherish its divergent blood types, united in the common bonds of nationality.

Experiences is a glowing account of Gwynn's life up to 1906 but, as its introduction suggests, bears the cultural scars of post-revolutionary Ireland. It tells of his upbringing in Donegal, school days in Dublin, university education in Oxford, school-mastering around England, literary activities in London and finally his return to Ireland. It offers no account of his political career, the Great War or the Irish revolutionary years. This was not his intention: he merely ran out of room. He did, in fact, write a second volume of memoirs for the same publisher, Thornton Butterworth, but it was never published. In 1936, Gwynn submitted a manuscript to Butterworth with the title 'From Westminster to Flanders', but received what he described as a 'querulous report' from the firm's reader. After making alterations, Gwynn found that the contract had been terminated. He offered the proposed book to Macmillan, but frustratingly nothing came of it.[93] This potential 'Experiences of a political man' remains lost; the symbolism of this should not be underestimated. Following the publication of *Experiences of a literary man*, Gwynn committed himself to purely literary pursuits, taking no part in political activities beyond the occasional article for the *Observer* and public lecture. *Experiences* represented a turning point in his life, coming full circle to where he began. His finest works after 1926 would be historical and literary biographies; it is no coincidence that his subjects – Henry Grattan, Jonathan Swift, Oliver Goldsmith – were classic examples of the eighteenth-century Anglo-Irish at their height. Despite his protestations regarding the label, Gwynn, like his great contemporary Yeats, came to identify more with the Anglo-Irish *mentalité* during independent Ireland's first few decades.

Contemporary reviewers of *Experiences* praised Gwynn's crisp narrative, the prose of an established essayist. Robert Lynd identified 'a strain of melancholy running through it, for, in immoderate days it fell to Mr Gwynn to play the ungrateful part of the moderate man'.[94] Despite his position on the losing side of a revolution, Gwynn's memoir was, according to his cousin W. F. P. Stockley, 'so unembittered, so forgetful of wrongs'.[95] John St Loe Strachey, whose attitude to Gwynn had greatly warmed in response to the toughness of his *Observer* articles during the War of Independence and the Civil War, sent Gwynn a letter congratulating him on the book, one with 'not a trace of egotism or self-complacency'.[96] The incisive former literary editor of the *Freeman's Journal*, J. W. Good, probed *Experiences* in the pages of the *Irish Statesman*: 'If the volume has a moral, which Mr Gwynn I imagine would deny, it is the absurdity of making party badges and labels acid tests of nationality, oblivious of the fact that the cross-divisions accepted by one generation are repudiated by the next'.[97] It is not clear that Gwynn would have denied this moral. Yet he was certain that nationality was not a political matter.

Notes

1 Stephen Gwynn, 'Hatred', in *Fond opinions* (London: Frederick Muller, 1938), p. 37.
2 *Irish Independent*, 16 January 1922.
3 Stephen Gwynn, *Ireland* (London: Ernest Benn, 1924), pp. 197–8.
4 This is not to downplay O'Brienism, but candidates associated with William O'Brien tended to cluster around constituencies in Munster.
5 *Observer*, 26 February 1922.
6 Mark Sturgis, *The last days of Dublin Castle: the Mark Sturgis diaries*, ed. Michael Hopkinson (Dublin: Irish Academic Press, 1999), p. 227 (15 January 1922).
7 Gwynn, *Ireland*, p. 197.
8 Alan F. Parkinson, *Belfast's unholy war: the troubles of the 1920s* (Dublin: Four Courts Press, 2004), pp. 229–39. Nixon's involvement in the murders has never been categorically proved – or, indeed disproved. He later went on to enjoy a lengthy career as an Independent Unionist for the Woodvale district of Belfast in the Northern Irish parliament: for this, see Colin Reid, 'Protestant challenges to the "Protestant state": Ulster unionism and independent unionism in Northern Ireland, 1921–1939', *Twentieth Century British History*, 19:4 (2008), pp. 419–45.
9 *Observer*, 26 March 1922.

10 *Observer*, 2 April 1922.
11 Peter Hart, *Mick: the real Michael Collins* (London: Macmillan, 2005), p. 383.
12 *Observer*, 9 April 1922.
13 *Observer*, 23 April 1922.
14 Stephen Gwynn to Andrew Bonar Law, 31 October [1922]; Andrew Bonar Law to Stephen Gwynn, 29 November 1922; Lord Derby to Andrew Bonar Law, 12 December 1922; Andrew Bonar Law to Stephen Gwynn, 17 December 1922; Stephen Gwynn to Andrew Bonar Law, 20 December [1922], Andrew Bonar Law papers, Parliamentary Archives, London (PAL), BL/114/1–13.
15 *Observer*, 7 January 1923. Also see Stephen Gwynn, 'Irish soldiers and Irish brigades', *Cornhill Magazine*, December 1922, pp. 737–49.
16 *Observer*, 25 June 1922.
17 Nevil Macready, *Annals of an active life* (London: Hutchinson and Co., two vols, n.d. [1942]), vol. II, pp. 652–3.
18 *Observer*, 2 July 1922.
19 *Observer*, 30 July 1922.
20 *Observer*, 13 August 1922.
21 Hart, *Mick*, p. 401.
22 John M. Regan, 'Michael Collins, General Commander-in-Chief, as a historiographical problem', *History*, 92:307 (2007), p. 346.
23 *Observer*, 27 August 1922.
24 Michael Hopkinson, *Green against green: the Irish Civil War* (Dublin: Gill and Macmillan, 1988), p. 181.
25 *Observer*, 22 October 1922.
26 Eunan O'Halpin, *Defending Ireland: the Irish state and its enemies since 1922* (Oxford: Oxford University Press, 1999), p. 30.
27 *Observer*, 3 December 1922. Also see Richard English, *Irish freedom: the history of nationalism in Ireland* (London: Macmillan, 2006), p. 312.
28 *Observer*, 10 December 1922.
29 *Ibid*.
30 Joseph M. Curran, *The birth of the Irish Free State 1921–1923* (Alabama: University of Alabama Press, 1980), p. 260.
31 *Observer*, 14 January 1923.
32 *Observer*, 21 January 1923. For this incident, see J. B. Lyons, *Oliver St John Gogarty: the man of many talents: a biography* (Dublin: Blackwater Press, 1980), pp. 127–8.
33 *Freeman's Journal*, 2 February 1923.
34 *Freeman's Journal*, 22 February 1923 and 2 April 1924.
35 Father John Ryan to Myles Dillon, 14 February 1923, in Joachim Fischer and John Dillon (eds), *The correspondence of Myles Dillon 1922–1925: Irish–German relations and Celtic studies* (Dublin: Four Courts Press, 1999), p. 92.
36 *Observer*, 4 February 1923.
37 *Observer*, 18 February 1923.
38 See the pamphlet *A record of some mansions and houses destroyed, 1922–23*, which was published by the Irish Claims Compensation Association. There is a copy of the pamphlet in the Andrew Bonar Law papers, PAL, BL/144/1/45.
39 *Observer*, 11 March 1923.
40 *Observer*, 18 March 1923; reprinted in Stephen Gwynn, *Collected poems* (Edinburgh: William Blackwood and Sons, 1923), pp. 39–47.
41 *Irish Statesman*, 13 October 1923.
42 *Observer*, 20 May 1923.
43 *Observer*, 9 March 1925.
44 David Fitzpatrick, 'Commemoration in the Irish Free State: a chronicle of

embarrassment', in Ian McBride (ed.), *History and memory in modern Ireland* (Cambridge: Cambridge University Press, 2001), pp. 184–203.
45 Kevin O'Higgins to Stephen Gwynn, n.d. [1926], Stephen Gwynn papers, National Library of Ireland (NLI), MS 8600 (13).
46 *Observer*, 1 and 15 July 1923.
47 *Irish Times*, 25 August 1923. Also see Lennox Robinson, *Bryan Cooper* (London: Constable and Co., 1931), pp. 142–6.
48 *Freeman's Journal*, 6 October 1923; *Irish Independent*, 24 September 1923; *Observer*, 23 September 1923; *Irish Times*, 8 February 1924.
49 Gwynn, *Collected poems*, p. 1.
50 *Irish Statesman*, 13 October 1923.
51 Edith Somerville to Stephen Gwynn, 21 March 1925, Stephen Gwynn papers, NLI, MS 8600 (16).
52 Terence de Vere White, *Kevin O'Higgins* (London: Methuen and Co., 1948), p. 239.
53 Patrick Buckland, *The factory of grievances: devolved government in Northern Ireland 1921–39* (Dublin: Gill and Macmillan, 1979), pp. 221ff.
54 *Observer*, 21 October 1923. Also see *Observer*, 11 November 1923.
55 St John Ervine, *Craigavon: Ulsterman* (London: George Allen and Unwin, 1949), p. 563. Gwynn seems to have enjoyed a friendly relationship with Craig, and he presented him with a book in 1927. Lord Craigavon to Stephen Gwynn, 16 May 1927, Stephen Gwynn papers, NLI, MS 8600 (3).
56 R. F. Foster, *W. B. Yeats: a life. Vol. II: The arch-poet* (Oxford: Oxford University Press, 2003), p. 245.
57 W. B. Yeats, *Autobiographies*, ed. William H. O'Donnell and Douglas N. Archibald (Basingstoke: Palgrave, 1999), p. 410.
58 *Observer*, 18 November 1923.
59 Stephen Gwynn to George A. Macmillan, 13 November [1924], Macmillan archive, British Library (BL), box M44.
60 *Irish Independent*, 24 December 1923; *Connacht Tribune*, 29 December 1923; *Irish Times*, 11 January 1924; *Studies*, 13 (March 1924), pp. 161–3; *Observer*, 23 December 1923.
61 *Irish Statesman*, 5 January 1924.
62 *Freeman's Journal*, 26 January 1924.
63 Stephen Gwynn, *The history of Ireland* (London: Macmillan and Co., 1923), p. vi.
64 *Catholic Bulletin*, January and February 1924.
65 Margaret O'Callaghan, 'Language, nationality and cultural identity in the Irish Free State, 1922–7: the *Irish Statesman* and the *Catholic Bulletin* reappraised', *Irish Historical Studies*, 24:94 (1984), p. 235. For the *Catholic Bulletin*'s hounding of Yeats, see Foster, *The arch-poet*, pp. 255–6.
66 R. B. McDowell, *McDowell on McDowell: a memoir* (Dublin: Lilliput Press, 2008), p. 75; Brian Inglis, *West Briton* (London: Faber and Faber, 1962), p. 27.
67 *Observer*, 13 July 1924.
68 Stephen Gwynn, *Ireland* (London: Ernest Benn, 1924), p. 12.
69 *Ibid.*, pp. 37, 222.
70 *Ibid.*, p. 47.
71 *Ibid.*, pp. 218–19.
72 *Catholic Bulletin*, November and December 1924.
73 *Catholic Bulletin*, November 1924.
74 Shan Bullock to Richard Rowley, 27 July 1926, quoted in Robert Greacen, *Rooted in Ulster: nine northern writers* (Belfast: Lagan Press, 2000), p. 21. Greacen quotes from five letters between Bullock and Rowley from 1924–31,

which are held in private hands. The present author has been unable to trace them.
75 Kevin O'Higgins to Stephen Gwynn, n.d. [1926], Stephen Gwynn papers, NLI, MS 8600 (13).
76 *Observer*, 6 December 1925.
77 *Observer*, 16 March 1924.
78 Kevin O'Higgins to Stephen Gwynn, 26 March 1924, Stephen Gwynn papers, NLI, MS 8600 (13); *Observer*, 30 March 1924.
79 *Irish Independent*, 26 January 1926.
80 *Irish Times*, 4 February 1926.
81 *Observer*, 4 April 1926.
82 J. Anthony Gaughan, *A political odyssey: Thomas O'Donnell: MP for West Kerry 1900–1918* (Dublin: Kingdom Books, 1983), p. 149.
83 John Dillon to Thomas O'Donnell, 17 June 1926, Thomas O'Donnell papers, NLI, MS 15,461 (1).
84 Minutes of Irish National League meeting, 1 October 1926, Thomas O'Donnell papers, NLI, MS 16,186.
85 *Irish Independent*, 8 September 1926.
86 Thomas O'Donnell to Stephen Gwynn, 30 November 1926, Thomas O'Donnell papers, NLI, MS 15,461 (5).
87 *Observer*, 12 September 1926.
88 Foster, *The arch-poet*, pp. 299, 719, n. 16.
89 Gwynn, *Ireland*, p. 33.
90 Stephen Gwynn, *Experiences of a literary man* (London: Thornton Butterworth, 1926), p. 11.
91 P. S. O'Hegarty to Stephen Gwynn, 16 October 1929, Stephen Gwynn papers, NLI, MS 8600 (13).
92 Gwynn, *Experiences*, pp. 11–13.
93 Stephen Gwynn to Macmillan, 11 July [1936], Macmillan archive, BL, box M44.
94 *Observer*, 19 December 1926.
95 *Irish Monthly*, September 1927.
96 John St Loe Strachey to Stephen Gwynn, 15 December 1926, Stephen Gwynn papers, NLI, MS 8600 (16).
97 *Irish Statesman*, 15 January 1927.

9
Experiences of a literary man
1927–50

It is no fun to outlive one's generation. (Stephen Gwynn to Harold Macmillan, 1944)[1]

WITH the publication of *Experiences of a literary man*, and a reluctance to participate in the political programme of the Redmondite-tinged National League, Gwynn crossed a personal Rubicon. His had been a political mind, single-minded in its pursuit of self-government and a unified Ireland since the years of the Great War; in his sixty-third year, Gwynn re-dedicated himself to writing. As the scale and range of the works he produced from 1927 to his death in 1950 testify, this was in literary terms the most intensely productive stage of a busy life. The absence of politics resulted in a scattering of his creative energies, as he tirelessly moved from literary project to literary project, straddling a range of genres and styles. The later stages of Gwynn's life echoed the pattern of his early days, before politics became an obsession, as he relentlessly worked on travel guides and literary and historical criticisms. He rekindled his relationship with the Macmillan Company, reading manuscripts for the publishing house. Gwynn also moved continuously between Ireland and England. Completing the symmetry with Gwynn's earlier life was a return to school-mastering in the late 1930s, the profession he detested in the 1890s.

Gwynn thus stood aloof from the major political and cultural battles that defined the Irish experience of self-government from the foundation of the Free State to the declaration of the Republic in 1949. Hubert Butler, then a young emerging voice of the Anglo-Irish tradition, later painted a cheerless picture of the lack of plurality in the public space of the Free State, and delineated Ireland between the collapse of George Russell's *Irish Statesman* in 1930 and the foundation of Sean O'Faolain's *The Bell* in 1940 as a cultural wasteland. With the likes of Russell and Plunkett dejectedly leaving Ireland for England, it was O'Faolain who, in Butler's words, saved the 'nobody's children' of the dwindling Anglo-

Irish intelligentsia.[2] Gwynn's contribution to *The Bell*, as it was to the *Statesman*, was limited to only a few articles, which appeared towards the end of his life. While Yeats produced some of his greatest poems in the 1930s, the mantle of Anglo-Irish literature was passing to a younger generation of authors, such as O'Faolain, Frank O'Connor and Denis Johnston. While admiring the breadth of Gwynn's life's work (not least his amorism), O'Faolain for one believed that the former MP 'found us younger men much too unconventional for his taste'.[3] The age of the late Victorian man of letters had most definitely passed.

New directions

WHILE he was immensely productive in the last decades of his life, it is difficult to 'place' Gwynn in the literary culture of independent Ireland. Unshackled from politics, unity of thought was difficult to sustain across the genres which preoccupied him; finding a personal niche within the new state proved impossible and he made relatively few public appearances. He remained a supporter of the Cosgrave administration, which he praised for its courage in steering the twenty-six counties through the post-revolution turbulence, while remaining critical of the forces that brought Cumann na nGaedheal into being.[4] Partition remained a blot on the map of nationalist Ireland and the failure of a common identity to germinate remained of deep concern to Gwynn. Rather than providing a temporary means to reconcile Irish differences and to promote moderation on both sides of the border, partition merely entrenched the disparities and permitted space for their growth. As the *Observer*'s editor, J. L. Garvin, affirmed to Gwynn, 'the self-conscious polarisation of opposite mentalities ... is going on here before our eyes'.[5] For very different reasons, Gwynn was as alienated from contemporary Ireland as the republican intellectual Ernie O'Malley. Their two ideals – Redmondite nationalism and revolutionary purity – were both compromised and destroyed by the realities of Irish life in the 1920s and 1930s.[6] Gwynn's was one lost Ireland among many.

Not that this hindered his desire to write. Despite moving restlessly between two addresses in Dublin and London over the next few years, Gwynn immersed himself in a range of literary projects, often working on several at any given time. During the later 1920s, he produced an imposing two-volume edition of letters of his distant kinsman (whom he never met), the British diplomat Sir Cecil Spring Rice. Gwynn's plea for three volumes was rejected by the American publisher, Houghton Mifflin; even then, they were 'a little staggered' by the 520,000-word manuscript he submitted in 1928.[7] Spring Rice was the British ambassador to the United States during the Great War; the large collection of letters that make up Gwynn's volumes reveal a man adept at diplomacy, with a genuine humane touch. The medium of private letters written during the period of the Great War was one to which Gwynn returned in the mid-1930s, with the publication of *The anvil of war: letters between F. S. Oliver and his brother 1914–1918*. Oliver, the champion of imperial federation, died in 1934, and Gwynn was enlisted by his widow to compile a lasting monument to his political thought. Gwynn wrote warmly about his late friend, claiming he had 'a genius for friendship', and outlined his contribution to the political culture of his lifetime.[8] The main thread of the letters was Oliver's passionate support of national service and his ideal of a conscripted 'New Model Army'.[9] While the volume was generally welcomed, it was savaged by one of Oliver's ideological opponents. Describing Oliver as little more than 'a stupid man', an anonymous reviewer in the *Manchester Guardian* condemned him as 'a fascist in embryo', reflecting how dramatically political culture and language had changed from the heady days of Edwardian Britain to the fearful mid-1930s.[10]

The *Observer* continued to offer an outlet for Gwynn, but on a drastically reduced level from the early 1920s. Between 1927 and 1932, Gwynn contributed to the pages of the *Observer* more as a book reviewer than as a feature writer. The spirit of the old Irish Party was not far from many of his writings for the paper, overtly and covertly. Gwynn penned a heartfelt tribute to his former parliamentary colleague 'Long' John O'Connor upon his death in 1928, in which he expressed his fondness for the gregarious ex-Fenian.[11] Similar sentiments were professed for Tim Healy, the maverick former MP and the Free State's first Governor-General, after his death in 1931. While Healy was more against John Redmond than with him, Gwynn recognised his genius for public life. The point was not lost on Gwynn that it was Healy – the independent nationalist, non-Redmondite and 'a leaderless man' – who emerged as 'the only one of the old fighters who found a part to play' within the new state.[12] Redmondism was resurrected during an interview Gwynn conducted with President of the Executive Council, William Cosgrave, in December 1931, on the tenth anniversary of the Treaty. In the resulting *Observer* article, Gwynn praised Cosgrave's courage in the face of the continuing IRA threat and the rise of Éamon de Valera's Fianna Fáil, and commented that Redmond would have approved of the course plotted by the Cumann na nGaedheal government.[13] Gwynn backed the pragmatic Cosgrave on the eve of the 1932 general election; he feared that the coming of Fianna Fáil would be catastrophic for Anglo-Irish relations, the Irish economy and the hope of building bridges to Ulster unionism.[14] His trepidation was realised with the first handover of power in the Free State, as de Valera claimed the presidency of the Executive Council. Gwynn reported on this landmark occasion for the *Observer*, but the angry tone which saturated his article landed him and the paper in legal trouble. Headed 'The Free State polls: a decisive verdict: the return of the gunman', Gwynn took particular offence at the election of Dan Breen under the Fianna Fáil banner: 'I had thought Ireland wanted to hear no more of the gunmen, but Tipperary has returned, at the head of the poll, Mr Dan Breen, who in his day was the gunman *par excellence*'.[15] Breen, a former IRA man, had previously been a target of Gwynn's pen. On the release of Breen's memoirs, *My fight for Irish freedom*, in 1924, Gwynn lampooned the fact that several thousand copies were sold across Ireland in a few months. 'Mr Dan Breen, most famous of gunmen, has done something more difficult than shooting policemen', wisecracked Gwynn; 'he has made Ireland buy a book'.[16] Breen let this quip pass without comment; but as a public representative in 1932, he did not ignore Gwynn's second slander. Several months after the 1932 election, Breen filed for £10,000 damages for alleged libel against Gwynn and the *Observer* at the High Court in Dublin, citing the (dubious) fact that the article implied that the Tipperary Teachta Dála (TD) would 'force Mr de Valera, as head of the State, to support, connive or condone the assassination of those opposed to or who gave evidence against the IRA'.[17] Gwynn and the newspaper strongly denied that the report impugned Breen, but constituted a 'fair and *bona-fide*' expression of opinion.[18] The case was dropped in November, with Breen accepting an undisclosed settlement.[19] Gwynn's contributions to the *Observer* notably slackened further during and after the case, leaving him only an occasional opinion writer and book reviewer for the paper after 1932.

Gwynn was, in truth, writing little about politics in the Free State (or Northern Ireland for that matter) before the Breen case. He complained in 1931 that the Dáil was 'rather a drab assembly': 'It has not had eloquence, and, above all, it has had very few scenes'.[20] This viewpoint was amplified by a glib comment in the introduction to his travel guide *The charm of Ireland*, published a few years later: 'the stranger in Ireland has nothing to be afraid of. We are peaceable now to the point of dullness'.[21] Gwynn instead filled his days with literary pursuits. He re-entered the Macmillan orbit, reading and correcting numerous manuscripts for the house from the 1920s to the 1940s. This offered a regular, if fluctuating, income, ranging from £15 for revising submitted manuscripts (such as pruning Lady Minto's colossal *India, Minto and Morley, 1905–1910*),[22] to three guineas for reporting on individual book proposals. The final major work he revised was E. H. Carr's seminal *The twenty years' crisis, 1919–1939*.[23] Gwynn also used his rekindled relationship with Macmillan to aid members of his family, recommending works by his brother Charles and his son Aubrey for publication.[24] Success was forthcoming for Charles: the recently retired major-general published *Imperial policing* through Macmillan in 1934, a book which provided an insight into the policing functions of the British Army across the Empire. Oddly,

FIGURE 6. Sketch of Stephen Gwynn, by Hooper Rowe.

perhaps, the example of Ireland was missing from the book.[25] Aubrey, however, was less fortunate than his uncle: his bibliography contains no work published by Macmillan. Gwynn himself did not publish many books through Macmillan during his final decades, and his position as a reader for the firm did not guarantee success on his own proposals. The company turned down a second volume of his memoirs, as well as an idea Gwynn had for 'a study of Ireland from the death of Parnell to the death of Yeats', both rejected in 1940. With obvious parallels to F. S. L. Lyons's scholarly study published in 1979, *Culture and anarchy in Ireland* (which had the same bookends), Gwynn's 'Ireland since Parnell' (his provisional title) proposed to tie literature and politics together in the half century under scrutiny to produce a 'lively' account of Ireland's revolutionary moment.[26] The book never saw the light of day.

A great number of books did, however, come to completion from the late 1920s to the 1940s. The most important – and numerous – of these were biographical treatments of a range of figures, historical and contemporary. In chronological order of publication, Gwynn wrote about the lives of: the Antarctic explorer Captain Robert Falcon Scott; the Scottish novelist and poet Sir Walter Scott; the eighteenth-century politician and writer Horace Walpole; the English explorer, and Gwynn family friend, Mary Kingsley; the satirist Jonathan Swift; the Scottish explorer Mungo Park; the Anglo-Irish writer Oliver Goldsmith; the Protestant Patriot Henry Grattan; and the Victorian literary giant Robert Louis Stevenson.

The common themes which run through Gwynn's biographical treatments of the trio of explorers are the heroism of sacrifice and patriotic dedication. Scott, Kingsley and Park all met their deaths as a result of their endeavours in faraway places: Scott perished in the freezing cold of the South Pole; Kingsley contracted typhoid near Cape Town during the Boer War; and Park drowned after being attacked by natives on the banks of the river Niger. Gwynn presented all three of these figures as case studies of extreme valour in the face of danger, who pushed the boundaries of civilisation beyond the western world and marched towards what appeared inevitable oblivion in their quests for adventure. Gwynn's treatment of Kingsley in particular was empathetic, coloured by his friendship with her during the 1890s. 'This book', proclaimed Gwynn, 'is written and published with the hope to revive not merely her memory, but her vivifying influence'.[27] Gwynn eulogised Kingsley as the humane face of British imperialism, the greatest advocate of the African people in the nineteenth century. Through her published work – in particular *Travels in West Africa* and *West African studies* – Kingsley defended aspects of African culture which bewildered many in Europe. Gwynn reiterated her position that successful British imperial expansion in Africa required fairness and respect for native traditions and institutions: 'She stood for the light of justice and for the honour of England'.[28] This, too, was Gwynn's own brand of imperialism, and the righteousness of this worldview shines throughout the Kingsley book, the Park biography and the introduction Gwynn wrote to Dorothy Wellesley's study of Sir George Goldie, the founding father of British Nigeria.[29] Taken together, as one reviewer from the Royal African Society did, these texts did much 'to present the history of British influence in West Africa in a more revealing light than prejudice, due to many causes, has in the past been inclined to accord'.[30] These were esteemed examples of the triumph of imperialism in an age, from the vantage point of the inter-war years, long since past.

The Scott and Kingsley books were successful enterprises for Gwynn, both going on to paperback editions through Penguin. Gwynn picked up the James Tait Black memorial prize for biography for *The life of Mary Kingsley* in 1932. This was a considerable honour: past winners included G. M. Trevelyan, Lytton Strachey and John Buchan. Shortly after the publication of *Kingsley*, Gwynn received a letter from Henry Guillemard, an old friend of Kingsley who revised her manuscript of *Travels in West Africa*. Guillemard forcibly told Gwynn that Kingsley had exaggerated her African adventures, warping truth for the sake of a good story.[31] Gwynn seemingly refuted this contention, as no such charge was made in the second edition. At the height of their friendship in 1899, Kingsley confided in Gwynn that he was 'the only person I know who so far has shown signs of understanding me underneath in this African affair'.[32] But there were limitations to this, as Gwynn admitted in the biography:

> I knew, indeed, that her habitual jesting was a mask, emphasising the deep seriousness which appeared always when she dropped the mask, as often happened, but concealing also an extreme melancholy.... Of herself, of her life as a simple human being, we never spoke: it was as if she existed only in her purposes.[33]

The irony of Gwynn's work was that it did much to cement this viewpoint of Kingsley.[34]

Anglo-Irishness in the Free State

THE dramatic lives of explorers offered one literary outlet for Gwynn during the 1930s; his other intellectual impulse was the eighteenth-century Anglo-Irish *mentalité*, explored through biographies of Swift, Goldsmith and Grattan. While Gwynn had long been a student of the Irish eighteenth century, the subject took on a new complexity in the 1930s, in the aftermath of revolutionary violence, partition and independence. The *Catholic Bulletin* continued its war on Gwynn, Yeats and others associated with what it deemed the 'New Ascendancy' throughout the inter-war years. After Gwynn delivered a lecture on Goldsmith at Trinity College Dublin in December 1928, the *Bulletin* somewhat flatteringly described him as 'the most astute of the literary adjutants of the New Ascendancy'.[35] While Gwynn was writing (according to the *Bulletin*) 'English biographies of very English people',[36] his fascination with the eighteenth century overlapped with that of the *Bulletin*'s chief target, W. B. Yeats, who spent much of the 1920s and 1930s immersed in the literary worlds of Swift, Goldsmith, Bishop Berkeley and Edmund Burke, reacting against the grubbiness of twentieth-century Irish realities. The murder of Kevin O'Higgins in 1927, for instance, was bitterly invoked by Yeats in his poem 'Blood and the moon', which contrasted the blood-soaked nature of modern Ireland's 'abstract hatred' with what he interpreted as the intellectual utopia of the eighteenth century, the century that bore witness to the rise of Protestant Patriotism. 'Blood and the moon' was Yeats's boldest declaration of his identification with the Ascendancy tradition.[37] In his reading of the eighteenth century, Yeats found the Irish Enlightenment, permitting an exploration of his conception of 'unity of being', the truest state of a soul. 'I read Swift for months together, Burke and Berkeley less often but always with excitement, and Goldsmith lures and waits', Yeats declared in 1934: 'I collect materials for my thought and work, for some identification of my beliefs with the nation itself, I seek an image of the modern mind's discovery of itself, of its own permanent form, in that one Irish century that escaped from darkness and confusion'.[38] The real Ireland, for Yeats, lay in the tombs of the Ascendancy.

Gwynn was much more circumspect in his reading of the Irish eighteenth century, with his interpretations calmed by a critical rationality. Nevertheless, he gained a similar nostalgic inspiration from it, which resonated throughout his work. While he expressed sympathy with the Ascendancy, Gwynn's eighteenth-century Ireland, as recorded in his *History of Ireland* (1923), 'was an undeveloped country, and the endeavours of its people to develop its resources were very largely checked by successive laws, from which fact lassitude and discouragement resulted'.[39] Gwynn was attuned to the 'colonial' aspect of the Irish experience of the eighteenth century but, like Yeats, found redemption in the Ascendancy mind. This found clearest expression in Gwynn's *Henry Grattan and his times*, published in 1939, which also bears the unmistakable imprint of the Redmondite tradition. Grattan in Gwynn's reading is an Irish hero, a leader who represented the spirit of constitutional struggle, but who was doomed to a sad fate. In this narrative, particularly Gwynn's handling of the frustrations of Grattan's post-Union career, the ghost of John Redmond haunts the biographical landscape.[40] In Gwynn's view, the essence of Grattan, like Redmondism, represented the best hope of national reconciliation in Ireland. Grattan 'attached more value to national unity than to national distinctness'; he, not the revolutionary-minded Wolfe Tone and the United Irishmen, was the greatest advocate of binding Catholic and Protestant together in a union of nationality.[41] Gwynn declared:

> The race of men which the Grattans and the Parnells represented has, owing to an unfortunate political evolution, been lost almost completely to the service of Ireland, except in Ulster. One of the happiest results to be hoped from a union of North and South would be a gradual return to public life all over Ireland of the class which gave us Charles Stewart Parnell, and, two generations earlier, had given us Henry Grattan.[42]

Modern Irish nationality, in other words, should strive for pluralism: Anglo-Irish did not imply anti-Irish. One reviewer of *Henry Grattan and his times* amplified the book's political undertones:

> Grattan was a great Liberal, overwhelmed by the intolerant forces that are born of force and panic. It is significant that Mr Gwynn, himself an Irish Liberal whose party suffered a similar fate, looking wistfully at modern Ireland, can find no descendant of the Grattan school in the politics of Eire.[43]

While Gwynn combed Anglo-Irish history for political exoneration and Yeats for intellectual freedom, Daniel Corkery, the Gaelic zealot and critic, in 1931 published his influential survey *Synge and Anglo-Irish literature*, which attacked the national foundations of Protestant Ireland. Not only did Corkery reject the notion that modern Anglo-Irish literature could form a genuinely national literature, he deemed the 'Ascendancy mind' to be seemingly genetically 'alien to the genius of Ireland'.[44] He felt Anglo-Irish literature was trapped by the same historical forces which had produced the Ascendancy in Ireland. The first Irish writers who used the English tongue, Corkery rationalised, saw themselves as Englishmen living in Ireland; as the Ascendancy developed, it became more 'colonial' in its worldview, not 'Irish'.[45] While Gwynn continued to stress that 'the "separateness" of the Anglo-Irish stock has been habitually exaggerated',[46] there was no amalgamation of the new and old Irish after the seventeenth century in Corkery's reading of history. While Synge was afflicted by the inherent prejudices of the Anglo-Irish worldview, his attachment to peasant Ireland was real, according to Corkery. Synge, alone of the modern Anglo-Irish writers, 'went into the huts of the people and lived with them', before he created an intrinsically Irish masterpiece: *Riders to the sea*. 'It is the unique example where an Ascendancy writer entered with any effective intimacy into the life of the Catholic Gaelic people'.[47] Corkery recalled attending a hurling match at Thurles, County Tipperary: looking around the crowd, he 'became acutely conscious that as a nation we were without self-expression in literary form'. Under this narrow definition of the national consciousness there was no place for the literature of Yeats and his circle. As Corkery put it, 'the writers would not belong' at a hurling match; how, then, could their work represent the nation?[48]

Through *Synge and Anglo-Irish literature*, Corkery presented a sophisticated version of the argument of D. P. Moran a generation before, although he emphasised the need for Gaelic authenticity in contrast to Moran's reactive anti-Englishness.[49] The publication of Gwynn's *The life and friendships of Dean Swift* in 1933 gave Corkery the opportunity to develop his assault on Anglo-Irish literature. Gwynn's treatment of Swift's literary reputation was fairly orthodox; but a somewhat confused portrait of the dean's national identity blighted the book. Swift is presented as an Englishman – 'as he always regarded himself' – at the beginning of the biography, but also as the founder of the Ascendancy:

> What should be made clear is that when he was born that type which we call Anglo-Irish scarcely existed, and was not recognized, but before he died, it was strongly developed, beginning to be organized, and conscious of its own separate interest and allegiances. In fact, he created it. This Englishman was the first who taught the Anglo-Irish to think of themselves as a nation; he was their acknowledged leader.[50]

Having outlined this thesis, Gwynn then alternated between the labels 'Englishman' and 'Irishman' in describing Swift. While not a nationalist in the modern sense, he was a 'nation-builder'; he 'stood for Ireland against England'.[51] 'Ireland' here, of course, refers only to the Protestant Church of Ireland interest.[52] Despite a fluctuating national identity, Gwynn positioned Swift, with some justification, as a prototype of the Irish Protestant Patriotism of the age of Grattan; indeed, as one authority as noted, Swift's legacy to Ireland was the 'rich fund of rhetoric, argument, and imagery' he provided for the Patriot tradition of the late eighteenth century.[53]

Gwynn's study of Swift was published around the same time as W. D. Taylor's *Jonathan Swift*, and Mario Rossi and Joseph Hone's *Swift, or the egoist*. Corkery reviewed the three books in an extended essay in *Studies*, which dwelt on the theme of identity. Swift's 'Irishness' was deeply complex – the indecision over his identity in Gwynn's book offers one such insight into its ambiguities – but for Corkery the very nature of the 'Ascendancy mind' was the elephant in the room.[54] Corkery believed that Swift was, *pace* Gwynn, Irish, in virtue of being born in Ireland. Yet Swift's mindset was very different from that of his contemporaries in Ireland, such as Carolan, O'Rahilly and Ó Doirnín, 'poets who were journalists in the sense that Swift himself was a journalist':

> The dominant factor, the scale of values, native to the mind of these poets was a 'glow' transmitted from the Gaelic past. The 'glow' in Swift's mind

came to him from the past of the English nation; the dominant factor in his mind was English. Mr Gwynn admits that Swift was not an Irish nationalist; he will not admit, however, that the dominant factor in him was English.[55]

Corkery revised Gwynn's assertion that Swift was a 'nation-builder': 'the *un*national Irish became a nation'.[56] Swift's true legacy, Corkery asserted, was thus missed by Gwynn:

> So it was that the Dean opened a way for a disintegrating matter to flow into the brain of the Ascendancy.... When that matter had worked long enough on them, the Ascendany knew no longer what they were, nation or colony or lost tribe, nor have they known ever since what it is that they stood for. That they did not know, George Henry Moore, Standish O'Grady, Captain Shawe-Taylor, and others of their own people found out when they tried to get them to act on principle.[57]

This was the most powerful argument against Gwynn's and Yeats's separate appropriations of Swift as an Irish Patriot. Gwynn accepted Swift as English but a powerful Irish force; Corkery believed that the dean was Irish but English in mentality. 'Anglo-Irishness' in the eighteenth century, as in the 1930s, did not conform to a single model of identity.

Gwynn remained committed to Anglo-Irish history and literature after the publication of *Dean Swift*. His sympathetic biography of Goldsmith appeared in 1935 and was followed a year later by his survey *Irish literature and drama in the English language*. *Irish literature*, in many ways an Irish companion to Gwynn's earlier *The masters of English literature* (1904), offered a defence against the restricted versions of 'Irishness' pedalled by Corkery and the *Catholic Bulletin*.[58] Corkery's focus on the Gaelic tradition in literature was used against him:

> It is in English that Professor Corkery has written a series of very admirable tales of southern countryfolk.... In English also, he has written that book, *The hidden Ireland*.... In English, again, he has written a book on Synge, which challenges the right of any writer to call himself Irish who does not conform to Professor Corkery's definition; and he allows that it almost excludes Synge.

'We all grow a little tired of this exclusiveness', Gwynn concluded wearily.[59] The definition of modern Irish literature he offered was broad, commencing with Thomas Moore and ending (ironically) with Corkery. Given Gwynn's previous publications, one reviewer asked, not unfairly, why was Swift not the founding father of Irish literature in English? Another attacked several of Gwynn's critical judgements ('To say that Austin Clarke in the main seems derivative from Yeats is enough to startle any genuine poetry reader out of their wits').[60] The book's importance, though, lay in its pluralistic vision of the history of Irish writing, at a time when literary life in the Free State was stunted by the much hated Censorship Board, established in 1929, and the cultural insulation promulgated by the political elites.

Gwynn's ongoing commitment to Anglo-Irish writing and intellectual freedom brought two appointments in 1932, almost his seventieth year. Following the retirement of Richard Ashe-King, Gwynn became the President of the Irish Literary Society of London, the organisation he had helped to develop in the early 1900s.[61] He also became an associate member of the Irish Academy of Letters, a literary council established by George Bernard Shaw and Yeats ostensibly to combat Church-inspired censorship.[62] Headed by Shaw and Yeats, the Academy boasted an impressive list of full members, including Austin Clarke, Oliver St Gogarty, F. R. Higgins, Frank O'Connor, Peadar O'Donnell, Lennox Robinson, Edith Somerville and James Stephens. These academicians were selected for their creative work; the associate membership bracket, which included John Eglinton (pen-name of William Magee), Walter Starkie and L. A. G. Strong, was for those literary figures whose work did not fall completely within this definition. Gwynn was co-opted onto a committee, alongside Higgins, Joseph Hone, T. C. Murray, O'Connor and Sean O'Faolain, in 1936, which was mandated to 'consider ways and means to accelerate the work of the Academy'.[63] The first measure the committee pushed through was the abolition of the associate membership bracket from 1937, with every member of the Academy granted the academician rank. Despite the Academy's distinguished cast list, not every Irish writer was behind the enterprise. James Joyce was asked to join as a founding member in 1932 but declined the invitation; Douglas Hyde and Daniel Corkery refused membership because they maintained that an Irish Academy should consist of writers in Irish.[64] In any event, the Academy was centred on Yeats, who in Austin Clarke's estimation was 'trying to set up a Hitler dictatorship'.[65] Edith Somerville was in contact with Gwynn while he served on the working committee through 1936 and 1937, and pressed him to suggest new members to challenge the dominant influence of 'the Pale' within the Academy:

> I cannot help saying that it seems to me a pity to make the Academy quite a parochial affair! I've heard this complaint made about the Dublin Intelligentsia (but don't tell them I said so!). I think we ought to import fresh outside blood.[66]

Somerville, seemingly with the support of Gwynn, attempted to get the Cork-born literary scholar Nevill Coghill elected to the Academy in 1937, but was rebuffed because he did not reach 'the standard required'. Success came, though, with Gwynn's nomination, Elizabeth Bowen (Gwynn's sister married Bowen's father in 1918), who was elected with the support of Somerville.⁶⁷ 'I am not shouting "up county Cork!"', Somerville (rather unconvincingly) confided in Gwynn, 'only urging a wider outlook and less provincialism'.⁶⁸

The Irish Academy of Letters lost its guiding light with the death of Yeats in 1939. 'Poets who live too long confound their critics', one reviewer of John Pollock's *William Butler Yeats* hypothesised in 1935;⁶⁹ given the vastness of published and unpublished Yeatsian criticism since then, this dictum has been proved largely correct. Gwynn, who first encountered Yeats in the 1880s, wrote an incisive obituary of his old friend for the *Observer*, outlining the artistic dignity and integrity that shaped the poet's life. Yeats's influence on the Irish cultural landscape was profound:

> First and last [wrote Gwynn], he was smashing idols in the market place; at first, the cheap rhetoric of drum-beating ballads, false models in poetry; later, justifying work which his artistic sense approved as vital, while the crowd denounced it as 'an insult to Ireland'. First and last, he was a champion of freedom – but above all, against the tyrannies of democracy. And in the end, the democracy which he never spared to resist and rebuke marches, to its credit, behind his coffin.⁷⁰

In 1919, Gwynn had contrasted the cultural ethos of Yeats's circle with that of the Gaelic League: 'Yeats and Synge have showed how completely it is possible to be Irish while using the English language'.⁷¹ Irish literature was much more fluid than the definitions stressed by (among others) the extremities of the Gaelic League, Daniel Corkery and the *Catholic Bulletin*. For Gwynn, Yeats injected Irish literature with new modes of expression and cemented its genius in the English language. Like the former Orange Tory-cum-Home Ruler Isaac Butt, several generations before, Yeats helped to create a more pluralistic sense of Irishness.⁷²

Immediately after Yeats's death, an official biography was commissioned by Macmillan, with Joseph Hone handed the challenge of interrogating the poet's 'unity of being'. Daniel Macmillan looked to Gwynn for confirmation that Hone was the right man for the job:

> I should be grateful of you could let me know whether you think he could do it adequately. One advantage is that he certainly would write the book, whereas there are some other perhaps better writers like [the English literary critic] Desmond MacCarthy who would probably undertake to do it, but never finish it. Anyhow, I should be glad to know whether you can think if [there is] any other obvious person who ought to be asked.⁷³

Gwynn was forthcoming in his reply:

> As to the Yeats biography. It should be done by someone who has known Dublin for a long time, instinctively. This would rule out Desmond McCarthy [*sic*]. The obvious ones would be Lennox Robinson, John

Eglinton and – less obvious – Hone. I talked it over yesterday in strict confidence with my wife and Aubrey, and they both think that Hone would be better than Lennox Robinson; I agree. His book on George Moore, a difficult subject, surprised me by its excellence, for it conveyed faithfully and most distinctively, his own critical estimate of Moore's character without the least disparagement of Moore's work.

Gwynn believed that Robinson was unsuitable because his handling of Yeats's 'philosophical' side would be 'incompetent'; he was also too closely attached to the Abbey Theatre to offer the necessary critical analysis. Eglinton 'could do a very brilliant and interesting appreciation; he is a far better judge of poetry than either of the other men'. Gwynn feared, though, that the Yeats family would regard him as too critical for the task of constructing an authorised biography. Given the options, Gwynn asserted, probably fairly, Hone was the logical choice.[74]

Hone's study appeared in 1942: Yeats's sister Lily thought it 'good, written with grace & dignity'.[75] Macmillan pre-empted the authorised biography in 1940 with the publication of a collection of essays written by Yeats's contemporaries, edited by Gwynn. The idea for *Scattering branches: tributes to the memory of W. B. Yeats* came from Sir William Rothenstein, and the format was partly based on the tribute volume edited by A. W. Lawrence, *T. E. Lawrence by his friends*, published in 1937. Macmillan contacted Gwynn in the summer of 1939 to gauge his opinion on the venture, suggesting a dozen papers by the likes of Oliver St John Gogarty, Thomas Sturge Moore, Edmund Dulac, Ezra Pound, J. B. Yeats and Rothenstein, under his editorship.[76] Gwynn was enthusiastic about the project, envisaging the book as an intimate portrait of the master poet, constructed from a number of very different perspectives, and not necessarily those recommended by Macmillan:

> Putting my thoughts together, I think, first that Shaw *ought* to be asked. He was joined with Yeats and AE in starting the Irish Academy of Letters and is now President of it.... Next, that for the theatre, both Lennox Robinson and St John Ervine should have a say, as their minds and standpoints are unlike.... Then for the intimacy of association, Jack Yeats and Maud Gonne. Add Rothenstein and John Eglinton, making seven. Gogarty, eight, Sturge Moore, nine. I think Cecil Day Lewis for the younger school of poets, and Corkery for a not enthusiastic Irish estimate. This seems to me a good eleven.[77]

Gwynn also asked T. S. Eliot to contribute, but the invitation was declined.[78] In any event, the final book looked rather different from Gwynn's ideal. There were no contributions from Shaw, Sturge Moore, Corkery or, disappointingly given his previous praise, Eglinton. *Scattering branches* carried tributes from Gonne, Rothenstein, Robinson, the actor W. G. Fay, Dulac, the poet F. R. Higgins, Day Lewis and the writer

L. A. G. Strong. The title came from the tale of the sacrifice of the Trojan princess Polyxena, whose body was covered with leaves and branches. 'When an Irish poet had lived valiantly', Gwynn proclaimed with purpose in his introduction, 'it was only right that some such tribute should be paid, above all by those of his own allegiance'.[79] Gwynn dwelt on themes that would have been familiar to his long-time readers: meeting Yeats in the 1880s, the quality of his poetry, his unflappable courage. Yeats's championing of Synge at the highpoint of the *Playboy of the western world* controversy did Ireland a favour that was not repaid. On his poetic legacy, Gwynn declared a preference for the 'middle period', with 'A prayer for my daughter' his Yeatsian highlight.[80] An elegiac mood permeated the book; the Irish literary revival had symbolically closed, at least as far as publishing opportunities at Macmillan were concerned.[81]

Final years

WHILE Gwynn was one of the most industrious writers of his generation, his books did not generate him much wealth. *The masters of English literature* – 'the only book, my father used to say, from which he had a small, but steady income', recalled Aubrey Gwynn[82] – received a welcome second edition in 1938. Included was a new discussion of twentieth-century literature, including the Anglo-Irish revival writers ('One can't well omit George Moore, though I think him absurdly over-rated', Gwynn cheekily told Daniel Macmillan).[83] Gwynn ensured that *Masters* was used as the core textbook for English at Bradfield College, where he returned to work in 1939, at the age of seventy-five.[84] Bradfield was where he had been a school-master in 1888; he seemed to enjoy this second stint much more than his first. 'I am preparing young gentlemen with a view to scholarships & the like', Gwynn confided to William Rothenstein. 'I prefer it to writing more books which nobody reads & which I didn't want to write'.[85] He remained at Bradfield for only a few months, though, and still, despite protestations to the contrary, had several books in him.

As he was constantly on the move, the dynamics of Gwynn's relationship with his wife, May, during the 1920s and 1930s remain obscure. They certainly split up after his affair with Grace Henry in the early 1920s, but this was a temporary arrangement. They remained at least on friendly terms, attending various functions together, such as an exhibition at the Royal Hibernian Academy in Dublin in April 1931.[86] Gwynn moved between Dublin and Berkshire during the late 1930s, however, sharing a cottage ('Paradise Cottage') in England with Florence Lucas, the widow of E. V. Lucas. In a tantalising letter to Harold Macmillan in 1940, addressed from the Stephen's Green Club in Dublin, Gwynn reveals that 'I have to stay on at this club, & can't get into my own house, as I had hoped to do'.[87] It is quite possible that May locked him out; no reason is given by Gwynn, however, for this state of affairs. May died in a convent in Meath in 1941; just before her funeral, Gwynn composed a short poem in her memory, stressing the conviction of her religious belief, but curiously avoiding personal feeling or affection.[88]

Gwynn lived in Paradise Cottage with Lucas for the bulk of the war years. 'Since the war began', Gwynn told Thomas Bodkin, a former Director of the National Gallery in Dublin, in 1941, 'I have been here continually as paying guest with Mrs Lucas.... Ireland is not very attractive to me at present'.[89] His allegiances during the Second World War were in no doubt. That same year, Gwynn published a slim volume of poetry, *Salute to valour*, which celebrated the virtues of the Allies. His own advancing years were clearly on his mind in the composition of several of the verses, such as 'We that are old':

> But should death swoop down from the sky
> With rush and roar,
> An old man may be proud to die
> Who dies in war.[90]

'I marvel at your ability to write poetry at your time of life', Bodkin enthused.[91] Gwynn was 'bidden to suppress' one poem, 'Song of a neutral', which remains unpublished.[92] Despite his sympathies for the Allied cause, Gwynn was sensitive to Ireland's neutral stance. Much hinged on de Valera's need for national unity (within the twenty-six counties) in the face of a major European war; neutrality was the least divisive option. Gwynn differentiated between the politics of war and the thousands of Irish people joining the Allies in various guises: this was pro-British neutrality. De Valera's attitude, Gwynn wrote at the beginning of 1940, 'will be that of a neutral pushing benevolence so far as possible without compromising his independence of action'.[93] As the war drew to a close, Gwynn analysed the Irish experience from an English perspective: 'It seems likely to me, having lived almost continuously in England since 1937, that people outside of Ireland have no adequate view of the course which Mr de Valera felt called upon to take'. But Gwynn, having recently returned to Ireland, believed that the policy of neutrality had been 'justified'. Had de Valera entered the theatre of war in 1939, he asserted, civil war could have followed. Yet in avoiding strife in the twenty-six counties, partition became more entrenched, with Northern Ireland playing a leading role in the United Kingdom's war effort.[94] Reconciling divisions in Ireland seemed an impossible task.

Gwynn left the heavenly sounding Paradise Cottage in 1944, his eightieth year. 'I am going back to Ireland for good (if that is the right word)', he informed Bodkin.[95] Gwynn's final home was in Tenenure, just outside Dublin. He was still physically fit and active, despite his lament to his son Aubrey on one occasion while being helped up steps in Lesson Street: 'Don't go beyond eighty!'[96] He lost an eye while cutting firewood in 1947,[97] but continued to write, becoming increasingly preoccupied with the contours of his life and the biography of his country. Two reflective essays appeared in *The Bell* in 1947 and 1948. The first was a biographical piece, proudly outlining the 'old order' which existed in the Donegal of his childhood; the second was a more general critique of Irish life in the 1940s, belittling the forced Gaelicisation of political culture in the aftermath of independence.[98] The finer aspects of Gwynn's life received coverage in *Memories of enjoyment*, a collection of previously published essays, which was released in 1946. This celebrated his chief interests: wine, conversation, companionship, reading, writing and fishing. It was clear that his life's journey was drawing to a close. 'The worst part of being over eighty', admitted Gwynn, 'is that when any name is mentioned, carrying association back into the past, our first impulse is to ask if that person still lives'. By the close of the Second World War, many of his generation were dead; 'For the old, life tends to be bounded within an always narrowing circle'.[99]

In his later years, Gwynn received a number of awards in recognition of his long service to Irish life. Two honorary doctorates came his way: the National University of Ireland celebrated his life in 1940, while Trinity College Dublin followed suit five years later. Gwynn had briefly served on the National University's Senate after its formation in 1908,[100] but his opposition to compulsory Irish as a matriculation requirement left him a minority voice. As the University presented him with a degree over thirty years later, Gwynn could not resist noting that his position had been vindicated:

> Parnell would have stared if you told him that he was less Irish because he spoke the language into which every man on his estate had been bred or born. Pearse was a great champion of Gaelic but when Pearse stirred the mind of Ireland it was by his speech [in English] about the Fenian dead.... Today, I am sorry to say Eire is a name that divides; Ireland unites us.[101]

A year before his death, Gwynn, at the age of eighty-five, sounded out the possibility of publishing a short autobiographical work through Macmillan, but this came to nothing.[102]

But one final honour came in April 1950, as the Irish Academy of Letters commended his lifetime contribution and commitment to literature with the Lady Gregory Medal, a special award made every three years in recognition of a distinguished service to Irish letters. As all the previous winners of the medal – Gregory, Yeats, George Russell, Douglas Hyde, George Bernard Shaw and Eoin MacNeill – had passed away by 1950, the ceremony carried a certain poignancy for Gwynn, the last of his generation of authors. Acknowledging his award, Gwynn recorded his gratitude to the Academy, 'because as a man well over eighty it made him feel that he was still alive'.[103] Just two months later, on 11 June 1950, Gwynn died peacefully at his home in Dublin. Newspaper obituaries around the country saluted a life dedicated to Ireland, tolerance and intellectual life. The Belfast unionist daily the *Northern Whig* paid tribute to Gwynn's 'love of freedom, respect for the convictions of others, a readiness to subordinate his own when he thought it right, qualities much needed in Ireland'[104] – high praise from a former political enemy. Despite his vast catalogue of publications, Gwynn never made significant money from the writing trade: his estate, which was left to his daughter Shelia, was valued at only £125 on his death.[105] Gwynn's remains were lowered into the earth of a Church of Ireland cemetery at Tallaght, south of Dublin, at a service which brought together the Irish President, Sean T. O'Kelly, the Taoiseach, John A. Costello, literary figures, scholars and Army officers from Gwynn's disbanded regiment, the Connaught Rangers. It was fitting company for one whose long life had spanned politics, literature and war. Yet the Irish soil which covered Gwynn's remains was not of the Ireland he anticipated. Stephen Gwynn's Ireland – reconciled, pluralist and above all united – lies with him in his grave. 'He sought no rewards and received few', Mabel Dearmer's son, Geoffrey, wrote on Gwynn's death; 'perhaps the knowledge of services too valuable to be computed was the greatest of them, and certainly gave him the greatest pleasure'.[106]

Notes

1. 21 October [1944], Macmillan archive, British Library (BL), box M44.
2. Hubert Butler, '*The Bell*: an Anglo-Irish view', in *Independent spirit: essays* (New York: Farrar, Straus and Giroux, 1996), p. 86.
3. Sean O'Faolain, *Vive moi! An autobiography* (London: Rupert Hart-Davis, 1965), p. 270.
4. Stephen Gwynn, 'Ireland since the Treaty', *Foreign Affairs*, January 1934, pp. 319–30.
5. J. L. Garvin to Stephen Gwynn, 28 September 1924, Stephen Gwynn papers, National Library of Ireland (NLI), MS 8600 (5).
6. For O'Malley, see Richard English, *Ernie O'Malley: IRA intellectual* (Oxford: Oxford University Press, 1998).
7. Mr Greenslet to Stephen Gwynn, 10 October 1928, Houghton Mifflin papers, Houghton Library, Harvard University, bMS Am 1925 (737), folder 4 (22).
8. Stephen Gwynn (ed.), *The anvil of war: letters between F. S. Oliver and his brother 1914–1918* (London: Macmillan and Co., 1936), pp. 1–34; quote on p. 3.
9. Stephen Gwynn to Daniel Macmillan, 17 August [1935], Macmillan archive, BL, box M44.
10. *Manchester Guardian*, 5 March 1936.
11. *Observer*, 16 January 1928. This essay later appeared in expanded form in Gwynn's *Memories of enjoyment* (Tralee: Kerryman, 1946), pp. 81–7.

12 *Observer*, 29 March 1931. See Gwynn's review of Healy's *Letters and leaders of my day* in *Observer*, 2 December 1928, for the 'leaderless man' quote.
13 *Observer*, 6 December 1931.
14 *Observer*, 7 February 1932.
15 *Observer*, 21 February 1932.
16 *Observer*, 21 September 1924.
17 *Irish Times*, 19 April 1932.
18 *Irish Times*, 3 May 1932.
19 *Irish Independent*, 10 November 1932.
20 *Observer*, 18 January 1931.
21 Stephen Gwynn, *The charm of Ireland: her places of beauty, entertainment, sport and historic association* (London: George G. Harrap and Co., 1934), p. 20.
22 Harold Macmillan to Stephen Gwynn, 20 April 1934, Macmillan archive, BL, 55751/624.
23 Stephen Gwynn to Harold Macmillan, 12 January [1940], Macmillan archive, BL, box M44.
24 Stephen Gwynn to Daniel Macmillan, 4 March 1932, Macmillan archive, BL, box M44; Gwynn to Macmillan, n.d. [March 1932], Macmillan archive, BL, box M44.
25 Charles Gwynn, *Imperial policing* (London: Macmillan and Co., 1936; first published 1934), pp. 8–9.
26 Stephen Gwynn to Macmillan, 17 July [1940], Macmillan archive, BL, box M44.
27 Stephen Gwynn, *The life of Mary Kingsley* (London: Macmillan and Co., 1932), p. 263.
28 *Ibid.*, p. 175.
29 Stephen Gwynn, 'The making of Nigeria: a historical introduction', in Dorothy Wellesley, *Sir George Goldie: founder of Nigeria* (London: Macmillan and Co., 1934), pp. 3–87.
30 Review of *Mungo Park*, *Journal of the Royal African Society*, 34:136 (1935), p. 357.
31 Henry Guillemard to Stephen Gwynn, 21 November 1932, Stephen Gwynn papers, NLI, MS 8600(5).
32 Mary Kingsley to Stephen Gwynn, 16 February 1899, Stephen Gwynn papers, NLI, MS 8600(9).
33 Gwynn, *The life of Mary Kingsley*, pp. 24–5.
34 The heroic aspects of Kingsley's life have been emphasised in more recent biographical treatments, particularly Katherine Frank's *A voyager out: the life of Mary Kingsley* (Boston: Houghton Mifflin Co., 1986).
35 *Catholic Bulletin*, January 1929.
36 *Catholic Bulletin*, December 1933.
37 R. F. Foster, *W. B. Yeats: a life. Vol. II: The arch-poet* (Oxford: Oxford University Press, 2003), p. 346.
38 W. B. Yeats, *Wheels and butterflies* (London: Macmillan and Co., 1934), p. 7. For a discussion of 'unity of being' in relation to Yeats's interpretation of the eighteenth century, see Richard Ellman, *Yeats: the man and the masks* (New York: W. W. Norton and Co., 1978; first published 1948), pp. 268–71.
39 Stephen Gwynn, *The history of Ireland* (London: Macmillan and Co., 1923), p. 365.
40 For this, see Patrick Maume, 'Gwynn, Stephen Lucius', in James McGuire and James Quinn (eds), *Dictionary of Irish Biography* (Cambridge: Cambridge University Press, 2009), vol. IV, pp. 338–42. I am indebted to Dr Maume for discussions on this aspect of Gwynn's later writings.

41 Stephen Gwynn, *Henry Grattan and his times* (Dublin: Browne and Nolan, 1939), pp. 391–3.
42 *Ibid.*, pp. 393–4.
43 *Manchester Guardian*, 30 May 1939.
44 Daniel Corkery, *Synge and Anglo-Irish literature* (Cork: Mercier Press, 1966; first published 1931), p. 38.
45 See Patrick Maume, *'Life that is exile': Daniel Corkery and the search for Irish Ireland* (Belfast: Queen's University Belfast, 1993), pp. 109–10.
46 *Times*, 16 January 1929.
47 Corkery, *Synge*, pp. 27, 109.
48 *Ibid.*, pp. 12–13.
49 Foster, *The arch-poet*, p. 423.
50 Stephen Gwynn, *The life and friendships of Dean Swift* (London: Thornton Butterworth, 1935, first published 1933), pp. 14–15.
51 *Ibid.*, pp. 228, 285.
52 Ian McBride, *Eighteenth-century Ireland: the isle of slaves* (Dublin: Gill and Macmillan, 2009), p. 273.
53 Stephen Small, *Political thought in Ireland 1776–1798* (Oxford: Oxford University Press, 2002), p. 45.
54 For the changing perceptions of Swift's Irishness see Robert Mahony, *Jonathan Swift: the Irish identity* (New Haven: Yale University Press, 1995).
55 Daniel Corkery, 'Ourselves and Dean Swift', *Studies*, June 1934, p. 210.
56 *Ibid.*, p. 215.
57 *Ibid.*, p. 218.
58 See, for example, the attack on Gwynn and Anglo-Irish literature in the *Catholic Bulletin*, July 1931.
59 Stephen Gwynn, *Irish literature and drama in the English language: a short history* (London: Thomas Nelson and Sons, 1936), pp. 224–5.
60 *Irish Monthly*, November 1936; *Dublin Magazine*, July–September 1936.
61 *Irish Times*, 7 May 1932.
62 G. B. Shaw and W. B. Yeats to Gwynn, n.d. [1932], Stephen Gwynn papers, NLI, MS 8600 (16).
63 W. B. Yeats to St John Ervine, February 1937, in John Kelly (ed.), *The collected letters of W. B. Yeats* (Oxford: Oxford University Press, InteLex electronic edition, 2002).
64 Gwynn, *Irish literature*, pp. 232–6.
65 Quoted in Foster, *The arch-poet*, p. 450.
66 Edith Somerville to Stephen Gwynn, 8 July 1937, Stephen Gwynn papers, NLI, MS 8600 (16).
67 Edith Somerville to Stephen Gwynn, 9 August 1937, Stephen Gwynn papers, NLI, MS 8600 (16).
68 Edith Somerville to Stephen Gwynn, 23 July 1937, Stephen Gwynn papers, NLI, MS 8600 (16).
69 *Irish Book Lover*, July/August 1935.
70 *Observer*, 5 February 1939. Also see Roy Foster's essay on Yeats's obituaries, '"When the newspapers have forgotten me": Yeats, obituarists and Irishness', in *The Irish story: telling tales and making it up in Ireland* (London: Allen Lane, 2001), pp. 80–94.
71 Stephen Gwynn, *Irish books and Irish people* (Dublin: Talbot Press, 1919), p. 4.
72 R. F. Foster, 'Varieties of Irishness: culture and anarchy in Ireland', in *Paddy and Mr Punch: connections in Irish and English history* (London: Allen Lane, 1993), p. 27.

73 Daniel Macmillan to Stephen Gwynn, 10 February 1939, Macmillan archive, BL, 55819/246.
74 Stephen Gwynn to Daniel Macmillan, 13 February 1939, Macmillan archive, BL, box M44.
75 Foster, *The arch-poet*, p. 655.
76 Harold Macmillan to Stephen Gwynn, 22 August 1939, Macmillan archive, BL, 55828/381.
77 Stephen Gwynn to Harold Macmillan, 25 August [1939], Macmillan archive, BL, box M44. Original emphasis.
78 Stephen Gwynn to Thomas Mark, 21 May [1940], Macmillan archive, BL, box M44.
79 Stephen Gwynn, 'Scattering branches', in Stephen Gwynn (ed.), *Scattering branches: tributes to the memory of W. B. Yeats* (London: Macmillan and Co., 1940), p. 3.
80 *Ibid.*, p. 12.
81 Forthcoming work by Warwick Gould shows that Macmillan recruited no new Irish writers after the death of the Yeats. I am grateful to Professor Gould for sharing this work with me.
82 Aubrey Gwynn, 'Unfinished history of the Gwynn family', Aubrey Gwynn papers, Irish Jesuit Archive (IJA), J10/89 (180)
83 Stephen Gwynn to Daniel Macmillan, 21 May [1938], Macmillan archive, BL, box M44.
84 Stephen Gwynn to Harold Macmillan, 12 December [1939], Macmillan archive, box M44.
85 Stephen Gwynn to William Rothenstein, 29 September [1939], William Rothenstein papers, Houghton Library, Harvard University, bMS Eng. 1148 (134).
86 *Irish Times*, 14 April 1931.
87 Stephen Gwynn to Harold Macmillan, 1 January [1940], Macmillan archive, BL, box M44.
88 Stephen Gwynn, 'On one dying in a convent', in *Aftermath* (Dundalk: Dundalgan Press, 1946), p. 20.
89 Stephen Gwynn to Thomas Bodkin, 8 March [1941], Thomas Bodkin papers, Trinity College Manuscript Department, Dublin (TCD), MS 6996/687.
90 Stephen Gwynn, 'We that are old', in *Salute to valour* (London: Constable and Co., 1941), p. 14.
91 Thomas Bodkin to Stephen Gwynn, 14 March 1941, Thomas Bodkin papers, TCD, MS 6996/688.
92 Stephen Gwynn to Thomas Bodkin, 25 March 1941, Thomas Bodkin papers, TCD, MS 6996/689.
93 Stephen Gwynn, 'Ireland and the war', *Foreign Affairs*, January 1940, p. 313.
94 *Manchester Guardian*, 5 January 1945.
95 Stephen Gwynn to Thomas Bodkin, 6 August [1944], Thomas Bodkin papers, TCD, MS 6996/696.
96 Geoffrey Hand, 'Aubrey Gwynn: the person', *Studies* (1992), p. 382.
97 Stephen Gwynn to Roger Gwynn (his nephew), 3 July 1947, letter in the possession of Roger Gwynn, Stroud.
98 Stephen Gwynn, 'From Donegal I wandered', *The Bell*, 15:3 (December 1947), pp. 26–36; 'Thoughts about Ireland', *The Bell*, 15:6 (March 1948), pp. 54–7.
99 Gwynn, 'Anno Domini', in *Memories of enjoyment*, p. 146.
100 See Chapter 3, pp. 84–5.
101 Copy of Gwynn's after-dinner speech, papers in the possession of Fergus Kelly, Dublin.

102 Stephen Gwynn to Harold Macmillan, 1 March [1949], Macmillan archive, BL, box M44.
103 *Irish Times*, 28 April 1950.
104 *Northern Whig*, 12 June 1950.
105 Stephen Gwynn's will, National Archives of Ireland, 1072.
106 *Times*, 19 June 1950.

Conclusion

On the centenary in 1964 of Stephen Gwynn's birth, the *Irish Times* devoted an editorial to his memory; Gwynn had already become largely forgotten in independent Ireland. The article lamented the defeat of Gwynn and the final generation of Home Rulers in 1918 and the lack of opportunities they had in the forging of the new Ireland thereafter. The landscape of memory within Irish political culture is a notoriously difficult terrain to navigate. For the generation who oversaw the march to independence in 1921, the revolutionary 'year 1' was 1916; the long nineteenth-century constitutional nationalist perspective was in effect erased from Irish political consciousness with the achievement of the Free State. The Easter Rising was a revolt not only against British rule in Ireland but also against John Redmond's Irish Party: the very legitimacy of Sinn Féin and the IRA partly rested on discrediting constitutional nationalism. The chain of leaders who kept the flame of Home Rule alive for over fifty years – Isaac Butt, Charles Stewart Parnell, John Redmond and John Dillon – were not commemorated by the post-1921 Irish political elite; expunged from the public mindset, the constitutional struggle for Irish self-governance from 1870 to 1916 was left for later historians to excavate.[1] This was the context for the *Irish Times*'s plea for Gwynn to be permitted to take his rightful place 'in the pantheon of good Irishmen'; failure to do so would demonstrate the narrow exclusivity of contemporary Irishness.[2]

It was not to be. Gwynn's brand of Protestant nationalism, imbued with a strong imperial identity and reconciliatory ethos, was a victim of the revolutionary impulses that swept through Ireland during the Great War and after. Unable to compete with a more idealistic nationalism which stressed the integrity of the nation and territory, Gwynn's nationalism, like Redmondism more generally, was swiftly eliminated from Irish political culture.

'Unobtrusively he lived and died, but for patriotism, scholarship, and integrity he was the greatest figure in the Ireland of his time'. This

Conclusion

was how Oliver St John Gogarty eulogised Gwynn in the *Dictionary of national biography* in 1959. Gogarty also described Gwynn's life philosophy as 'a kindly stoicism'.[3] Geoffrey Dearmer, whose mother had an affair with Gwynn, praised his 'selfless loyalty to causes even when the trend of events was to prove them lost'.[4] This was a central component of Gwynn's psyche: he never reneged on a cause which he believed was right. His political and cultural worldview was one of dogmatic realism: malleable in shape, but inflexible in substance. Nowhere was this more apparent than in Gwynn's political manoeuvrings during the years 1919–21, when he argued the case (in sequence) for federalism, dominion Home Rule and limited devolution with partition, each with the premise of uniting moderate nationalists and unionists. The fate of the causes Gwynn championed during his career would have broken a lesser individual: he was a fearless and righteous operator. He fought every major political and cultural battle – figuratively and literally – which Ireland experienced between 1906 and 1921, and lost every one. From the vantage point of 1926, when he retreated to write his memoir, constitutional nationalism, and particularly the imperially minded and cosmopolitan vision which John Redmond possessed, had been destroyed. The sacrifices of the war generation had led to nothing. Gaelic League militancy now received state backing, with scant regard for the spiritual effects of compulsory learning of the Irish language, never mind its divisiveness. Yeats, Synge and Gregory had fought tooth and nail for artistic freedom; now censorship threatened the integrity of the Irish imagination. In this context, the longevity of Gwynn's presence in Irish life is nothing short of remarkable. As St John Ervine wryly commented in a review of Gwynn's *Irish books and Irish people* in 1919, 'the quality of his character is such that he is incapable of surrendering to despair'.[5] Gwynn was unflappable in the face of defeat, even when every ideal he possessed was violated by political and cultural revolution.

Explaining the failure of Gwynn's career illuminates many of the forces that defeated him. From Gwynn's early advocacy of the Gaelic League's idealistic programme to his break with Irish-Ireland over language compulsion, from his unbending commitment to self-government in Ireland to his realisation that Ulster's distinctiveness needed to be adequately addressed, his career encapsulates the chief ideological dilemmas of early twentieth-century Irish nationalism. He articulated a vision for Ireland's future in which north and south were reconciled under a pluralistic definition of Irishness. The scale of his ambition was immense and was fuelled by more than mere Redmondite rhetoric; with Gwynn at the heart of the action, southern unionism and constitutional nationalism came tantalisingly close to reaching a deal during the Irish Convention in 1918. The historic significance of this is often overlooked; it would take another eighty years for an agreement between unionism and nationalism to be reached. The Convention – and its ultimate failure – was symbolic of a changing Ireland, as Gwynn hinted in a contemporary review:

> When the history of the Irish Convention comes to be fully recorded, it will be seen that a great desire was universally felt, cordially uttered, in that assembly, to bridge over the gulf which divides us from yesterday in Ireland, and to recover for the future much of what was admirable, valuable and lovable in a past that is not unkindly remembered.[6]

For Gwynn, contemporary notions of 'Irishness' without Ulster unionism and Protestantism were not really 'Irish' at all: 'Complete nationhood can only be achieved by a reconcilement of the divergent ideals' on the island.[7] The model of the Irish Convention remained the practical method to deliver an Ireland based on the abstract language of inclusiveness; that such an approach was rendered impotent by the politics of extremism was a devastating blow for Gwynn personally, and the shrinking brand of conciliatory nationalism which he represented.

What effect did a public career blighted by failure have on the man? Gwynn was a private individual and the surviving archival material does not offer many insights into his home life. His sense of humour was black, touching on morbid. Evelyn Sharp visited the Gwynns during the summer of 1921, shortly after the truce was agreed between the IRA and Crown forces. Sharp told her hosts that a friend, Leland Buxtons, was thinking of coming to Ireland for a fishing holiday as he was 'fond of killing things'. 'Stephen wrinkled up his face and smiled his characteristic wry smile, and observed, "Then he'd better not come to Ireland just now, because for the moment we're having a close time in killing"'.[8] Fishing, wine and travelling throughout Ireland were his great passions away from the political sphere; perhaps sex can also be added to this list. Gwynn had at least two affairs, both hidden from the public eye: a long-standing relationship with Mabel Dearmer and a shorter, intense liaison with Grace Henry. Those who were aware of his extra-marital activities perhaps raised a wry smile at his observation from 1921 that a writer's life required two strands for general wellbeing: 'The big concern of sex – always present, to help or hinder – is a preoccupation rather than an occupation; and nothing but a regular occupation can supply to the mind something intimately familiar, yet extraneous, to mix into the web drawn spiderwise from its own entrails'.[9] Gwynn's relationships with his wife and children are difficult to probe. May Gwynn's politics were more 'advanced' than her husband's, most notably in her support for Sinn Féin during the War of Independence. The toil of Stephen's affairs appears to have driven May to the Catholic Church in 1902, and the couple separated at various times throughout their lengthy marriage. By 1911, Gwynn was living with Mabel Dearmer; in February of that year, May told their children that their father 'will live at home no more'.[10] Gwynn did, however, return to the family home, under which circumstances it would have been impossible to hide his extra-marital activities from his children. Nevertheless, the Gwynn children appear to have basked in their father's attentions, even into adulthood. Gwynn's daughter Sheila was very fond of her father.[11] His second son, Aubrey, who became a distinguished Jesuit medieval scholar, remembered that his father 'was by his own temperament and by the changing fortunes of his life a very restless though loveable human being'.[12] Gwynn's third son, Denis, who became a professor of history in Cork in the 1940s, was more circumspect in voicing an opinion of his father for the historical record, but their political and ideological leanings were similar. Like his father, Denis fought in the Great War; he also was a committed Redmondite, as demonstrated by his sympathetic treatment of the Irish Party leader in his *The life of John Redmond*, published in 1932. Denis was more of a professional historian than his father, but lacked the sense of personal empathy which made Gwynn senior's histories more relevant: it is this trait which makes *John Redmond's last years* a more penetrating and insightful book than the archival-dominated *Life of John Redmond*. Nevertheless, Denis, as a respected member of the academic community and a committed Catholic, was well integrated into the Irish state, something his father never achieved.

Gwynn's life was dominated by his pursuit of an imagined Ireland, and not just in a political sense. He was deeply attached to Irish topography, history and lore. Gwynn published a dozen books of Irish travel writings, all of which record an immense love for his country. The 'hidden Ireland', which Gwynn walked time and time again while researching these books, attuned his thinking and offered new perspectives on facets of Irish life. 'In Ireland', he wrote in 1935, 'the distinction between east and west is more real than between north and south'. The natural landscape of Ireland offered solace from political realities.

> The east faces the Channel, and it is, moreover, nearer to the English way of life. Lough Foyle is the dividing-line between east and west, and would be even if no political boundary existed. Inishowen is already Western Ireland; the Gaelic language still lives there; and if you explore Inishowen thoroughly in its mountainous length you will get a fairly good idea of the sea-bordering parts of Donegal, which are the most famous for beauty.[13]

The delights which the hidden Ireland offered Gwynn were, however, tinged with sadness after the Great War. In towns and villages across the country, Gwynn found and celebrated ex-servicemen who had become reintegrated into normal life. 'You find yourself at Glencar fishing with a man from the Munster Fusiliers; on Beltra, in Mayo (at least, if you have any luck), with a Connaught Ranger'. In such company another hidden Ireland was found but could not be recovered: 'We keep our own pride among ourselves'.[14]

Gwynn's early interpretation of the Home Rule ideal was firmly positive, lacking any Anglophobia or insular provincialism. Home Rule would bind Ireland to the British Empire, reconciling Irish nationalism and imperialism. He also argued in 1903 that the concession of Home Rule would transform Irish life, creating a new breed of politician more concerned with socio-economic issues than with the national question, weakening the political power of the Catholic Church and granting a new role for the declining landed classes.[15] The great blind spot in this analysis, though, was Ulster's place in this new order: as did nationalists more generally, Gwynn underestimated the lengths to which Ulster Protestants would go to oppose any constitutional change to the status quo. Gwynn's major contribution to the self-governing debate, *The case for Home Rule*, failed to take seriously unionism's multi-faceted argument against the nationalist project, as he focused solely on addressing Protestant fears of Catholic intolerance.[16] The Great War, however, radically altered Gwynn's interpretation of the Irish question, in both a positive and a negative sense. Gwynn's experiences on the battlefields of Europe were profound. He and Redmond hoped the theatre of war could provide the context for the breaking down of ancient divisions between Irishmen. Relations between officers of the Irish and Ulster Divisions were cordial; Gwynn also was deeply moved by instances of Catholic and Protestant servicemen working together in the face of a common enemy. He described one such scene in his book *The charm of Ireland*:

> I saw, too, in France a couple of these same little Northern Catholic Belfast boys, machine-gunners, in the crater of a mine whose sides still reeked and crumbled from the explosion, working with the fury of wild cats to get their Southern Protestant officer out from under a shelter that had blown in on him; with tears streaming down their faces and appalling blasphemy proceeding from their lips. They got him out.[17]

Gwynn became more sympathetic to unionist concerns during the war, and this was heightened after the Easter Rising, which pushed him towards seeking a political settlement with Ulster, on Ulster's terms. According to his reading, the Easter Rising and the revolutionary hatreds which it unleashed destroyed the unity of Ireland that the war had created.[18] Such an explanation ignored crucial factors such as the unpopularity in Ireland of the bloody and seemingly endless war, as well as the political impact of the conscription crisis; but the righteousness of Gwynn's convictions spurred him on. 'History will judge between the Irish Nationalists who went out with Willie Redmond and Tom Kettle and those who stayed at home and let loose the Rising of Easter Week',

Gwynn proclaimed in May 1918.[19] Ultimately it did, but history was against him. Gwynn was parodied in Sinn Féin propaganda and the anti-Treaty IRA targeted him in 1923.[20] While his post-1916 political stances endeared him to the London *Times* – its obituary of Gwynn claimed that 'As a politician he deserved a much higher reputation than his fellow-countrymen after the rise of Sinn Féin were prepared to concede him'[21] – it did little to enrapture his fellow Irish nationalists, and his reputation suffered accordingly.

In literature, as in politics, Gwynn's reputation suffered the fate of changing trends. Gwynn prided himself on being a 'man of letters', a cultivated individual with a wide range of literary interests. Yet this label was in essence extinct in post-war Britain and Ireland, with the unstoppable rise of professional intellectuals and the 'specialist' rendering obsolete the musings of enlightened critics cut from the cloth of the late-Victorian period.[22] The books which Gwynn produced over his lengthy life have mostly been forgotten; aside from *The masters of English literature*, none of his works received multiple editions or remained in the public domain for very long. Yet there is much to be found in Gwynn's extensive oeuvre: the calm analysis of his historical work; the charm of his travel writings that chart an Ireland long gone; the enjoyment gained from life which was mapped out through many essays. While he celebrated and lamented Ireland in print throughout his life, he found solace in a range of other interests, from the vineyards of Burgundy to Claude Monet. The breadth of Gwynn's worldly knowledge was imposing.

Failure blots Gwynn's career, but there was nothing inevitable about this. He emerged as one of the strongest supporters of John Redmond and gave constitutional nationalism an intellectual muscle and propagandist energy that the movement sorely lacked. Gwynn's pro-active leadership of the Irish Press Agency did much to keep Ireland's struggle for Home Rule in the British newspapers during its quieter moments in Westminster, and helped to bolster Redmond's position in Britain and Ireland at the close of the Edwardian period. The vibrancy of the Home Rule cause during Gwynn's time serves to further the tragedy of his career, while indicating the importance of considering his contributions to political and cultural nationalism. Gwynn was a politician, writer, intellectual, soldier and journalist, a man of considerable energy and talent. His worldview offers a sharp insight into Redmondite psychology, its attractions and weaknesses. Gwynn personified a strand of moderate Irish nationalism that became unfashionable in the Ireland which emerged from the Great War; his experiences were also emblematic of the new state's attitudes to the legacy of the war and constitutional nationalism from previous generations. Gwynn was a fearless commentator: his weekly *Observer* columns during the revolutionary years offer penetrating accounts of the excesses of militant republicanism and the self-defeating nature of the British reprisal campaign. It was the violence of the IRA, according to Gwynn, that renewed and entrenched the Irish divisions which partition reflected, and pushed him to a greater degree of sympathy with Ulster unionism's efforts to ensure the survival of Northern Ireland during its difficult birth. His commentary on the revolution, written from a Redmondite perspective, revealed the stark contrast between republican idealism and national realism, while also providing insights into Irish nationalism's turbulent ideological reconfigurations from the leadership of John Redmond to William Cosgrave. Gwynn is one of the more compelling early-twentieth-century Irish Party members, the only nationalist MP who also sat on the Gaelic League's executive body, fought in a World War and controversially supported the Act that partitioned Ireland. A tribute that Gwynn wrote to Redmond, the figure who most influenced his political thought, perhaps serves as a fitting epitaph for his own life:

> To have served long and faithfully without reward – to have given all of life to one high purpose – to have faced a great crisis greatly – these are claims enough for Redmond that the allegiances of his comrades and followers may be justified when it is judged. The grave has closed over him, and the rest is for us to do, that a coping-stone may be set on his life's labours, and that reparation final and conclusive, for what he suffered undeservedly, may yet be offered to the dead.[23]

Notes

1 David Fitzpatrick, 'Commemoration in the Irish Free State: a chronicle of embarrassment', in Ian McBride (ed.), *History and memory in modern Ireland* (Cambridge: Cambridge University Press, 2001), p. 189.
2 *Irish Times*, 13 February 1964.
3 Oliver St John Gogarty, 'Gwynn, Stephen Lucius (1864–1950)', in L. G. Wickham Legg and E. T. Williams (eds), *Dictionary of national biography, 1941–1950* (London: Oxford University Press, 1959); online edition http://www.oxforddnb.com/view/olddnb/33621, accessed 20 September 2010.
4 *Times*, 19 June 1950.
5 *Observer*, 16 November 1919.
6 Stephen Gwynn, 'Yesterday in Ireland', in *Irish books and Irish people* (Dublin: Talbot Press, 1919), p. 110.
7 Stephen Gwynn, *Ireland* (London: Ernest Benn, 1924), p. 13.
8 Evelyn Sharp, *Unfinished adventure: selected reminiscences from an Englishwoman's life* (London: John Lane the Bodley Head, 1933), p. 227.
9 Stephen Gwynn, 'A poet under a cloud', in *Garden wisdom: or from one generation to another* (Dublin: Talbot Press, 1921), p. 49.
10 W. B. Yeats to Lady Gregory, n.d. [5 February 1911], Lady Gregory papers, Henry W. and Albert A. Berg collection, New York Public Library.
11 Michael Hurley, 'Rough typescript notes on Aubrey Gwynn's family', 16 December 1981, Aubrey Gwynn papers, Irish Jesuit Archive (IJA), J10/55.

12 Aubrey Gwynn, 'Unfinished history of the Gwynn family', Aubrey Gwynn papers, IJA, J10/89(2).
13 Stephen Gwynn, *Ireland in ten days* (London: George G. Harrap and Co., 1935), p. 145.
14 Stephen Gwynn, *The charm of Ireland: her places of beauty, entertainment, sport and historic association* (London: George G. Harrap and Co., 1934), pp. 281–2.
15 Stephen Gwynn, *Today and tomorrow in Ireland: essays on Irish subjects* (Dublin: Hodges, Figgis, and Co., 1903), pp. xiv–xix.
16 Stephen Gwynn, *The case for Home Rule: with an introduction by John E. Redmond* (Dublin: Maunsel and Co., n.d. [1911]), pp. 88–106.
17 Gwynn, *The charm of Ireland*, p. 3.
18 Stephen Gwynn, *Fond opinions* (London: Frederick Muller, 1938), p. 37.
19 *Irish Independent*, 20 May 1918.
20 Gwynn appeared as a 'political pauper' in an anonymous spoof of Lady Gregory's *The workhouse ward. The worked-out ward: a Sinn Féin allegory*, which is included in Lady Gregory, *The collected plays. Vol. I: The comedies*, ed. Ann Saddlemyer (Gerrard's Cross: Colin Smythe, 1970), pp. 299–304.
21 *Times*, 12 June 1950.
22 John Gross, *The rise and fall of the man of letters: English literary life since 1800* (London: Penguin, 1991; first published 1969), p. 9; Stefan Collini, *Absent minds: intellectuals in Britain* (Oxford: Oxford University Press, 2006), pp. 451–72.
23 Stephen Gwynn, *John Redmond's last years* (London: Edward Arnold, 1919), p. 341.

Select bibliography

Primary sources

1. Books by Stephen Gwynn

Memorials of an eighteenth century painter (James Northcote) (London: T. Fisher Unwin, 1898).
Highways and byways in Donegal and Antrim (London: Macmillan and Co., 1899).
The repentance of a private secretary (London: John Lane, 1899).
Tennyson: a critical study (London: Blackie and Son, 1899).
The decay of sensibility and other essays and sketches (London: John Lane the Bodley Head, 1900).
The old knowledge (London: Macmillan and Co., 1901).
The queen's chronicler and other poems (London: John Lane, 1901).
John Maxwell's marriage (London: Macmillan and Co., 1903).
Today and tomorrow in Ireland: essays on Irish subjects (Dublin: Hodges, Figgis, and Co., 1903).
Fishing holidays (London: Macmillan and Co., 1904).
A lay of Ossian and Patrick: with other Irish verses (Dublin: Hodges, Figgis, and Co., 1904).
The masters of English literature (London: Macmillan and Co., 1904).
Thomas Moore (London: Macmillan and Co., 1905).
The fair hills of Ireland (Dublin: Maunsel and Co., 1906).
The glade in the forest and other stories (Dublin: Maunsel and Co., 1907).
A holiday in Connemara (London: Methuen and Co., 1909).
Robert Emmet: a historical romance (London: Macmillan and Co., 1909).
Beautiful Ireland (London: Blackie and Son, 1911).
The case for Home Rule: with an introduction by John E. Redmond (Dublin: Maunsel and Co., n.d. [1911]).
With T. M. Kettle, *Battle songs for the Irish brigades* (Dublin: Maunsel and Co., 1915).
The famous cities of Ireland (Dublin: Maunsel and Co., 1915).
The life of the Rt. Hon. Sir Charles W. Dilke: begun by Stephen Gwynn; completed and edited by Gertrude M. Tuckwell (London: John Murray, two vols, 1917).
Mrs Humphry Ward (London: Nisbet and Co., 1917).
For second reading: attempts to please (Dublin: Maunsel and Co., 1918).
To the electors of the University of Dublin (pamphlet, 1918, copy held in the National Library of Ireland, ILB300P4 (100)).

Select bibliography

Irish books and Irish people (Dublin: Talbot Press, 1919).
John Redmond's last years (London: Edward Arnold, 1919).
Garden wisdom: or from one generation to another (Dublin: Talbot Press, 1921).
The Irish situation (London: Jonathan Cape, 1921).
Collected poems (Edinburgh: William Blackwood and Sons, 1923).
The history of Ireland (London: Macmillan and Co., 1923).
Duffer's luck: a fisherman's adventures (Edinburgh: William Blackwood and Sons, 1924).
Ireland (London: Ernest Benn, 1924).
The student's history of Ireland (Dublin: Educational Company of Ireland, 1925).
Experiences of a literary man (London: Thornton Butterworth, 1926).
In praise of France (London: Nisbet and Co., 1927).
Captain Scott (London: John Lane the Bodley Head, 1929).
Essays of today and yesterday (London: George G. Harrap and Co., 1929).
Saints and scholars (London: Thornton Butterworth, 1929).
Burgundy: with chapters on the Jura and Savoy (London: George G. Harrap and Co., 1930).
The life of Walter Scott (London: Thornton Butterworth, 1930).
The life of Horace Walpole (London: Thornton Butterworth, 1932).
The life of Mary Kingsley (London: Macmillan and Co., 1932).
The life and friendships of Dean Swift (London: Thornton Butterworth, 1935; first published 1933).
The charm of Ireland: her places of beauty, entertainment, sport and historic association (London: George G. Harrap and Co., 1934).
Claude Monet and his garden: the story of an artist's paradise (London: Country Life, 1934).
Mungo Park and the quest of the Niger (London: John Lane the Bodley Head, 1934).
Sir Henry Simpson: a memorial (London: Richard Clay and Sons, 1934).
Ireland in ten days (London: George G. Harrap and Co., 1935).
Oliver Goldsmith (London: Thornton Butterworth, 1935).
The happy fisherman (London: Country Life, 1936).
Irish literature and drama in the English language: a short history (London: Thomas Nelson and Sons, 1936).
River to river: a fisherman's pilgrimage (London: Country Life, 1937).
Dublin old and new (London: Geo. G. Harrap and Co., 1938).
Fond opinions (London: Frederick Muller, 1938).
Two in a valley (London: Rich and Cowan, 1938).
Henry Grattan and his times (London: Browne and Nolan, 1939).
Robert Louis Stevenson (London: Macmillan and Co., 1939).
Salute to valour (London: Constable and Co., 1941).
Aftermath (Dundalk: Dundalgan Press, 1946).
Memories of enjoyment (Tralee: Kerryman, 1946).

2. Books edited and/or with contributions by Stephen Gwynn

(ed.), *Comedies by Alfred De Musset* (London: Walter Scott, n.d. [1890]).
'Introduction', William Makepeace Thackeray, *Vanity fair: a novel without a hero* (London: Methuen and Co., three vols, 1899).
'Introduction', William Makepeace Thackeray, *The history of Pendennis* (London: Methuen and Co., three vols, 1900).
(ed.), *The odes of Horace* (London: Blackie and Son, 1902).
'Introduction', William Makepeace Thackeray, *Christmas books* (London: Methuen and Co., 1903).

'Introduction', William Makepeace Thackeray, *The history of Henry Esmond, esq.* (London: Methuen and Co., 1903).
'Sarsfield', in R. Barry O'Brien (ed.), *Studies in Irish history 1649–1775* (London: Macmillan and Co., 1903), pp. 251–87.
(ed.), *Memoirs of Miles Byrne: a new edition with an introduction by Stephen Gwynn* (Dublin: Maunsel and Co., two vols, 1907).
(ed.), *Charlotte Grace O'Brien: selections from her writings and correspondence with a memoir by Stephen Gwynn* (Dublin: Maunsel and Co., 1909).
(ed.), *What Home Rule means and other leaflets issued by the Irish Press Agency* (Dublin: Maunsel and Co., n.d. [1909]).
(ed.), *A brotherhood of heroes: being memorials of Charles, George and William Napier* (London: A. R. Mowlray and Co., 1910).
Dearmer, Mabel, *Letters from a field hospital: with a memoir of the author by Stephen Gwynn* (London: Macmillan and Co., 1916).
'Irish regiments', in Felix Lavery (ed.), *Great Irishmen in war and politics* (London: Andrew Melrose, 1920), pp. 149–86.
'Foreword', A. M. Cogswell, *Ermytage and the curate* (London: Edward Arnold and Co., 1922), pp. 5–7.
'Foreword', Ministry of Fisheries, *The angler's guide to the Irish Free State* (Dublin: Stationery Office, 1924), pp. v–x.
(ed.), *The personal history of Walmer Castle and its lords warden* (London: Macmillan and Co., 1927).
(ed.), *The scholar's treasury: a book of Irish poetry* (Dublin: The Educational Company, n.d. [1927]).
(ed.), *The letters and friendships of Sir Cecil Spring Rice: a record* (London: Constable and Co. two vols, 1929).
'Foreword', Roger Pocock, *Chorus to adventurers* (London: John Lane, n.d. [1930]), pp. vii–ix.
'Introduction', R. H. Kiernan, *Little brother goes soldiering* (London: Constable and Co., 1930), pp. 9–20.
'Oliver Goldsmith', Lascelles Abercrombie *et al.*, *Revaluations: studies in biography* (London: Oxford University Press, 1931), pp. 20–44.
'Introduction', R. F. Patterson, *Six centuries of English literature: passages selected from the chief writers and short biographies* (London: Blackie and Son, six vols, 1933), vol. IV, pp. xiii–xxv.
'The making of Nigeria: a historical introduction', in Dorothy Wellesley, *Sir George Goldie: founder of Nigeria* (London: Macmillan and Co., 1934), pp. 3–87.
With Maud Lowry Cole (eds), *Memoirs of Sir Lowry Cole* (London: Macmillan and Co., 1934).
(ed.), *The anvil of war: letters between F. S. Oliver and his brother 1914–1918* (London: Macmillan and Co., 1936).
(ed.), *The art and technique of wine* (London: Constable and Co., 1936).
'Foreword', Ella Blanche Home, *Mr Justice Day of Kerry, 1745–1841* (Exeter: W. Pollard and Co., 1938), pp. 1–2.
Kathleen Scott, *Homage: a book of sculptures: with a commentary by Stephen Gwynn* (London: G. Bles, 1938).
'Foreword', C. H. Rolleston, *Portrait of an Irishman: a biographical sketch of T. W. Rolleston* (London: Methuen and Co., 1939), pp. vii–x.
'Introduction', Sydney Fairbrother, *Through an old stage door* (London: Frederick Muller, 1939), pp. 11–17.
(ed.), *Scattering branches: tributes to the memory of W. B. Yeats* (London: Macmillan and Co., 1940).

Select bibliography

'Foreword', Mina Lenox-Conyngham, *An old Ulster house and the people who lived in it* (Dundalk: Dundalgan Press, 1946), pp. v–vi.
'Foreword', C. E. R. Sinclair, *Coarse fishing in Ireland* (London: H. F. and G. Witherby, 1947).
(ed.), *Poems of Alfred Lord Tennyson* (London: Oxford University Press, 1949).

3. Manuscript material

Belfast Central Library (BCL)
Sir Horace Plunkett diaries (microfilm).

Bodleian Library, Oxford
H. H. Asquith papers.
Augustine Birrell papers.
H. E. Duke papers.
Ian Macpherson papers.

British Library, London (BL)
J. H. Bernard papers.
John Burns papers.
Sir Charles Dilke papers.
Macmillan archive.
George Bernard Shaw papers.

Burns Library, Boston College
Shane Leslie papers.

Churchill College Archives, Cambridge
Winston Churchill papers.

Dublin Diocesan Archives (DDA)
William J. Walsh papers.

Harry Ransom Humanities Research Center, University of Texas (HRHRC)
W. B. Yeats papers.

Henry W. and Albert A. Berg Collection, New York Public Library
Lady Gregory papers.
W. B. Yeats papers.

Houghton Library, Harvard University, Boston
Houghton Mifflin papers.
George Roberts papers.
Sir William Rotherstein papers.

Imperial War Museum Library, London (IWML)
Lord French papers.

Irish Jesuit Archive, Dublin (IJA)
Aubrey Gwynn papers.

The National Archives, London (TNA)
Sir John Anderson papers.

Colonial Office papers.
Lord Midleton papers.
Ministry of National Service papers.
War Office papers.

National Archives of Ireland, Dublin (NAI)
Stephen Gwynn's will.

National Archives of Scotland, Edinburgh (NAS)
Lord Lothian papers.

National Library of Ireland, Dublin (NLI)
F. S. Bourke papers.
Roger Casement papers.
Gaelic League minute books and executive attendance books.
Stephen Gwynn papers.
Joseph Holloway diaries (microfilm).
J. J. Horgan papers (microfilm).
Michael MacDonagh papers.
Eoin MacNeill papers.
O'Brien family papers.
William Smith O'Brien papers.
Thomas O'Donnell papers.
Sir Lawrence Parsons diaries.
John Redmond papers.
Robertson papers.
Sheehy Skeffington papers.
Theatre of Ireland minute book.

National Library of Scotland, Edinburgh (NLS)
F. S. Oliver papers.

New York Public Library (NYPL)
Macmillan Company papers.
John Quinn papers.

Papers in private hands
Papers in the possession of Professor Fergus Kelly, Dublin, Ireland.
Papers in the possession of Lord Aberdeen, Haddo House, Aberdeenshire, Scotland.
Papers in the possession of Roger Gwynn, Stroud, England.

Parliamentary Archives, London (PAL)
Andrew Bonar Law papers.
David Lloyd George papers.
Stansgate papers.
John St Loe Strachey papers.

Public Record Office of Northern Ireland, Belfast (PRONI)
Rev. J. B. Armour papers.
Sir Edward Carson papers.
Robert Lynn papers.
McCaughlen family papers.

Select bibliography

Queen's University Library, Belfast (QUB)
Somerville and Ross papers.

Trinity College Manuscript Department, Dublin (TCD)
Thomas Bodkin papers.
John Dillon papers.
Edward Dowden papers.
J. O. Hannay papers.

University College Dublin Library (UCD)
Thomas Kettle papers.

Wiltshire and Swindon Record Office (WSRO)
Walter Long papers.

4. Parliamentary papers and other official documents

Parliamentary Debates, 4th and 5th series.
Report of the proceedings of the Irish Convention (1918).

5. Newspapers and magazines

The Bell, British Review, Catholic Bulletin, An Claidheamh Soluis, The Columban, Connacht Champion, Connacht Tribune, Contemporary Review, Cornhill Magazine, Daily Chronicle, Dana, Dublin Review, Dublin University Review, Eire–Ireland, Fortnightly Review, Freeman's Journal, Galway Express, Irish Freedom, Irish Monthly, Irish News, Irish Province News, Irish Review, Irish Statesman, Irish Times, Irish Worker, Leader, Londonderry Journal, Manchester Guardian, Meath Chronicle, Nationality, Nineteenth Century and After, Northern Whig, Observer, Pall Mall Gazette, Peasant, Punch, Quarterly Review, Round Table, The Shanachie, Sinn Féin, Spark, Spectator, Times, Tuam Herald, Westminster Gazette.

6. Contemporary works and memoirs

Begbie, Harold, *The lady next door* (Dublin: University College Dublin Press, 2006; first published 1914).
'Birmingham, George A.', *The seething pot* (London: Edward Arnold and Co., 1932; first published 1905).
'Birmingham, George A.', *Pleasant places* (London: William Heinemann, 1934).
Birrell, Augustine, *Things past redress* (London: Faber and Faber, 1937).
Boland, John, *Irishman's day: a day in the life of an Irish MP* (London: MacDonald and Co., n.d. [1944]).
Bowen, Elizabeth, *The mulberry tree: writings of Elizabeth Bowen*, ed. Hermione Lee (London: Vintage, 1999).
Boyce, D. George (ed.), *The crisis of British unionism: Lord Selborne's domestic political papers, 1885–1922* (London: Historians' Press, 1987).
Brown, T. E., *Poems of T. E. Brown*, eds H. F. B. and H. G. D. (London: Macmillan and Co., 1908).
Cary, Joyce, *A house of children* (London: Michael Joseph, 1955; first published 1941).
Chesterton, G. K., *Irish impressions* (New York: John Lane Co., 1920).
Chesterton, G. K., *Autobiography* (London: Hutchinson and Co., 1936).
Corkery, Daniel, *Synge and Anglo-Irish literature* (Cork: Mercier Press, 1966; first published 1931).

Davis, Richard and Marianne Davis (eds), *The rebel in his family: selected papers of William Smith O'Brien* (Cork: Cork University Press, 1998).
Denson, Alan (ed.), *Letters from AE* (London: Abelard-Schuman, 1961).
Feilding, Rowland, *War letters to a wife: France and Flanders 1915–1919* (London: Medici Society, 1929).
Fischer, Joachim and John Dillon (eds), *The correspondence of Myles Dillon 1922–1925: Irish–German relations and Celtic studies* (Dublin: Four Courts Press, 1999).
Ginnell, Laurence, *Land and liberty* (Dublin: James Duffy and Co., 1908).
Godley, Alexander, *Life of an Irish soldier* (London: John Murray, 1939).
Gonne MacBride, Maud, *A servant of the queen: reminiscences* (London: Victor Gollancz, 1974; first published 1938).
Gough, General Sir Hubert, *The fifth army* (London: Hodder and Stoughton, 1931).
Gough, General Sir Hubert, *Soldiering on* (London: Arthur Barker, 1954).
Griffin, Gerald, *The wild geese: pen portraits of famous Irish exiles* (London: Jarrolds, n.d. [1938]).
Gwynn, Charles, *Imperial policing* (London: Macmillan and Co., 1936; first published 1934).
Gwynn, Denis, *The life of John Redmond* (London: George G. Harrap and Co., 1932).
Gwynn, Denis, *The history of partition 1912–1925* (Dublin: Browne and Nolan, 1950).
Gwynn, May, *A birthday book: being a book of wise and pithy sayings for each day in the year* (London: Methuen and Co., n.d. [1899]).
Gwynn, May, *Stories from Irish history* (Dublin: Brown and Nolan, 1904).
Hackett, Francis, *Ireland: a study in nationalism* (New York: Huelsch Inc., 1920; first published 1918).
Hannay, J. O., *Is the Gaelic League political?* (Dublin: Gaelic League, 1906).
Healy, T. M., *Letters and leaders of my day* (London: Thornton Butterworth, two vols, 1928).
Herbert, Dorothea, *Retrospections of Dorothea Herbert 1770–1806* (Dublin: Town House, 1988; first published as two vols, 1929 and 1930).
Horgan, John J., *Parnell to Pearse: some recollections and reflections* (Dublin: Richview Press, 1948).
Inglis, Brian, *West Briton* (London: Faber and Faber, 1962).
Jones, Thomas, *Whitehall diary, vol. III: Ireland 1918–1925*, ed. Keith Middlemass (London: Oxford University Press, 1971).
Jourdain, H. F. N. and Edward Fraser, *The Connaught Rangers* (Cork: Schull Books, three vols, 1999; first published 1928).
Joyce, James, *Occasional, critical, and political writing* (Oxford: Oxford University Press, 2000).
Kelly, John *et al.* (eds), *The collected letters of W. B. Yeats* (Oxford: Oxford University Press, four vols, 1986–2005).
Kerr-Smiley, P., *The peril of Home Rule* (London: Cassell and Co., 1911).
Kettle, T. M., *Home Rule finance: an experiment in justice* (Dublin: Maunsel and Co., 1911).
Le Gallienne, Richard, *The romantic '90s* (London: G. P. Putnam's Sons, 1926).
Londraville, Janis and Richard Londraville (eds), *Too long a sacrifice: the letters of Maud Gonne and John Quinn* (London: Associated University Presses, 1999).
Lucas, E. V., *Reading, writing and remembering: a literary record* (London: Methuen and Co., 1933; first published 1932).
MacDonagh, Michael, *The Irish at the front* (London: Hodder and Stoughton, 1916).
MacNeill, Eoin, *Irish in the National University of Ireland: a plea for Irish education* ([Dublin]: [An Cló-Cumann], [1909]).

Macready, Nevil, *Annals of an active life* (London: Hutchinson and Co., two vols, n.d. [1942]).
MacVeagh, Jeremiah (ed.), *Religious intolerance under Home Rule: some opinions of leading Irish Protestants* (London: Irish Press Agency, 1911).
McDonald, Walter, *Some ethical questions of peace and war: with special reference to Ireland* (Dublin: University College Dublin Press, 1998; first published 1919).
McDowell, R. B., *McDowell on McDowell: a memoir* (Dublin: Lilliput Press, 2008).
Midleton, Lord, *Records and reactions 1856–1939* (New York: E. P. Dutton and Co., 1939).
Mikhail, E. H. (ed.), *The Abbey Theatre: interviews and recollections* (London: Macmillan, 1988).
Molony, J. Chartres, *The riddle of the Irish* (London: Methuen and Co., n.d. [1927]).
Moran, D. P., *The philosophy of Irish Ireland* (Dublin: University College Dublin Press, 2006; first published 1905).
Morgan, Charles, *The house of Macmillan (1843–1943)* (London: Macmillan and Co., Ltd., 1944).
Murphy, Daniel J. (ed.), *Lady Gregory's journals* (Gerrards Cross: Colin Smythe, two vols, 1978 and 1987).
Nic Shiubhlaigh, Maire, *The splendid years: recollections of Maire Nic Shiubhlaigh as told to Edward Kenny* (Dublin: James Duffy and Co., 1955).
O'Brien, Conor Cruise, *Memoir: my life and themes* (Dublin: Poolbeg Press, 1998).
O'Brien, William, *The Irish revolution and how it came about* (Dublin: Maunsel and Roberts, 1923).
O'Conor, Norreys Jephson, *Changing Ireland: literary backgrounds of the Irish Free State 1889–1922* (Cambridge, MA: Harvard University Press, 1924).
O'Donnell, F. Hugh, *The stage Irishman of the pseudo-Celtic drama* (London: John Long, 1904).
O'Faolain, Sean, *Vive moi! An autobiography* (London: Rupert Hart-David, 1965).
O'Hickey, Michael P., *An Irish university, or else —* (Dublin: M. H. Gill and Son, 1909).
O'Malley, William, *Glancing back: 70 years' experiences and reminiscences of press man, sportsman and member of parliament* (London: Wright and Brown, n.d. [1933]).
'Pacificus', *Federalism and Home Rule* (London: John Murray, 1910).
Pethica, James (ed.), *Lady Gregory's diaries 1892–1902* (Gerrards Cross: Colin Smythe, 1996).
Redmond, John E., *The Irish nation and the war: extracts from speeches made in the House of Commons and in Ireland since the outbreak of the war* (Dublin: Sealy, Byers and Walker, 1915).
Riddell, Lord, *Lord Riddell's intimate diary of the Peace Conference and after 1918–1923* (London: Victor Gollancz, 1933).
Rosenbaum, S. (ed.), *Against Home Rule: the case for the Union* (London: Frederick Warne and Co., 1912).
Rothenstein, William, *Men and memories: recollections of William Rothenstein* (London: Faber and Faber, two vols, 1932).
Scott, C. P., *The political diaries of C. P. Scott 1911–1928*, ed. Trevor Wilson (London: Collins, 1970).
Sharp, Evelyn, *Unfinished adventure: selected reminiscences from an Englishwoman's life* (London: John Lane the Bodley Head, 1933).
Shaw, George Bernard, *The matter with Ireland*, ed. David H. Greene and Dan H. Laurence (London: Rupert Hart-Davis, 1962).
Street, C. J. C., *The administration of Ireland, 1920* (London: Philip Allan and Co., 1921).

Sturgis, Mark, *The last days of Dublin Castle: the Mark Sturgis diaries*, ed. Michael Hopkinson (Dublin: Irish Academic Press, 1999).
Sullivan, A. M., *Old Ireland: reminiscences of an Irish KC* (London: Thornton Butterworth, 1927).
Tynan, Katharine, *Twenty-five years: reminiscences* (London: Smith, Elder and Co., 1913).
Tynan, Katharine, *Memories* (London: Eveleigh Nash and Grayson, 1924).
Valentine, John, *Irish memories* (Bristol: St Stephen's Press, n.d. [c. 1928]).
Wells, Warre B., *Irish indiscretions* (London: George Allen and Unwin, 1922).
Whitton, Frederick Ernest, *The history of the Prince of Wales's Leinster Regiment (Royal Canadian)* (Aldershot: Gale and Polden, n.d. [1924]).
Yeats, W. B., *A book of Irish verse* (London: Routledge, 2002; first published 1895).
Yeats, W. B., *Wheels and butterflies* (London: Macmillan and Co., 1934).
Yeats, W. B., *Autobiographies*, ed. William H. O'Donnell and Douglas N. Archibald (Basingstoke: Palgrave, 1999).

7. Reference works

Brasenose college register 1509–1909 (Oxford: Oxford University Press, 1909).
Burke, Bernhard, *Burke's Irish family records* (London: Burke's Peerage, fifth edition, 1976).
Foster, Joseph (ed.), *Alumni Oxonienses: the members of the University of Oxford, 1715–1886: their parentage, birthplace, and year of birth, with a record of their degrees* (Oxford: Parker and Co., 1888).
Legg, L. G. Wickham, and E. T. Williams (eds), *Dictionary of national biography, 1941–1950* (London: Oxford University Press, 1959).
Leslie, J. B., *Clergy of Connor: from patrician times to the present day* (Belfast: Ulster Historical Foundation, 1993).
McGuire, James, and James Quinn (eds), *Dictionary of Irish biography* (Cambridge: Cambridge University Press, 2009).
Rutherford, George, *Old families of Carrickfergus and Ballynure: from gravestone inscriptions, wills and biographical notes*, ed. Richard Clarke (Belfast: Ulster Historical Foundation, 1995).
Walker, Brian M. (ed.), *Parliamentary election results in Ireland, 1801–1922* (Dublin: Royal Irish Academy, 1978).

Secondary sources

8. Books, articles and theses

Adams, R. J. Q., *Bonar Law* (London: John Murray, 1999).
Allen, Nicholas, *George Russell (AE) and the new Ireland, 1905–30* (Dublin: Four Courts Press, 2002).
Anderson, Benedict, *Imagined communities: reflections on the origin and spread of nationalism* (London: Verso, 1983).
Bew, Paul, *Conflict and conciliation in Ireland 1890–1910: Parnellites and radical agrarians* (Oxford: Oxford University Press, 1987).
Bew, Paul, *Ideology and the Irish question: Ulster unionism and Irish nationalism, 1912–1916* (Oxford: Oxford University Press, 1994).
Bew, Paul, *John Redmond* (Dundalk: Dundalgan Press, 1996).
Bew, Paul, 'Moderate nationalism and the Irish revolution, 1916–1923', *Historical Journal*, 93:3 (1999), pp. 729–49.

Bew, Paul, *Ireland: the politics of enmity 1789–2006* (Oxford: Oxford University Press, 2007).
Blackie, John, *Bradfield 1850–1975* (Bradfield: St Andrew's College, 1976).
Blunt, Alison, *Travel, gender and imperialism: Mary Kingsley and West Africa* (New York: Guilford Press, 1994).
Bourke, Marcus, *John O'Leary: a study in Irish separation* (Tralee: Anvil Books, 1967).
Bowman, Timothy, 'The Irish recruiting and anti-recruiting campaign, 1914–1918', in Bertrand Taithe and Tim Thornton (eds), *Propaganda: political rhetoric and identity 1300–2000* (Thrupp: Sutton Publishing, 1999), pp. 223–38.
Bowman, Timothy, *Irish regiments in the Great War: discipline and morale* (Manchester: Manchester University Press, 2003).
Boyce, D. George, *Englishmen and Irish troubles: British public opinion and the making of Irish policy 1918–1922* (London: Jonathan Cape, 1972).
Buckland, Patrick, *Irish unionism. Vol. I: The Anglo-Irish and the new Ireland 1885–1922* (Dublin: Gill and Macmillan, 1972).
Buckland, Patrick, *The factory of grievances: devolved government in Northern Ireland 1921–39* (Dublin: Gill and Macmillan, 1979).
Butler, Hubert, *Independent spirit: essays* (New York: Farrar, Straus and Giroux, 1996).
Callan, Patrick, 'Recruiting for the British Army in Ireland during the First World War', *Irish Sword*, 17:66 (1987), pp. 42–56.
Campbell, Fergus, *Land and revolution: nationalist politics in the west of Ireland 1891–1921* (Oxford: Oxford University Press, 2005).
Campbell, Fergus, *The Irish establishment 1879–1914* (Oxford: Oxford University Press, 2009).
Christie, O. F., *A history of Clifton College 1860–1934* (Bristol: J. W. Arrowsmith, 1935).
Collini, Stefan, *Absent minds: intellectuals in Britain* (Oxford: Oxford University Press, 2006).
Collini, Stefan, *Common reading: critics, historians, publics* (Oxford: Oxford University Press, 2008).
Cooper, D., *Haig* (London: Faber and Faber, two vols, 1935).
Curran, Joseph M., *The birth of the Irish Free State 1921–1923* (Alabama: University of Alabama Press, 1980).
Curtis, Jr, L. P., *Apes and angels: the Irishman in Victorian caricature* (Newton Abbot: David and Charles, 1971).
Daly, Dominic, *The young Douglas Hyde: the dawn of the Irish revolution and renaissance 1874–1893* (Dublin: Irish University Press, 1974).
Denman, Terence, *Ireland's unknown soldiers: the Sixteenth (Irish) Division in the Great War, 1914–1918* (Dublin: Irish Academic Press, 1992).
Denman, Terence, *A lonely grave: the life and death of William Redmond* (Dublin: Irish Academic Press, 1995).
Edwards, Ruth Dudley, *Patrick Pearse: the triumph of failure* (Dublin: Irish Academic Press, 2006; first published 1977).
Ellman, Richard, *Yeats: the man and the masks* (New York: W. W. Norton and Co., 1978; first published 1948).
English, Richard, *Irish freedom: the history of nationalism in Ireland* (London: Macmillan, 2006).
Ferguson, Niall, *The pity of war* (London: Penguin, 1999; first published 1998).
Fitzpatrick, David, *Politics and Irish life 1913–1921: provincial experience of war and revolution* (Dublin: Gill and Macmillan, 1977).
Fitzpatrick, David, *Irish emigration 1801–1921* (Dundalk: Dundalgan Press, 1990; first published 1984).

Fitzpatrick, David, 'The logic of collective sacrifice: Ireland and the British Army, 1914–1918', *Historical Journal*, 38:4 (1995), pp. 1017–30.
Fitzpatrick, David, 'Commemoration in the Irish Free State: a chronicle of embarrassment', in Ian McBride (ed.), *History and memory in modern Ireland* (Cambridge: Cambridge University Press, 2001), pp. 184–203.
Fitzpatrick, David, *Harry Boland's Irish revolution* (Cork: Cork University Press, 2003).
Foster, John Wilson, *Irish novels 1890–1940: new bearings in culture and fiction* (Oxford: Oxford University Press, 2008).
Foster, R. F., *Lord Randolph Churchill: a political life* (Oxford: Oxford University Press, 1981).
Foster, R. F., *Paddy and Mr Punch: connections in Irish and British history* (London: Allen Lane, 1993).
Foster, R. F., *W. B. Yeats: a life. Vol. I: The apprentice mage 1865–1914* (Oxford: Oxford University Press, 1997).
Foster, R. F., *The Irish story: telling tales and making it up in Ireland* (London: Allen Lane, 2001).
Foster, R. F., *W. B. Yeats: a life. Vol. II: The arch-poet* (Oxford: Oxford University Press, 2003).
Frank, Katherine, *A voyager out: the life of Mary Kingsley* (Boston: Houghton Mifflin Co., 1986).
Frazier, Adrian, *Behind the scenes: Yeats, Horniman, and the struggle for the Abbey Theatre* (Berkley: University of California Press, 1990).
French, Frances Jane, 'A history of the house of Maunsel and a bibliography of certain of its publications' (Dublin: TCD MLitt thesis, 1969).
French, R. B. D., 'J. O. Hannay and the Gaelic League', *Hermathena: a Dublin university review*, 102 (spring 1966), pp. 26–52.
Gailey, Andrew, *Ireland and the death of kindness: the experience of constructive unionism 1890–1905* (Cork: Cork University Press, 1987).
Gaughan, J. Anthony, *A political odyssey: Thomas O'Donnell: MP for West Kerry 1900–1918* (Dublin: Kingdom Books, 1983).
Gorman, David, *Imperial citizenship: empire and the question of belonging* (Manchester: Manchester University Press, 2006).
Gould, Warwick, '"Playing treason with Miss Maud Gonne": Yeats and his publishers in 1900', in Ian Willison, Warwick Gould and Warren Chernaik (eds), *Modernist writers and the marketplace* (Basingstoke: Macmillan, 1996), pp. 36–65.
Greacen, Robert, *Rooted in Ulster: nine northern writers* (Belfast: Lagan Press, 2000).
Gross, John, *The rise and fall of the man of letters: English literary life since 1800* (London: Penguin, 1991; first published 1969).
Hart, Peter, *The IRA and its enemies: violence and community in Cork, 1916–1923* (Oxford: Oxford University Press, 1998).
Hart, Peter, *Mick: the real Michael Collins* (London: Macmillan, 2005).
Hennessey, Thomas, *Dividing Ireland: World War I and partition* (London: Routledge, 1998).
Hobsbawm, Eric J., *On history* (London: Abacus, 1998; first published 1997).
Hopkinson, Michael, *Green against green: the Irish Civil War* (Dublin: Gill and Macmillan, 1988).
Hopkinson, Michael, *The Irish war of independence* (Dublin: Gill and Macmillan, 2004; first published 2002).
Hutton, Clare (ed.), *The Irish book in the twentieth century* (Dublin: Irish Academic Press, 2004).
Jackson, Alvin, *The Ulster party: Irish Unionists in the House of Commons, 1884–1911* (Oxford: Oxford University Press, 1989).
Jackson, Alvin, *Sir Edward Carson* (Dundalk: Dundalgan Press, 1993).

Select bibliography

Jackson, Alvin *Home Rule: an Irish history 1800–2000* (London: Weidenfeld and Nicolson, 2003).
Jalland, Patricia, *The Liberals and Ireland: the Ulster question in British politics to 1914* (Brighton: Harvester Press, 1980).
James, Elizabeth (ed.), *Macmillan: a publishing tradition* (London: Palgrave Macmillan, 2002).
Jeffery, Keith, *Field Marshal Sir Henry Wilson: a political soldier* (Oxford: Oxford University Press, 2006).
Jenkins, Roy, *Dilke: a Victorian tragedy* (London: Papermac, 1996; first published 1958).
Jenkins, Roy, *Asquith* (London: Collins, 1969; first published 1964).
Johnstone, Tom, *Orange, green and khaki: the story of the Irish regiments in the Great War, 1914–18* (Dublin: Gill and Macmillan, 1992).
Kelly, M. J., *The Fenian ideal and Irish nationalism, 1882–1916* (Woodbridge: Boydell Press, 2006).
Kennedy, S. B., *Paul Henry* (New Haven: Yale University Press, 2000).
Kidd, Colin, *Union and unionisms: political thought in Scotland, 1500–2000* (Cambridge: Cambridge University Press, 2008).
Kilroy, James, *The 'Playboy' riots* (Dublin: Dolmen Press, 1971).
Kotsonouris, Mary, *Retreat from revolution: the Dáil courts, 1920–24* (Dublin: Irish Academic Press, 1994).
Laffan, Michael, *The resurrection of Ireland: the Sinn Féin party, 1916–1923* (Cambridge: Cambridge University Press, 2005; first published 1999).
Levitas, Ben, *The theatre of nation: Irish drama and cultural nationalism 1890–1916* (Oxford: Oxford University Press, 2002).
Lewis, Gifford, *Edith Somerville: a biography* (Dublin: Four Courts Press, 2005).
Loughlin, James, 'The Irish Protestant Home Rule Association and nationalist politics, 1886–93', *Irish Historical Studies*, 24:95 (May 1985), pp. 341–60.
Loughlin, James, 'Creating "a social and geographical fact": regional identity and the Ulster question 1880s to 1920s', *Past and Present*, 195 (2007), pp. 159–96.
Lyons, F. S. L., *The Irish Parliamentary Party, 1890–1910* (London: Faber and Faber, 1951).
Lyons, F. S. L., *John Dillon: a biography* (London: Routledge and Kegan Paul, 1968).
Lyons, J. B., *Oliver St. John Gogarty: the man of many talents: a biography* (Dublin: Blackwater Press, 1980).
MacKenzie, John M., *Propaganda and empire: the manipulation of British public opinion, 1880–1960* (Manchester: Manchester University Press, 1984).
Mahony, Robert, *Jonathan Swift: the Irish identity* (New Haven: Yale University Press, 1995).
Malcomson, A. P. W., *Virtues of a wicked earl: the life and legend of William Sydney Clements, 3rd Earl of Leitrim (1806–78)* (Dublin: Four Courts Press, 2009).
Manning, Maurice, *James Dillon: a biography* (Dublin: Wolfhound Press, 1999).
Mathews, P. J., *Revival: the Abbey Theatre, the Gaelic League and the co-operative movement* (Cork: Cork University Press, 2003).
Matthews, Kevin, *Fatal influence: the impact of Ireland on British politics 1920–1925* (Dublin: University College Dublin Press, 2004).
Maume, Patrick, *'Life that is exile': Daniel Corkery and the search for Irish Ireland* (Belfast: Queen's University Belfast, 1993).
Maume, Patrick, *The long gestation: Irish nationalist life 1891–1918* (Dublin: Gill and Macmillan, 1999).
May, James Lewis, *John Lane and the nineties* (London: John Lane the Bodley Head, 1936).
McBride, Ian, *Eighteenth-century Ireland: the isle of slaves* (Dublin: Gill and Macmillan, 2009).

McConnel, James, 'The Irish Parliamentary Party, industrial relations and the 1913 Dublin lockout', *Saothar*, 28 (2003), pp. 25–36.
McConnel, James, 'The franchise factor in the defeat of the Irish Parliamentary Party, 1885–1918', *Historical Journal*, 47:2 (2004), pp. 355–77.
McConnel, James, 'The Irish Parliamentary Party in Victorian and Edwardian London', in Peter Gray (ed.), *Victoria's Ireland? Irishness and Britishness, 1837–1901* (Dublin: Four Courts Press, 2004), pp. 37–50.
McConnel, James, 'Recruiting sergeants for John Bull? Irish nationalist MPs and enlistment during the early months of the Great War', *War in History*, 14:4 (2007), pp. 408–28.
McDiarmid, Lucy, *The Irish art of controversy* (Dublin: Lilliput Press, 2005).
McDowell, R. B., *The Irish Convention 1917–18* (London: Routledge and Kegan Paul, 1970).
McGarry, Fearghal, *Eoin O'Duffy: a self-made hero* (Oxford: Oxford University Press, 2005).
Mitchell, Arthur, *Revolutionary government in Ireland: Dáil Éireann 1919–22* (Dublin: Gill and Macmillan, 1995).
Murphy, Cliona, *The women's suffrage movement and Irish society in the early twentieth century* (London: Harvester Wheatsheaf, 1989).
Murphy, Desmond, *Derry, Donegal and modern Ulster 1790–1921* (Londonderry: Aileach Press, 1981).
Murphy, William M., *Prodigal father: the life of John Butler Yeats (1839–1922)* (London: Cornell University Press, 1978).
Murray, Bruce K., *The People's Budget 1909/10: Lloyd George and Liberal politics* (Oxford: Oxford University Press, 1980).
Nicholls, David, *The lost prime minister: a life of Sir Charles Dilke* (London: Hamble Continuum, 1995).
Nolan, J. A., *Ourselves alone: women's emigration from Ireland 1885–1920* (Lexington: University Press of Kentucky, 1989).
O'Brien, Donough, *History of the O'Briens: from Brian Boroimhe AD 1000 to AD 1945* (London: B. T. Batsford, 1949).
O'Brien, Grania R., *These my friends and forebears* (Whitegate: Ballinakella Press, 1991).
O'Brien, Ivar, *O'Brien of Thomond: the O'Briens in Irish history 1500–1865* (Chichester: Phillimore and Co., 1986).
O'Brien, Patrick, 'Is political biography a good thing?', *Contemporary British History*, 10:4 (1996), pp. 60–6.
Ó Broin, Leon, *The Chief Secretary: Augustine Birrell in Ireland* (London: Chatto and Windus, 1969).
O'Callaghan, Margaret, 'Language, nationality and cultural identity in the Irish Free State, 1922–7: the *Irish Statesman* and the *Catholic Bulletin* reappraised', *Irish Historical Studies*, 24:94 (1984), pp. 226–45.
O'Connell, Anne, 'Charlotte Grace O'Brien', in Mary Cullen and Maria Luddy (eds), *Women, power and consciousness in nineteenth-century Ireland: eight biographical studies* (Dublin: Attic Press, 1995), pp. 231–62.
O'Leary, Cornelius and Patrick Maume, *Controversial issues in Anglo-Irish relations 1910–1921* (Dublin: Four Courts Press, 2004).
Ó Síocháin, Séamas, *Roger Casement: imperialist, rebel, revolutionary* (Dublin: Lilliput Press, 2008).
Parkinson, Alan F., *Belfast's unholy war: the troubles of the 1920s* (Dublin: Four Courts Press, 2004).
Pašeta, Senia, *Before the revolution: nationalism, social change and Ireland's Catholic elite, 1879–1922* (Cork: Cork University Press, 1999).

Pašeta, Senia, 'Ireland's last Home Rule generation: the decline of constitutional nationalism in Ireland, 1916–1930', in Mike Cronin and John M. Regan (eds), *Ireland: the politics of independence, 1922–49* (Basingstoke: Macmillan, 2000), pp. 13–31.

Pašeta, Senia, *Thomas Kettle* (Dublin: University College Dublin Press, 2008).

Patterson, Henry, 'Independent Orangeism and class conflict in Edwardian Belfast: a reinterpretation', *Proceedings of the Royal Irish Academy*, 80:1 (1980), pp. 1–27.

Peatling, G. K., *British opinion and Irish self-government, 1865–1925: from unionism to liberal commonwealth* (Dublin: Irish Academic Press, 2001).

Potter, Simon J. (ed.), *Newspapers and empire in Ireland and Britain: reporting the British Empire, c. 1857–1921* (Dublin: Four Courts Press, 2004).

Regan, John M., 'Michael Collins, General Commander-in-Chief, as a historiographical problem', *History*, 92:307 (2007), pp. 318–46.

Reid, Colin, 'Protestant challenges to the "Protestant state": Ulster unionism and independent unionism in Northern Ireland, 1921–1939', *Twentieth Century British History*, 19:4 (2008), pp. 419–45.

Reid, Colin, 'The Irish Party and the Volunteers: politics and the Home Rule army, 1913–1916', in Caoimhe Nic Dháibhéid and Colin Reid (eds), *From Parnell to Paisley: constitutional and revolutionary politics in modern Ireland* (Dublin: Irish Academic Press, 2010), pp. 33–55.

Sisson, Elaine, *Pearse's patriots: St Enda's and the cult of boyhood* (Cork: Cork University Press, 2004).

Sloan, Robert, *William Smith O'Brien and the Young Ireland rebellion of 1848* (Dublin: Four Courts Press, 2000).

Small, Stephen, *Political thought in Ireland 1776–1798* (Oxford: Oxford University Press, 2002).

Stone, Norman, *World War I: a short history* (London: Allen Lane, 2007).

Taylor, Brian, *The life and writings of James Owen Hannay (George A. Birmingham) 1865–1950* (Lewiston: Edwin Mellen Press, 1995).

Townshend, Charles, *The British campaign in Ireland 1919–21: the development of political and military policies* (Oxford: Oxford University Press, 1975).

Townshend, Charles, *Easter 1916: the Irish rebellion* (London: Allen Lane, 2005).

Turner, John, *Lloyd George's secretariat* (Cambridge: Cambridge University Press, 1980).

Waller, Philip, *Writers, readers and reputations: literary life in Britain 1870–1918* (Oxford: Oxford University Press, 2008; first published 2006).

Ward, Alan J., 'Lloyd George and the 1918 Irish conscription crisis', *Historical Journal*, 17:1 (1974), pp. 107–29.

West, Trevor, *Horace Plunkett: co-operation and politics, an Irish biography* (Gerrards Cross: Colin Smythe, 1986).

Wheatley, Michael, 'John Redmond and federalism in 1910', *Irish Historical Studies*, 32:127 (May 2001), pp. 343–64.

Wheatley, Michael, *Nationalism and the Irish Party: provincial Ireland 1910–1916* (Oxford: Oxford University Press, 2005).

Whelan, Diarmuid, *Conor Cruise O'Brien: violent notions* (Dublin: Irish Academic Press, 2009).

White, G. K., *A history of St Columba's College 1843–1974* (Dublin: Old Columban Society, 1980).

White, Terence de Vere, *Kevin O'Higgins* (London: Methuen and Co., 1948).

Wilson, John, *C.B.: a life of Sir Henry Campbell-Bannerman* (London: Constable and Co., 1973).

Yeates, Pádraig, *Lockout: Dublin 1913* (Dublin: Gill and Macmillan, 2001; first published 2000).

Index

Abbey Theatre, Dublin 54, 67, 76, 98, 99, 176, 233
Aberdeen, Lady 54
Act of Union (1800) 13, 16
Aestheticism 39
Agar-Robartes, Thomas 108–9
All-for-Ireland League (AFIL) 99
Ancient Order of Hibernians 113, 116
Anderson, Benedict 77
Anderson, Sir John 184
Anglo-Irish Treaty (1921) 191, 192, 193, 198, 199, 203, 213, 222
Anti-Partition League 172, 177
Archer, William 53
Ardilaun, Lord (Arthur Guinness) 115
Armour, Reverend J. B. 106
Ashe, Thomas 154
Ashe-King, Richard 231
Asquith, Herbert H. 97, 113, 117, 127, 133, 150, 178
Asquith, W. W. 36
Austen, Jane 40

Bagwell, John 203
Barlow, Jane 45
Beardsley, Aubrey 39
Beerbohm, Max 39
Begbie, Harold
 Lady next door, The (1914) 106
Bell, The 220–1, 236
Berkeley, Bishop George 227
Bernard, John H. 35, 181
Bigger, F. J. 64, 106
Biography 5
Birmingham, George A. *see* Hannay, J. O.
Birrell, Augustine 63, 80, 81, 84, 104, 109
Black and Tans 185–6, 188, 201
Blackwood Company 37
Blackwood's Magazine 40, 42, 44
Blunt, Wilfred Scawen 110
Bodkin, Thomas 235

Boer War, second (1899–1902) 4, 42, 43, 45
Boland, Harry 192
Boland, John 76, 88, 113, 115
Boru, Brian 11, 14
Boundary Commission 192, 213
Bowen, Elizabeth 38, 231
Bowen, Henry 38
Brady, Patrick J. 115, 117
Brasenose College, Oxford 20, 21–2, 27, 28, 35, 100
Breen, Dan
 My fight for Irish freedom (1924) 223
Brett, George 54, 55, 63–4, 98
British Army 1, 19, 21, 42, 86, 127, 134–5, 140, 144, 174, 178, 225
 SG joins 131
 SG and recruitment campaigns for 129–30, 132–3, 152, 160, 161, 162, 163, 164
 Sixteenth (Irish) Division 130, 132, 134, 135, 139, 140, 142, 143, 144, 246
 Thirty-Sixth (Ulster) Division 131, 139, 140, 142, 143, 151, 165, 246
British Empire 1, 3, 4, 44, 77, 95, 96, 126, 157, 173, 175, 177, 192, 225, 246
British Library 6
British Weekly 107
Brown, T. E. 36
Browning, Robert 51
Buchan, John 226
Buckley, William
 Croppies lie down (1903) 46
Bullock, Shan 212
Burke, Edmund 227
Burke, Thomas 21
Butcher, S. H. 80–1
Butler, Hubert 220–1
Butt, Isaac 1, 4, 126, 203, 232, 242
Buxtons, Leland 244
Byrne, Miles 98

264

Index 265

Campbell-Bannerman, Henry 77
Carleton, William 45, 46
Carlisle, Lord (George Howard) 16
Carolan, Turlough 229
Carr, E. H.
  Twenty years' crisis, The (1939) 223
Carson, Sir Edward 108, 118, 133, 138, 139, 144, 161
Cary, Joyce
  A house of children (1941) 15
Casement, Sir Roger 64, 77, 138
Catholic Bulletin 210–11, 212, 226–7, 230, 232
Catholic Church (Irish) 22, 70, 71, 73, 74, 84, 85, 87–8, 102–3, 116, 159, 190, 246
  SG's view of 99, 112, 156, 208
Catholic Truth Society 104
Cavendish, Frederick, Lord 21
Censorship Board (Ireland) 231
Chamberlain, Joseph 110
Chaucer, Geoffrey 65
Chesterton, G. K. 43, 51, 163
Childers, Erskine 203
Church of Ireland 1, 10, 18, 19, 237
Churchill, Randolph 107
Churchill, Winston 104, 107, 108, 127, 199
Civil War (Irish) 3, 198, 201–5, 207, 216
Claidheamh Soluis, An 64, 84
Clancy, J. J. 152, 157
Clarke, Austin 230, 231
Clifton College, Bristol 36, 37
Coffey, George 25
Coghill, Nevill 231
Cogswell, A. M.
  Ermytage and the curate (1922) 134
Collins, Michael 192, 199, 200, 201
  death of (1922) 202
Collins, Wilkie 65
Columban, The 19, 20
Connacht Champion 82–3
Connacht Tribune 161
Connaught Rangers 134–5, 140, 200, 207, 237, 246
  SG and 133, 141–2, 143
Conscription 133, 158, 163
  crisis (1918) 158–9
  SG's view on 127, 160, 161, 164
Conservative Party (British) 19, 35, 100, 108, 117, 127, 133, 138, 173, 181
Constable Company 38
'Constructive unionism' 83
  SG's attitude towards 44
Contemporary Club 25–7
Contemporary Review 40
Cooper, Major Bryan 207
Corkery, Daniel 230, 231, 232, 233
  Synge and Anglo-Irish literature (1931) 228–9

Cornhill Magazine 40
Cosgrave, William 202, 206, 221, 222, 248
Costello, John A. 237
Craig, Sir James (Lord Craigavon) 103, 192, 199, 208, 209
Craig, W. J. 34
Cumann na nGaedheal 207, 211, 213, 214, 221
Curragh 'incident' (1914) 119, 135, 173
Curtis, Edmund 209–10

Dáil Éireann 173, 179, 182, 184, 187, 190, 192, 193, 207, 223
Daily Mail 138
D'Alton, Father John 85
Dana 66
Davis, Thomas 27, 45, 132, 208
De Valera, Éamon 126, 162, 186, 187, 191, 192, 193, 198, 199, 201, 205, 222, 223, 235
De Vere, Aubrey 98
Deakin, Alfred 77
Dearmer, Geoffrey 53, 237, 243
Dearmer, Mabel 39, 41, 49, 55, 104, 127, 188, 237, 244
Dearmer, Reverend Percy 39
Derby, Lord (Edward Stanley) 200
Devlin, Charles 73
Devlin, Joseph 96, 101, 103, 111, 118, 152, 156
Devolution 5, 66, 74, 77, 182, 243
Dickens, Charles
  Tale of two cities, A (1859) 65
Dilke, Sir Charles 35, 110
Dillon, John 44, 68, 70, 73, 74–5, 82, 83, 84, 85, 86, 87, 88, 95, 107, 111, 113, 118, 127, 140, 151, 152, 153, 156, 214, 242
  on the Easter Rising (1916) 137–8
  as leader of the IPP 157, 158, 159, 162, 164, 165
Dillon, Myles 204
Dixon, Sir Daniel 64
Dockrell, Sir Maurice 160, 163
Dolan, Charles 78
Dominion Home Rule 151, 175, 177, 178, 182, 184, 185, 243
Dooley, Father Peter 85
Dougherty, Sir James B. 152
Dowden, Professor Edward 23–5, 26, 35, 51
Doyle, Arthur Conan 36, 111, 112, 132
Dublin lockout (1913) 114–17
Dublin University Review 23
Duffy, Charles Gavan 27
Duke, Henry E. 152, 154
Dulac, Edmund 233
Dunraven, Lord (Windham Wyndham-Quin) 66

Easter Rising (1916) 3, 64, 89, 119, 135, 136, 137, 140, 171, 180, 200, 213, 242, 246
Edgeworth, Maria 45, 46
Edinburgh Review 40
Edward VII 100
Edward Arnold and Company 38, 42
Edwards, Ruth Dudley 136
Eglinton, John (William Magee) 231, 232–3
Elections
 Irish Free State 1922: 200
 Irish Free State 1923: 207
 Northern/Southern Ireland 1921: 190
 United Kingdom January 1910: 99
 United Kingdom December 1910: 102
 United Kingdom 1918: 164, 165
Eliot, T. S. 233
Ellis, Havelock
 New spirit, The (1890) 41
Emmet, Robert 67, 98, 136
Ervine, St John 233, 243
Esmonde, Sir Thomas 78, 195
Extra-marital affairs
 SG and 39, 55, 104, 127, 188, 244–5

Farmers' Party (Irish) 200
Fay, W. G. 53, 67, 233
Federalism 100, 105, 179, 181, 182
 SG and 4, 101, 153–4, 165, 172, 173–4, 175, 243
Feilding, Rowland 141, 143, 151
Fenianism 21, 22, 26, 27, 236
Fianna Fáil 222, 223
Figgis, Darrell 213
Fingall, Lord (Arthur Plunkett) 177
First World War (1914–18) 3, 4, 21, 86, 96, 110, 119, 126–44, 158–9, 163, 164, 176, 178, 180, 182, 191, 215, 220, 221, 222, 242, 245, 246, 247, 248
Fortnightly Review 37, 40, 53
Foster, John Wilson 49
Freeman's Journal 77, 87, 95, 115, 116, 117, 127, 132, 172, 180, 185, 216
French, John, Lord 160, 164, 171, 172, 174

Gabbett, Elizabeth (SG's great-aunt) 15
Gaelic League 3, 7, 22, 37, 55, 63, 67, 69, 76, 77, 98, 136, 211, 232, 243, 248
 Canon Hannay controversy 70–3
 Coiste Gnótha (executive) 68, 70, 71, 72, 73, 78, 85, 89, 136, 248
 and compulsory Irish 84, 85, 87, 88, 89
 SG's attitude towards 50–1, 176
 SG joins 49
 special feis in Antrim (1904) 64–5
Gallipoli, battle of (1915) 132
 Dardanelles commission on 139
Galway City parliamentary seat 67, 69, 102, 164
 by-election (1906) 73–5

Galway Express 73, 74, 75
Garvin J. L. 175, 221
Ginnell, Laurence 79, 80, 81
Gladstone, William Ewart 21, 54
Glynn, Monsignor 68
Godley, Alexander 143
Gogarty, Oliver St John 203, 206, 231, 233, 242–3
Goldie, Sir George 226
Goldsmith, Oliver 7, 216, 225, 226, 227
Gonne, Maud 25, 26, 47, 52, 117, 144, 233
Good, J. W. 216
Gorman, David 5
Gough, Brigadier-General Hubert 135, 173
Government of Ireland Act (1920) 179, 181, 183, 184, 186, 187, 190, 192, 208–9
Grattan, Henry 7, 216, 225, 226, 227–8, 229
'Grattan's Parliament' (1782–1800) 13, 209
Graves, Robert
 Goodbye to all that (1929) 134
Great War *see* First World War (1914–18)
Green, Alice Stopford 206
 Making of Ireland and its undoing 1200–1600, The (1908) 105
Green, Mrs J. R. 43
Gregory, Augusta, Lady 45, 46, 52, 54, 63, 67, 68, 104, 110, 127, 159, 209, 236, 243
 Twenty-five (1903) 53
Grey, Sir Edward 105, 127
Griffin, Gerald 131
Griffith, Arthur 54, 71, 72–3, 87, 161, 198, 200, 201–2
Gross, John 39, 63
Guillemard, Henry 226
Guinness family 115
Gwynn, Arthur (SG's brother) 15
Gwynn, Father Aubrey Osborn (SG's son) 1, 6, 14, 15, 19, 20, 21, 36, 39, 45, 55, 65, 86, 98, 178, 188, 204, 223, 225, 233, 234, 236, 245
 joins Jesuit order 99
Gwynn, Brian (SG's brother) 15
Gwynn, Brigadier-General Charles (SG's brother) 15, 42, 143
 Imperial policing (1934) 223, 225
Gwynn, Professor Denis (SG's son), 6, 36, 86, 98, 131, 136
 Life of John Redmond, The (1932) 245
Gwynn, Edward (SG's brother) 15
Gwynn, Edward Lucius (SG's son, known as Lucius) 36, 178–9
Gwynn, Reverend John (SG's father) 9–10, 11, 14, 18, 23, 26, 144, 178
Gwynn, John Tudor (SG's brother) 15
Gwynn, Lucius (SG's brother) 15, 19, 54

Index

Gwynn, Lucy (SG's sister) 15
Gwynn, Lucy Josephine (SG's mother, née O'Brien) 9, 11, 14, 18, 34
Gwynn, Madeline (SG's daughter, known as Peggy) 38, 55
Gwynn, Mary (SG's sister) 15, 38
Gwynn, Mary Louisa (SG's wife, known as May) 34–5, 36, 38, 39, 66, 86, 104, 115, 136, 188, 189, 204, 233, 234–5, 245
 Stories from Irish history (1904) 64
 conversion to Catholicism 55, 99, 244
 and women's suffrage 114
Gwynn, Owen (SG's son) 55, 86, 173, 178
Gwynn, Robert (SG's brother, known as Robin) 15, 117
Gwynn, Shelia (SG's daughter) 36, 37, 53, 170, 188, 237, 245
Gwynn, Stephen Lucius
 Anvil of war, The (1936) 222
 Battle songs for the Irish brigades (with T. Kettle, 1915) 132
 Case for Home Rule, The (1911) 106–7, 246
 Charlotte Grace O'Brien (1909) 98
 Charm of Ireland, The (1934) 223, 246
 Collected poems (1923) 188, 207–8
 Experiences of a literary man (1926) 6, 7, 9, 63, 134, 206, 213, 215, 216, 220
 Fair hills of Ireland, The (1906) 75
 Fishing holidays (1904) 49
 Garden wisdom (1921) 188
 Glade in the forest and other stories, The (1907) 82
 Henry Grattan and his times (1939) 227–8
 Highways and byways in Donegal and Antrim (1899) 16, 48, 75, 97
 History of Ireland, The (1923) 64, 206, 209–10, 212, 227
 Holiday in Connemara, A (1909) 81, 97–8
 In praise of France (1927) 33–4, 208
 Ireland (1924) 198, 206, 211–12
 Ireland in ten days (1935) 245
 Irish books and Irish people (1919) 176, 243
 Irish literature and drama in the English language (1936) 6, 230–1
 Irish situation, The (1921) 6, 191
 John Maxwell's marriage (1903) 48, 49
 John Redmond's last years (1919) 6, 118, 129, 130, 135, 152, 153, 180–1, 214, 245
 Letters and friendships of Sir Cecil Spring Rice, The (1929) 221–2
 Life and friendships of Dean Swift, The (1933) 229, 230
 Life of Mary Kingsley, The (1932) 225–6
 Life of the Rt. Hon. Sir Charles W. Dilke, The (with G. Tuckwell, 1917) 110
 Masters of English literature (1904) 51, 65, 230, 234, 247
 Memories of enjoyment (1946) 236
 Mungo Park and the quest of the Niger (1934) 226
 Odes of Horace, The (1902) 28
 Old knowledge, The (1901) 48, 49
 Oliver Goldsmith (1935) 230
 Queen's chronicler, The (1901) 49
 Repentance of a private secretary, The (1899) 40
 Robert Emmet (1909) 64, 98
 Salute to valour (1941) 235
 Scattering branches (1940) 233–4
 Students' history of Ireland, The (1925) 209
 Tennyson (1899) 40
 Thomas Moore (1905) 64, 65
 Today and tomorrow in Ireland (1903) 16, 44, 46, 64, 73, 81
 What Home Rule means (1909) 95
Gwynne, Catherine (SG's great-grandmother, née Rolleston) 10
Gwynne, Reverend John (SG's great-grandfather) 10
Gwynne, Mary (SG's grandmother, née Stevens) 10
Gwynne, Reverend Stephen (SG's grandfather) 10
Gyles, Althea 39

Haig, Field Marshal Douglas 21
Haldane, Richard, Lord 105
Halpin, James 68
Hannay, Canon James Owen 76, 98, 106
 and Gaelic League controversy 70–3
 Seething pot, The (1905) 69–70, 71
Harbison, Thomas 152
Hardy, Thomas 39
Harland, Henry 39
Harrison, Henry 151, 175, 177, 183–4, 214
Hayden, Mary 88
Hazleton, Richard 88, 113
Healy, John 85
Healy, Tim 77, 82, 97, 101, 102, 203, 222
Henry VIII 11
Henry, Grace 104, 188, 189, 234, 244
Henry, Paul 188, 189
Herbert, Dorothea 10
Hewlett, Maurice
 Forest lovers, The (1898) 40, 41
Hickey, General William 134
Higgins, F. R. 231, 233
Higginson, Barkley 34
Higginson, Nesta 6, 34, 38
 Songs of the Glens of Antrim (1900) 37, 46

Hobsbawm, Eric 2
Hobson, Bulmer 64
Holloway, Joseph 99
Home Rule, Irish 1, 4, 5, 7, 22, 45, 77, 78, 80, 110, 114, 135, 138, 158, 173, 181, 182, 198, 242, 243, 247
  and the cultural revival 51, 76
  Fourth Bill (1920) 179, 181, 183, 184, 186, 187, 190, 192
  and the Liberal Party 97, 104–5
  SG's attitude towards 35, 55, 66–7, 139, 140, 157–8, 161–2, 188
  SG's propagandising of 79, 95–6, 106–7
  SG's vision of 17, 44, 98, 99, 100–1, 102–3, 105, 112, 203, 246
  and southern unionism 153, 154–5, 156
  Third Bill (1914) 106, 108–9, 111, 117–18, 127, 133, 151, 170, 178, 179, 180
Hone, Joseph 67, 68, 69, 231
  Swift, or the egoist (1934) 229
  W. B. Yeats, 1865–1939 (1942) 232–3
Horgan, John J. 89, 106, 162
Horniman, Annie 53, 54, 67
Houghton Mifflin 221
Hurley, Michael 188
Hyde, Douglas 24, 25, 26, 27, 33, 37, 49, 50, 72, 85, 89, 99, 106, 206, 231, 236

Independent Orange Order 66
Inglis, Brian 211
Irish Academy of Letters 231, 232, 233
  SG awarded Lady Gregory prize 236–7
Irish Catholic Women's Suffrage Association (ICWSA) 114
Irish Centre Party 4, 135, 152, 173, 174, 177, 178, 190, 214
Irish Citizen Army 117, 129, 171
Irish Convention (1917–18) 150, 151, 152–8, 159, 165, 170, 172, 243–4
Irish co-operative movement 4, 44, 48
Irish Council Bill (1907) 77, 78, 79, 80, 82, 83, 84, 97
Irish Demobilisation Committee 172, 174, 175
Irish Dominion League 4, 153, 177, 178, 179, 180, 181, 182, 183, 184, 185, 208
Irish Free State
  government of 198, 201, 202–3, 206, 211, 213, 235
Irish identity 229–30
  SG on 17–18, 20–1, 22, 49, 209, 215, 228, 244
Irish Independent 114, 129, 140, 160, 179, 191
Irish language 3, 37, 50, 51, 65, 68, 70, 72, 76, 86, 98, 99, 164, 176, 179, 211, 243
  position of in the National University of Ireland 84, 85, 87–9, 202, 236

Irish Literary Society of London 23, 45, 55, 151–2
  SG as president of 231
  SG as secretary of 49–50, 51, 52, 53
Irish Literary Theatre 50, 52
Irish Monthly 49
Irish National League 214, 220
Irish National Theatre Society (INTS) 52–4, 67
Irish nationalism
  and the First World War (1914–18) 129–30, 133, 136, 143, 144, 161
  Protestantism and 4, 105, 111–12
  SG's version of 3, 22–3, 43, 44, 45, 49, 76, 152, 154, 156, 165, 180, 181–2, 209, 215, 228, 242, 243
Irish Parliamentary Party (IPP) 4, 7, 19, 22, 33, 44, 45, 63, 64, 66, 67, 68, 70, 73, 74, 77, 82, 83, 99–100, 101, 102, 106, 107, 111, 139, 143, 144, 150, 151, 161, 162, 165, 170, 175, 176, 182, 198, 202, 203, 206, 211–12, 213, 214, 215, 222, 242, 248
  and agrarian radicalism 79–81
  and the cultural revival 76
  and the First World War 126, 129–31, 133, 138, 158–9
  and the Irish Convention (1917–18) 152–8
  and the Irish Universities Bill (1908) 84, 88
  and labour politics 112, 114–15, 117
  and partition 118–19, 138, 139–40, 162, 180
  and the 'People's Budget' (1909) 96–7
  SG resigns from (1918) 164
  SG wins parliamentary seat for (1906) 75
  and women's suffrage 112–13
Irish Party *see* Irish Parliamentary Party (IPP)
Irish Press Agency (IPA) 79, 85, 95, 105, 111, 139, 247
Irish Protestant Home Rule Association 25
Irish Recruiting Council (IRC) 160, 161, 162, 163, 164, 171–2, 182
Irish Reform Association 66
Irish Republican Army (IRA) 3, 178, 179, 182, 184, 185, 186, 190, 191, 192, 199, 212, 222, 223, 242, 244, 248
  anti-Treatyite 198, 200, 201, 202, 203, 204, 205, 247
  and Dáil Éireann 187
Irish Republican Brotherhood (IRB) 26, 117, 129, 192, 213
Irish Statesman 177, 183, 208, 209–10, 216, 220, 221
Irish Times 74, 75, 131, 140, 151, 161, 163, 184, 189, 242

Index

Irish Transport and General Workers' Union (ITGWU) 114, 116, 117
Irish Universities Act (1908) 84
Irish Volunteers 117, 119, 127, 129, 130, 133, 142, 178
Irish Women's Franchise League (IWFL) 112, 113, 114
Irish Worker 114–15

Jackson, Alvin 109, 151
James Tait Black memorial prize, SG wins (1932) 226
Jameson, Andrew 207
John Lane company 38, 39, 40, 41
  see also Lane, John
Johnston, Denis 221
Johnston, Lionel 37
Joyce, James 63, 231
  Dubliners (1914) 67
Joyce, Michael 83

Kavanagh, Rose 27
Keats, John 65
Kenny, P. D. 80
Kerr, Philip (Lord Lothian) 181, 183, 187, 188, 190
Kerr-Smiley, Peter 143
  Peril of Home Rule, The (1911) 107
Kettle, Andrew 117
Kettle, Tom 80, 83, 106, 131, 132, 141, 246
  death of (1916) 140
Kidd, Colin 3
Kiernan, R. H.
  Little brother goes soldiering (1930) 134
Kingsley, Mary 43
  Travels to West Africa (1897) 42, 225, 226
  West African studies (1899) 225
Kipling, Rudyard 39
Kitchener, Horatio, Lord 127, 129, 130
Knox, Vesey 19

Labour Party (Irish) 200
Land Act
  of 1870: 16
  of 1881: 15
  of 1903: 66
  of 1909: 81, 82
Land League 21, 117, 212
Land War (1879–81) 17, 19, 22, 81, 114
Landlordism
  SG's views on 16–17, 81, 111
Lane, Hugh 115
Lane, John 39–40, 41
  see also John Lane company
Lang, Andrew 40
Lansdowne, Lord (Henry Petty-Fitzmaurice) 97, 138, 139
Larkin, James 114, 115, 117

Laurier, Sir Wilfred 44, 77
Law, Andrew Bonar 117, 187, 200
Law, Hugh 117, 130, 159, 162
Lawless, Emily 45, 132
Lawrence, A. W.
  T. E. Lawrence by his friends (1937) 233
Le Fanu, Sheridan 45
Le Gallienne, Richard 38, 39
Leader 52, 96, 101, 114, 133
League of Nations 177
Lee, Hermione 5
Leinster Regiment 131, 132, 137
Leitrim, Lord (William Clements) 15–16
Lenox-Conyngham, Colonel John 137, 140, 141
Leslie, Shane 115, 150
Lever, Charles 45, 46
Lewis, Cecil Day 233
Liberal Party (British) 19, 76, 77, 79, 83, 96, 97, 99, 100, 102, 103, 105, 106, 112, 117–18, 119, 127
Lloyd George, David 66, 96, 104–5, 141, 150, 152, 156–7, 158, 160, 161, 165, 181, 186, 187, 190, 191
  Home Rule initiative of (1916) 138–9
Logue, Cardinal Michael 52, 208
Londonderry Journal 17
Long, Sir Walter 138, 160, 171, 172, 174, 179, 180, 181, 184
Loreburn, Lord (Robert Reid) 105
Loughlin, James 48
Lucas, E. V. 40, 64, 104, 234
Lucas, Florence 40, 104, 234, 235
Lynch, Arthur 113, 160
Lynch, Liam 203, 205
Lynd, Robert 216
Lyons, F. S. L. 74
  Culture and anarchy in Ireland (1979) 225

MacBride, John 144
MacCarthy, Desmond 232
McCarthy, Justin 97
McCaughlen, Amelia 142
MacDonagh, Michael
  Irish at the front, The (1916) 134
McDonald, Walter
  Some ethical questions of peace and war (1919) 181
MacDonnell, Sir Antony 133
McDonogh, Martin 156
McDowell, R. B. 211
McGarry, Fearghal 192
Macken, Canon T. F. 70–1, 72, 73
Macken, Mary 25
MacKenzie, John M. 96
McLaughlin, Henry 160, 172
McMahon family murders 199
Macmillan, Daniel 232, 234

Macmillan, Frederick 41, 104
Macmillan, George 41, 43, 46, 48, 51, 65
Macmillan and Company, London 6, 41, 42, 49, 51, 63, 64, 65, 75, 97, 98, 104, 127, 215, 220, 223, 225, 234, 236
  commissions biography of Yeats 232–3
  SG recommends Yeats to 46–7
Macmillan and Company, USA 46, 50, 51, 63, 98
Macmillan's Magazine 40, 42, 45
MacNeill, Eoin 37, 49, 64, 85, 87, 88, 119, 129, 130, 133, 236
Macready, Sir Nevil 185, 201
MacVeagh, Jeremiah
  Religious intolerance under Home Rule (1911) 105
Maeterlinck, Maurice 52
Magdalene College, Cambridge 20
Mahaffy, John 28
Malcomson, A. P. W. 16
Manchester Guardian 40, 75, 222
Martin, Violet 106
Martyn, Edward 52
Maunsel and Company 75, 82, 95
  SG co-founds 67–8
Messire, Monsieur 34
Methuen and Company 40, 64
Midleton, Lord (William Brodrick) 153, 154, 155, 156, 157, 158, 172, 177, 190
Milligan, Alice 64
Milton, John 41
Minto, Mary, Lady
  India, Minto and Morley, 1905–1910 (1935) 223
Moles, Joseph Alexander 153, 165
Monet, Claude 247
Monteagle, Lord (Thomas Spring Rice) 177
Montefiore, Dora 116
Moore, George 46, 47, 98, 204, 230, 233, 234
Moore, Thomas 65–6, 98, 230
Moore, Thomas Sturge 233
Moran, D. P. 50, 52, 74, 229
Morgan, Sydney, Lady 45
Morley, John 41, 46, 47, 63, 66, 97
Morning Leader 53
Morning Post 103
Morris, Mowbray 41, 46, 47
Morris, William 26
Motu Proprio decree (1911) 107–8
Mount St Benedict, Gorey 86
Mulcahy, Richard 192
Murphy, William Martin 114, 115
Murray, T. C. 231

Nation, The 27
National Gallery of Ireland 235
National Library of Ireland 6

National University of Ireland 3, 84–5, 87, 88, 89, 99, 116, 176, 202, 211, 236
National Volunteers (Redmondite) 129, 130, 131, 133
Nationality 161
Ne Temere decree (1908) 107, 108
  and the McCann case 102
Nic Shiubhlaigh, Maire 53
Nicoll, Sir William Robertson 107
Nixon, John 199
Northern Ireland, government of 192, 201, 208
Northern Whig 64, 66, 237
Norway, Arthur
  Highways and byways in Devon and Cornwall (1897) 48
Nugent, General Oliver 142–3
Nugent, Sir Walter 108, 115, 159

O'Brien, Charlotte (SG's great-grandmother, née Smith) 13
O'Brien, Charlotte Grace (SG's aunt) 14, 22–3, 43, 98
  Light and shade (1878) 22
O'Brien, Conor Cruise 5
O'Brien, Dermod (SG's cousin) 20
O'Brien, Donough 11
O'Brien, Sir Edward (SG's great-grandfather, fourth Baronet of Dromoland) 13
O'Brien, Francis Cruise 100, 101, 177
O'Brien, Lucius (thirteenth Baron Inchiquin) 13
O'Brien, Sir Lucius Henry (third Baronet of Dromoland) 13
O'Brien, Murrough 11
O'Brien, R. Barry 50
  Two centuries of Irish history 1691–1870 (1907) 105
O'Brien, William 4, 77, 82, 83, 99, 102, 119
O'Brien, William Smith (SG's grandfather) 11, 13–14, 27, 28, 69, 74, 98
Observer 165, 211, 216, 221, 247
  SG writes for 175, 176, 177, 179, 182, 184, 185, 186, 187, 190, 191, 192, 198, 200, 202, 203, 204, 206, 208, 212–13, 214, 215, 222–3, 232
O'Connell, Daniel 13, 14, 50, 84, 206
O'Connell, J. J., 'Ginger' 201
O'Connor, Frank (Michael O'Donovan) 221, 231
O'Connor, John 222
O'Connor, Rory 200
O'Connor, T. P. 97, 118
Ó Doirnín, Peadar 229
O'Donnell, Frank Hugh 52
O'Donnell, John 82, 83
O'Donnell, Bishop Patrick 155, 156, 157
O'Donnell, Peadar 231

Index

O'Donnell, Thomas 88, 206, 214
O'Faolain, Sean, 104, 220, 221, 231
O'Grady, Standish 98–9, 230
O'Growney, Father Eugene 37
O'Hegarty, P. S. 210, 215
O'Hickey, Father Michael
  An Irish university, or else — (1908) 87–8
O'Higgins, Kevin 202, 206, 208, 213, 227
O'Kelly, Sean T. 237
Oldham, Charles Hubert 23, 24, 25, 173
O'Leary, John 26–7
Oliver, F. S. 49, 100, 101, 137, 138, 143, 144, 153, 174, 222
O'Malley, Ernie 221
O'Malley, William 114, 130, 164, 180
O'Neill, Moira *see* Higginson, Nesta
O'Rahilly, Egan 229
Osborne, Walter 23, 26, 36
O'Shee, J. J. 113
Oxford, University of 20, 21–2, 23, 26, 28, 33, 34, 35, 43, 112

Park, Mungo 225, 226
Parliament Act (1911) 104, 105
Parnell, Charles Stewart 20, 21, 22, 33, 36–7, 43, 44, 50, 70, 98, 100, 143, 198, 209, 212, 225, 228, 236, 242
Parsons, Sir Lawrence 130–2, 134, 155
Partition 108–9, 117–18, 138, 150, 154, 155, 206, 221, 235, 243, 248
  SG on 3, 5, 7, 109, 118–19, 139, 140, 162, 164, 179, 180, 181–2, 183, 185, 191, 214, 215
Pater, Walter 20
Pearse, Patrick 33, 86, 135, 136, 137, 138, 144, 236
Peasant 80
Peel, Robert 13
Penguin Ltd (publisher) 226
Phillips, Stephen 40, 41–2, 46
  Paolo and Francesca (1902) 42
Plunkett, Count 143
Plunkett, Sir Horace 4, 44, 64, 106, 152–3, 154, 155, 158, 204, 220
  and the Irish Dominion League 177, 180, 183, 185
Pollock, John
  William Butler Yeats (1935) 232
Pound, Ezra 233
Powell, General C. H. 143
Powell, John 153
Prescott-Decie, Brigadier-General Cyril 184
Punch 21
Purser, Sarah 23

Queen's University, Belfast 84
Quiller-Couch, Arthur 36
Quinn, John 119, 189

Ranch War 79
  SG on 80–2
Read, Herbert 34
Redmond, John 4, 14, 44, 66, 68, 73, 76, 79, 80, 81, 82, 83, 95, 96, 97, 100, 105, 106, 108, 111, 115, 126, 127, 137, 138, 144, 150, 151, 158, 160, 162, 202, 204, 206, 222, 227, 242, 243, 246, 247
  death of (1918) 157
  and federalism 101
  and the First World War (1914–18) 129, 130–1, 133, 134, 142
  and the Irish Convention (1917–18) 152, 153, 154, 155–6
  and partition 117–18, 139
  SG on 118–19, 133, 136, 157, 165, 175, 180, 203, 212, 248
  and women's suffrage 112
Redmond, William (Willie) 103, 113, 132, 135, 137, 140, 142, 143, 173, 204, 246
  death of (1917) 151–2
Redmond, William Archer (John Redmond's son) 206, 214
'Redmondism' 45, 76, 126, 129, 135, 142, 143, 150, 157, 165, 170, 203, 204, 206, 222, 227, 242
Regan, John 202
Reid, Mayne
  Forest exiles, The (1855) 15
Repeal Movement 13
Rhymers' Club, London 37
Rhys, Ernest 37
Rice, Reverend Robert 18
Riddell, George, Lord 181
Ritchie, Charles 35
Roberts, George 53, 54, 67, 69
Robinson, Sir Henry 171
Robinson, Lennox 209, 231, 232, 233
Rolleston, T. W 10, 23, 24, 25, 27, 37
Rosenbaum, Simon
  Against Home Rule (1912) 108
Ross, Martin *see* Martin, Violet
Rossall College, Lancashire 34
Rossi, Mario
  Swift, or the egoist (1934) 229
Rothenstein, Sir William 43, 133, 160, 189, 233, 234
Round Table 151
Round Table movement 100–1, 174, 181
Rowland, Richard (Richard Valentine Williams) 189, 212
Royal African Society 226
Royal Dublin Fusiliers 139
Royal Hibernian Academy 234
Royal Irish Constabulary (RIC) 173, 178, 184, 186, 187
  Auxiliary Division of 185
Royal Irish Regiment 132
Russell, C. H. 36

Russell, George (AE) 44, 67, 115–16, 117, 152, 205, 207–8, 220, 233, 236
  Divine vision and other poems, The (1904) 46
Ryan, Frederick
  Laying of the foundations, The (1902) 53
Ryan, Father John 204

St Andrew's College, Bradfield 34, 35, 36, 234
St Columba's College, Dublin 9, 10, 14, 18–19, 38
St Enda's School, Dublin 86, 136
Samuel, Herbert 105
Samuels, Arthur 165
Sarsfield, Patrick 132
Sassoon, Siegfried
  Complete memoirs of George Sherston, The (1937) 134
Saturday Review 40
Saunderson, Somerset 143
Scanlan, Thomas 139
Scott, C. P. 150–1
Scott, Captain Robert Falcon 225, 226
Scott, Walter 3, 36, 45, 225
Second World War (1939–45) 235, 236
Sennett, A. R. 41
Shaftesbury, Ninth Earl of (Anthony Ashley-Cooper) 185
Shanachie, The 68
Sharp, Evelyn 39, 114, 189, 244
Shaw, George Bernard 68, 111, 112, 115, 116, 117, 153, 163, 231, 233, 236
Shawe-Taylor, Captain John 66, 67, 74–5, 230
Sheehy, David 114, 117
Sheehy Skeffington, Francis 88, 138
Sheehy Skeffington, Hanna 114, 117
Shelley, Percy 65
Shortt, Edward 163
Sigerson, George 55
Sinclair, David 41
Sinn Féin 71, 72, 87
Sinn Féin 4, 43, 72, 76, 77–8, 104, 126, 133, 138, 144, 151, 154, 155, 157, 158, 159–60, 161, 162, 165, 170, 171, 172, 174, 175, 176, 178, 181, 185, 186, 189, 191, 206, 208, 242, 244, 247
  and the Anglo-Irish Treaty (1921) 192, 193, 198, 200
  by-election victories (1917–18) 143, 150, 152
  and Dáil Éireann 173, 179, 182, 184, 190
  and the IRA 187
Skrine, Walter 35
Sloan, Thomas 66
Smiley, Sir Hugh 64
Smith, F. E. (Lord Birkenhead) 138
Smith, William 13

Somerville, Edith 113, 208, 231–2
Somme, battle of (1916) 139, 140, 141
Southern unionism 138, 153, 154–5, 156, 157, 158, 190, 243
Spark 133
Spectator 37, 40, 43, 44, 45, 49, 50, 79, 80, 81, 82, 100, 181
Spring Rice, Sir Cecil 221–2
Staniforth, J. H. M. 137
Starkey, James 67
Starkie, Walter 231
Stephen, Walter 41
Stephens, James 231
Stevens, Katharine (SG's great-aunt) 34
Stevenson, Robert Louis 37, 225
Stockley, John (SG's cousin) 23
Stockley, W. F. P. (SG's cousin) 23, 25, 49, 216
Strachey, John St Loe 37, 50, 80, 216
Strachey, Lytton 226
Strong, L. A. G. 231, 234
Studies 229
Sturgis, Mark 187, 199
Sullivan, A. M., Serjeant 160, 162, 163, 182
Swift, Jonathan 7, 216, 225, 226, 229–30
Synge, J. M. 48, 54, 67, 69, 75, 209, 232, 243
  Playboy of the western world (1907) 51, 76, 176, 234
  Riders to the sea (1904) 54, 228

Taylor, J. F. 24
Taylor, W. D.
  Jonathan Swift (1933) 229
Tennyson, Alfred, Lord 40
Thackeray, William Makepeace
  Christmas books (1903 edn) 40
  History of Henry Esmond, esq, The (1903 edn) 40
  History of Pendennis, The (1900 edn) 40
  Vanity fair (1899 edn) 40
Theatre of Ireland 67
Thomson, Hugh 48
Thornton Butterworth 215
Times 53, 75, 100, 102, 159, 175, 247
Tone, Theobald Wolfe 228
Trevelyan, G. M. 226
Trinity College, Cambridge 13
Trinity College Dublin (TCD) 10, 11, 14, 22, 23, 25, 27, 28, 35, 84, 117, 181, 211, 227, 236
  SG contests parliamentary seat of (1918) 165
Tuam Herald 75, 82
Tuckwell, Gertrude 110
Tudor, General Hugh 185
Tynan, Katharine 23, 27
Tyrrell, Robert 28

Ulster Day (1912) 111, 127
Ulster Special Constabulary 204

Index

Ulster unionism 4, 48, 102, 108, 109, 117, 118, 119, 140, 152, 153, 154, 155, 156, 157, 158, 165, 172, 173, 177, 179, 181, 182, 183, 214, 222, 244, 248
  SG on 103, 139, 162, 174, 175, 180, 191, 208–9, 246
Ulster Unionist Party 190, 209
Ulster Volunteer Force (UVF) 117, 127, 129, 131, 142
United Irish League (UIL) 68, 74, 75, 76, 79, 81, 83, 139, 161
United Irishman 54
United Irishmen 228
University College Dublin 86, 178

Valentine, John 180

Walkley, A. B. 53
Walpole, Horace 225
Walsh, William, Archbishop 85, 86–7, 114, 116
Wanklyn, James L. 102
War of Independence, Irish (1919–21) 172–3, 175, 178, 179, 182, 185–6, 191, 206, 214, 216, 244
Wellesley, Dorothy 226
Wells, H. G. 39, 51
Wells, Warre B. 177
Welsh, James 39
West Africa 225–6
  SG on 40, 42
West Clare parliamentary seat 68, 74
White, Patrick 113

Wilson, Field Marshal Sir Henry 134, 201
Women's suffrage 112
  SG and 113–14, 164
Woolf, Virginia 5
Wordsworth, John 35
Wylie, W. E. 173

Yeats, Jack 233
Yeats, John Butler 24, 68
Yeats, Lily (Susan) 233
Yeats, W. B. 6, 24, 26, 27, 33, 37, 45, 46, 51, 54, 63, 65–6, 76, 111–12, 115, 117, 127, 159, 206, 207, 214, 216, 221, 225, 227, 229, 230, 231, 236, 243
  Countess Cathleen (1892) 51–2
  Cathleen ni Houlihan (with Lady Gregory, 1902) 52–3
  Hour-glass, The (1903) 53
  King's threshold, The (1904) 53
  and Maunsel and Company 67, 68–9
  Pot of broth, The (with Lady Gregory, 1904) 53
  rejects SG's dramatic play 67
  SG on 25, 50, 52, 176–7, 209, 232, 234
  on SG's affair with Mabel Dearmer 104
  SG recommends to Macmillan 46–7
  Shadowy waters, The (1900) 50, 54
  Wanderings of Oisin and other poems, The (1889) 25, 37
Yellow Book 39
Young Irelanders 11, 27, 45, 65
  and rebellion (1848) 13
Young Liberals 101

EU authorised representative for GPSR:
Easy Access System Europe, Mustamäe tee 50,
10621 Tallinn, Estonia
gpsr.requests@easproject.com

www.ingramcontent.com/pod-product-compliance
Ingram Content Group UK Ltd.
Pitfield, Milton Keynes, MK11 3LW, UK
UKHW021847140426
5217IPUK00022B/1643